Y0-BUN-820

SOCIAL CASEWORK IN THE FIFTIES

Selected Articles, 1951–1960

SOCIAL CASEWORK IN THE FIFTIES

Selected Articles, 1951-1960

CORA KASIUS, *Editor*

Reprinted from *Social Casework*

FAMILY SERVICE ASSOCIATION OF AMERICA
44 East 23rd Street New York 10, N.Y.

Printed in U.S.A.  3 *Price, $6.00*

CONTRIBUTORS

Present positions and affiliations are listed.

Nathan W. Ackerman, M.D., Clinical Professor of Psychiatry, Columbia University; Lecturer, New York School of Social Work, Columbia University; Supervising and Research Psychiatrist, Family Mental Health Clinic, Jewish Family Service, New York; Director of the Professional Program, Family Institute, Inc., New York, New York

Lucille N. Austin, Professor of Social Work, New York School of Social Work, Columbia University, New York, New York

Frances Levinson Beatman, Executive Director, Jewish Family Service, New York, New York

Fred Berl, Ph.D., Case Consultant, Jewish Family and Children's Service, Baltimore, Maryland

Werner W. Boehm, D.L., Professor of Social Work, School of Social Work, University of Minnesota, Minneapolis, Minnesota

Jacob Chwast, Ph.D., Director, Mental Health Consultation Service, Educational Alliance, New York, New York

Eleanor Cockerill, Professor of Social Casework, Graduate School of Social Work, University of Pittsburgh, Pittsburgh, Pennsylvania

Jessie P. Dowling, Mental Health Consultant in Social Work, U.S. Public Health Service, Regional Office, Chicago, Illinois

David Fanshel, D.S.W., Associate Professor of Social Work, New York School of Social Work, Columbia University, New York, New York

Samuel Finestone, Associate Professor of Social Work, New York School of Social Work, Columbia University, New York, New York

M. Robert Gomberg, Ph.D., deceased, formerly Executive Director, Jewish Family Service, New York, New York

CONTRIBUTORS

Emanuel Hallowitz, Staff Associate for Youth and Correction, Department of Public Affairs, Community Service Society of New York, New York, New York

Gordon Hamilton, LL.D., L.H.D., Professor Emeritus, New York School of Social Work, Columbia University, New York, New York

Florence Hollis, Ph.D., Professor of Social Work, New York School of Social Work, Columbia University, New York, New York

Irene M. Josselyn, M.D., Member, Southern California Psychoanalytic Institute; Editor, *Journal* of the American Academy of Child Psychiatry

Alfred Kadushin, Ph.D., Professor, School of Social Work, University of Wisconsin, Madison, Wisconsin

Othilda Krug, M.D., Professor and Director of Child Psychiatry, Department of Psychiatry, College of Medicine, University of Cincinnati, Cincinnati, Ohio

Louis J. Lehrman, Professor of Social Casework, Graduate School of Social Work, University of Pittsburgh, Pittsburgh, Pennsylvania

Maurice E. Linden, M.D., Director, Division of Mental Health, Community Health Services, Philadelphia Department of Public Health; Assistant Professor of Psychiatry, University of Pennsylvania School of Medicine, Philadelphia, Pennsylvania

Mary J. McCormick, Ph.D., Associate Professor and Director, Social Welfare Program, Department of Sociology and Social Welfare, University of San Francisco, San Francisco, California

Russell R. Monroe, M.D., Professor of Psychiatry, Director of Graduate Training, The Psychiatric Institute, University of Maryland School of Medicine, Baltimore, Maryland

Gardner Murphy, Ph.D., Director of Research, The Menninger Foundation, Topeka, Kansas

Helen Harris Perlman, Professor, School of Social Service Administration, University of Chicago, Chicago, Illinois

CONTRIBUTORS

Otto Pollak, Ph.D., Professor of Sociology, Wharton School of Finance and Commerce, University of Pennsylvania, Philadelphia, Pennsylvania

Muriel W. Pumphrey, D.S.W., Research Social Worker and Assistant Professor, Department of Psychiatry and Neurology, Washington University Medical School, St. Louis, Missouri

Quentin F. Schenk, Ph.D., Chairman, Department of Social Work Extension, University of Wisconsin, Milwaukee, Wisconsin

Frances H. Scherz, Director of Casework, Jewish Family and Community Service, Chicago, Illinois

Jean M. Snelling, Director of Studies, The Institute of Almoners, London, England

Bernice Stephens, Assistant in Professional Education, Department of Family Services, Community Service Society of New York, New York, New York

Elliot Studt, D.S.W., Director, Inmate-Staff Community Project in Berkeley, Institute for the Study of Crime and Delinquency, Sacramento, California

Irving Weisman, Ed.D., Associate Professor, Hunter College School of Social Work, New York, New York

Viola W. Weiss, Director of Casework, Family Service Society, New Orleans, Louisiana

Corinne H. Wolfe, Chief, Division of Technical Training, Bureau of Family Services, Social Security Administration, U.S. Department of Health, Education, and Welfare, Washington, D.C.

CONTENTS

Part I: Concepts

Part II: Casework Practice

CONTENTS

Introduction

This collection of outstanding *Social Casework* articles of the fifties is designed as a companion volume to *Principles and Techniques in Social Casework,* which was published by the Family Service Association of America about ten years ago. The chief reason for publishing the earlier collection, which covered the decade of the forties, was to meet the requests—particularly from social workers in other countries—for articles that were out of print. The continued demand for the volume suggests that such a collection serves a number of useful purposes, one of which is to make significant papers readily accessible for reference. It seems likely that a series of time-focused collections would have the additional value of facilitating comparative study of the major developments in the field during particular periods.

The planning of this volume presented some editorial problems that needed to be resolved. The first pertained to the title. Had the possibility of a series been anticipated at the time the first volume was published, an appropriate over-all title might have been chosen. The best solution at this point seemed to be to select such a title now. The second editorial question pertained to the advisability of including articles that have been published in reprint pamphlets. Since many of these articles have had wide circulation and are currently available, it seemed desirable to give preference to those that had not already been reprinted.

The organization of this volume follows the pattern of *Principles and Techniques in Social Casework.* The articles are divided into three sections, and, with one exception, the same sectional headings are used. In the earlier volume the general articles were entitled "Philosophy," while in this one they appear under the title "Concepts." This change seemed appropriate because of the shift in emphasis in the papers. In fact, the chief characteristic of social work in the fifties is its effort to construct a conceptual framework that encompasses and specifies the profession's values, theories, and methods. This quest for a framework has led to critical re-examination of accepted psychological premises and to attempts to identify social science theories that have relevance to social work operations.

Extension of Theory

The trend toward utilizing social science concepts is evident not only in the general papers but also in the articles dealing with practice and teaching. The psychosocial framework established in the thirties has not been discarded in recent years, but the social component has been amplified and given greater weight. In retrospect, it is evident that the profession's preoccupation with psychological theory, particularly with individual psychodynamics, resulted in neglect of the situational aspects of the client's problems. For a number of years, relatively little attention was given to the impact of social and cultural forces on personality development, attitudes, and behavior.

The increased emphasis on the social component in the theoretical framework stimulated the casework field to re-evaluate its traditional diagnostic base. Questions were raised about the validity of a clinical diagnosis for purposes of casework treatment, since psychological theory does not encompass such social phenomena as situational stress, family processes, cultural norms, or value systems. It is true, of course, that the diagnostic formulation in casework, particularly since the advent of ego psychology, has not been limited to an appraisal of the individual's psychodynamics but has included his external stresses and his ego capacity to cope with them. The basic issue, which precipitated considerable controversy, pertained to the adequacy of the assessment of the sociocultural influences when ego psychology was used as the main frame of reference.

A number of articles in this volume deal with the extension of the diagnostic framework. Role theory is examined, and new insights are offered about cultural influences and social control factors. Several papers in this volume deal specifically with family processes and present schemes for assessing family dynamics.

Emphases in Practice and Education

The extension and revision of theory have had profound effects on practice. Caseworkers' increased awareness of the social forces that affect the lives of people, and of their motivations to utilize or evade offers of help, has stimulated them to experiment with new methods and techniques. The expanding knowledge about family interaction and group processes has also served as a stimulus for developing new treatment approaches.

Of particular note has been the effort of caseworkers in various types of agencies to develop procedures designed to further their understanding of family dynamics. Home visiting, which had fallen into disrepute, has been reinstated as a respectable technique. Family members now are interviewed, at home or in the office, in pairs, in triads, or in other combinations, partly for the purpose of gaining an understanding of the roles played by each and the nature of their patterns of interaction. Experimentation with the technique of multiple-client interviewing indicates that the caseworker can also effectively intervene in negative interactions and, as part of the intervention, can help the members find more constructive ways of handling family conflicts.

Concern about the plight of persons and families with serious social pathology and about their limited ability to utilize helping service has prompted a number of agencies to experiment with new procedures and techniques. Both sociologists and psychologists have thrown light on the patterns and mechanisms that interfere with the ability of certain clients to accept offers of help or to enter into a therapeutic relationship. The literature of the past decade contains many reports of attempts to find a *modus operandi* with multiproblem families, delinquents, alcoholics, and other "hard-to-reach" groups. In the main, the approach involves considerable activity on the part of the caseworker, such as seeking out the client, giving continuous assurance of concern and interest, and manipulating the environment. After rapport has been established, the worker is often able to help these clients develop greater capacity to handle their social responsibilities and personal relationships.

Another noteworthy development in casework agencies during the past decade has been the establishment of group treatment programs. The treatment groups may be composed of men, women, adolescents, or children, either of one sex or of both sexes combined, who are faced with similar social or developmental problems. The goals are identical with those of individual treatment, and the two approaches may be combined or used alternately with the same client. The group approach seems to have particular value for clients who fear or resist a close individual relationship. An example of this form of treatment is included in this volume.

Mention should also be made of the increased use of research techniques by agencies and schools, both for validating theory and for testing treatment procedures. In the schools, greater attention is being given to theory formulation and to helping students develop a scientific approach to problem-solving efforts. Schools have also endeavored to bridge the gap between specializations by giving greater weight to the generic aspects of social work theory.

The trend in field instruction and supervision has turned sharply away from the former overprotective procedures, which often precipitated hostility and dependency in students. Educational goals have been more clearly defined, group teaching is used to supplement tutorial teaching, and students and staff members are expected to take greater responsibility for their own professional advancement.

It seems fitting to conclude this brief review of trends in the fifties with mention of the profession's heightened awareness of its responsibility in the realm of social policy. Two penetrating analyses on the leadership function are included in this volume, one by Gordon Hamilton, dean of American casework, and the other by Jean Snelling, a distinguished British colleague. The authors point to factors that have impeded the development of leadership qualities in social work, noting that the requirements for engaging in social action are different from those for providing a helping service. Both place high priority on the responsibility to shape social institutions, indicating that a profession is not truly a profession if it fails to discharge this function.

Acknowledgments

Appreciation is extended to the authors for permission to reproduce their articles in this volume. The Association is also indebted to the National Conference on Social Welfare and other organizations for making papers presented at their meetings available for publication in *Social Casework*.

CORA KASIUS
Editor

December 1, 1962

Part I
Concepts

MARY RICHMOND'S PROCESS OF CONCEPTUALIZATION [1]

Muriel W. Pumphrey

THERE ARE TWO persistent themes in current social work literature—a lament that creative leadership of high caliber is not rising to the top of the profession, and the observation that our research is limited in its effectiveness by lack of skill in conceptualization. Many authorities on the development of social casework believe that Mary Richmond did more than anyone who preceded her to help practitioners see the treatment of individuals as a total process—a conceptual whole within the larger whole of social work. Here was a leader from the ranks who possessed that rare, much-sought ability to conceptualize. In this paper, I shall concentrate only on the essential features of her thought processes. These processes offer provocative suggestions for discovering new areas of research.

Conceptualization involves arranging many separate observations from experience and many hypotheses growing out of philosophic speculation in such a way that they form an ordered pattern of abstractions. One of the characteristics of a concept is that it can be transmitted in unitary form and used as a framework within which diverse realistic manifestations take on enlarged meaning through new understanding of their interrelatedness.[2]

[1] Published in *Social Casework*, October 1957. Presented at the National Conference on Social Welfare, Philadelphia, May 24, 1957.

[2] For an extended description of conceptualization as process, consult William J. Goode and Paul K. Hatt, *Methods in Social Research*, McGraw-Hill Book Co., New York, 1952, pp. 41–48.

In considering the methods Mary Richmond used to bring theory and experience together into one conceptual whole, one should look first at the stages in her understanding at various points in her career, and then at some of the devices she continually used to stimulate her own thinking.

Beginning Stages of Understanding

Mary Richmond's first reaction to charity organization, nearly seventy years ago, was an emotional affirmation of its goals expressed in generalized terms. "The best work of all is . . . the gradual building up among the less fortunate of habits of cleanliness, industry and self-control," she wrote in an early report.[3]

The ideology of charity organization in 1889 consisted of an accumulation of slogans concerning general purposes and of minute instructions for the personal behavior of friendly visitors, with almost no attempt to unify the two. Pronouncements like "The causes of want and suffering are to be removed even if the process be painful," and "Make the unworthy worthy," were common. For her first two years in the Baltimore agency, as assistant treasurer, while her major responsibilities were to interest new contributors and recruit volunteer friendly visitors, such platitudes satisfied Mary Richmond's need to feel that she knew what she was doing and why she did it. She assumed that the necessary techniques would be self-evident to any friendly visitor who exercised the qualities required in everyday contacts—"simple friendliness," "tact," and "good will."[4]

As a beginning frame of reference, she inherited a skeleton idea of a series of procedural steps that had gradually evolved in relation to the persons who customarily did each task rather than out of a conceptual conviction about the inherent separateness of these tasks. Investigation by a paid agent, case planning by a committee of volunteers, and "restoration" by a volunteer visitor formed the nucleus from which developed the ideas of study, diagnosis, and treatment.

The next stage came shortly after she became general secretary of the Baltimore Charity Organization Society. A person who had always done well at whatever she had set out to accomplish, she

[3] Mary Richmond's initial impressions are described in Muriel W. Pumphrey, *Mary Richmond and the Rise of Professional Social Work in Baltimore,* Chaps. II and III, D.S.W. dissertation, New York School of Social Work, Columbia University, New York, 1956. University Microfilms Publication No. 17,076.

[4] Mary E. Richmond, *The Long View,* Joanna C. Colcord and Ruth Z. S. Mann (eds.), Russell Sage Foundation, New York, 1930, pp. 41–42.

tried valiantly to apply every precept she could locate in COS literature. It was a tremendous jolt to discover that, in spite of all her effort, restoration of individuals was not taking place consistently. The climax came when she first tried to supervise new agents. She was appalled to find how little real help she or experienced visitors could offer them. An associate remembered Mary Richmond's vivid account of one particularly downcast moment when she was working late at night reading reports and growing more and more discouraged. She had a sudden realization—her first large over-all view—of the current state of knowledge. What visitors, agents, and district committees really did was to act intuitively and use common sense gained in other relationships. Any success depended more on little-understood "character" factors in the worker and recipient than on any logically conceived process and foreknowledge of predictable results. Mary Richmond called this process of random selection of method "blundering" and used to compare it to a person trying to do detailed work in gathering twilight. She decided that night that if haphazard blundering was the basis of operation, a way should be devised to learn from blunders.

There followed a period of frenzied groping when she tried to discover ways of identifying component parts in what she thought ought to be a much larger concept. In effect, she was setting new immediate goals, partializing segments of experience for organization into manageable sub-concepts, formulating many hypotheses and developing crude research methods for testing them. She scrutinized factors related to the person being helped, factors in the helper, and factors in the agency, neighborhood, and community where the helping was taking place. She isolated the individual case as the major unit which would probably produce the key to process, and she developed a technique for case analysis, "examining each case as though it were a new one." [5] Two of the persons who watched her work between 1895 and 1900 remembered a slogan she coined, "If we know more, we can do more."

First Complete Concept

A fourth major advance in her conceptual understanding occurred at another moment of tension, the two-month period after

[5] *The Charities Record*, publication of the Charity Organization Society of Baltimore, Vol. I (December, 1893), p. 32.

her resignation from her first job in Baltimore and before taking up her new duties in Philadelphia. Her old associates had requested a new manual that would incorporate all her established ideas and practices. Her new employers had set her the frightening task of reorganizing an agency according to the most advanced standards. For the first time in her career she could devote herself exclusively to professional thinking. The result was a rough draft of her famous diagram of concentric circles representing the family, personal, neighborhood, civic, private charitable, and public charitable forces "with which the charity worker may co-operate." [6] She saw process as considered selection of these forces, and the criterion of their usefulness was their closeness to the family, which was the matrix.

All purposeful social work activities had a place in this conceptual scheme. If forces were lacking or harmful, social reform should be utilized; if forces were not well understood, research was indicated; if forces conflicted, or were of insufficient strength, co-operative effort was required. All efforts were to be directed toward "strengthening the forces within the family itself." Charity work became a matter of philanthropic logistics, the calculated deployment of forces and personnel. The selection and provision of these forces now seemed to require special training and experience instead of good will alone—a hint of a beginning concept of a profession. The demonstrated potentialities of each force, and the way in which the strength of these forces could be assessed in each individual example, formed the core of knowledge required by the charity worker. She thought that two sub-concepts in individual treatment had now been fairly well delineated: investigation and planning. Again she also pointed out what was lacking by hinting that within the family there were many individual and interpersonal forces which eventually must be understood and utilized.

Testing in Practice

This, then, was the state of Mary Richmond's comprehension of total process when she arrived in Philadelphia fifty-seven years ago [i.e., in 1900]. Although she gradually ceased to rely on the

[6] "The Work of a District Agent, Instructions and Suggestions Compiled for the Charity Organization Society of Baltimore by its General Secretary, Mary E. Richmond," May 1, 1900, unpublished manuscript in the Mary E. Richmond Archives, Library of the New York School of Social Work. Much of the textual material in the manual was incorporated in more finished style in "Charitable Co-operation," *The Long View, op. cit.*, pp. 186–202.

diagram of forces, she never made any major change in the over-all conceptual view of process. Most of her later efforts were elaborations of single component parts selected for closer scrutiny.

The Philadelphia years were a period of application of this enlarged concept in solving the problems of practice, a testing of the idea to see if it jibed with reality. It was also a period focused intellectually on perfecting three component parts of the concept: the kind of person who should direct the forces (the trained social worker); the nature of the force that kept the whole process going (the charitable spirit); and the principles that determined the balanced use of effort (the relation of social reform to individual treatment). She was intent on discovering how the whole concept could be put in a form that would be transmissible through interpretation and teaching.

Also in Philadelphia, an abortive attempt to develop the third step in casework process—treatment—led Mary Richmond into the next stage of conceptualization. She was well along on a book which was cordially praised by several well-known social workers to whom she had shown the rough draft, but she became disillusioned when they suggested that several passages might be further clarified.[7] She decided that casework was still an individual art, not yet ready for generalization. Blocked in this attempt to explore unformulated areas, she reluctantly began a completely new study of the process of decision-making—investigation and treatment planning. Started as a spare-time pursuit, it became her central interest after she went to the Russell Sage Foundation in 1909. The diagnostic summary with its appraisal of assets and liabilities [8] was thus the conceptual product of at least thirteen years of research and philosophic speculation. In developing a conceptual picture of how treatment methods ought to be selected, she constantly offered hints about missing knowledge, with emphasis on the need to know mechanisms within the individual personality and more about the nature of affectional ties within the family.

The enthusiastic, almost fanatical response to *Social Diagnosis* in 1917 stimulated its author to further conceptualization. At first she viewed the wholesale acceptance of her offering with modest appreciation, and then with something akin to alarm. The zeal

[7] Mary E. Richmond Archives contain part of the manuscript and correspondence regarding its revision.

[8] Mary E. Richmond, *Social Diagnosis,* Russell Sage Foundation, New York, 1917, pp. 360–361.

for ritualistic application of a specific technique, which she saw as a small piece of a large, involved process, became a matter of increasing concern. At one convention she threw herself on a bed after a particularly exuberant meeting and, in a tone of deep disappointment at having been completely misunderstood, exclaimed, "I never intended they would always do it all to one client!" She tried to stimulate an interest in treatment,[9] a subject about which she had planned to write a companion book. The growing body of conflicting knowledge about mechanisms within the individual made her hesitate. She could see that this knowledge had a bearing on treatment but felt that its validity had not been established.

Relation of the Parts to the Whole

Another of her concerns was what she detected as a professional lack of interest in social reform. *What Is Social Case Work?* [10] was an effort to clarify the whole casework process and place social investigation and diagnostic procedure in proper perspective, to show casework's relations with other kinds of social work, and especially to make clear the relationship between providing social forces and the skilled selection of forces. Her best-known definition of social casework—that it is a process of individual adjustment between man and his social environment [11]—thus represented the culmination of her lifetime effort to present work with individuals as a unified idea. Again she called attention to areas where additional knowledge was still needed, concerning what went on within families and within small groups.

In her final years Mary Richmond re-examined her original concept and reaffirmed that the focus of social casework and all other social work was the family. Understanding the family, which was primarily responsible for the development of individual personality and which provided experience required for participation in a democratic society, would provide an index to ways of moving forward on the task of human betterment. Obviously, therefore, the study of effective ways of improving the family should be the chief object of social work research and social action. She had thus returned to her original primitive conceptual position, an

[9] For example: "Some Next Steps in Social Treatment," *The Long View, op. cit.,* pp. 484–491.
[10] Mary E. Richmond, *What Is Social Case Work?,* Russell Sage Foundation, New York, 1922.
[11] *Ibid.,* Chapter IV.

acceptance of social work goals toward which the whole process was moving, but had redefined it. Ultimate goals had always been in her mind during every excursion in developing conceptual sub-patterns, but now she was interested in determining which had primary importance.

In brief, the stages we have seen in her thinking were these:

1. A firm conviction that the concept she was selecting to work on, as expressed in ultimate purposes, was worth while, deserving of immediate attention, plausible, and possible of clarification for use in practice. In essence this conviction was that unhappy individuals could be helped by the consciously controlled effort of others.

2. Objective appraisal of the extent to which this goal was being attained and of the state of current conceptualization. In Mary Richmond's experience, this appraisal consisted largely of recognizing that a state of non-conceptualization existed.

3. Experimentation with sub-patterning to identify and conceptualize components out of which a large, over-all design might be constructed.

4. Organization of a tentative pattern which incorporated a major portion of these sub-patterns. This pattern revealed a central focus and the absence of certain components.

5. Application of the concept to the realities of practice and perfecting the details of conceptualization of sub-patterns, for meaningful transmission to others.

6. Selection of one unsatisfactory sub-pattern (social investigation) for complete reconceptualization which involved study of further sub-patterns, organizing them into a design, and testing them in experience.

7. Re-examination of the entire concept with a new appraisal of relationships among the parts.

8. Selection of the next major sub-pattern that required intensive conceptual formulation.

Suggestions for Future Conceptualization

When, today, we feel the need to examine our theoretical positions, it might be useful to consider the steps by which we have arrived at our own formulations and see what further steps Mary Richmond's process might suggest. Such comparison might help us determine whether we are working on a small component of a larger whole and what kinds of knowledge will be needed to make our assumptions complete and consistent. Recapitulation of such a conceptual process might reveal the possibilities of whole new arrangements of our component ideas, giving hints of lacunae, and inviting new frontiers. For example, with our present knowledge of psychodynamics, what do we consider the focus of our efforts—the individual or the family?

Those of us who feel pressed by the exigencies of day-to-day practice may be encouraged by noting that the groundwork of Mary Richmond's entire theoretical system was laid during the twenty years when she was administering diverse functions in understaffed agencies. Sandwiched between dealings with a landlord who refused to fix a leaky roof, a client whose emergency could not wait, a disgruntled board member who aspired to be president, and a newspaper reporter bent on showing the inhumaneness of "scientific charity," time was found in which she could discover the deeper implications in each separate case and community attitude and pursue their larger meaning. Although temperamentally she liked to read, think, and put things in order, nevertheless there were times when she had to push herself to keep ultimate goals in view.

Her published writings are so finished in style and so logical in presentation that they do not indicate the labored thinking and many false starts that were involved. For evidence of these efforts we must turn to her personal papers, which contain letters to friends in which she aired her speculations, brief reading notes of apt phrases and germinal ideas, marginal annotations in her personal library, and raw data, research notes, and endless rough drafts of most of her research. Added to these sources are the memories of some seventy-five personal and professional associates who knew her between 1888 and 1927, with whom she shared her hunches and whom she pressed for cues to new insights.[12]

Professional Sources of Stimulation

How did Mary Richmond manage to pursue the large goals while pressed with each day's tasks? First, she continually related what she

[12] Mary E. Richmond Archives. The list of interviews and much of their content will be contained in a biography being written by the author under grant from the Russell Sage Foundation.

was doing and observing to existing social work abstractions. She never wavered from her initial commitment that the essential job was one of human reconstruction. She saw continued need to reaffirm and rephrase this "devotion to the whole." In *What Is Social Case Work?* she spoke of the "great task of furthering social advance," and in her last public utterance urged that "while remaining loyally devoted to our own specialty," it was essential "to work from the basis of the whole and to see the multiform interrelations of the whole." [13]

Against this large purpose, Mary Richmond was continually measuring success in each small venture. Each of her major steps in conceptualization was a result of her encounter with some obstacle. She used candid appraisal of failure as a way of finding meaning in what was, and should be, going on. Her method of case analysis, which she devised as a tool for better understanding of the whole process, came as a result of her willingness to admit that restoration of individuals showed very few successes. The diagram of forces was produced when she was feeling that she knew too little about the best standards of practice. She launched what proved to be her *magnum opus* when she saw that the process of treatment of individuals was not as well conceptualized as she had supposed. The best-known definition of casework which has yet been formulated came as a result of her disappointment that a contribution to technique was too often seen as an end instead of a means. Can we, today, with equal candor refuse to delude ourselves that the techniques in which we take pride are infallibly successful, and maintain a willingness to experiment and modify?

Second, she was always sensitive to the suggestions to be found in the literature and practice of all branches of social work. Her use of history was not to find institutional arrangements that could be adopted, but rather to seek insights into both dangers and possibilities. Often she examined past failures to see if there possibly was some merit in what her predecessors had been trying to do. She considered whether their failures might have been due to the limitations they faced and whether in her own time their ambitions were possible of attainment. An example is her careful study of the work of Thomas Chalmers. She disagreed with a good share of Chalmers' ideas, especially his belief that relief-giving in any form or circum-

[13] *What Is Social Case Work?*, *op. cit.*, p. 242; *The Long View*, *op. cit.*, p. 615.

stances was deleterious, but she salvaged from his voluminous writings the concept that the chief aim of efforts to help people should be to develop their own capacities, and that without care, dependent attitudes could easily be fostered. Late in her life she referred, in a personal letter, to Chalmers' fine understanding of the psychology of relief before psychology was known.

In the same way she utilized the experience of her contemporaries. Oftentimes she thought the older ones "inordinately proud" of "mere machinery," and said the "solemn cawings of older birds" were sometimes "dull and uninteresting." [14] Nevertheless, she found many meaningful hints in their observations and would expand a small reference made in passing in a committee meeting or a chance phrase in a book into an entirely new idea. She leaned much on Charles Loch, but he probably never dreamed that his almost casual reference to "social evidence" [15] would be transformed into a large section of a book that was to become the "bible" of a generation of practitioners.

Probably the most fruitful source of all Mary Richmond's efforts to find new ways of thinking was her painstaking attention to the initial reaction of newcomers in the field. While she was initiating them to the accumulated wisdom of the profession, she was ever alert to their impressions.[16] With a remarkable lack of defensiveness about established practices in which she had faith, and an amused tolerance of naïve and short-sighted observations, she gently urged them to tell her exactly what they were seeing. She found very early that people who had not become accustomed to limited results and cumbersome routines could often sense an exaggeration of unimportant components and express a sense that something essential was missing, even though they might not realize what it was. The first new agent she supervised led her to re-evaluate the presumption that receiving relief over a long period was harmful, and from then on she worked on the concept of relief as a tool rather than as a necessary evil. A visitor-in-training first proposed the idea that some of the newer insights from Freud, Rank, and Jung

[14] *The Long View, op. cit.*, pp. 45, 50.

[15] Charles S. Loch, *How to Help Cases of Distress* (3rd ed.), Charity Organisation Society, London, 1884, p. 8. Cf. *Social Diagnosis*, Chaps. II, III, IV, pp. 38–80.

[16] Elizabeth R. Day, "The Preparation of *Social Diagnosis*," *The Family*, Vol. IX, No. 10 (1929), pp. 345, 347; *The Long View, op. cit.*, p. 481.

might enrich the concept of the relationship a worker had with a client. The list of recruits whom Mary Richmond cultivated in this way reads like a later roster of National Conference speakers, indicating that the experience must have been mutually stimulating and rewarding.

Laymen offered similar, but not exactly the same, ideas for further examination. She spoke of them as people with "less jaded minds" and "more varied experiences." [17] From them she was able to draw conclusions as to whether her tentative formulations were timely and workable in view of the state of public attitudes. She believed firmly that the idea of social casework must emanate from the desires of the public at large.

Some, but not as many, fertile suggestions came to her from exceptionally gifted, experienced practitioners. She often used them to check and amplify her own formulations. Often one of her ideas was far ahead of the times, and there were not many examples of how it fitted into practice. If persons of unusual insight thought it might be applicable, they were often induced to experiment. One training institute was devoted to "study of the unusual and unorthodox." The case readers hunting for material to be used in *Social Diagnosis* sometimes wished they could examine the usual run of practice rather than seek out instances that Mary Richmond's lengthy process of conceptualization led her to think must exist.

We take as a matter of course our obligation to borrow from the newest creative thinking of noted contemporaries, but we might ask ourselves whether we are equally conscious of the particular kinds of contributions each of our associates is able to make. Are we anxious to conserve the philosophic perspectives from the varied experiences of those nearing retirement? Are we alert to the new insights to be drawn from the reactions of the youngest student? With our sophisticated knowledge of learning difficulties, and our complicated supervisory arrangements, are we providing channels for their halting comments to get into the mainstream of professional thought while still fresh? The fact that a paper such as this present one was requested indicates that we are somewhat aware of the rich potential for professional stimulation which is buried in our agency archives and outmoded literature, but are we drawing sufficiently or systematically on this source of inspiration?

[17] *Social Diagnosis, op. cit.,* p. 348.

Utilization of Other Sources

When she felt herself going stale and taking each day's work as a matter of course, Mary Richmond invariably turned to reading outside the professional literature. Anyone who has dipped into the footnotes of *Social Diagnosis* and *What Is Social Case Work?* can testify to the wide range of her borrowings. She kept up with the newest concepts in the social sciences, from Spencer's description of society as an organism, which she read in 1889, to George Mead's expanding theory of the self, which she enthusiastically followed in the twenties. She paid particular attention to how other disciplines had altered their original concepts in the light of newer discoveries. For example, changes in legal philosophy which gave human welfare a more important place and the shift in medical education from the exclusive use of books to bedside teaching were some of the subjects of her extended study.

Scientific findings yielded fewer hypotheses to be pursued than did poetry and fiction. Every imaginary character and every description of human aspiration told her something that social work should seek for people, or human characteristics that had to be taken into account. Many of her close friends have agreed that it was a liberal education to be with Mary Richmond when she read a daily newspaper. She was as apt to find a suggestion for overcoming mistakes in the interpretation of agency records in an advertisement or a cartoon as in the most learned treatise on data analysis. Her first notations on the importance of democratic interaction within a family were made on the margin of an early funny paper.

Borrowing of ideas was almost automatic with Mary Richmond, but she was suspicious of the need for a profession to borrow much from any one source. She thought there was constant danger of losing professional identity. This is reflected in the remark she frequently made in the early twenties that charity had originally been in the trap of the clergy, had escaped only to slip into the noose of the economist, had freed itself again, and she hoped it could avoid the lasso of the psychiatrist. Her genius lay in her clear-sighted ability to draw on what she considered applicable, from whatever source, and still maintain a firm belief that social work was capable of producing a body of knowledge and theory distinctly its own.

Next to the provocative suggestions she obtained from newcomers to the profession, Mary Richmond probably got more of her conceptual ideas from the use of analogy than from any other source. Her own personal experiences, literary allusions, experiences of members of other professions, all could be used to draw poignant meaning for casework. Ordinarily she used the skill of the true scientist in seeing only one or two likenesses, and not pushing analogous reasoning too far. This may not be true of her two best-known analogies, the social physician and the charitable bookkeeper. Two Baltimore physicians, Dr. Shippen, a volunteer visitor, and the famous Dr. Osler, inspired her idea that people suffered from social sicknesses that could be diagnosed and for which appropriate treatment could be prescribed. She extended the analogy into so many facets that she may sometimes have lost sight of the differences between the two professions. While she was working on the book later abandoned, she was having difficulty in picturing what took place in the social worker's effort to weigh potentialities for treatment—the nature of social casework judgment. It suddenly occurred to her that conceptually this was a process similar to the use a corporation makes of its ledgers, and the concept of assets for reconstruction balanced against liabilities to be overcome and guarded against was developed. In this, her early experience in bookkeeping led her to place emphasis on the balance or the surplus, rather than on the dynamics of existing positives.

Brief mention should be made of her utilization of standard research techniques. We have already noted her skill in selecting single factors for study in isolation, and then relating them back to the whole concept she was developing. She routinely scanned available social statistics and was quick to note any shifts or inconsistencies that might indicate misconceptions or overlooked factors. All her life, from the time she began to study "blunders," she carried on comparative studies—the most successful cases contrasted with the unsuccessful, a group of clients with the same problems but different backgrounds, the varying ways in which different professions would regard the same problem. She often referred to the value of "the searchlight of difference," and the importance of "the point of intersection" with other activities.[18]

Finally, Mary Richmond believed that every small piece of theory should constantly be tested and applied. The only reason for devel-

[18] *The Long View*, *op. cit.*, pp. 481, 615; *What Is Social Case Work?*, *op. cit.*, p. 225.

oping the profession on the intellectual side was to ensure that the helping of people would not be haphazard and its results a gamble.

It is leadership of this type, based on ability, methodology, and hard work, which will make our present-day research productive of entirely new techniques and will uncover whole new areas of usefulness. We, looking back to Mary Richmond, would judge that she met her own specifications of the true professional person, dedicated to social advance.

> There can be no solid advance without patient attention to detail or without respect for workmanship. . . . The professional worker who, in any field, has imagination enough to deal effectively with concrete things . . . is also likely to be the one who can be trusted to see their larger relations. The great technicians, like Osler in medicine and Pasteur in chemistry, have been men highly sensitive to the relations of the part to the whole.
>
> As one of the newest of the professions, social work should strive to hold an even balance between the specializing and the generalization tendencies.[19]

[19] *What Is Social Case Work?*, *op. cit.*, p. 243.

THE OLD AND THE NEW IN CASEWORK[1]

Mary J. McCormick

THE BEGINNING OF CONTEMPORARY casework coincides, at least roughly, with the beginning of the present century—which means that it is little more than fifty years old. The development of casework as a professional discipline, some twenty years later, coincides with the emergence of dynamic psychiatry following World War I and the resulting application of analytic concepts to the understanding and treatment of human problems within the social setting. Although casework as we know it today is therefore very new,

[1] Published in *Social Casework*, December 1954.

examination of its principles and methods reveals the fact that much that is new had its origins in old theories and, conversely, old theories are clarified by the new insights.

This is especially true of at least three of the principles, and their corollaries in practice, which are basic to the diagnostic approach: human personality is capable of modification and change which can be self-determined and self-directed; the professional nature of the client-caseworker relationship is the primary medium of giving help; the client's present must be observed in relation to the past out of which it springs and the future toward which it strives.

The Capacity for Change

Casework theory is predicated on Freudian formulations. It utilizes the concept that the capacity for change and growth within the human personality is directly dependent on the ego, that is, on the existence within the human being of a "coherent organization of mental processes" which holds the central position in the psychic structure and through which a person "adapts himself to the outside world, securing from it the opportunity to express his fundamental drives and to meet his major needs." [2] In line with this thinking, the human being is conceived of "as fashioned by the interrelationship between his basic needs and his physical and social environment." [3]

Casework help is therefore based on an understanding of these needs (both psychological and social) and of the environment in which the person is hoping to satisfy them. Such help is described as goal-directed, that is, its aim is to enable the person to achieve improvement in some aspect of his social living and to do so by reinforcing his ability "to find suitable solutions to his problems and to operate on a more mature and satisfactory level." [4]

The casework process itself begins with what the person already possesses, with whatever positive resources—external and internal, psychological and physical—are at his disposal. It progresses through his conscious and repeated use of the greatest degree of self-direction of which he is capable. This calls for building up strengths rather than overcoming weaknesses, or, looked at from

[2] Florence Hollis, *Women in Marital Conflict,* Family Service Association of America, New York, 1949, p. 13.
[3] Cora Kasius (ed.), *A Comparison of Diagnostic and Functional Casework Concepts,* Family Service Association of America, New York, 1950, p. 10.
[4] *Ibid.,* p. 17.

another angle, overcoming weaknesses through building up strengths. The procedure itself is an essentially positive one in which the productive use of the person's own resources becomes the pivot around which the entire helping process revolves.

The principles and methods adopted by caseworkers in their efforts to employ this process constructively have been shaped largely out of experience—practical everyday experience in helping persons who are in trouble. As a result, currently accepted practices bear the unmistakable stamp of twentieth-century thought and action. The stamp of an earlier time, however, can be found on many of the principles on which these practices are based—principles that are traceable in their essentials to the thirteenth-century teaching of Thomas Aquinas. Much of this teaching as it bears on the "why" of human behavior has been clarified for the modern mind through the explorations of psychiatry. It is being put into practice in interesting fashion by contemporary caseworkers.

Within the framework of the Thomistic system, the possibility of development and change within the human personality hinges on the control of human actions, a control that is established by the deliberate will of man. This deliberate will is nothing more nor less than the human capacity or appetite for doing—for reaching out and ultimately possessing an object that appears to be desirable. This capacity, along with the intellect on which it depends for its information, belongs to the distinctly spiritual part of man's nature. Moreover, it is rational, that is, it is subject to the appraisal of reason. The will is also subject to the sensitivity of feeling. This must be so since man is human, and, according to Aquinas, wherever there is man there is emotion. By the same token, wherever there is human action there is human response to the pleasure or pain accompanying that action. The will's response is, therefore, a seeing, knowing, feeling response, not a blind or lethargic one. It leads a person, ultimately, to movement or action which is based on knowledge of a desired end and which is, in casework terminology, goal-directed.[5]

This means, according to Aquinas and his followers, that human activity stems from human will and moves toward the object of that will. The activity itself is molded according to the way

[5] Mary J. McCormick, *Diagnostic Casework in the Thomistic Pattern*, Columbia University Press, New York, 1954, pp. 15–16.

in which the human mind perceives that object and the strength of the will's desire to possess it. The sureness and determination with which the resulting activity is carried out depend, therefore, on two factors—*purposiveness* and *challenge*—factors which, in reality, are inseparable. Purposiveness stems from the intensity of the desire to reach the goal in question; challenge is dependent on the character of the object itself, on the qualities that make it desirable. Intensity of desire grows as the worth of an object becomes more keenly appreciated; and appreciation increases desire and spurs the person on to greater activity.[6]

This cycle is familiar to caseworkers. The parents of a spastic child will spend long and arduous hours supervising the muscular exercises that may correct the deformity. As they do so, both the desire to attain their objective—the child's health and happiness—and the value of the objective itself are intensified. So also is the part that each plays in bringing about activity that is controlled and directed toward a desired end.

This formulation about the character and the operation of human behavior is in essential agreement with many contemporary theories on the subject, including those that are basically Freudian. However, agreement does not extend to the origin of the control and the human qualities or faculties that account for it. According to Freud, both the origin and the qualities of control reside in the ego, that is, in a part of man's personality structure which is principally determined by experience and which is ultimately derived from bodily sensations.[7] The strength of this ego is "a variable factor, determined largely by the favorable or unfavorable course of the person's psychosocial development."[8] The ego is capable of modification and change in the face of pressures, whether external or internal, and its strength is determined principally by the individual's own experience, by the "accidental and current events" that belong to everyday living. In Freud's own words, "The ego represents what we call reason and sanity" and is "in control of voluntary movement."[9]

[6] *Ibid.*, p. 19.

[7] Sigmund Freud, *The Ego and the Id,* The International Psychoanalytical Library, No. 12, Hogarth Press, London, 1950, p. 31.

[8] *A Comparison of Diagnostic and Functional Casework Concepts, op. cit.,* p. 8.

[9] Sigmund Freud, *An Outline of Psychoanalysis,* W. W. Norton and Company, New York, 1949, pp. 15, 114; also *The Ego and the Id, op. cit.,* p. 30.

Aquinas, on the contrary, places this capacity for control, and for subsequent growth and change, in powers that are distinctly spiritual, in the intellect and will that belong not to the material, physical part of man's nature but to the life-giving principle or soul with which that material part is united. He sees this union of body and soul, of material and spiritual, as producing a single nature; one that is complete in itself and is wholly individual in that it is a reality and is capable of integrating and directing its own forces in its own way.[10]

In this power to direct and to integrate, Aquinas sees the combined operation of the human intellect, which is capable both of knowing and understanding and of doing. The appetite for doing is the capacity of every normal person for moving in the direction of getting something that he wants. In moving, he initiates activity that is controlled in that it is directed toward the attainment of a specific goal—toward the possession of a desired object. Personality development then consists in "extending those controlled acts that alone are human to every department of man's activities." [11] Actually, this is only a philosopher's way of stating the avowed objective of contemporary psychotherapy—the bringing of uncontrolled, instinctual drives under the control of the ego which is, to Freud, synonymous with reason.[12]

The desire and the ability to extend control in this way—a control that is spiritual rather than organic both in origin and in character—make it possible for a person to realize change and improvement which can become permanent and enduring. These changes are evaluated in terms of the extent to which the reason and will responsible for them are in conformity with the divine reason and the divine will from which the central direction of life actually stems. Final judgments are tempered by recognition of the pleasure and pain that the resulting action brings.

Within a framework such as this, the helping process becomes, ultimately, an attempt to extend that composite of divine and human direction to an ever-widening sphere in the hope that as many of man's activities as possible will be subject to its dictates and control.

[10] St. Thomas Aquinas, *Summa Theologica,* Benziger Brothers, New York, 1948, I, Q 76, Art. 1, pp. 370–372.
[11] Walter Farrell, *A Companion to the Summa,* Sheed & Ward, New York, 1940, Vol. II, p. 211.
[12] *The Ego and the Id, op. cit.,* p. 30.

The Professional Relationship

The primary medium of help in reaching the goal is, for the caseworker, the particular form of relationship which he has come to look upon as characteristic of his orientation. According to Gordon Hamilton the handling of this relationship "is what characteristically gives the professional quality to any social service." She describes it as an association in which the caseworker "gives of his understanding, of his own ego strength, and even of his own superego" and in which he uses "his whole self as consciously as possible" in the interests of another person.[13]

The central dynamic in all of this is, according to the same authority, a "special kind of love" called "acceptance," a love that "consists of warmth, concern, therapeutic understanding, interest in helping the person to get well," that is, to regain control of his own life and conduct. This love is further characterized by a "consistent neutrality and firmness" which make it a sincere expression of the caseworker's willingness "consciously to enter and share in" the life experiences of another. There may be some degree of reciprocity—the caseworker "may benefit indirectly or incidentally" from it—but that possibility is of minor importance.

The primary aim, both of the love and its expression, is the happiness of another human being—a happiness that can be brought about only by someone who is concerned with loving rather than with being loved. Hamilton sees this love as "a part of any real healing, but it must be a special sort of love—a disciplined concern, not indulgence for oneself." All of this represents a "clinical or professional development of a natural quality."[14]

Thomas Aquinas sees this "natural quality" as the beneficent love which is an external act of charity and as the "execution of good will" which has the character of friendship. It is the generous love in which "we love someone so as to wish good to him." This is the love that *"moves those, whom it unites, to a mutual friendship; it turns the inferior to the superior to be perfected thereby; it moves the superior to watch over the inferior."* The description in italics belongs to a fifth-century doctor of the Church whom Aquinas quotes frequently.[15] In its emphasis on the role of the

[13] Gordon Hamilton, *Psychotherapy in Child Guidance,* Columbia University Press, New York, 1947, pp. 126–127.

[14] *Ibid.,* pp. 124–126.

[15] St. Thomas Aquinas, *op. cit.,* II–II, Q 31, Art. 1, pp. 1320–1321.

"superior," that is, the person who is in a position to give from his own abundance, toward the inferior who is ready to receive and assimilate the gift, the statement can well become a part of any discussion of relationship in casework.

Aquinas says that, in this love, which is characterized by giving and not by receiving, by loving and not by being loved, "the lover stands in relation to that which he loves, as though it were himself or part of himself and this union with the object of love is the result and work of love." A recent commentator on this portion of Thomistic teaching says:

> Any human person is himself the first object of his love . . . but the secret of right living [or loving] is to regard other human persons as "other selves." That is what the second great Commandment implies . . . a man is not to love others merely with the love of desire; that is, as objects to be exploited to his own advantage. He must love others for what they are or can be; that is, he must love them with the love of friendship. . . .[16]

In his Yale lecture on *Psychoanalysis and Religion,* Erich Fromm says essentially the same thing in different words:

> There is no more convincing proof that the injunction "Love thy neighbor as thyself" is the most important norm of living and that its violation is the basic cause of unhappiness and mental illness than the evidence gathered by the psychoanalyst. Whatever complaints the neurotic patient may have, whatever symptoms he may present are rooted in his inability to love, if we mean by love a capacity for the experience of concern, responsibility, respect, and understanding of another person and the intense desire for another person's growth. *Analytic therapy is essentially an attempt to help the patient gain or regain his capacity for love.*[17]

Thus, fullness of personality is most surely attained through the exercise of a power that is uniquely human, a power that Hamilton sees as an essential part of any real healing. Such exercise, on the part of the caseworker, calls for sympathy with and understanding of the dynamics of human behavior; it also calls for careful application, to particular problems, of the knowledge and skill that are integral parts of any profession. Its focal point is the attempt "to strengthen the person's ability to deal with real life situations, helping him to meet his own basic needs, both economic and affectional." [18]

[16] Juvenal Lalor, "The Passions," in Appendix to Vol. III, *Summa Theologica,* p. 3228.

[17] Erich Fromm, *Psychoanalysis and Religion,* Yale University Press, New Haven, 1950, pp. 86–87.

[18] Gordon Hamilton, *op. cit.,* p. 124.

In all casework process there must be the discipline that makes it possible for the caseworker to identify himself with the one who is disturbed and, at the same time, to remain sufficiently separated from the disturbance itself so that he can control his own reaction to it and his own activity in meeting it. Intelligent sympathy must be combined with professional distance if this is to be accomplished. Only then can the caseworker maintain the balance between nearness and remoteness, between casualness and intimacy, between the protection of reserve and the encouragement of confidences which relationship in casework demands.

For the present-day caseworker, principles such as these have emerged largely from practice. The philosophy of Aquinas sees them as validly established principles that can be substantiated by reason as well as by experience. This point is exemplified in his brief discussion of *mercy,* a discussion that contains much that is pertinent to relationship in casework. For Aquinas, "mercy signifies grief for another's distress," grief that brings with it movement in the direction of relieving that distress. Such movement, if it is to be efficacious, "must proceed along rational lines to the goal of reason." It must be disciplined and controlled as well as sympathetic and altruistic.[19]

In this movement, "it belongs to one who is higher and better to supply the defect of another, in so far as the latter is deficient." The defects referred to have been known throughout the ages and have been specifically defined within the framework of current social welfare programs. They are the common deficiencies that every man may suffer; they stem, within the material order, from the need for food, clothing, and shelter and from the longing that every person has for support and encouragement in times of sickness, death, or incarceration. The process of supplying them embraces all the activities that the caseworker includes in treatment —activities that call for some form of relationship within the professional setting.[20]

The caseworker is uniquely equipped to supply these deficiencies by virtue of the education, the experience, the personal motivation, and the specialized affiliations that are the marks of his profession. Moreover, he has at hand the specific means for doing so, the professional relationship which can, for all practical purposes, be in-

[19] St. Thomas Aquinas, *op. cit.,* II–II, Q 30, Arts. 1, 2, 3, and 4, pp. 1317–1320.
[20] Mary J. McCormick, *op. cit.,* p. 197.

itiated whenever a person decides to move in the direction of specialized help.

Within the professional setting the incentive to give such help is sharpened by the "fact of individual presentation," that is, by the direct, personal contact that is the basis of relationship and around which the entire casework process is developed. This immediate contact with the reality of human problems as they are synthesized in the difficulties of a single human being gives rise to the caseworker's desire to do something about those difficulties here and now and to do it through the exercise of that special kind of love that plays so important a part in real healing, the kind of love that is the true basis of positive, constructive relationship.[21]

The Interrelationship of Past, Present, and Future

Casework has always emphasized the importance of past experiences as guides to understanding the present. Consequently, early interviews are usually exploratory ones which embrace some examination and evaluation of the past and of its meaning for a particular individual. This is one way of becoming familiar, not only with what a person wants in the present, but with what he has wanted in the past and what he hopes to possess in the future. The diagnostic cycle completes itself as caseworker and client consider both present and future in relation to past, finding in the past an explanation of the present and, hopefully, a foundation for the future.

This sequence is demonstrated in virtually every step of history-taking. The caseworker, at the beginning of any contact, encourages the recall of whatever experiences seem relevant to the present difficulty. In the resulting verbalization, some connection is inevitably established between a past that had, up to this time, perhaps seemed comfortably remote and a present that is alarmingly real.

As present and past are thus merged, their relationship to each other and to the future becomes clarified; the person himself should then be able to see all three in better perspective. Once this perspective is established, the human capacity for change and the readiness to act in such a way as to bring about that change should be strengthened; self-directed, goal-directed behavior thus becomes

[21] *Ibid.*, pp. 114–115.

easier to attain. All this represents sound diagnostic thinking; it also represents sound Thomistic teaching.

In his discussion of human action, Aquinas gives special consideration to the *act of command* by which a person finally gets results. This act contains within itself the two essentials of all human activity—control and movement. It can be described briefly as effective direction. The conditions with which Aquinas surrounds this act of command are interesting in their practicality and, for the caseworker, in their existing counterparts in the diagnostic process.

The first of these conditions is *foresight,* that specific ordering of means to end which carries "the notion of something distant to which that which occurs in the present has to be directed"; the second is *circumspection,* or cognizance of the particular circumstances that surround an action; the third is *caution,* or the avoidance of obstacles in so far as possible.[22] The significance of these three conditions in the light of the diagnostic approach to persons and their problems is not difficult to trace.

The foresight of which Aquinas speaks, the "something distant," finds its way into exploratory interviews as the caseworker attempts to get from a client some expression of what it is that he wants to have happen. Actually, these desires about the future constitute his real reason for coming to the social agency. The mother whose child is ill or disturbed wants to know what is wrong and how to right it. Before these questions can be answered for the future, however, there is need for some consideration, not only of the present in which they exist, but of the past out of which they grew. Such discussion may reveal situations as widely divergent as a focal infection that can be cleared up easily and with no damage involved, or a mental retardation which can never be changed and which has resulted in permanent damage.

In this kind of exploration, the sufferings of the past and the frustrations of the present are scrutinized, not because anything can be done to change either past or present, but because something can be done to shape the future to which each of them leads. In the words of Aquinas, "The past has become a kind of necessity, since what has been done cannot be undone. In like manner, the present has a kind of necessity; [the present illness or unhappiness persists in the present] . . . consequently, future contingents, in so

[22] St. Thomas Aquinas, *op. cit.,* II–II, Q 49, Arts. 6, 7, and 8, 1404–1406.

far as they can be directed by man to the end of human life, are the matter of prudence," that is, of the controlled actions that lead to the habit by which man gets things done.[23]

In this controlled and directed activity, attention must be given to circumstances; hence, the condition of circumspection. The importance of circumspection rests on the fact that, to Aquinas, "a thing may be good in itself and suitable to an end, and nevertheless become evil or unsuitable to the end, by reason of some combination of circumstances." The words "desirable" and "undesirable" can be substituted for good and evil in this context. Here, Aquinas is not discussing, specifically, the morality of a given action; that is, its conformity to reason. He is referring, rather, to any combination of circumstances surrounding that action which may affect, adversely, its benefits to the individual.

This situation is a familiar one to caseworkers. An attending physician may, for example, be convinced that the convalescent mother's place is in a rest home. The caseworker who knows about that mother's concern over long separation from her family will realize that separation may prolong her convalescence. The circumstances surrounding the total situation are such that the solution which is desirable or good in itself and in relation to the illness per se becomes undesirable or evil if it aggravates the illness by arousing anxiety and distress. In this instance, the future effects of such disturbances must, therefore, be weighed against the present value of further supervised care. In the process of weighing, it becomes possible to determine whether or not the means are suitable to the end in view of the circumstances. If they are not, then the caseworker will probably seek a compromise measure. He will not pursue a plan of action for its own sake if such action promises only to make more difficult an already difficult situation and perhaps ultimately impede the recovery that is so urgently desired.

The third condition that Aquinas sets up is caution, that is, the avoidance, in so far as possible, of the hazards that accompany action. Again, it is a condition with which caseworkers are familiar. In fact, this caution is an important element in casework. This is especially true in counseling, in which the caseworker is often faced with the task of helping a person to see that certain lines of action, although appearing to be desirable, are, on the contrary, hazardous;

[23] *Ibid.*, II–II, Q 49, Art. 6, p. 1405.

that in other activities positives and negatives are intermingled in such a way that their separation is, for all practical purposes, impossible; that still other actions, although desirable in themselves, are, by their very nature, bound to be accompanied by dangers, some of which can be avoided, others of which must be tolerated once the action is undertaken.

When a person looks in this way at the facts and feelings that surround his problem and accepts, at least to some extent, their reality, he normally develops an attitude of caution toward them. At least he does not plunge headlong into a plan of action once he realizes that there are elements of danger in it. On the contrary, he does some thinking and planning about these dangers and how they may be met; he does something, through this consideration of past and present, to prepare himself for the future and for the hazards it may bring.

In this interpretation of the conditions surrounding human actions, Aquinas establishes an intimate connection between past, present, and future; his entire system places emphasis on future contingencies as they affect the present and are affected by the past. Caseworkers establish this same connection whenever they make use of the human capacity to recall past experience and to interpret that experience in the light of a present problem and a future goal. They do the same thing, in another way, whenever they help an individual to evaluate a present difficulty through comparison with similar difficulties in the past and through consideration of a possible recurrence in the future.

Looked at in this way, the entire process of helping a person to achieve greater awareness and understanding and, consequently, to arrive at a fuller development of his total personality becomes synonymous with a deepened appreciation of the interaction of his past, his present, and his future. The understanding and the awareness, if sustained and encouraged, should facilitate that goal-directed activity which caseworker and philosopher alike see as the privilege of the human being, who, in his very nature, is endowed with reason and will and the capacity to love.

THE ROLE OF SOCIAL CASEWORK IN SOCIAL POLICY[1]

Gordon Hamilton

WHAT ARE THE DISTINCTIVE characteristics of social casework today? How can it be made more effective? We shall grant at once that social work has no monopoly on human welfare, which is the objective of civilization. The essence of the status of science today is the recognition that no one science or profession can become everything or do everything, that knowledge must be pooled, means of communication established, and various disciplines geared and integrated for the solution of all significant human problems. But the social sciences will be sterile unless their goals include ethics, humanities, and value systems as priorities. Neither science nor welfare can allow itself to be manipulated into anti-human practices and toward the destruction of civilization. As Alex Comfort says, we cannot remain neutral; as scientists, we must remain "on the side of man." [2] Social work in particular must affirm and reaffirm its unique responsibilties in the shaping of human events. It must make its special knowledge available in the public interest.

[1] Published in *Social Casework,* October 1952. Presented at the National Conference of Social Work, Chicago, May 1952.

[2] "Everything we sense as individuals, and very nearly everything we learn as social psychologists, makes it clear that any gesture of protest, any attempt to modify the course of events, must initially, if not throughout, be a personal one—a reassertion of our own responsibility towards other individuals. . . . I only know that in this world there are pestilences and there are victims, and it is up to us not to ally ourselves with the pestilences! . . . So strongly do I oppose not only atrocities of all kinds, but the pestilence itself from which I believe they spring, that a bald reassertion of what I have called 'humanity,' so far from being neutral, is a declaration of partisanship, of being, more specifically, on the side of man." "Morality, Science, and Art," *The Commonweal,* Vol. LV, No. 15 (1952), pp. 367–369.

Assuming Larger Responsibilities

In assuming an active role in the formation of social policy, the profession is guided by certain principles:

1. *The principle of competence, of professional knowledge in use.* As citizens we may speak and act in any way we choose. As citizens we have rights, freedoms, and obligations, but when we speak and act as social workers our role should be related to our area of competence—to the disciplines and responsibilities incurred through assimilating professional contents.

2. *The principle of professional ethics.* The social work obligation is always based on a commitment to welfare and an abiding belief in positive human relationships. Ethics includes normal self-interest as motivation, but social work does not subscribe to the "adversary principle." Social workers cannot permit themselves to act destructively. Ends can never justify destructive means. Whether in collective bargaining, group participation, or whatever else, social workers cannot regard community, board, administration, staff, or clients as an enemy to be overcome. Those things that cannot be compromised without sacrifice of belief in the brotherhood of man *should not be done.* Mankind has always known this in the innermost recesses of its heart. The central problem today is how to bring all the insight of faith and science toward the constructive solution of interpersonal relationships. This purpose rests upon a third principle:

3. *The principle of acceptance of difference.* This is indispensable to ethical adjustment and compromise; it involves a capacity for object relationships which is hard to achieve. Workers learn this (though not without difficulty) in treatment of clients, but the temptation to make common cause through hostile identifications whenever there are strained situations among co-workers and other groups is very great.

It is hard for social workers, when they leave the client focus, to accept divergence of opinion without anger; to be willing to make constructive compromises. I do not mean by this that a solution can be found in so-called "eclecticism," a current rationalization of some practitioners faced with divergent systems of principle and practice. One cannot become a good practitioner, or a good agency, or develop good programs by picking a little of this and a little of that. Everyone who practices practices as an artist. He is his own man, responsible for his own vision, knowledge, and behavior, but a professional person must also act on a systematic evolving body of knowledge, and, if in an agency, within the framework of consistent policy. Participation in policy formation at home or abroad requires a discipline of give and take, calling for flexibility of personality which permits concession and mutual modification because neither staff nor clients conform to an imposed system of ideas.

These three principles—professional knowledge in use; ethical goals in method (in human events, means and ends must equally be justified); and acceptance of the individual's right to be different—should guide the social worker's role in social action. A diagnostic approach to the larger social problems should give accurate and relevant data on which to formulate social action as well as treatment hypotheses and goals. Goals must be specifically, not vaguely, determined; what is to be modified, toward what goal, and through what means, must be purposefully decided. Social work has, to date, been more conscious of its rapidly developing professional process than of its distinctive contribution to the larger goals of welfare.

In casework the value system—the worth of the individual, the significance of the family, individual, group and intergroup responsibility, self-determination, self-involvement, and a mutually co-operative society—has been translated into process, into interviewing skill, into participant eligibility study, into the use of social resources and the life experience as means of treatment. Recognition, not only of human needs but of human rights and responsibilities, thus becomes incorporated into professional method as values and as techniques. There are two fundamental approaches: the protection of human rights and the weaving of rights and responsibilities, through social communication, into the fabric of interpersonal relations. Men cannot pull themselves up by their bootstraps. There must be adequate production and distribution of goods and services, but treatment is not something patched on to economics. The client must be helped to involve himself, to assume responsibilities for the better society toward which all are striving. Social work has much to offer here in both individual and group processes. Its knowledge, as well as its processes, must be formulated and communicated. One of the most important of such formulations is concerned with the possibility of the mobilization of ego strengths in the family, in the group, in the individual, not only toward a person's own rehabilitation, but toward the betterment of the society of which he is a member.

Goals and Role

Let me try to state in what ways social casework makes a special contribution within its own field of operation. That this contribution has been fragmentary and has often gone unacknowledged does not change the fact of its permeating influence. Since our objective is well-being for everyone, I am not afraid of the term "welfare state"; the first concern of any state, nationally or internationally, should be the welfare of all people. The contribution arises out of the conviction that all human events are composed of interacting psychodynamic and sociodynamic factors.

One broad aspect of human suffering may be said to lie within the economic-political-cultural area, in which forms of government, standards of living, production, and demographic trends are seen, and where appropriate programs for meeting needs must be constructed and administered. A second aspect lies in the area of interpersonal relationships, in which cultural, intergroup, and family tensions, discrimination and prejudice exist. These tensions interfere with men's ability to live together constructively, to communicate with and to help each other. These aspects are interdependent; the first is no more important than the second. One cannot successfully solve problems of interrelationships without a sound economic and political structure, but it is also true that one cannot solve—and this is less readily granted—economic problems without profound understanding of human behavior and psychodynamics. These two complementary areas must be integrated for policy and program, just as they become the unit of psychosocial treatment for the caseworker. When confronted by bad immigration policy, juvenile delinquency, niggardly or humiliating practice in social assistance, social workers must find more successful ways of bringing their insights into social legislation, but progress cannot be safeguarded only through legislation and other organized attempts toward social action. Informed social action can proceed only on deepening knowledge of the personality which determines and is determined by its society, as well as on the more familiar and accepted data of political and related science.

The first duty of any profession is to bring its knowledge and competence into direct focus for the use of its clients, and then to generalize, applying these principles in community programs, education, mental hygiene, public health, public welfare, within democratic forms of government. The educative process underlying and implementing social action can arise only from understanding psychodynamics and human behavior. To put it once more, the policy-maker or administrator is of little use in welfare unless he is grounded in professional practice, and the practitioner who tends to be fixated on primary levels of practice must be rededicated to bringing what he knows into the larger context.

Within social work's distinctive method I have placed first the bringing together of ethics with the knowledge and disciplines of science. Included are the ethics of human rights and responsibilities, respect for difference, and the dignity and worth of the individual. As a child of the social sciences, social work is culturally oriented. Whatever pure science discovers must be adapted ultimately to human betterment and human needs. Every treatment goal is culturally determined. American social workers believe in cultural pluralism; characteristic social work process incorporates cultural concepts. Our "one world" is a flexible, moving drama of interpersonal relationships. It is true that social work has produced no genius like Freud to create a new concept of personality, its structure and functioning; yet it is to the credit of caseworkers that they caught early the significance of Freud's contribution. Loch, Richmond, the Abbotts, Florence Kelly, Jane Addams, and others, through an increasingly exact discipline which is being continuously implemented within our profession, brought ethics, humanitarian values, into social process. These pioneer insights have been assimilated; every well-qualified social worker today takes the fusion of values, social science, and psychodynamics for granted.

A second characteristic position derives from the first, namely, that social work process is both psychosocial and interpersonal. Social workers have not been alone in recognizing the interaction of person and situation, inner and outer factors, but before dynamic psychology the nature of such interaction could scarcely have been grasped. The acceptance of this view of every human situation, basic to social work practice, has been of great significance and has acted as a constant, though not sufficiently accredited, stimulus in helping to reduce the distance between the environmentalist and the constitutionalist, the scientist and the therapist. The idea of the psychosocial event must now be brought into the wider stream of economic and interpersonal understanding and program making.

Determinism is certainly not the only principle of life; relativity is also a principle. The individual not only is shaped by biological and environmental forces, but is capable of modifying at least his environment, and probably of shifting some of the constitutional balance. At any rate, the strength of social work lies in its ability to operate at both ends of the psychosocial event, in its refusal to limit itself either to the manipulation of external factors alone, even though this is one of its traditional and proper concerns, or to the treatment of inner factors alone even though the latter has been vastly tempting. This conviction has been further reinforced by growing insight and skill in regard to interpersonal phenomena—the family and the small group constellation. In larger group interaction we believe that the principles of operation are the same. Knowledge of the nature of man, of how the personality functions in the life experience, must be joined with knowledge of society—the development of one is inextricably bound with the improvement of the other.

Another characteristic derives from the fact that social work is agency-geared. Its institutional design has necessitated that social workers use special techniques in the formulation and interpretation of policy. Much of the framework for the social services is statutory, but because of the commitment to interpersonal collaboration, policy has been made a living, communicable thing. Not only is Social Security coverage today inadequate, but we do not have the common sense to insist on rehabilitation as an inherent element in categories of assistance and insurance. Casework and other social work techniques are essential for effective social administration. Rehabilitation is not just a matter of physical restoration, occupational training, and placement. It must be entrusted to a professional staff who have knowledge of human behavior and psychodynamics. Sooner or later, too, policy makers must recognize the family's as well as the patient's role in recovery. Procedures in workmen's compensation, veterans' benefits, and so on are still laid down with minimal recognition of family and interpersonal factors. Science tells us that nobody need starve unless the group starves; but neither can anyone be rehabilitated toward social functioning in a vacuum. Rehabilitation is a many-sided approach in which the goal of adequate functioning requires the knowledge and skill of social work, especially in regard to interpersonal considerations. Social work is, perhaps, the only profession in which involvement of the whole person within the whole situation is the goal and process.

The right to financial assistance in a modern society should include the right to receive social and psychological help, particularly from persons trained to understand how to begin where people are—culturally and emotionally; who know how to release feelings around specific problems, how to reduce anxiety, how to give emotional and practical support, how to increase self-awareness, how to mobilize efforts toward self-help and self-realization within a social situation. These skills are not the private property of social work, but social workers have a long and valid experience in helping clients to use financial assistance, as well as medical, educational, recreational, and other programs for maximum benefit. Social work has brought administrative policy and agency structure into process but has lost ground meanwhile in the integration of those social and psychological therapies that are fundamental to welfare. The balance, I believe, is now being redressed.

Casework is not just a luxury developed within the American scene for, so to speak, the American trade. Casework is a reflection in process of political democracy and psychodynamics addressed to the most important problem of this or any other time —the social functioning of the personality. The charge is often made that social caseworkers are overconcerned with immediate practice. Every profession worthy of its name exacts the single-minded devotion of its practitioners. A social worker should be a well-rounded human being, but it is the objectives and day-by-day practice of the profession which stir and hold him. It is true that social work should produce more leaders, more administrators, more national and international figures, but it is also true that we see a great many leaders and administrators today, whether recruited from business or the professions, who lead to no good purpose because they have not the most elementary grasp of the principles of human relations, or of the skills involved in bringing about a good life for clients, staffs, and community. Because of their experience with operational policy, caseworkers have a peculiar responsibility to engage in social planning and social action on a broader scale. Casework insights and experience from the field of interpersonal relationships must be brought into program building for human welfare. As one of our social economists puts it:

> The increasing scope of income security programs, in a period of full employment, has led too to the recognition of a new risk, whose statistical importance, in this country at least, has been surprisingly large. This is the broken family (or more accurately the pathological family) as a cause of income insecurity.[3]

This important statement comes as no surprise to the caseworker.

Areas of Knowledge

In what areas has social work a special opportunity to make a contribution to the growing science of interpersonal relations? One is the area of family and child relationships. Medicine finds its patients among those having a disease process or bodily dysfunctioning. In general, doctors treat persons who show symptom formation. Medical treatment is mainly a psycho-biological operation, although medicine looks beyond this focus. Social work finds its clients, in general, among those who "act out" their conflicts through social and familial relations. As long as psychiatry was utilized largely for mental illness or addressed to unconscious "id" impulses, psychotherapy was seen primarily as a medical specialty; but when cultural and social factors and ego functions of the personality were given fuller attention, professional range had to be extended. Purely medical versions of psychotherapy will remain and also psychoanalysis, but the utilization of social therapy as an essential element in many forms of psychotherapy is inescapable. The psychotherapy of children requires therapeutic intervention as to the parental environment; for many adolescents, ego-building through social achievement is bound up with psychotherapeutic efficacy. For therapeutic casework we should select cases in which there is a genuine social component, just as medicine takes cases with a biological component, and law a legal component. The psychotherapeutic tools used should be in combinations appropriate to the goals and competence of the practitioner.

Social workers today, perhaps, know more about problems of family separation than any other one profession. Yet institutional policy, progressing slowly from custodial care and detention to treatment for the patient, hardly yet touches one of the most

[3] Eveline M. Burns, "Social Security in a Period of Full Employment," Annual Meeting of the Industrial Relations Research Association, Boston, December 29, 1951.

important angles, that is, the patient's relationship to his family, to the institutional personnel, and to the outside world. Has hospital administration faced the problem of how staffs deal with the anxiety perpetually aroused in patients and their families by mental illness? What might it not do for the recovery of patients if administrators knew how to enable constructive day-by-day relations in institutions? Suppose all institutional personnel had not only therapeutic attitudes toward the client, but helpful ones toward each other? Suppose social work agencies began to set an example through the use of casework principles in social administration?

The family as the unit of work was briefly abandoned as social work discovered the child as an entity, and later the fascination of the "patient." There is always a tendency to regress from the more complicated to the less complicated solution. Thus, in the difficulty of learning therapy some workers turned aside for a while from the interpersonal approach. There has been a flight to multiple workers even when inappropriate, just as there have been attempts to split apart the essential sociopsychological unity. We have shared the fear of the mystics that any reaching outward might contaminate intimate therapy. Fortunately caseworkers are returning with renewed conviction to social-psychodynamics.

As social work becomes competent to envisage family treatment goals, the courts may, perhaps, discard old lables of "neglect" and "juvenile delinquency" for more precise psychodynamic concepts. Social workers should renounce the obsolete division between "family" and "children's" agencies along with other provincial and out-moded isolationist categories. In child behavior problems, although the child may be the focus, the family should remain not merely the "context," but the essential core of treatment. Recognition of the importance of age levels, in diagnosis and treatment for the young child or the adolescent, should not lead to parallel structures like a youth authority set up without reference to established family and children's programs. We saw during the war years the tremendous expansion of day nurseries, introduced and operated often with very little reference to what was already known about the needs of children and interagency functions.

The "clinical" use of authority to supplement well-established therapeutic techniques of acceptance, ventilation of feeling, support, clarification of behavior and attitudes should be further tested and developed. Introduction of equally therapeutic techniques in limits and restraints might revolutionize some aspects of the field of delinquency. Casework is essential here also.

As a citizen, one may be for or against the policy of released time in the public schools for religious instruction. One may have a conviction about the roles of church and state, and many conscious and unconscious preconceptions, but as social workers we know what the effects of such a policy on children and on family and social attitudes are likely to be in interpersonal and intergroup terms. We know or can ascertain some of the things that teachers tend to do; some of the things that the children who are released and the children who are not released tend to feel and do. Such data should become available for the consideration of persons drafting social legislation.

Social work has data on money both as "income" and as "behavior"—data that are not learned in schools of business or on Wall Street. Social workers should be prepared to testify more often on what they know about attitudes toward money in social functioning; not only about what inadequate money grants do to people, important as this is, but to testify also about problems of marital tension and how these may become displaced on the financial situation; how workers, unless well trained, may use money grants to punish, to control, to threaten, to seduce. Probably few would advise that the social insurances should be administered wholly by social workers, but there are many functions that call for social work processes. A department of social work is as much needed within the insurance structure as in a school, court, or hospital.

New facilities for children and youth are urgently needed, but all resources should be planned from the base of family life and the development of personality. We are not yet paying family allowances to parents, nor yet to substitute parents, but for the most part niggardly board rates. We could find far more good substitute homes if economic subsidy were possible. Why don't we do something about it? A country cannot afford, in this most precious of endeavors, the waste of competitive programs, or the meager appropriations that skimp and distort. Children are not expendable even in the great immorality which is tolerated as war. At the last White House Conference on Children many of us were disheartened to sense the conflicting power groups, the vested interests, the prejudices which were operating. And why are we not trying more courageous experiments (whenever the fluidity of a cultural situation permits) with interracial adoptions? There are important demonstrations indicating the feasibility of such adoptions both in Canada and the United States, but otherwise progressive adoption legislation contains a number of culturally restrictive clauses. Why do we let such things happen?

Social workers have fought for public welfare—although not enough and not always in the best way—but they have not insisted upon the use of their knowledge that public welfare safeguards family life, and that it must be concerned not alone with eligibility for money grants, but with the family as a whole. Today social assistance, the first safeguard of children, is backed up against the wall; ill and incapacitated people are bracketed with chiselers on public lists. (True, investigations have not disclosed many chiselers, but the damage to people is already done.) Parents are devaluated and children go to school haunted and taunted because they have been given the assistance to which they and their families have a right. Perhaps the child welfare workers may stand aloof, thinking that "attacks on public assistance do not necessarily hurt the children's services." But wait—look around—the "night riders" are out again. Out-of-wedlock children who most need our protection are being menaced; mothers in some places are spied upon and their allowances withdrawn. Aid to Dependent Children itself may be seriously undermined. What do such movements cover but hatred toward human beings, hatred toward all children?

Perhaps, too, the private agencies may stand aloof. Perhaps if they do not vigorously back the public social services they will "get by," obtain more money in financial drives, and so on. Can anyone fail to see that the attack on the public services is on all forms of social service, on human relations, and on people? Treatment is not esoteric, is not something applied only in certain settings—it means understanding and caring for people in skilled ways. Casework method is as essential to the public as to the voluntary social services. The leaders and staffs of voluntary agencies who dare not stand up to be counted on the basic issues of social welfare and social justice cannot be counted on for quality of service either. Make no mistake about that. Social work will not have professional or economic security, or prestige, so long as it retains its ancillary or adjunctive position to medicine or law or other established professions, or to an abstraction called "setting"! Casework process is distorted whenever it loses its focus on client and community. Social work must learn to stand on its own feet, develop its own research, and make its unique contribution to a common science of behavior and of society.

An area in which social work knowledge and process must increasingly be used is social administration. Social work is an agency-geared profession; the framework for social welfare increasingly is that of statutes and regulations. Yet administration has been far too little influenced by knowledge of dynamics, of human channels, of interactions, and of adaptations. Administration has been described as the process of relating specific duties or functions within a co-ordinated whole; leadership in human relations is the art of educating and inspiring people through informed understanding. Leadership qualities are the same in all professions. There is no known training for leadership other than opportunity. As admissions policies in the schools reinforce the trend to the selection of relatively well-adjusted persons with good ego strengths, we shall get more persons with capacity for community leadership. But we must attract these potential leaders to the professional schools through better recruitment and enhanced professional status and reward.

There are those who urge social workers to become community organizers and administrators, but do not yet realize that an adequate concept of personality and behavior is as essential to sound legislation, to programs, to institutions, and to administration, as it is to treatment. A person may have excellent ego strengths, be well adjusted, be a good caseworker, but he may not choose to use himself in administrative practice. As a first-class practitioner he, too, is an indispensable leader. Casework insights should be combined with the administrative process in the making and use of policy. Administration begins with people and goes on with people. Since social services have the objective of positive welfare, this element must be central to all policy formulation. The administrative process should reflect sound principles, concepts, values, and methods of professional work. Good administration includes ability to formulate and to articulate, to conceptualize, to synthesize; to channelize and utilize staff abilities—not to strangle opposition and difference. Yet outstanding social workers in strategic places, both in public and private agencies, recently have been liquidated with some of the usual rationalizations—"reorganization," "economy," or the like.

The administrator should be an organizer and leader imbued with the concept of participation and respect for staff as deeply as is the caseworker with respect for clients. Administrators who do not respect staff usually do not care much about clients either. Respect for differences, opportunity afforded for special strengths and aptitudes, freedom to present opposing points of view, participation in policy and personnel practices at all levels, devices through which board, administrative, and staff activities can be channelized, communicated, and shared, should be assured. Sound administration means a strong board, administration, and staff, with clearly defined functions, mutual respect, and effective means of working together. The administrator is neither a creature of the board nor an advocate of staff, but a representative of the welfare community. Above all he should be trained in the psychodynamics of behavior and interpersonal relationships.

Symptoms of pathological organization show up when policies are either imposed by the board upon the agency or forced upon the staff by administration, without due process of study, discussion, and collaboration. Other symptoms are seen in personally based promotions, an inner circle with policies decided in executive session or behind closed doors. Factionalism practically always points to disintegration of leadership and a tendency on the part of board and/or executive to attract and reward partisans. The warning may come slowly or in disguised ways. There is always a denial or dilution of practice in regard to clients, always deterioration of personnel practices, always an insidious or open attack on staff participation, always a history of inadequate support for public issues and programs, except in the safest and least controversial areas. For whom the bell tolls!

The contention that major reorganization plans and personnel practices are of no concern to anyone outside the agency cannot be defended, or that "the agency belongs to the donors" in the sense even that a concern may "belong" to its stockholders. It simply is not true. Modern industry increasingly regards its operations as being those of public policy, public trust, and public service. Welfare agencies should be in the lead in furthering this concept. Probably the majority of social workers accept the fact of unions in social work, of collective bargaining as a human right, but if we are going to have unions we cannot merely conform to existing labor or management traditions; rather we must ask ourselves how professional knowledge should affect union operation in social work agencies. The "adversary principle," already mentioned, is not adequate for labor relations, least of all in welfare practice.

Accountability is a two-way, not a one-way, street. Neither staffs nor clients should be told they must accede to an edict or it will be held against them. Evaluation should not be made the instrument of supervisory and administrative doctrine. Procedures for fair hearings represent great advance, and so do collective bargaining and negotiation and arbitration, but beyond that the whole question of the formulation of policy for international and national issues, for states and local governments, for boards and staffs and clients, must be the responsibility of everyone. What *consent of the governed* was to our forefathers, *constructive participation* is to our own generation. An agency represents a group activity—it is not a strait jacket! Social workers must be on their guard lest conformity to established procedures be extolled as a virtue in itself. Agency policy must remain dynamic, not static; it must belong to all of us, constantly being reshaped to meet changing human needs and to reflect new professional knowledge and skill. Adjustment never means acceptance of injustice. And since interpersonal dynamics is an acknowledged skill in social work, why are we not moving more rapidly ahead on interracial staffing of agencies? The pending immigration bill [4] is a disgrace, but have we done our part on intergroup and interracial practices even in our own agencies and communities? What are we waiting for?

Integration with the Social Sciences

Social policy cannot be successfully developed until the gap is closed between the social sciences and social work. But the basis of the administration of social policy arises from the insights gained with clients out of practice and research in which practitioners are not regarded as second-class scientists.

A difficulty for any profession is the enormous spread of substantive knowledge which must be assimilated for use; in social work it includes a theory of personality, behavior, culture, economic

[4] Editor's Note: By the time this article was first published, the bill had been enacted into law.

systems, and government. Administrators cannot administer without adequate grounding in the primary objectives, ethics, and skills of human relationships, nor can practitioners develop competence without breadth, depth, and vision as to human needs, rights, and responsibilities. Nor can the social sciences be made accessible from outside. Nothing substantial can be achieved unless there is a two-way collaboration, with sharing of research and of practice. The practitioner learns from the scientist, and the scientist learns from the practitioner. Indeed, the ultimate knowledge of attitudes, feelings, and behavior cannot be acquired adequately at all save in the actual experience of practice—learning how to involve oneself in treating another person. Even important concepts like "the multidiscipline approach" are already being prostituted and popularized to evade the hard task of each profession's defining its goals and making education and training adequate for its shared responsibilities.

Perhaps what we can count on most today from the social sciences is methodology, but methodology cannot be superimposed; it must be tested in collaborative effort on problems of mutual significance. The professional disciplines must themselves be related through definition of goal and role. We cannot achieve what we are after by dilution of any given discipline or any form of imitation or spreading thin; integration is not achieved by boards' or administrators' imposing a structure upon practitioners; it is not achieved by sharing a building or an office, with co-operation resting upon vague assertions of good will. It is only achieved by people working together in a genuine experience as well as in a spirit of co-operation.

Social workers have suffered both from a true humility, which is the basis of any scientific attitude, and the inferiorities of a newcomer among the professions. We shall progress as a mature self-criticism replaces insecurity and false modesty. The golden age of medicine began with the assimilation of the physical and biological sciences with professional practice. The golden age of social work is still on the horizon. It will not come until the integration of the social sciences and social work is made more possible; but social workers must speak out with assurance on what they already know and what they are learning about human beings. Must social work be made respectable by being called "clinical sociology," or can the social sciences and social work at last come together in multi-disciplinary effort?

The next steps in policy-making call for a stronger alliance among the social sciences, such as cultural anthropology, social psychology, economics and political science, but there must be a true partnership, not snobbishness on one side and inferiority feelings on the other. Each science and professional discipline has its own frame of reference, terminology, and special methods. What must be recognized, however, is the deep-set character of the resistance, which certain social scientists reveal, to taking into account conscious and unconscious feelings and motivation. Indeed, the fundamental resistance is toward understanding the nature of personality itself. Social workers should, therefore, recognize not only their own inertia and resistance to research and social action, but they should also understand the widespread phenomenon of resistance to psychodynamics. Just now mental health is enjoying deserved popular and financial support, but how long will this last unless legislators are helped to understand that mental health cannot be achieved without Social Security? It cannot be divorced from social assistance, nor can it be divorced from the needs of children; it means social welfare, it means caring for people; and, conversely, social assistance cannot be divorced from personality. This is the revolutionary idea so long overdue, so little accepted. The interests of research and therapy not only are not in opposition, but will be brought together.[5]

Perhaps the root of the matter is that the purpose of social work is to help bring the psychosocial, psychodynamic concept into the larger scene, into the building of welfare programs and into their administration. If, as Charlotte Towle says, the role of social work is to mobilize the conscience of the community through processes addressed to interpersonal relations, all welfare programs will be person-centered, just as all true education is student-, not subject-, centered. Legislation alone cannot accomplish this end, although legislation is one of the most effective tools in a modern society. In order to develop feelings and attitudes that permit men to think and act constructively, there must be professional multidisciplinary efforts actively directed toward understanding the nature of man

[5] Chester C. Bennett, "Training of Clinical Psychologists: Some Growing Pains in Clinical Psychiatry" (Part 3 of Round Table), *American Journal of Orthopsychiatry,* Vol. XXII, No. 1 (1952), pp. 153–161.

and of society. Too often in education, research, social science, and social action, process is unrelated to human feelings and human existence. Social workers must take more leadership in constructing welfare platforms and programs; they must re-commit themselves to manipulating the social as well as the individual environment; but they must also increasingly bring what they know of human behavior and interpersonal adaptations into the fabric of welfare and community life. Resistance to looking at the nature of man is the last enemy to be overcome. As men become willing and able to understand personality, the vision of human brotherhood may be realized. If we can further knowledge and practice in the field of social as well as psychological dynamics, we can hold up our heads as the oldest, the newest, the most difficult, and the most radical of the professions.

PROFESSIONAL LEADERSHIP IN THE SOCIAL STRUCTURE[1]

Jean M. Snelling

"WITHIN THE RANKS of the professions are to be found most of those upon whose special skill the functioning of modern society depends."[2] Carr-Saunders wrote this in 1933; and, in the score of years that have followed, the place and importance of special skill in the community have not altered. Yet, throughout these years, there has been evidence of disappointment among professional people in the United States and Great Britain over the lack of pro-

[1] Published in *Social Casework,* July 1954.

[2] A. M. Carr-Saunders, *The Professions,* Oxford University Press, New York, 1933.

fessional leadership in our social structure. Carr-Saunders, in Britain, and the Inter-Professions Conference [3] held at Buck Hill Falls, Pennsylvania, in 1948, speak of this disappointment in the medical, legal, engineering, architectural, and business professions. Benjamin E. Youngdahl, addressing the American Association of Social Workers in 1947,[4] expressed one of several instances of similar disappointment among professional social workers.

Eveline M. Burns, writing in 1947, made a useful distinction between two kinds of leadership and activity, the truly professional type and the citizenship type.[5] In the second, professional people act in public affairs as ordinary, conscientious citizens without having a claim to special knowledge. In the first, they can claim to speak with particular authority on subjects coming within their professional area of knowledge. Mrs. Burns believed, for instance, that social workers have professional competence in their understanding of human behavior and its relations with environmental factors and social institutions, and that they have a sense of reasonable priorities in the social welfare field. With their unique access to special informational material and their particular perspectives on matters related to their own techniques, the professions have expert knowledge which they should offer to the community when it is needed in the solving of some broad problem. The sources referred to previously indicate that many people regard the professions as having failed in both kinds of leadership; yet possibly there is more concern over defective activity in areas of special knowledge.

So keen is the sense of loss and of self-questioning that it seems to imply a feeling that the professions have some obligation to do differently. Perhaps the time has arrived for adding this capacity for social leadership to the criteria by which we recognize true professions and distinguish them from avocations. If this is so, it would account, in part, for such widespread concern.

The criteria of professionalism still await satisfactory definition, but for the purposes of this paper Carr-Saunders' work [6] is helpful.

[3] *Education for Professional Responsibility:* Proceedings of the Inter-Professions Conference on Education for Professional Responsibility, Carnegie Press, Pittsburgh, Pa., 1948.

[4] Benjamin E. Youngdahl, "Social Workers: Stand Up and Be Counted," *The Compass,* Vol. XXVIII, No. 3 (1947), p. 21.

[5] Eveline M. Burns, "Social Action and the Professional Social Worker," *The Compass,* Vol. XXVIII, No. 4 (1947), p. 37.

[6] Carr-Saunders, *op. cit.*

He saw professional people as undertaking prolonged and specialized intellectual training and thereby developing a technique that would enable them to render a specialized service to the community. Such a technique might be scientific, or institutional, or partly aesthetic, and would be founded upon a basic field of inquiry (for example, biology, sociology, or law) which would be more clear-cut when scientific than when institutional. Carr-Saunders found that in true professionalism the technique always gives rise to certain attitudes and activities: attitudes of responsibility toward clients and of concern for the competence and honor of practitioners as a whole; activities involving tests of competence and enforced observance of certain standards of conduct. He recognized certain new professions (nursing, business administration) as wanting in their relationship to a basic field of inquiry, yet compensating somewhat in their attitudes or activities; these he placed on the periphery of the professional field.

Social work is coming well within the periphery, and it should move toward the center as the gap between it and the social sciences narrows. It seems that, in the modern world, this equipment of basic specialized knowledge, competence, and sense of responsibility to clients is being broadened, quite logically, into an obligation by a profession to serve the community—as one unit to a bigger unit. In that sense the widely held yet unspoken thought seems justified: a profession is not truly professional today if it fails in skilled leadership for social action.

The New Expectation

This sense of having failed nevertheless obscures the newness of the issue. In the main, professions have developed their principles, ethics, and techniques around the practitioner's relationship with his client. Basically this is a one-to-one relationship; and that fact has been fundamental to the patterning of the professions within Western society. The modern concept of the interdependence of men in a democratic society now demands that the professions maintain their one-to-one service unchanged, yet that they also accept a new and simultaneous responsibility as separate professional groups toward the community as a whole. A profession will have to do two things at once: it must keep up practitioner service to individuals and it must render group service to a group.

When the momentous nature of this dual expectation is considered, it is not surprising that the professions find themselves ill equipped. The situation bristles with questions. Is the newer group relationship of the same kind as the one-to-one relationship and just larger in scale, or is it fundamentally different? Can the one-to-one relationship be kept intact, or must it be modified in some way? In what direction should the first experiments be made if the new relationship is to be explored constructively and quickly? How far can the professions make common cause in learning their place in the society of tomorrow? How far must they venture forward separately? While experiments are being made, can professional education and practice be so modified that they can begin to move ahead as soon as a desired direction is identified? The fact that the newer and less well established professions are more persistent and alert in their questioning than the older ones is a complicating, if natural, factor.

Such a momentous change cannot develop overnight, and for some time the professions are likely to remain confused over what they should do and how they should do it. The purpose of this paper is to try to recognize some of the immediate obstacles that impede progress in working out this new relationship, and in particular to recognize obstacles confronting the profession of social work.

Handicaps for Professional People

Some of the difficulties that handicap professional people and prevent broad and responsible thinking in community affairs were analyzed by Elliott Dunlap Smith of the Carnegie Institute of Technology, speaking at the Inter-Professions Conference in 1948.[7] He remarked on the dichotomy in the professional man; he contrasted the sound competence, judgment, interest, and integrity offered to clients with the failure to apply such qualities to considering matters that seemed to be outside regular professional channels. He noted that professional study and work are so preoccupying that, were broad humanistic and social studies taught as part of professional courses, they would be in danger of being swallowed up by, and completely subordinated to, the professional interests. This point

[7] *Education for Professional Responsibility, op. cit.*

was made in relation to professional education; its broader application to a profession's whole way of thinking seems plain. However much social workers might feel disturbed to see this process occur when the very substance of their professional program and thinking is humanistic and social study, many of them would probably agree that this is a true observation and that it applies as much to social work as to other professions.

The dichotomy that was described by Dr. Smith points to a failure in maturing. Strecker and Appel's charming account of the mature individual [8] cannot be summarized without loss; yet the qualities they indicate as contributing to personal maturity are the very ones sought by the professions within themselves. These qualities are the ability to stick to a job and to give to it more than is asked; reliability and endurance; the ability to size things up and to make decisions independently; the capacity to co-operate, to work with others and under authority; patience, tolerance, flexibility, adaptability; the ability to wait and to compromise. "Basically, maturity represents a wholesome amalgamation of two things: (1) dissatisfaction with the status quo, which calls forth aggressive, constructive effort; and (2) social concern and devotion." Could the professions possess these qualities, they would be happier about their future adaptations.

In considering how the professions could move toward this state, we see clearly at once that maturity in a profession is partly a reflection of maturity in its practitioners. Knowledge and understanding of the components of maturity and their promotion are still in the beginning stage. Professional programs that first select practitioners carefully and then offer them through education and further education all possible help toward attaining maturity, within the professional framework, are of prime importance. Although social work educators do not consider themselves to be as far along in such developments as they would wish, nevertheless they are ahead of many other professions. The apparent unreadiness of some others to learn only puts more onus upon social work to crystallize and formulate this growing body of experience in order to have it available and relevant against the time when it is wanted.

[8] E. A. Strecker and K. E. Appel, quoted by G. B. Chisholm in "The Reestablishment of Peacetime Society: The Responsibility of Psychiatry," *Psychiatry*, Vol. IX, No. 1 (1946), p. 6.

Special Handicaps for Social Workers

It is well known that every profession tends to attract to itself some practitioners whose personal needs meet with some gratification within the professional technique. Thus each profession will have certain conditions that make for and against maturing. Social work has long been recognized as drawing workers who are sensitive to and needful of good relationships with other human beings within the prefabricated yet protecting framework of the profession. They need to feel themselves to be valued and liked by other people. It cannot be easy for such workers to step out beyond the safety of the professional framework and to accept the comparative loneliness or disapproval that sometimes faces innovators of social action. The fact that this is a particular and understandable handicap for social workers needs to be recognized and accepted, for part of the profession's problem of maturing lies in this dependency upon the approval of the community.

The absence of quiet, imperturbable confidence in the profession of social work is acknowledged among its practitioners, and the profession's hesitancy in taking social leadership can be attributed to it. The contributing factors must be many, and some of them are indicated briefly here.

The low level of salaries is often said to be related to the lack of self-confidence; and it is probably true that a professional group with personal need of the community's approving recognition will feel depreciated when the community seems to rate its services at a low value. This can set up a spiral, for the profession that feels inferior will have difficulty in convincing the community of its worth. But, despite its intrinsic truth, this argument is probably being used by social workers as a smoke screen to hide other unwelcome facts.

The American political climate of today is likely to make special difficulties for social workers who feel uncertain of themselves and of their profession; but a foreigner cannot easily be sure of the force and direction of various trends here.

The uncertainty of some workers must stem from their conflict over psychology. Gordon Hamilton has said, "Resistance to looking at the nature of man is the last enemy to be overcome."[9] Social

[9] Gordon Hamilton, "The Role of Social Casework in Social Policy," p. 44 of this volume. Reprinted from *Social Casework*, October 1952.

workers commonly speak as though this were a struggle between themselves (the lookers) and the community (the resisters). Yet it is surely true that within the profession there is uneasiness and perhaps rejection among some workers who were not able to come to terms personally with psychology during the short years of training and who have not done so subsequently; who have in fact remained unhappily stuck betwixt and between. Until their inner conflict is resolved in one way or another, these social workers are not likely to speak and act with confidence and to relate satisfactorily to the community. Resolution of the conflict will make for a move toward professional and personal maturity.

A further reason for the sense of inferiority among workers in both the United States and Great Britain comes from uneasiness in facing the task they know they must face, the sorting out of the job into grades. Although many social workers accept in general terms the idea that different degrees of skill are required for different functions within the wide and varied field, and recognize that a systematic survey is needed to ascertain and define the skills and functions, the survey has not been set up and the task is untackled. The two studies of training, the Hollis-Taylor report [10] in the United States and Younghusband reports [11] in Great Britain, lead up to pointing the need for the surveys and then have to stop short. The common hesitance to proceed is associated with the difficulties of knowing how to do so and who should do so, and with problems of personnel and funds; but there are deeper reasons. Most social workers sense, though few openly say so, that the top-grade skills in casework, group work, community organization, and social administration are beyond the reach of many workers and would remain so however much help could be given by training. The pattern of the future may lie in a small number of highly selected, highly trained, highly skilled professional people, a large number of sub-professional workers and a large number of skilled clerks, all the result of a refining and sloughing off that each profession in turn experiences, sometimes recurrently, at stages of its development. The profession's resistance to this development in social work has some foundation

[10] Ernest V. Hollis and Alice L. Taylor, *Social Work Education in the United States,* Columbia University Press, New York, 1951.

[11] Eileen L. Younghusband, *Report on the Employment and Training of Social Workers in Britain,* Carnegie United Kingdom Trust, Dunfermline, Scotland, 1947; *Social Work in Britain,* Carnegie United Kingdom Trust, Dunfermline, Scotland, 1951.

in the awareness or suspicion of many workers that both their own capacities and the duties they perform would place them and their jobs in the lower grades. There is a reality of vested interest to be faced which will not melt away with waiting.

In Britain the inevitable day of reckoning will be eased somewhat by the growing appreciation of population studies, which reveal both the proportionate insufficiency of the young-adult age group and the total shortage (in relation to demand) of intellects capable of undertaking skilled professional work; these findings will sugar the pill of need for job-analysis and for the acknowledgement that not everybody can perform in the first rank.

In the United States the population situation is different and there seems to be confidence that the total adult group can meet the heavy demands on young and old in the next quarter century. There is also confidence that American universities do not yet absorb all the good potential candidates for university education and that their nets could be cast more widely yet. Although this happy state of expansion may continue for some time, it is to be hoped that the American professions will benefit eventually by the grimmer experience of the British professions, by being able to look ahead to shortage through absorption before its actual arrival. Meanwhile the question of what proportion of graduates is suitable for skilled professional training for top-level social work will probably continue to receive attention; and a watch may need to be kept to see whether this matter of supply will come to have more bearing on the distribution of function within American social work than it has today.

Fragmentary Thinking

There is another side to the matter of intellectual quality. Mrs. Burns[12] observed that social action, in so far as it is attempted today, is not effective if its front becomes too broad and that it usually needs to be founded upon a concentrated study of a small area. In this way the problems can be identified and the hypotheses made, the evidence collected and solutions planned. This is the area of expert activity, and sound work here must precede the more spectacular stages of enlisting public support, and then carrying through and subsequently maintaining suitable social action. Social

[12] Burns, *op. cit.*

work, with its present inner uncertainty, might be expected to succeed in the early expert steps and then to falter at the stage of seeking public interest.

This is not what happens, however; the faltering comes earlier, for general social problems are often identified only partially, and few hypotheses are made about the causes, nor is supporting evidence acquired in fair proportion to the opportunities that exist. Social workers are more skillful in their ability to individualize a problem than in their ability to generalize about it, and this peculiarity must make for weakness in preparing for social or group action, unless the skill can deliberately be disciplined.

The reasons for this characteristic are not clear, and are probably multiple. Experience in selecting candidates for professional training in social work in England suggests a line for further thinking and inquiry. This experience indicates that some candidates put forward by knowledgeable people as having "excellent potential for social work" will do well in psychometric tests measuring verbal facility, and comparatively poorly in tests requiring a capacity for discerning similar qualities in apparently dissimilar material. (The subsequent performance of these individuals has usually borne out the findings of the tests). There is no conclusive evidence—yet the proposition deserves more consideration—that social work tends to recruit workers whose powers of verbalizing are greater than their powers of co-ordinating ideas; and verbalizing that is not controlled by a pull toward generalization may go toward excessive individualization and fragmentation. If this is basically a fault in maturing, it must be a very deep-seated one. Some compensation for its effects in individual practitioners may be found in self-awareness and conscious control and by educational modifications, but proper correction for the whole profession would entail revision of recruiting programs. If, in the future, the profession aimed to be able to think as a group about general community problems, correction of this trend in personnel qualities would be important.

A peculiarly American phenomenon that may further encourage fragmentary thinking is the rapid migration among social workers. To a foreign observer, a disproportionate amount of professional time and energy appears to be bound down in teaching and learning the routines of new jobs. The workers who are overly and recurrently preoccupied in this way are not free for thinking of general trends or deeper issues, and thereby they seem to delay their own professional maturing.

Ways and Means To Help Thinking

When once the practitioners in any profession have the ability to formulate ideas and sort evidence (and they could hardly claim to be a profession without a good number of such practitioners), they still require, according to Carr-Saunders,[13] four essential aids to promoting the continued development of professional knowledge —the knowledge, that is, upon which social action and leadership are based. These four aids are an active contact with universities and their thinking; a broad and continuous study program for qualified practitioners which flourishes through the professional association; an accessible library for the use of practitioners; and at least one periodical published within the profession as a vehicle for sharing studies. It would not be difficult to test these findings and relate them to the intellectual vigor and activity of different professions; general observation would seem to confirm their validity.

Effective use of such channels, however, raises the question of spending time and expending money on further studies. The time issue is roughly this: If the community expects its professional people to find a way of using their expert knowledge and thinking in public affairs, and if it is accepted that continued study is a necessary part of so doing, then professional time should be used both for the public activity and for the preliminary study. Good thinking on public affairs is hardly possible when practitioner duties consume the best working hours entirely and study and creative thinking are relegated to the hours of fatigue and private choice; nor would such a method of time expenditure indicate due appreciation of the wider duties. Since this question of the proper use of professional time is common to all the professions, an expert body should be set up to study it and to make recommendations for a better investment of the working day. This body would probably need to study the relations between known methods of payment (fees, salaries) and the time given already by practitioners to study and to public affairs.

A more important financial issue would relate to study programs, university contacts, libraries, and magazines. Whether a profes-

[13] Carr-Saunders, *op. cit.*

sional association could support these adequately, and what size of membership would be needed for doing so, again would be matters for expert assessment. Public funds and employers might be expected to contribute, and their financial participation would reflect their general concern for the efficient functioning of professional life. This is therefore a much broader issue than finance alone, and it leads straight back to the question of the future relationship between the professions and the total community.

Conclusion

On considering these professional problems in one country and the other, and then between various professions within the two countries, we find the striking feature to be the commonness of the problems. This seems to indicate that they are mainly problems of growth rather than problems of error. Growth can be frightening, but the Western world in which these professions are reared has come to look upon sound growth as something good leading to something better.

Social workers are keenly aware of their late start in the professional world and of the unformed state of their professional knowledge, in comparison with other disciplines. However, in the matter of a responsible attitude to community affairs, which here has been put forward as a mark of professionalism, social workers do not lag behind other disciplines. Their very discontent and their fumbling for understanding of their responsibility place them well forward in this aspect of professionalism today. That a new profession can attain this position after a half century of growth promises well for its developing powers and future progress. Social work cannot take comfort in its own discomfort over social responsibility, but it can rightly be cheerful for having come so far.

THE INTERDEPENDENCE OF THE PROFESSIONS IN HELPING PEOPLE [1]

Eleanor Cockerill

THE FLYLEAF OF Mary Richmond's *Social Diagnosis* presents a provocative quotation from the writings of Hans Gross, a lawyer, which might well be read by all of us at least once a day as a reminder of the interdependent relationship we hold with other professional groups who, like ourselves, are seeking to acquire increased understanding of man and his society and to promote the welfare of both. In his book dealing with criminal investigation, Gross declares: "Only the sham knows everything; the trained man understands how little the mind of any individual may grasp, and how many must co-operate in order to explain the very simplest things." [2] In other words, the more actual knowledge we possess about man and his environment, the less likely we are to feel competent to encompass the whole or to operate independently. In a professional sense, the "sham" is a person who behaves as though he had some choice about his interdependent relationships with others who deal with human problems. There is, however, no actual choice, since denial of this interdependent relationship has to be purchased at the cost of a distorted view of man and his problems.

The human organism is a physiological, psychological, and social being, and its totality is the product of the interaction of its three

[1] Published in *Social Casework,* November 1953. Presented at the National Conference of Social Work, Cleveland, June 1953.

[2] Mary E. Richmond, *Social Diagnosis,* Russell Sage Foundation, New York, 1917, flyleaf (quoting from Hans Gross, *Criminal Investigation,* translated by Adam and Adam, A. Krishnamachari, Madras, India, 1906).

components. Moreover, the individual "cannot live alone nor achieve fulfillment except in interrelated living. Man and his society, therefore, constitute an organic whole in which the welfare of each is dependent on the other."[3] Aspects of man or of society may be selected for investigative purposes at any given time, but this is an artificial device, utilized by man in order to study phenomena. "The process of understanding is not complete until separate aspects have been re-integrated."[4] Special needs or problems of man and his society may also be isolated for purposes of instituting specialized kinds of corrective or remedial action developed by various groups of experts. Such division of labor, with differentiation of professional function, is a necessary device utilized by society in order to provide the range of services required to meet human needs and to ensure that they are rendered with expertness. The effectiveness of any partialized form of remedial action, however, rests ultimately upon comprehension of the full context of the problem, delineation of over-all objectives, recognition of the full range of approaches required for reaching them, and the integration of each approach with the total problem-solving operation. This imperative stems from the organic wholeness of human and social problems and must be obeyed if problem-solving objectives are to be fully realized.

Dr. Elliott Smith, an engineer by profession, has pointed out that unless professional problems are considered in relation to all their aspects it is not possible to ask the truly professional question: "What, all things considered, should be done?" "Otherwise," says Dr. Smith, "we are confined to the technical half-question, 'How can I do my stuff?', the answer to which is a dangerous half-truth."[5]

Since human and social problems are organic in nature, they pay no attention to professional boundaries. "Although the specific roles and functions of various professions and disciplines may have an apparent clarity when viewed separately, there is considerable evidence that the boundaries and something more than the boundaries becomes fuzzy when an attempt is made to work together on a common problem. A partial, but only a partial, explanation of

[3] Eleanor Cockerill and others, *A Conceptual Framework for Social Casework*, School of Social Work, University of Pittsburgh, University of Pittsburgh Press, 1952, p. 2.

[4] *Ibid.*, p. 7.

[5] *Education for Professional Responsibility:* Proceedings of the Inter-Professions Conference on Education for Professional Responsibility, Carnegie Press, Pittsburgh, Pa., 1948, p. 198.

the fuzziness is that it is probably inherent in the multidiscipline approach that roles become modified in the process. The remainder, and much the larger part of the explanation is that clarity is more apparent than real." [6]

The challenge to the professions then becomes one of learning how to work together in such a way as to be able to bring to bear upon the solution of the problems of the individual and of society —without distorting their unitary nature—the fruits of segmental investigation and the expertness that accrues from accumulated experience in dealing with specific problems in specialized functions.

Although barriers between the professions have been frequently lowered, if not eradicated, in the attack upon pressing and important human and social problems, certain real difficulties associated with interprofessional and interdisciplinary endeavor continue, which must be recognized and handled. Dr. Henry Brosin, an eminent psychiatrist and medical educator, has urged every worker in an interdisciplinary program to work conscientiously at the "problem of the observer" and to examine, as systematically as possible, the emotional roots of his prejudices no matter how well rationalized they may be. Interdisciplinary learning, Dr. Brosin points out, "often means the sacrifice of one's own certainties and the willingness to expose one's cherished views to critical inspection." [7]

In discussing the task and problem of philosophy in days of transition, Dewey points out that poetry, art, and religion are precious things that cannot be maintained by "lingering in the past and futilely wishing to restore what the movements of events in science, industry, and politics have destroyed." "It is possible," declared Dewey, "to expedite the development of the vital sources of religion and art that are *yet to be.*" [8] The immediate task of the helping professions would seem to be that of expediting the further development and utilization of those vital sources which have not eventuated—which are *yet to be.* The ideals and practices embodied in the concept of democracy afford the best way we know to accomplish this objective, since they describe the method by

[6] Institute Proceedings, *Social Work Practice in the Medical and Psychiatric Setting,* School of Social Work, University of Pittsburgh, June 1951, p. 121 (mimeographed).

[7] *Ibid.,* p. 69.

[8] John Dewey, *Reconstruction in Philosophy,* A Mentor Book, New American Library of World Literature, New York, 1950, p. 164.

which we can give all sides a fair hearing and thus utilize and benefit from the specialized knowledge and skills of all individuals and groups who share the common purpose of furthering the welfare of mankind.

Characteristics and Tasks of a Profession

In all true professions there exists potential capacity to respond to social and scientific change, although the attainment of this capacity is clearly related to the stage of maturity achieved by the particular profession. Dr. Tyler identifies two essential characteristics of a true profession. The first is the existence of a recognized code of ethics which commits the members of the profession to certain social values above the selfish ones of income, power, and prestige, with the expectation that the individual member will seriously dedicate himself to these higher values. The second distinguishing feature of a profession noted by Dr. Tyler is the basing of its techniques of operation upon principles rather than rule-of-thumb procedures or simple routine skills. In elaborating upon this second characteristic, Dr. Tyler asserts that as a profession "becomes more mature it recognizes that the principles used in the profession must be viewed in an increasingly larger context and that, correspondingly, the science needed by the profession must be continually extended to more basic content rather than restricted only to the obvious applied science." [9]

The late Dr. Lindeman proposed a number of criteria for measuring the maturity of a profession. These criteria included the following: the capacity to absorb relevant data and devices from ever-widening and varied sources so long as these assimilations do not lead to confusion with respect to the major hypothesis; adaptability to differing auspices and controls without loss of methodological integrity; capacity to adapt to the dynamics of the society in which it operates; and, finally, the ability to merge the content which derives from empirical sources (experience) with that which comes from science (theoretical) into a unifying stream of applicable knowledge.[10] Carr-Saunders and Wilson have stressed

[9] Ralph W. Tyler, "Distinctive Attributes of Education for the Professions," *Social Work Journal,* Vol. XXXIII, No. 2 (1952), p. 56.

[10] Eduard C. Lindeman, "Social Case Work Matures in a Confused World," an address given at the New York State Conference of Social Work, 1946, *The Compass,* Vol. XXVIII, No. 2 (1947), pp. 3–9.

particularly the responsibility of professions for contributing their specialized skill and viewpoint to the appropriate problems of their surrounding societies.[11]

These authorities emphasize that certain essential characteristics of a profession are the outgrowth of a maturation process. Growth of a profession, in other words, results from an orderly process of dealing with a series of developmental tasks, each of which must be achieved if the profession is to deal effectively with subsequent developmental tasks. In the early stages of a profession, the task of differentiation is primary and central. Several of the older professions were reasonably successful early in their development in coming to grips with this requirement of defining their essential functions and the particular segment of human experience to which they were primarily related. Social work, on the other hand, has failed to address itself vigorously to this task; progress along a number of fronts has been impeded because we have, to date, evolved no truly informative definition of social work. This failure undoubtedly influences the security with which social work is able to participate in interdisciplinary endeavor and also limits its ability to proceed with some of the further steps required for its professional growth.

Dr. Lee's discussion of the cultural implications of delimitation emphasizes the values of definition. Referring to our culture, Dr. Lee points out that "we need definition of knowledge, and we value it as security. We judge intelligence by ability to define and delimit. We consider clear definition essential in dealing with any situation; otherwise we cannot 'grasp' it. An object, a thought, a situation, a project, must have a limiting line around it to differentiate what it *is* from what *is not,* to show us where it ends and something else begins; otherwise we cannot act, we are immobilized. Besides, a vague situation makes us feel uncomfortable and insecure: 'We don't know where we are.' "[12]

Differentiation should aid professional interchange; its purpose is not merely to distinguish one profession from others, which might result in habits of non-co-operation and lead to separation and divorce. In fact, one of the primary purposes of definition is to

[11] A. M. Carr-Saunders and P. A. Wilson, "Professions," *Encyclopedia of the Social Sciences,* Macmillan Company, New York, 1937, Vol. VI, p. 479.

[12] Dorothy Lee, "Some Implications of Culture for Interpersonal Relations," *Social Casework,* Vol. XXXI, No. 9 (1950), p. 356.

facilitate communication between professions. Father Bowers has stated that "definition provides the definer with a precise thought content with which to carry on his own thinking, and gives to others a mode of weighing and measuring concepts and their correspondent terms." [13]

In addition to defining its function, a second developmental task for a profession is to establish interrelationships with the sciences that underlie its practice. As a profession moves toward maturity, its use of scientific knowledge must be continually extended; relevant data and devices from ever-widening and varied sources must be absorbed. This task is related to the broader one of merging the content that derives from empirical sources (experience) with that which comes from science (theoretical) into a unifying stream of applicable knowledge. This developmental task is vital for the growth of social work as a profession. The extensive social work literature dealing with the problem of establishing a scientific base affords evidence that the importance of this task is widely recognized. The obstacles to its achievement are not sufficiently relevant to this paper to justify enumeration here. It is important to note, however, that during recent years there has been increasing emphasis upon the necessity for establishing a theoretical base, since it is recognized that all "professional practice proceeds from a set of clear principles and concepts about human beings and their needs which are consciously held, teachable as such, and which constitute the logical justification for the practice." [14] A further consideration is that participation in interprofessional or interdisciplinary collaborative undertakings is, in many respects, dependent upon the possession of a systematized body of professional theory, and the capacity to deal with concepts and generalizations.

Interrelationships Between Sciences and Practice

How, then, do the basic and derived behavioral sciences influence the movement of a profession toward the establishment of a body of tested and useful theory, and how are these sciences influenced by this relationship? This reciprocal relationship is vividly illustrated in the revolutionary changes that occurred both in

[13] Swithun Bowers, O.M.I., "The Nature and Definition of Social Casework: Part I," *Journal of Social Casework,* Vol. XXX, No. 8 (1949), p. 312.

[14] Cockerill *et al., op. cit.,* p. 5.

medicine and in the biological sciences when these sciences were brought into the medical school. Although introduced initially for the purpose of making medicine more scientific, the sterile biological sciences themselves moved ahead more rapidly when this relationship came into being. "Even a cursory glance at medical history, or better, at Flexner's significant Carnegie report of 1910 will enable one to learn of the evolutionary steps which have taken place in physiology, bacteriology, and their application at the bedside." [15] David French, in a recent report, states: "When we consider the way in which other fields of practice have been able to contribute in quite fundamental ways to the sciences to which they are related, we can see the importance of not overlooking this possibility in the field of social work." [16]

Basically, the contribution of the sciences to the various helping professions would appear to be that of affording a more complete level of analyzing problems, through minimization of what Robert Merton terms "overlooked variables," [17] and of affording a broader base for identifying various approaches to the solution of these problems.

Pollak has noted that lack of necessary conceptual equipment may lead to the failure of the social worker to take certain important factors into account in the consideration of a professional problem since "phenomena for which technological terminology is not available to the practitioner tend to remain unconsidered." He thus concludes that enlargement of his conceptual base increases the "perceptual equipment" of the practitioner.[18] Grace Coyle has identified a number of useful concepts drawn from the field of cultural anthropology which illuminate professional social work problems in a recent article in which she discusses the new insights that are available to the social worker from the social sciences.[19]

[15] John Romano, "The Physician as a Comprehensive Human Biologist," *Education for Professional Responsibility, op. cit.*, p. 198.

[16] David G. French, *An Approach to Measuring Results in Social Work:* A Report on the Michigan Reconnaissance Study of Evaluative Research in Social Work Sponsored by the Michigan Welfare League, Columbia University Press, New York, 1952, p. 85.

[17] *Ibid.*, p. 84.

[18] Otto Pollak, "Relationships Between Social Science and Child Guidance Practice," *American Sociological Review,* Vol. XVI, No. 1 (1951), 61–67.

[19] Grace L. Coyle, "New Insights Available to the Social Worker from the Social Sciences," *Social Service Review,* Vol. XXVI, No. 3 (1952), pp. 289–304.

French has urged social work to state its problems and principles in terms that can be related to the thinking being done in the social sciences, so that we can obtain more reliable access to the knowledge of other professions working in the field of human relations. He comments upon the increasing interest of such fields as education, industrial management, and counseling in this activity and points out that as we become involved in a similar process we shall become related to the work that is going on in a much broader field of practice.[20]

In the maturation process of any profession it is essential to avoid the danger of premature crystallization which is inevitable if the profession becomes so engrossed in refining its current practices and strengthening its current institutions that it fails to take into account totally new approaches to its characteristic problems. In the field of dentistry, for instance, the fluoridation of water to retard tooth decay has afforded a new approach to dental problems which extends far beyond traditional methods. French has pointed out that research in social work must not only have freedom but also the responsibility for examining problems from every relevant perspective in order that various approaches to problems confronting social work may emerge. He quotes Dr. Alan Gregg, who said in his introduction to Dr. Kinsey's study of sexual behavior in the human male, "Seen from four points of the compass a great mountain may present aspects that are very different one from the other—so different that bitter disagreements can arise between those who have watched the mountain, truly and well, through all the seasons, but each from a different quarter." French emphasizes the fact that "it is by bringing together observers who have been watching the mountain from different sides and getting them to compare and try to put together their pictures of it that all relevant factors bearing on social work programs are going to be considered and studied." [21]

There is yet another developmental task that deserves emphasis, and that is the development of social responsibility and the capacity of the profession to respond to the dynamics of the society in which it operates. "Competence to assume this social responsibility and to respond to the dynamics of surrounding societies must rest not on emotion or intuition alone but on a solid foundation of knowledge

[20] French, *op. cit.*, p. 83.
[21] *Ibid.*, p. 57.

about that society which is to be affected."[22] The social sciences would seem to be one important source of that knowledge.

Interrelationship of the Professions

Having identified some of the essential characteristics of a profession and noted certain developmental tasks that it must achieve if it is to attain maturity, I shall now turn to a consideration of the major obligation of all helping professions in this age of specialization and diversified expertness. The obligation is that of refining further their ways of working together so that their efforts will be attuned to the unitary nature of man and his problems. Essential to the achievement of this objective is the commitment to the principle of the organic wholeness of human and social problems—on the part of professions as a whole and by their individual members on all operating levels. If this principle is firmly established, it will serve as the criterion by which professional service is evaluated, even though, because of obstacles, it cannot always be fully applied. Numerous new approaches will need to be employed in order to achieve correction of the problems that obstruct the integration of diversified bodies of knowledge and diversified kinds of specialized expertness. In fact, a new kind of specialist is already emerging—the person who, by virtue of the nature of his education and experience, is able to integrate within his own problem-solving efforts diversified approaches and to share the outcome of this with others. However, specialists in integration will always necessarily be limited in number and we shall have to depend primarily upon the co-operative effort of many persons.

The responsibilities of the professional person in *creating* effective teamwork have been ably defined by Ruth Hubbard. It is essential to recognize, when we examine these responsibilities, that teamwork is something that is *created* and that responsibility for its operations and outcomes must be shared by each participant. "To be part of a team means that one must be extremely well prepared in his own field, that he must see himself in relation to the contribution of others, that he must sense constantly the changing needs of the individuals whom he and the group are serving, that he must accept the corresponding changes in his contribution and the contributions

[22] Grace L. Coyle, quoted from an unpublished paper dealing with the relationship of the social sciences to professional education.

of other team members to these needs, that he must have the courage to say what he can do and why he feels that he can do that thing better than another, that he must have the grace to give up what he likes to do if another can do it better. It means further that he must learn to do things which do not come easily if they can best be done by him for the good of all. It means the will to pull with others and the integrity to withdraw from those parts of an undertaking which are not his. It means the enduring belief that together we can do things which none of us individually could do alone, and that the togetherness makes possible a concept of the job which is greater than the sum of the individual parts." [23] Dr. F. Fraser Darling, noted English biologist and ecologist, in referring to the essential nature of teamwork, says that each specialist should have "the quality of delighting in another man's work and linking his own to it." [24]

Several of the personal and professional capacities and attributes identified by Hubbard as essential for participation in the creation of teamwork merit further elaboration. The first of these is that "one must be extremely well prepared in his own field." The point needing emphasis here is that this preparation should be of a fundamental nature in terms of systematized *knowledge* of the concepts and principles comprising the theoretical base of the field so that they can be communicated clearly to others, and in terms of ability to perform well the functions characteristic of the field. The second is that the practitioner must be able to see himself in relation to the contribution of others. This implies, of course, general knowledge of other fields and also some capacity to think within their conceptual schemes. As was noted earlier, a professional problem cannot be viewed solely in terms of what it is possible for a particular practitioner to do about it; the step of defining the problem is implicit in a professional undertaking. Defining the problem may lead to the use of other resources, if knowledge and skills not possessed by the practitioner are required for its solution. Thus, both recognition of the instances that require a different kind of knowledge and competence and knowledge about where that competence is to be found are essential.

[23] Ruth Hubbard, "The Nurse on the Healing Arts Team," abstracted from an address given at the annual meeting of the Pennsylvania State Nurses Association, November 9, 1948.

[24] F. Fraser Darling, "The Ecological Approach to the Social Sciences," *American Scientist,* Vol. XXXIX, No. 2 (1951), p. 254.

A third important professional requirement is that the changing needs of the individuals being served must be sensed constantly. Thus, the clues for the determination of leadership responsibility are always to be found in the requirements of the problem situation. Leadership in the team situation, in this sense, is related to authority of ideas and competence and must be assumed freely and securely by the person or group best able to supply what is needed. Leadership responsibility, in terms of bringing specialized competence to bear upon the solution of a particular problem, therefore, cannot be permanently attached to any one person or group since it must always be responsive to reality considerations stemming from the nature of the problem at a particular point and the source of the competence required for its solution or modification. This kind of leadership responsibility should not be confused with that which stems from delegated administrative and over-all responsibility for co-ordinating and synthesizing the multiple approaches that may be required in the total problem-solving operation.

Education for co-operative effort would seem to be an important objective of both general and professional education. In the Inter-Professions Conference on Education for Professional Responsibility it was pointed out by Dr. Elliott Smith that "to deal with historical problems following the common professional-scholarly method gives exercise in weighing evidence and in the process of sifting out of a confused mass of events the issues which constitute the fundamental problems to be dealt with. . . . It thus teaches the student important aspects of the general art of problem solving difficult to teach as well in other fields. . . . Moreover, it makes the student aware of the several sectors which constitute the full circle of understanding of any problem, social or professional. When a student so taught in history, later approaches a problem from the angle of law, medicine, economics, or psychology, his work in history will help him to discover what the true problem is and to recognize that to look at it solely from the angle of one field, in spite of apparent clarity which results, does not constitute realism but a half-realism as unreliable and deceptive as any other half-truth." [25]

A further useful principle in training for co-operative effort is advanced by Dr. George Kelly, who points to the need of "training for professional adjustment to a world of emerging ideas rather than to a world of fixed doctrines. . . . The clinical psychologist

[25] *Education for Professional Responsibility, op. cit.,* p. 197.

must be trained not merely to occupy a present status of professional adjustment through the acquisition of contemporary sophistication, but he must be ready to relinquish some of the very concepts in which he is being trained, and to embrace new ideas as they may emerge." [26]

After an extensive review of the objectives of educational programs of a number of the professions and of the knowledge and competencies defined as essential for the practice of these professions, Wilber I. Newstetter, Dean of the Pittsburgh School of Social Work, declared that "the traditional subject-by-subject matter, single discipline approach to education for living, education for earning, and education for professional responsibility is on the way out so far, at least, as curriculum organization is concerned. It must be replaced by an interdisciplinary approach in general education, graduate education, and professional education. I believe a revolution in the organization of teaching content, media, method, and man-power is already upon us, whether we like it or not. The extent of *common* objectives, problems, method, and philosophy in *professional* education constitutes the handwriting on the walls of institutions of higher education." [27]

In a more fundamental sense, the many-faceted and interacting problems and needs of mankind consititute the handwriting on the wall and are the source of the interdependence of the professions at all levels of operation—practice, research, and education. This interdependence, which we are now beginning to recognize more fully, has been clear and insistent for some time but ability to relate to it and to engage in the co-operative effort needed can be acquired only through an evolutionary growth process. We have actually had very little time in which to develop capacity for co-operative effort—a fact that is often overlooked.

A professor of biology, in lecturing to a group of social work students, undertook, in the following paragraphs, to help them to appreciate the "newness of man" and the relatively limited span of time that people have had in which to learn how to live and work together:

In the whole stretch of two thousand million years man, as Homo sapiens, has

[26] George A. Kelly, "Training for Professional Function in Clinical Psychology: Principles of Training in Clinical Psychology," *American Journal of Orthopsychiatry*, Vol. XXI, No. 2 (1951), pp. 312–313.

[27] *Social Work Practice in the Medical and Psychiatric Setting, op. cit.*, p. 60.

been here less than one-half million. Perhaps the perspective will be more fully visualized if we condense geological time on this earth to one calendar year—January 1 to midnight December 31. On this scale life begins to appear vaguely in February in the form of microscopic units not yet fully cellular. Even in early April there are only unicellular organisms in the waters of the earth, and it is not until May that the first primitive multicellular invertebrates appear. At the half-way mark on July 1 there are still no multicellular plants and no vertebrates, and the land is utterly barren and waste. During the summer land plants appear and quickly spread into moist places. Invertebrates and finally vertebrates crawl out of the water and follow them. Evolution is gaining momentum, but it is not until September that the dry upland regions of the earth are covered with grasses and flowering plants and deciduous trees. Huge reptiles appear and disappear in the fall and there begins in November a magnificent and very rapid radiation of mammals and birds.

The primate monkey races ahead of all other mammals and the promise of Man is in the air. All through December the primates diverge, but it is not until near the last week of the year that the anthropoid apes appear. Now the rumor of Man is very strong. "Near Men" are being rushed forward by evolution moving at a tremendously accelerated pace, and then, on the last day of the year, December 31, just some four hours before midnight, Man appears. An hour or so later he makes tentative efforts at social life, but it is not until the last minute of the year that his first civilization is organized.[28]

According to this biologist, men have had, relatively speaking sixty seconds in which to learn how to get along with each other!

[28] Dr. George McKinley, from a lecture to students in the School of Social Work, University of Pittsburgh.

THE GENERIC AND SPECIFIC IN SOCIAL CASEWORK RE-EXAMINED [1]

Florence Hollis

IT SEEMS APPROPRIATE to discuss the generic and specific aspects of social casework again because the field is at this very moment at a point of crystallization in the formation of two extremely important social work organizations, the recently born National Association of Social Workers and the still quite young Council on Social Work Education. The National Association of Social Workers is just now in the process of establishing the actual practical form in which its divisions will operate, and the Council on Social Work Education is hammering out an answer to the question of whether or not specialization is to be emphasized in its accreditation procedures. There is real danger that in gaining the form, the appearance, of social work unity and wholeness we may yet lose its substance—its implementation in reality.

The generic and specific factors in social work *education* are the particular concern of this paper. A brief look into the historical background should help to give us perspective. Before the turn of the century there were two major fields of social casework—child welfare and family welfare. In the first decade of this century medical social work, school social work, and psychiatric social work became separate entities. National associations interested in the promotion of standards of work sprang up in all these fields. The first was the Family Service Association of America, founded in 1911 by the family field, and the last was the American Association of Psychiatric Social Workers, organized in 1926 by the field of psy-

[1] Published in *Social Casework,* May 1956. Presented at the Massachusetts Conference of Social Work, Boston, December 1955.

chiatric social work. Three of these national associations are exclusively professional membership organizations, while the other two—in the child and family welfare fields—combine professional and nonprofessional individual memberships and organizational memberships. Each of these national associations has been active in promoting standards of professional training. The Family Service Association of America, for example, speaks for almost 2,000 fully trained social workers in the family field, and has issued reports recommending content and standards for both classroom and field work, although it is not primarily a professional membership organization and represents only a portion of the workers in family agency settings.

The three organizations limited solely to professional membership have acted as bodies to approve specialized sequences of study in schools for practice in particular settings. They have related their individual membership qualifications, in part, to these approved sequences, and have attempted to influence agency employment practices through their emphasis on these sequences. The child welfare and family service organizations, on the other hand, did not attempt, by membership regulations, to force schools to adopt specific sequences of study, but rather exercised influence on the schools only through individual faculty members who were identified with these fields by their own practice.

In actuality it has been common practice to build curriculum sequences around child welfare, family casework, medical social work, and psychiatric social work. A few schools have also offered special courses in school social work, delinquency, and other specific areas. The term "specialization" has sometimes been applied to all of these settings and has sometimes been restricted to those settings represented by professional organizations that have set up membership requirements related to approved educational sequences.

Curriculum Developments

About fifty years ago, when training for social work first moved from in-service agency training to education in schools of social work, it was natural for school courses to be established along agency lines. But as soon as workers from different settings became members of the same faculty and became familiar with one another's work, they began to see that common principles underlay social work and casework in different types of settings. The first real leadership in the direction of a generic approach came from the committee known as the Milford Conference, which declared in 1929 that "generic social case work is the common field to which the specific forms of social case work are merely incidental."[2] The report went on to suggest that "the trend in training should be towards the development of courses in the methods which are common to all fields of social case work divorced from their specific application in any one field."[3]

The Milford Conference report and the point of view it represented had an enormous influence on education for social work. The following year the first Curriculum Committee of the American Association of Schools of Social Work was appointed. The report of this committee in 1932 led to the adoption of the first minimum curriculum requirements. These requirements had the effect of broadening the educational base but did not deal with the question of whether casework should be taught as a unified subject or along agency lines. Actually, some schools had a basic first-year casework course at that time although the second-year courses almost universally followed agency field lines. There was usually only one field placement.

During the thirties a first-year generic casework course became still more common, and it also became widespread practice to require at least two field placements, thus getting farther away from the apprenticeship type of field placement characteristic of earlier years.

In 1944 an additional step in the direction of generic study was taken by the American Association of Schools of Social Work in the report of its Curriculum Committee which, under the leadership of Charlotte Towle, outlined eight basic areas of study and practically assured a generic first year.[4] The second year, however, in most schools was still organized entirely, or almost entirely, along agency specialization lines.

The 1948 report of the Curriculum Committee, under the chairmanship of Florence Day, pointed out that this difference between

[2] *Social Case Work: Generic and Specific; A Report of the Milford Conference*, American Association of Social Workers, New York, 1929, p. 11.

[3] *Ibid.*, p. 80.

[4] Leona Massoth, "The Basic Eight," *The Family*, Vol. XXV, No. 10 (1945), pp. 384–387.

the first- and second-year curriculum had led to the erroneous assumption that generic content should be thought of as beginning casework, and specific as advanced. It was the opinion of the committee that "generic casework is conceived to include all that is common to casework knowledge and skill at any level of practice, and all that is adaptable to any casework setting." [5] The committee went on to describe the different emphases in the first and the second years in terms of increasing complexity of content, regardless of setting; it could see "no theoretical objection to extending generic casework instruction through the third or even the fourth semester," [6] and urged experimentation with the inclusion of specific content in courses to be taken in common by all casework students.

Since that time, many schools have been developing generic casework content for the second year of study. The School of Social Service Administration in Chicago should be mentioned especially for its leadership in this direction. The New York School of Social Work has established a sequence of four basic casework courses, and offers specialization in only one elective course for each of the major settings, each of which is open to all students regardless of their field placement. The Smith College School for Social Work was the very first school to take a stand for generic rather than specialized courses. Many other schools have moved in this direction. Throughout the whole field the vast majority of caseworkers in all settings and in all national casework organizations have moved steadily in recent years toward recognition of the fact that casework is a single discipline with only minor differences in the way in which it is used in different settings.

Nevertheless, at the moment the place of the content thought to be specific to particular settings is still a matter of controversy. The new Council on Social Work Education is actively working on the problem but has not yet taken final action. Many schools are still operating along the old lines of settings specialization. Representatives of the major casework settings now have an opportunity through the newly created, field-wide professional and educational organizations to pool their knowledge and effort in working for a sound educational base for all caseworkers instead of wasting themselves in separatist strivings.

[5] Florence R. Day, "Current Developments in the Graduate Curriculum," *Journal of Social Casework,* Vol. XXIX, No. 9 (1948), p. 338.
[6] *Ibid.,* p. 340.

The student who majors in casework is expected upon graduation from a school of social work to take responsibility for the care of people who are in serious—sometimes in desperate—trouble. Often these are people who are at a point of crisis in their lives where what the caseworker does or fails to do may be decisive as to whether a child is to be brought up in hostile, neglectful turmoil or in the relative security of a foster or adoptive home; whether a marriage is to continue or be broken; whether or not a family is to be adequately clothed, sheltered, and fed; whether a mentally sick person is to reach a hospital for care or end his life in suicide; whether a patient is to undergo an operation for cancer or run away in fear from medical advice. Obviously, the caseworker cannot make such decisions for others, but the way in which he relates to and talks with people day in and day out plays a major part in determining whether clients take action toward a better life or a worse. Basic skill in casework treatment the school graduate must have; otherwise we have failed in preparing him for the immediate job that will be entrusted to him by the community. It is our responsibility through professional and other national organizations to see that this objective of social work education is amply met.

In reality, all fields of social work are reaching for the same objective—to man our agencies with workers of the highest possible quality. We have for many years been in agreement that this requires at least two years of graduate training. We are all in agreement that it is impossible to teach the student in these two years all that is needed for competent practice in any setting, and that at least two years of subsequent practice under good supervision are needed before the average worker reaches mature competence. Some fields speak of "internships"; many agencies have some form of postgraduate in-service staff training. There is increasing interest in formalized third-year and doctoral training programs. At the same time the healthy emphasis on training for social work rather than narrowly for casework, on broad professional education rather than narrow technical training, is increasing. Thus it is imperative that we make the most of each educational hour and that we weigh carefully what can best be given in the basic master's program, and what can most safely be delayed for the worker's later development.

There is also general agreement, I think, that casework includes both generic and specific content and that both are important. Just as there is no doubt that certain generic content is basic to practice in all agencies, so it is also agreed that some content is specific to practice in certain types of agencies and not in others, and even that some content is specific to one agency and not to others. This fact, however, does not answer for us the questions of how much of this specific material can be taught in the master's program, in what units it is to be organized, and what methods are administratively and educationally best for assuring its teaching.

Before discussing some of the basic issues involved, I should like to outline, as a frame of reference, the content that I should like to see included in the education of all caseworkers.

Basic Content

It should be kept in mind that the emphasis of this paper is on the training of the *caseworker.* Therefore, in what follows I am not attempting to discuss these issues as they apply to group work or other types of social work. First of all, I believe that casework is a *basic major* or area of concentration within social work education. Casework itself can be considered a specialization, but I prefer to use the term "major" instead of "specialization" because of the present use of the term "specialization" to describe by setting the various subdivisions of the total field of casework. Group work is another such area of concentration. Whether community organization, administration, and research are also basic majors is debatable. They are certainly processes within the field of social work, but perhaps as majors they represent content to be studied at an advanced level after one of the basic methods has been mastered.

Every student preparing to practice in the casework field should master the broad social work curriculum as well as the content in his own major field. This broad social work curriculum should provide the student with knowledge of the field of social work as a whole, its historical development, and its current place and function in our culture. It should inform him about the present structure of social services, public and private. It should orient him to the philosophical premises upon which social work rests and to his role as a practitioner who carries responsibility for the welfare of other human beings. It should give him knowledge of the social, physical, and psychological factors in the development and adjustment of the individual. It should equip him with beginning skills in research. In addition to undertaking this broad social work curriculum, the student majoring in casework should study intensively the process of social casework itself; the group work student, the process of social group work; and so on.

It is not necessary in developing the subject of this paper to discuss in detail the actual structure of courses in which all this subject matter would be taught, but only to comment on areas that have been emphasized as requirements for specialization. I would suggest for all casework majors a one-semester course in medical problems and two semester courses on aspects of the dynamics of behavior with one or two more courses on this subject available as electives in the second year. In social casework itself I would suggest four semesters of basic casework courses with additional courses available as electives. I would prefer to see casework majors spend three days a week in field work—on the assumption that this would occupy half their actual study time—spending this in two agencies in successive years, preferably one in a primary social work setting and one in a secondary setting, an agency that has as its basic function something other than social work. In all field work I would like to see attention given not only to direct work with clients but also to aspects of practice which draw upon the subject matter of other than casework courses in the curriculum.

Where would specific content be placed in such a curriculum? A variety of patterns is possible. With proper planning most of the specific content can be incorporated into the basic courses. A good deal of it would be placed in the casework sequence and some in other areas of basic content—that is, community organization content in the community organization course, group work aspects in group work, administration in the administration course, and so on. Additional specific emphasis could be given in elective courses open to all casework students. These elective courses would, perhaps, resemble present settings courses, or on the other hand might take on a new pattern, drawing upon similar specific content found in different settings.

Basic Casework Courses

Let us look first at the so-called generic casework courses. We have learned that it is not only undesirable, but impossible, to teach generic content divorced from specific content. A properly constructed basic casework sequence draws its materials from all types of agency settings. Inevitably, cases reveal specific as well as generic factors. Take a child placement case. Before the decision to place the child is made and the specific foster home is decided upon, a social study has to be undertaken which differs very little from that made in a family agency dealing with parent-child adjustment, in a child guidance clinic, in a hospital offering service to a child with a long-standing illness affecting his family relationships, or in a school setting where intensive help is given to the child who is truanting. Indeed, perhaps some of the differences that do appear should not be there and would not be there had there been more cross-fertilization between casework settings.

But, you say, there are other special features about the application for placement of a child: the parent is in conflict about placement, guilty about it, protective, and reluctant to talk. Do not partially rejecting parents and parents unable to care adequately for their children almost always feel guilty and reluctant to face, or talk frankly about, painful aspects of their lives, no matter to what type of agency they turn for help?

But, the argument continues, sometimes the parent does not even come voluntarily; he is referred because someone else thinks his child should be placed. Have you ever read about the involuntary nature of *medical* referrals? That it is often the doctor, not the patient, who requests the medical social worker? In *psychiatric* social work, what of the relative of the patient? What about "aggressive" work in the *family* field? "Intrusive" [7] casework in the psychiatric field?

The advocate of specialties contends that one must understand the child's feeling about *separation.* Indeed, it is important to understand that, and a child's placement record is a very good resource in teaching about it, because child welfare has developed good content around that problem which the rest of us very much need to know. Several writers in the medical field have attested to the contribution of child welfare to their understanding of the reaction of the child to hospital and convalescent care. What about

[7] Rudolph F. Boquet, "The Use of an 'Intrusive' Technique in Casework with Chronic Mentally Ill Patients," *Journal of Psychiatric Social Work,* Vol. XXIV, No. 1 (1954), pp. 31–35.

the separation factor in the school phobia? In prolonged parental illness? In desertion by a parent? In divorce? In death?

If you read the articles describing the content specific to each of the major fields, the thought constantly occurs, "But this happens in other fields, too." One article states that the medical social worker has to learn to work with patients from the upper income brackets. What about child welfare work with adoptive and foster parents? What about the fee-paying cases in family agencies? Another writer states that the medical social worker has great opportunity to work with incipient problems. What about the public welfare worker or the school social worker?

It is true that certain agencies deal repetitively with certain types of problems and therefore accumulate detailed knowledge about these problems and facility in dealing with them. This is true, for instance, for the child placement agency in respect to problems of placement, the selection of foster homes, work with foster parents; for the state hospital and sometimes for the out-patient psychiatric clinic in their work with psychotics. It is true for the child guidance clinic in its work with certain types of disturbed children; for the hospital in relation to physical illness; for the private family agency in treatment of marital problems and problems of parent-child adjustment; for the public assistance agency in problems of self-support; and so on.

This greater skill is acquired by years of practice and should be fed back into the main stream of casework, since giving help with human problems is not confined to specific agency settings. Problems are multiple. The medical worker's problem may begin with a broken leg, but before the work is ended it may very well turn into a problem of school adjustment. Schizophrenia is appearing with increasing frequency among the clients of family agencies, partly because patients in partial remission are encouraged by hospitals to return to the community, and partly because caseworkers are better able to recognize schizophrenia in its incipient and less severe forms. The client, to be sure, does not come for treatment of his schizophrenia. He may come because of an unsuccessful marriage, but knowledge of schizophrenia and of casework with this specific type of mental illness is essential to the proper handling of the client. The student who has studied a case of schizophrenia from the files of a psychiatric agency puts that knowledge to good use when he meets the same problem in a family, medical, or child welfare setting. The graduate employed in a veterans' psychiatric clinic may be greatly strengthened in playing his part on the clinical team if he has studied cases from a family agency which have revealed the degree of distortion sometimes present in descriptions given of each other by husband and wife in marital conflict situations.

The student years are pre-eminently the years for the student to learn from the special, the specific knowledge of a great *variety* of agencies. A number of workers never again will have this opportunity, since they will remain in one type of agency throughout their working lives, even though the majority of workers eventually practice in a variety of settings. Graduates will have plenty of time in which to build up skill in the specifics of their own setting, but this may be the only time that they will have a chance to study what caseworkers in other agency settings have discovered and developed. There are much greater advantages to be gained from exposing the student to the rich specifics of a variety of settings than from concentrating in the second year on the one setting in which he may spend the rest of his professional career.

The required basic casework sequence could well be supplemented by elective courses that will give the student a chance for concentration upon some aspect of casework in which he is particularly interested or which the faculty is particularly well equipped to teach. These courses might or might not fall strictly along field lines. There would be advantages in experimenting with different patterns. One of the advantages of our present settings courses is that they give the student a chance to study certain types of problems more repetitively than is possible in the basic courses which emphasize variety of problems rather than concentrated comparative study of cases having similar features. In our present family casework course, for instance, we have a number of marriage counseling cases. By seeing several different types of reactions to the same social adjustment problem, students deepen their understanding of marriage adjustment in a way that goes beyond what they can do in the basic course. A preferable alternative to building these elective courses around settings might be to build them around a series of cases having a common denominator either in the social problem or in clinical diagnosis.

Thus far I have neglected teamwork. Collaboration with other disciplines and the general problem of fitting into a secondary type of setting (to use the terminology of Helen Perlman [8]) are the most frequently cited hallmarks of "specialization." School social work, medical social work, psychiatric social work, and probation and parole all meet this problem in varying ways. Relationships between professions are complicated, and in a secondary setting they differ from those in a primary setting, but they do belong to the same genus if not the same species. Helen Perlman has already dealt with this problem very well in her article on the University of Chicago curriculum.[9] She points out that general principles are involved in such staff relationships, which take different forms in different types of agencies.

This is an area in which comparative study might be particularly fruitful. Administrative courses might well be enriched by the analysis of this and other types of administrative relationships in different agencies. Study of the psychiatric collaboration common in the family agency, for instance, might have much to offer to practice in secondary settings. Indeed, I know of one very good psychiatric hospital that now uses two kinds of psychiatric teamwork. The conventional type is used for work with the patient, but in addition to this a senior psychiatrist is made available to staff members of the social work department as a consultant on work with relatives. The team relationship here has many similarities to that ordinarily found in primary settings. Certain aspects of interdisciplinary collaboration, of course, inevitably appear also in the basic casework sequence, for they are a part of the specifics of many cases from all fields. This same principle of incorporation of pertinent material about settings could well be applied to other courses in the curriculum, particularly The Field of Social Work, Community Organization, and Public Welfare. These all deal in one way or another with resources in relation to need and with the structure of social work fields. Restudy of their content with this in mind might lead to a sequence comparable to the basic casework sequence and the human behavior sequence.

It is obvious, of course, that it is in field work that the student learns most about the specific aspects of any particular setting. When a student spends three days a week for eight months in an

[8] Helen Harris Perlman, "Generic Aspects of Specific Case-Work Settings," *Social Service Review,* Vol. XXIII, No. 3 (1949), p. 295.

[9] *Ibid.,* pp. 293–301.

agency, he is given substantial opportunity for drill in whatever is special to that agency and the field of which it is a part.

On close examination, the organization of teaching along field lines does not appear to have too much logic. There is just as much difference between the knowledge needed in different types of agencies in the same field as there is between agencies in different fields. Some child guidance clinics and mental hygiene agencies, for instance, are closer in both structure and type of problem dealt with to the family agency than to the state hospital. The out-patient psychiatric clinic is closer to the out-patient medical clinic than to the child guidance agency. The work of the children's worker in an institution may be closer to that of the medical worker in a children's convalescent home or of a psychiatric worker in a residential treatment center than to that of a worker in a foster home agency. And certainly it is no longer true that one setting requires greater knowledge of the dynamics of human behavior than another. In a workshop for psychiatric social workers and family and children's workers in New York in 1953, it was pointed out [10] that the family worker takes more responsibility for diagnosis than the average psychiatric worker does. There are many psychiatric settings in which the caseworker is excluded from the use of treatment methods commonly required in many family agencies. I do not mean by this to imply that family casework requires more skill than psychiatric, but merely to call attention to the fact that, in reality, differences in specifics do not follow field lines alone.

Present Requirements

I should like to turn now to consideration of some of the specific requirements that are at present in force in many schools of social work. For example, a frequent requirement is that the student's second-year placement be in his specialization. At first thought this seems reasonable enough, but it is based on the assumption that the student knows in what field he wants to specialize before he enters the school, so that the school can assign him to a different field for his first-year placement. Sometimes this plan can be followed, but often the student discovers his interest in a certain field only

[10] "Current Trends in Psychiatric Settings and in Family and Children's Agencies," *Journal of Psychiatric Social Work,* Vol. XXIV, No. 3 (1955), p. 163.

after he has had experience in it quite by chance in his first year. More and more we are learning that, although all fields prefer second-year students, they all are able to provide a substantial number of first-year placements. Beginning work and advanced work definitely do not follow field lines.

Many considerations other than choice of field enter into assignment of students to second-year placements. Quality of supervision is certainly one of these. It not infrequently happens that the best supervisor for a particular student is to be found in a field other than the one he thinks he wants to enter. Should he be advised to take a less suitable placement in order to meet specific field requirements even though that means that he will be less well prepared to practice in that field? If a superabundance of good placements existed in all fields, some of these specifications would be more practical than they actually are. I think we can assume that a student who knows what type of agency he wants to work in and who has not already had a first-year placement in it will choose this kind of agency for his second year, other things being equal. We do not have to legislate this. If other things are not equal, they should be given consideration, and the student, upon graduation, should not be handicapped in getting a job in the field of his choice because it seemed better from an educational viewpoint for him to receive his field training in another setting.

Similar considerations apply to the popular requirement that the student do his thesis in the field in which he proposes to work. By and large the student will choose such a subject, but sometimes there are good reasons for his pursuing some other line of investigation. He may know of some particularly interesting group project in progress. He may have become especially interested in some problem encountered in his first year of study which he can profitably pursue further. Why should we legislate on a matter like this? Are there not enough rigidities in life without creating unnecessary ones?

Another proposed requirement is that the student take a settings course in the field in which he intends to work. Again it is true that, other things being equal, a student will elect courses according to his interests. He will not need to be coerced into doing so. If he does not choose a course related to his vocational plans it is probably because he believes the course is not as well taught or does not have as valuable content as others with which it is competing. Is it not better to know this situation exists so that it can be improved, rather than to obscure the matter by requiring the student to take such a course? Such a requirement also, of course, makes it extremely difficult to experiment with new curriculum patterns and creates vocational handicaps for the student graduating from a smaller school, which cannot offer a large number of special courses.

Most shortsighted of all is the policy of making faculty appointments and faculty assignments primarily along settings lines. This policy is based on the theory that, to train students who are to enter a particular field, a school must have a faculty member who is qualified for membership in the professional organization in that field (or, to bring us up to date, for membership in that section of NASW). Since, thus far, only three professional groups have pressed for this policy, some of the larger schools could comply. But if this idea is pushed, why will not other fields ask for the same recognition? Ultimately, then, each school would need also a family caseworker, a child welfare worker, a delinquency worker. And then, why not a rehabilitation instructor, perhaps one in geriatrics, and in whatever new fields emerge in the rest of the century? It would be a practical impossibility for all but the largest schools to meet all the claims for special treatment which could, with equal validity, be made. Already smaller schools, instead of being able to choose faculty on the basis of scholarship, competence in practice, and teaching skill, are having to give preference to candidates who have technical specializations in the three fields represented by membership organizations. This is wrong, very wrong, and inevitably it will lead to less well prepared graduates for *all* settings.

Once on a faculty, such a specialized instructor is expected to carry as his assignment all field work placements within his type of setting. This seems logical only because we have all been brought up with stereotypes about field lines and we are caught in the mesh of our own errors. At the New York School of Social Work we have now had three years of experimentation in assigning faculty members to field placements in agency settings in which they have never practiced. Inevitably this plan called for an initial learning period for the adviser before all the nuances of the new type of agency could be understood. But did we have complaints from agencies on this ground? On the contrary, agencies have been enriched and faculty members have been greatly broadened in their knowledge and perspective by this cross-fertilization. In fact, this is one of the best ways of improving the basic casework courses.

If we insist on keeping ourselves in ironclad, isolated compartments, of course we shall continue to be ignorant both of the extent to which we are now similar and of whatever content is specific in any field other than our own. But why should we allow ourselves to be caught in this growth-restricting, isolationist trap? We need to combine our strength in order to bring all caseworkers to a higher level of competence so that clients and patients will be met with thorough psychosocial understanding and adequate treatment skills, whatever the agency their self-recognized problems initially lead them to.

Why is this objective more likely to be met by emphasizing basic training than training for special settings? Because there is now more than enough basic social work and basic casework content to fill the two years of training for the master's degree. Because the student is best prepared for actual practice when he knows something of the specifics of several settings rather than concentrating on one. Because it is better to avoid unnecessary rigidities in training. Because schools of social work can offer better professional education when they are not fettered in choice of teaching personnel and in the assignment of faculty responsibilities by settings requirements.

For all these reasons, I believe that we must continue along the path we have so recently chosen of subordinating our old separatist loyalties to the task of building a profession fit to serve the hurt and the troubled wherever they are to be found.

CULTURAL DYNAMICS IN CASEWORK [1]

Otto Pollak

In order to analyze the problem of cultural dynamics in casework, the phenomena that are blanketed by this term must be identified. The identification of these phenomena requires in turn a concurrent presentation of the concepts assigned to the phenomena. In approaching both these tasks I should like to state that I am aware of the considerable amount of attention that has been given in the social work literature [2] to cultural phenomena and their impact on professional performance. It seems to me, however, that these discussions do not clearly identify and define phenomena that are conceptualized in the social sciences.

An outstanding example of this absence of definition in the casework literature pertains to the concept of *culture* as such. It is true that divergent definitions of culture are proposed in social science literature itself, but it seems to me that social work—a field that emphasizes cultural phenomena—would benefit by the selection of a definition that fits its particular need.

Definitions of culture vary from those of a high level of abstrac-

[1] Published in *Social Casework,* July 1953. Based on a paper given at the Massachusetts Conference of Social Work and on material presented at the Institute of the School of Social Work of the University of Michigan and the Institute of Supervisors arranged by the School of Social Work of the University of Louisville, both in March 1953; and the Field Work Supervisors' Institute of the School of Social Work of Atlanta University in April 1953. The author wants to express his appreciation to the members of these institutes for stimulation and impetus for clarification of the ideas presented.

[2] *New Emphasis on Cultural Factors,* papers reprinted from *The Family* and *Journal of Social Casework,* Family Service Association of America, New York, 1946–1948; William Gioseffi, "The Relationship of Culture to the Principles of Casework," *Social Casework,* Vol. XXXII, No. 5 (1951), pp. 190–196; Sol Wiener Ginsburg, M.D., "The Impact of the Social Worker's Cultural Structure on Social Therapy," *Social Casework,* Vol. XXXII, No. 8 (1951), pp. 319–325.

tion to those of great concreteness and specificity. An example of the first type of definition is simply that culture is a way of life or a pattern of existence.[3]

A definition of the latter type is that "culture is the accumulation of the group's experience, its way of solving the problems of life's demands and needs, the attitudes, folkways, mores, ways of behaving and feeling that have been invented, tested, approved, and perpetuated in a particular people's history. All these habits and ways of doing things become organized into complexes and patterns, institutions for meeting economic needs, organizing political relations, expressing religious worship, regulating marriage and family relations, and the sum total of these we call the culture of that people." [4]

It seems to me that neither type of definition is appropriate for use in casework practice. The blanket type is so abstract that it fails to identify the manifestations of life which might be subsumed under it; the second type is so specific that no one, in practice, would remember all its facets. The enumerative definition referred to above, however, does stress one aspect of cultural expression which is of interest and practical usefulness to social caseworkers—the aspect of feelings which, by content and frequency of occurrence, distinguishes the members of one cultural group from another. Since social casework is eminently concerned with feelings, a definition, if it is to be useful to the field, should contain the feeling aspects of cultural phenomena. In my opinion, the most useful definition of culture for social casework practice, if not for social work in general, based on Clyde Kluckhohn's analysis of the concept,[5] might be formulated as follows: Culture is the composite of specific ways of thinking, feeling, and acting which differentiates one group from another.

A concept closely related to that of culture is the concept of *national character*. This term is used to describe the phenomenon that members of different societies have different personality norms. By national character is meant a modal personality or a basic

[3] Robert L. Sutherland and Julian L. Woodward, *Introductory Sociology* (4th ed.), J. B. Lippincott Co., Philadelphia, 1952, p. 18.

[4] Maurine Boie, "The Case Worker's Need for Orientation to the Cuture of the Client," *The Family*, Vol. XVIII, No. 6 (1937), p. 197.

[5] Clyde Kluckhohn, *Mirror for Man*, McGraw-Hill Book Co., New York, 1949, pp. 17-44.

personality type.[6] The anthropologists who have pinpointed this phenomenon and who use its conceptualization recognize, of course, that individual differences in personality exist in every society; they maintain, however, that within the range of individual differences, each society has a specific personality configuration which, on purely statistical grounds, must be considered normal for that society. This modal personality provides the norm by which, in that society, aberration is assessed. Dynamically, the phenomenon of the modal personality suggests the phenomenon of the basic personality. In other words, the personality type that is found to exist most frequently in a given society seems to be the one that is most approved of in that society and permits the individual who has it to live most comfortably under the conditions of that society. This, in turn, suggests that cultural factors play a vital role in shaping the personality of the vast majority of its members. On the other hand, the fact that every society shows aberrations from the norm indicates that factors other than cultural ones determine personality development.

In their application to the concerns of social casework, the concepts of culture and national character, as well as of basic personality, pose an important question in the diagnostic process. This question has been formulated by the anthropologist Sapir. He points out that it is fallacious to think in terms of a simple contrast between social patterns and individual behavior since the only reality of social patterns is the behavior of individuals. He suggests that the diagnostician must inquire into the "meaning of culture in terms of individual behavior and whether the individual can, in a sense, be looked upon as the effective carrier of the culture of his group." [7]

Culture Conflict

To utilize the concepts of culture and basic personality in diagnosis in casework, obviously one requires knowledge about the culture of the client. Acquiring this knowledge, however, is a particularly complicated task in this country which has a variety of sub-cultures. Even more significant, perhaps, is that the profession

[6] Ralph Linton, "Problems of Status Personality," in *Culture and Personality* (S. S. Sargent and M. W. Smith, eds.), Viking Fund, New York, 1949, pp. 163–170.
[7] Edward Sapir, "Cultural Anthropology and Psychiatry," *Journal of Abnormal and Social Psychology,* Vol. XXVII, October–December (1932), p. 233.

of social work itself constitutes a sub-culture. The co-existence of the various groups and sub-groups creates the phenomenon of *culture conflict.* In this country, this phenomenon is frequently obscured. Out of historical necessity, people from many different ethnic backgrounds developed a method of reaction to cultural differences which is propounded as the *acceptance of cultural relativity.* The concept of cultural relativity is exemplified by the commonplace observation that, in this country, people from different cultural backgrounds have developed different methods of solving problems of living that are essentially the same. On the surface everyone seems to accept the fact that different groups have different preferences for the types of food with which they satisfy their hunger, have different ideas about the manner in which one should worship, have different beliefs about the values of various measures of child discipline and child rearing, and so on. Actually this acceptance of cultural relativity is maintained only as long as personal contact between members of different groups does not become very close. When closeness is established, the proposition that one way of living may be as successful as another encounters a great deal of resistance.

People usually are able to recognize such cultural divergences with considerable ease but find it exceedingly difficult to relinquish their belief that their own way of life is after all the best and the "most natural" one. Rare indeed is the person who, when confronted with someone not belonging to his own culture, does not have the impression of meeting a deviant individual who would be benefited by change. In social work practice this phenomenon is one of the great obstacles to establishing an effective relationship between helper and client. Social workers, as well as other persons, doubtless find it relatively easy to talk about cultural differences as a phenomenon of cultural relativity. In working closely with people, however, they must find it exceedingly difficult not to experience, as conflict, differences between the culture of the client and their own. In impersonal relationships it is easy enough to accept divergent ways of living. When, however, one has to deal with a person whose way of life is divergent from one's own, the temptation to assume that this person requires a reorientation that will bring him into line with one's own culture is tremendous.[8]

[8] Thorsten Sellin, *Culture Conflict and Crime: A Report of the Subcommittee on Delinquency of the Committee on Personality and Culture,* Bulletin 41, Social Science Research Council, New York, 1938, pp. 66–67.

The human tendency to react to the experience of cultural relativity in terms of culture conflict is particularly observable in the generation conflict between immigrants and their children. What perhaps is not realized with sufficient clarity is that this type of conflict has a significant dynamic basis. In our early years, we receive our culture primarily from our parents; in later development periods, from our peers; and in adulthood, from persons to whom we transfer feelings that we originally formed in the primary group contacts with parents and peers. In other words, culture becomes part both of our superego and of our ego structures. To accept emotionally all the implications of cultural relativity would mean, in the last analysis, to deny one's superego and one's ego structure. By the dynamically oriented person, this task obviously will be viewed as an exceedingly difficult, if not an impossible, one.

This phenomenon of culture conflict between two persons in meaningful contact, such as the casework relationship, appears to me to present a number of difficulties in diagnosis, in establishing a treatment plan, and in setting the treatment goal. It also may interfere with communication between caseworker and client in these three phases of the casework process. In diagnosis, a culture conflict may lead the caseworker to interpret a cultural difference as an aberration; in establishing a treatment plan, it may lead the caseworker to suggest measures or initiate procedures that are culturally unacceptable to the client; and in setting the treatment goal, it may involve the risk of expecting the client to go farther in the process of change than his cultural limitations permit him to go. In communication, it may bring the caseworker up against taboos about certain topics and about the ways in which they may be displayed. Over and beyond these difficulties cultural differences may carry implications of attitudes toward members of another culture, or toward members of one's own culture, that can interfere with the most essential aspect of casework—the establishment of a relationship. It might be argued that a good relationship between caseworker and client can have the power to overcome culturally based taboos and antagonistic attitudes. I should like to submit for consideration the question of whether the opposite might not be true, at least in the initial phases of the casework process—that cultural taboos and culturally based antagonistic attitudes will interfere with the establishment of a relationship.

Social Work Culture

Having posed these problems in purely theoretical form, I should like now to apply these propositions to a specific situation—the social work situation. I should like to make a tentative comparison between the characteristic traits of the culture of the wider American community and traits that may be considered as characteristic of the special sub-culture of social work. Such an analysis may have the value of alerting caseworkers to possible points of difficulty that may result from a failure to perceive their own culture as a phenomenon relative in time and place. To overlook the obvious is one of the most frequent errors in perception and one's own culture always seems to be obvious to the culture carrier.[9]

The comparison I am attempting is based on limited data; the American culture, in general, and the professional culture of social work, in particular, are relatively uncultivated fields of investigation. The identification, however, of a few cultural traits that are divergent between the two configurations may prove to be useful.

It is generally recognized that the culture of this country has been strongly influenced by Puritan thinking. In one of the classical works of sociology, Max Weber points out that in the countries of Western civilization Protestants frequently seem to hold higher economic positions than Catholics and that among the Protestant denominations the Calvinists seem to have developed a way of life, and particularly spiritual beliefs, that are conducive to great economic efficiency and to that specific type of economic institution that we call capitalism.[10] In his fascinating study he discusses the psychological impact of theological beliefs upon economic behavior. He postulates that Calvin's doctrine of predestination presented the believers with a tremendous problem about the criteria for salvation—who were to be saved and who were destined to damnation. In the development of Calvinistic doctrine, the first criterion established was that one must not doubt one's own salvation; the advice given on the best way to combat doubt was to be purposefully active in the here and now. Popular interpretation of this doctrine led to the belief that success itself was the criterion because the result of the activity often led to success.

[9] Gustav Ichheiser, "Misunderstandings in Human Relations," special issue of *The American Journal of Sociology*, Vol. LV, No. 2 (1949), Part 2, pp. 2, 40–41, 50.

[10] Max Weber, *The Protestant Ethic and the Spirit of Capitalism*, Charles Scribner's Sons, New York, 1930.

The tremendous influence of the Puritans and their offspring on the development of American thought in general—aided by the actual opportunities for successful activity which the opening of this continent offered to the energetic—has resulted in making success a part and parcel of the American belief system; success is the criterion of worth of the individual. Obviously, the basic philosophy of casework does not go along with this characteristic belief of the wider American culture; in casework, the worth of the individual is considered basic without qualifications.[11] By and large, individuals who are unsuccessful in one way or another are the ones who become agency clients.

Another aspect of the American culture is an almost magical belief in the value and effectiveness of material things. We are the nation of toolmakers par excellence; the mastery of nature through machinery is one of the outstanding achievements of this nation. A person in need of help from a professional person will therefore find it easier to believe in the power of such help if it can be communicated to him, at least in part, through the utilization of material things or through the perception of material symbols of competence of the practitioner. The medical patient, for instance, can perceive the specificity of the help he receives from the physician who uses instruments or prescribes medication. Even the psychoanalyst has at least the material symbol of the couch by which he communicates to the patient the specificity of the process. The client of the lawyer sees an array of law books which impresses him visually with the fact that specific funds of knowledge, not accessible to others, are at the disposal of this professional helper. The teacher works with textbooks and blackboards, the minister or rabbi with the paraphernalia of a church or synagogue. In social work, and particularly in casework agencies, no tools or symbols of professional competence are evident to a client when he enters the office.

As a consequence of the Anglo-Saxon ideal of the gentleman and the lady, free expression of feelings, particularly negative and hostile ones, are improper in our culture. Christianity, too, has inculcated concepts of controls and restraints of negative feelings. Social caseworkers, in contrast, endeavor to help the clients express their real

[11] Gordon Hamilton, *Theory and Practice of Social Casework* (2d ed., rev.), Columbia University Press, New York, 1951, p. 8; Gordon Hamilton, "The Role of Social Casework in Social Policy," pp. 28–44 of this volume, reprinted from *Social Casework,* October 1952.

feelings, which may be negative ones, and "must be willing to enter into the feeling experience of another." [12] Obviously, here is another culture conflict which is likely to operate at least in the initial phases of the casework process.

In the wider American culture there is a frequent distinction made between professional persons and "workers." In American terminology, a person goes to a physician, not to a medical worker; to a lawyer, not to a legal worker; to a minister, not to a church worker; to a teacher, not to an educational worker. He expects the help of a nurse, but not of a hospital worker. It is a strange phenomenon, worthy of note, that social work is the only profession on the American scene that uses in its designation the term "worker." This designation may well have a status implication to the client and the donor which is adverse to the interests of the client as well as of the caseworker.

One more aspect may show divergence between the culture of social casework and the culture of the wider community. The wider community values experience in the professional. The sick person prefers a resident to an intern, a private practitioner to a resident, and a mature private practitioner to a young one. The person in legal difficulties tries to find an experienced lawyer. Students who have a choice would rather have a professor than an instructor. All these professions keep their experienced members in that part of practice that maintains direct contact with the group it serves. In social casework, however, experience tends to remove the practitioner from direct client contact; he is utilized for supervision, administration, and teaching. The client, therefore, who may expect and value a mature person as his helper will, in all probability, find that he must rely on the services of a relatively young person.

The conflicting expectations and reaction patterns between the culture of minority groups and the culture of social casework create a special type of barrier. Inherent to all cultures of minority groups is a concern about the relationship to the majority, an apprehension about being discriminated against, a feeling of loyalty to one's own group when discussing it with a member of the majority group, a tendency to refuse the expression of negative judgment about the members of one's own group when communicating with an outsider. Minority groups also develop special methods of adaptation to their

[12] Hamilton, *Theory and Practice of Social Case Work, op. cit.*, p. 28.

social disadvantages which require intensive development of certain types of effort that members of majorities need not display. Owing to their professional training and experience, caseworkers are likely to be sensitive to such behavior patterns and to have sympathy for the persons placed in these disadvantageous positions. It is open to question, however, whether a client can readily recognize such sensitivity from the start or even accept the understanding attitude of the caseworker.

Problems of Adjustment

Obviously these culture conflicts require specific kinds of adjustment in casework if the process is to succeed. Adjustment has been defined by Donald Young, in striking simplicity, as a solution of problems of getting along with one another.[13] The social worker and his client certainly must be able to do this. The social work task, however, is complicated by the fact that the social worker and the client not only have to get along with each other, but also must get somewhere in terms of helping and utilizing help. The essence of this problem and of its solution, where culture conflict between worker and client exists, seems to me to lie in a process that has been conceptualized in cultural anthropology as *acculturation*. According to this concept, people from different cultural backgrounds who come into meaningful contact with one another can be successful in solving the culture conflict by a partial and unequal, but always somewhat reciprocal, assumption of their respective cultural traits. The concept can be adapted, I believe, in relation to particular conditions, to various phases of the helping process. To start from the end, it seems to me that a treatment goal determined entirely by the culture of the client would represent an undesirable and a dynamically impossible objective. Culture creates problems as well as solves them. Social work, as a profession, has developed certain insights, funds of knowledge, and value judgments about human needs, affects, and behavior. These values cannot be lightly set aside because they are alien to the client and his culture. It would seem to me impossible, if not professionally unethical, for social workers not to apply their professional knowledge to the problem at hand. To be sure, treatment goals must take into

[13] Donald Young, "Memorandum on Suggestions for Research in the Field of Social Adjustment," *The American Journal of Sociology,* Vol. XLVI, No. 6 (1941), p. 873.

account the extent to which the surrounding culture will permit the client to go, but go he must, if he is to benefit from casework help. Without some loosening of the grip his culture has had on him, change and movement are likely to be impossible. On the other hand, in the process of making a diagnosis and evaluation of the client's difficulty, the client's culture might well receive procedence over the culture of the caseworker.

In essence this means that caseworkers must re-examine the question of whether it is possible for them, as professional persons, to help a client adjust to his own culture and whether it would be desirable to do so. Every profession is not only a product of the culture but also a creator of culture. It is so in a relatively active way. For example, the cultural impact of medicine upon the American society as a whole has been very great. It might well be that social casework will play a similar role. By helping the client, it frequently will involve the client in a process of *cultural change,* which is the final concept that I wish to present.

Some cultures are relatively static; others are dynamic. The American culture is distinctly dynamic and rapidly changing. In this process of change, the culture carriers take a more or less active part. In primitive cultures it is the inventor and the innovator, that is, some particularly gifted individual, who takes the distinctively active role in the process. The others are less active, but not really passive, since they take up the innovation or invention. In complex societies such as ours, the role of the active agent of change is frequently taken on by the professions. The role of the less active, but none the less effective, participation in the process of cultural change is taken by the clients of the profession. Culture conflict between client and caseworker therefore will have to be solved always in terms of cultural change in which both the caseworker and the client participate. The direction, the speed, and the effectiveness of the process, of course, are dependent upon the manner in which the professional obligation is discharged.

NEW KNOWLEDGE ABOUT FAMILY DYNAMICS[1]

Gardner Murphy

THOSE WHO WORK in a practical way to help families with their problems and those who make social science investigations of the changing dynamics of American family life seem to be coming closer together. They are developing a common language for the sharing of ideas and are contributing to better understanding of family life as a pivotal aspect of our changing American culture. New and important light on family dynamics is coming not only from new factual material, but also from sudden vistas of new understanding, as old ideas take on new meaning. Even the newest factual materials spring, of course, from old contexts, and many of them are already known to those who have been working with families. But recent studies have furnished, as it were, a filling in of detail and and enrichment of the scene. It is as if we are now supplied with the spectrum of a new and powerful lamp, capable of bringing out coloring and shading that give fresh vitality to the whole picture.

Family psychology is a clue to world psychology. I do not mean only that men everywhere conceive of the world order in terms of their own early experiences in the family. I mean that in studying the family we can more intimately understand some of the world trends that help to forecast what man may become in the years ahead. World changes not only influence family change, but family changes affect world change. Perhaps we shall find that American family patterns will be melted in the crucible of our own social change, but will in their own way influence American culture and

[1] Published in *Social Casework,* July 1959. Presented at the Biennial Meeting of the Family Service Association, Washington, D.C., April 1–3, 1959.

political evolution. Family strife and family harmony may even influence our readiness for one or another kind of world society.

The Contribution of Cultural Anthropology

The material that I am going to present comes primarily from three broad sources: cultural anthropology, psychoanalysis, and social psychology. The cultural anthropologist has documented for us, from societies widely diverse in form and function, the thesis that the basic factors forcing changes in families may be very remote indeed from the family life itself. There may be far-flung economic changes across the globe which alter available jobs, available male-female differentiation of roles, and available concepts as to how children should be reared. The economic and military transformation wrought in the Manus people of New Guinea by World War II, as described by Margaret Mead,[2] dramatically documents the thesis that the family, in the white heat of social transformation, changes its shape under the hammer blows of a world-wide social convulsion. Moreover, such remote factors interact intimately with the personalities of local individuals, so that a new social pattern expresses the relation between the remote change and the available human material with its potentialities for growth at a particular time when decisions are made.

Intimately related to this point is the fact that those in authority may be absolutely blind to family change or they may perceive it with extraordinary clarity. From this fact we derive not only a sense of the impersonal, massive forces with which most of us have to deal most of the time, but also the more optimistic conception that thoughtful men and women may strike while the iron is hot, may play into situations as they are played upon by situations in such a way as to use critical points of choice in the direction of social evolution.

It follows that we no longer look down our noses at the conception of planning, as we did, for example, before the depression. It has become plain that an explicit plan dealing realistically with difficulties may entail not only top- but middle-level leadership. Extraordinary examples can be found in modern India, notably in the integration of top-, middle-, and lower-level agricultural leaders.

[2] Margaret Mead, *New Lives for Old: Cultural Transformation—Manus, 1928–1953,* Morrow, New York, 1956.

When those who are specially gifted and trained find expanding opportunities for usefulness, leadership can emerge and man can take social evolution into his own hands.

The family not only reflects these various changes, distant and immediate, but it absorbs and adapts them and thus changes the world. The American family pattern, varying so widely in Colonial days between New England and the Old Dominion, played a real part among the many forces at work in generating the new conception of legitimate and normal variation in modes of human organization. And when the Midwest was settled, people of the two different kinds of family pattern, familiar with both and respecting both, could build with some confidence a kind of social freedom for America as a whole, which went deeper than all phrases, however cherished, regarding democracy.

In an even wider theater of action, American family patterns began in the mid-nineteenth century to impress themselves on distant lands as Americans wandered as missionaries, tradesmen, or travelers to Asia, the Middle East, and Africa. The special types of democracy which had been achieved in American family living began to make their mark, as Van Wyck Brooks tells us, on the attitude patterns of distant peoples. We are beginning to understand that whatever we discover for better or for worse about new forms of human relationship will not only set the standards by which American life is to be judged, but serve as entering wedges in the thinking of awakening masses of Asia and Africa.

There are many, I believe, who understand this role of the family in social change far more thoroughly than we Americans do. Take, for example, the violence with which Communist China has developed its anti-Confucian message to a point where the young man or woman must not only repudiate his allegiance to father and mother and all his obligations to his ancestors, but must learn to deride and vilify his parents as narrow, bigoted, petty, cheap, mean, and coarse exponents of a vicious tradition. It is through the breaking of the Confucian family, say the Red leaders, that a new pattern of human interdependence must be created. If this is so, we may well take note of the ways in which our own alteration of family structure may alter American life at large, and what it may portend for the world as a whole. I am suggesting that from family to world order is a two-way street. World order may bear down upon and remold our family life into new forms, but so also, to some small degree, in reciprocal action, changes in family life may alter human destiny in the world arena.

Finally, while still quoting from the teachings of anthropology, I should like to stress the fact that we must view the family in terms of a value system which is part of American culture as a whole. Thus, although we may repudiate the commercial character of our civilization—what Fromm calls the mercantile man—we may continue to measure our clients, our communities, and ourselves in terms of a yardstick essentially mercantile. We may protest the encroachments of impersonal science upon the more delicate, iridescent richness of interpersonal relations, but may still carry out a sort of cost accounting, asking how much of this is worth one unit of that. Our values, as Max Weber would say, reflect the sociology of knowledge of our era as a whole. We "size up" the work of a sociologist or social caseworker by a process essentially like that used in sizing up the work of a blacksmith or a die-maker. Indeed, we could do worse, for the blacksmith and the die-maker have professional craftsmanship, and this is something to be proud of in itself. Perhaps, however, we can aspire to a sensitivity commensurate with our passage from the age of the blacksmith to the age of the electronics engineer. We can gain in subtlety while retaining craftsmanship, but we can also reflect a readiness, like that of the electronics engineer, to recognize that what we know today is not only inadequate for tomorrow but bound to be reflected in the values men will espouse tomorrow.

In a certain sense, a family is a barometer indicating not only what is going on in the world now, but what will be going on tomorrow and the day after tomorrow. This is partly because the family is sensitive to trends that have not yet become generally visible, and it is partly for the very plain reason that children immediately reflect the changes affecting family living around them. Even if their own family is not directly engulfed by the changes, the great majority of children are, sooner or later, engulfed by them and, as they grow into adulthood and the establishment of their own families, they inevitably live out what was sensitively impressed in the marrow of their lives.

Psychoanalytic Approaches

According to Freud's conception of the family, family structure and functioning determine, in a broad sense, the nature of social aggregates—groups and crowds, parliamentary bodies, and institutionally organized forms of social association, such as the church and the army. In *Group Psychology and the Analysis of the Ego,* Freud spelled out the way in which the father-son relationship and, by implication, all the subtle relationships within the family, are concerned and projected at an unconscious level into the patterns of group life.[3] Not only is a strong leader a "father surrogate"; not only are the relations between brothers unconsciously reinstated in co-working groups in industry and in politics; in social life, generally, group atmospheres of strength, tenderness, or chaos are realized in the accepted community patterns. The irreconcilable conflicts in the home find a way of giving rise to conflict relations in group after group, as the conflictful person, unaware of what he is doing, relives the old sense of frustration and the old blind ways of trying to avoid pain, to master difficulties, and to maintain in his own eyes his sense of adequacy and power, or his sense of guiltlessness and a martyr's role.

The whole modern conception of the psychology of social roles, as it has developed in group work and in sociology generally, has been partly derived from, and is also a strong support to, this conception of the unconscious psychology of the family. Just as the priest or the Pope, or even God himself, may to some degree be a father surrogate, so all that is meaningful in community life may need to be seen in a psychoanalytic light in terms of the reliving of early family experience.

Some readers may have noted the republication of Gregory Bateson's extraordinary volume on social roles, which is at the same time an expression of cultural anthropology and of psychoanalytic modes of dealing with unconscious interpersonal relationships.[4] I shall single out here the way in which the theory of social roles fits into what has just been said. Bateson describes, among the Iatmul people of New Guinea, patterns of male-female differentiation, which, to our ears, sound very strange at first. When at peace, these martial head-hunting males spend most of their time in the men's house, arguing with one another, vilifying one another, comparing their own clan or those who live on their own side of the Sepik River with the other clans or those who live across the river. It is as if the quantities of aggression were limitless and continuous

[3] Sigmund Freud, *Group Psychology and the Analysis of the Ego,* The International Psycho-Analytical Press, London, 1922.

[4] Gregory Bateson, *Naven,* 2nd ed., Stanford University Press, Stanford, Calif., 1958.

verbal aggression offered the only outlet. The women, on the other hand, are gentle, quiet, practical people who do most of the work. At the time of a great ceremony, however, the women may put on martial regalia, stride magnificently through the town, and walk over the prostrate forms of males. What is this all about? This suggests that in the ordinary family situation the woman has lost the opportunity for certain kinds of self-assertion which may channel themselves through this martial display. The men, throughout the year, have been overdoing their pattern of aggression and bragging, and are glad to throw off the burden for a moment and play very vigorously the part of subordinates. Each role, therefore, is a double role; there are two male roles, two female roles. Indeed, as each sex group carries out its normal role as one might think of it, it is preparing for an antithetical role which is a sort of compensation.

Perhaps, in all families everywhere, there are secondary roles which arise to make up for something missing in the primary roles. This line of thought, combined with the unconscious reworking of that which has not been adequately expressed, gives us more understanding of the so-called inconsistency of roles. We understand the domineering person's becoming gentle as he passes from his job to his home; or the curious reversal in which the man so meek that butter wouldn't melt in his mouth may become—not just through frustration, but because of a deep feeling for release of an unexpressed component in his selfhood—vigorous and strong, at home. A woman may whirl from passivity to domination, as she moves from a sick child or a frightening domestic burden to an opportunity for vigorous independence and self-assertion where the interpersonal pattern permits it. The family becomes a crazy quilt of interconnected patches of color; but not so crazy if the ultimate design requiring transition from one role to another is grasped. At the same time, the family, in its own crazy-quilt pattern, reflects the crazy quilt of unresolved and incomplete tension patterns being worked through by others in the community or in the nation as a whole.

Social and Clinical Psychology

I turn here to the materials of social and clinical psychology, as roles are studied by new experimental methods. Particularly useful and brilliant here are the concepts of Sherif,[5] who has shown, as certain pressures are applied to a boys' camp group, how to evaluate the like-mindedness, the uniformity of the group outlook, so that a certain standardized group attitude, a certain standardized inability to free oneself of group-centered bias, becomes deeply established. The group begins to develop a pseudo unity, like the pseudo unity of the members of a family pressed by circumstances into maintaining a common front against an adverse world, however deeply suspicious and deeply incompatible the various family members might otherwise seem.

Sherif, however, went beyond this point and showed how two such groups, each highly homogeneous and highly hostile to the other, could, through wise leadership, achieve a sense of a common goal, a goal big enough to serve the needs of all; and then how the two groups could be fused into a larger co-working group. Many social workers have had a part in such a process, as fragmented families have been brought together, and as groups of families at each other's throats have learned to see a community interest as big as that of an ethnic or village totality, or even, in fortunate cases, as big as a larger pattern in which ethnic, religious, and other groups could discover a common destiny, replacing previous civil strife. The development of this experimental procedure, using the technicalities of modern experimental psychology, may seem to the practical sociologist or social worker a little too precious, a little too fancy. Yet basically each group, the technical and the practical, has much to learn from the other; and the experimentalist can often build into his design all that has been developed by those who have started with an immediate practical goal.

Individualized Approach to Family Dynamics

Up to this point I have been discussing trends that relate to the American family as a whole in its broadest contexts. Some of these generalizations may make social workers uneasy. Much is true of one family which is not true of a family across the street, however similar the economic, ethnic, and other background factors may be. I turn now, therefore, to the kind of material, very characteristic of today's observation and research, in which the spotlight is thrown

[5] Muzafer Sherif, *et al., Experimental Study of Positive and Negative Intergroup Attitudes between Experimentally Produced Groups*, Norman, Oklahoma, 1954. (Privately distributed.)

on the individual family—its texture, its way of life, and the mark that it makes upon its individual members—and, under still sharper focus, upon the individual member of the family who can sometimes teach us, through his own individuality, what membership in the American family of such-and-such attributes may actually mean. What kind of light on family dynamics does the more individualized approach give us?

Our discussions of the American family have often implied an ideal, a standard or norm, for the American mother. She is expected to be warm, strong, direct, to enjoy her femininity and her motherhood, to give affection and support, to protect her children, to be firm but not overbearing, tender but not mawkish; to provide stimulus and support for the child's growth and his ultimate achievement of independence. We have recently begun to learn, however, that in this picture a number of basic realities are missing; for one thing, the factor of individual differences. What is really simple, direct and warm, and natural for the mother to provide, may not meet the needs of every child. The research group making intensive studies of children as they grow up in Topeka has observed an affectionate, tender mother whose infant boy wanted more vigorous handling, wanted to bounce and jounce, developing from early months a puppy-dog-like need for energetic activity. He not only put pressure on the mother to be something that she could not become, but to the mother's bewilderment the child seemed incapable of fitting into the elemental tenderness pattern which she had assumed was adequate mothering. In another case a strong, vigorous mother found in her little son a need for sensitivity and tenderness which was actually beyond what she was capable of giving. One might say, in a fairy-tale manner, that the children had arrived at the wrong homes.

Despite both the biology of the hereditary tie and the family continuity, which leads the mother to conserve and re-enact a good deal from her own girlhood, at times there are these wide discrepancies in what is physiologically wanted by the child and what the mother is physiologically capable of giving. A very verbal child and an active motor mother result in a story-telling hour demanded by the child but boring to the mother. Some children when taken to the supermarket will sit still looking at comics or movies, but not all mothers have this type of child. One mother takes her 3-year-old to the supermarket expecting him to keep still like the others while she sorts out soaps, onions, and cookies. But this 3-year-old is fascinated by a puppy he discovers, and if he cannot pull his tail and squeeze his neck, puts on a howling act.

Like all human relationships, the family relationships are intensely individualized, and the good mother who is equally good for all the children cannot always be found in the individual home. In one family there may be children with different temperaments, each of whom may or may not get what is needed for optimal growth at a particular time. This situation is sometimes balanced, sometimes complicated, by the fact that the father's temperament may fit into the child's needs or fail to fit in at any given time. Families have been observed in which the mother seldom responded to the child's moods, but the father often did. One father was capable of a "roughhouse" relationship with a demanding tomboy of a girl, which was exactly what the little girl, who felt remote from her mother, wanted. This home situation complicated the child's psychosexual development a year or two later, and had indirect repercussions upon her relation to the mother. Indeed, it also apparently affected the relations between the parents. If the father is at home a good deal, he may play a major role in the cuddling, protecting, and growth-stimulating functions, with many subtle or not so subtle positive and negative results for different children.

I have been speaking of the so-called biological family—the family of the parents and their children. Complications are added by the extended family, involving the pattern of in-laws living in the home, which developed to such a degree during the depression years, and even more during the housing shortage after the war. Matters are also complicated, of course, by changing patterns of nationwide travel in all directions, as young couples look for new jobs and neighborhoods, sometimes towing the old folks with them, sometimes falling back upon them for long visits. The presence of the extended family or, as they say in Asia, the joint family, comprising the spouses of members of a brother-sister group, and often grandparents, may sometimes reduce the intensity of the pressure of mother-child relationships. It may also serve as a protective factor for young children by preventing their having to come into new situations too fast or without preparation. The Topeka data suggest that children with joint family experience are better protected against that shock of newness and strangeness which is likely to overwhelm children of pre-school age when they encounter strange people. Moreover, the presence of cousins in the joint family group may make contact with strange children far easier to accept and enjoy.

Sequences in the Family Drama

All such generalizations, which I am offering tentatively for consideration, are too static, in the sense that they cut cross sections through the experience of a family at a given time. A family that is managing in a self-sufficient and even happy way at one time may be caught in personal adversity or distress or a nationwide economic squeeze and may go downhill. In other instances—as we found in the Topeka group—families often achieve greater security as the father becomes more established in his vocation. A family history can be enormously constructive if it compares what is going on at different phases in the development of both the parents and the children. It is relatively easy to understand those factors that strengthen or weaken family solidarity and are external to the family, but internal factors are changing as well. Consider, for example, the cases in which the nature of the relationship of husband and wife, and the relationship of both to their children, promise well for the family at one period in the family's development, and not so well in another. We see young couples who enjoy their youth, their intimacy, their intensity, and enjoy producing and caring for infants upon whom they may lavish physical affection and warm support in the earliest years. As physical intensity gradually subsides and the children cease to be satisfying babies and become kindergartners or school-age children, they may neither want nor need the original primitive affection, but want and need more thought, more attention in verbal terms, a little more study of their problem. The parents, already vaguely feeling that life is less intense than it used to be, will be superhuman if they do not feel some resentment.

As the children are away from home more and more during daytime hours and put pressure on their parents for time and help and companionship in the evenings, the time parents have with each other is reduced and there may be an increase in the tendency of each parent to blame the other for a disintegration they do not understand and cannot control. There are, fortunately, also families in which the process of the parents' genuine discovery of each other takes some years; in which the babies come so soon that they are actually experienced as a force dislocating the relation of the parents; but in which the children gradually win a place in the affection, respect, and need systems of their parents, so that by elementary-school age each child as a complete person means more and more to both father and mother, so that the parents may be drawn together. General statements about the solidarity or the wholesomeness of a particular family or of the meaning of family background for the growing child need to be supplemented by considerations of these sequences in the family drama.

It may be felt that this way of thinking is too "clinical." It is certainly clinical in the sense that it calls for a good deal of care in observation, and sensitivity in description. If, however, the term "clinical" is used to describe the easy habit of applying the thinking on one pathological case to another, or to a normal person, it can lead us far astray. The term has sometimes been applied to the easy habit of finding Freudian symbolism everywhere and looking for essentially the same oedipal problems in all families, working themselves out to the same ultimate destiny. We might discontinue such use of the term and reserve it for the more appropriate use of individualized study. Indeed, this method of individualized study has come into the modern social sciences and into social casework just as much by virtue of the directly observed facts of human family life as through the subtleties of the clinical interview and the interchange between the analyst and the patient on the couch. Our modern clinical knowledge has come from a wide variety of types of observation, and it will often be the privilege of the social worker or the applied sociologist to observe relationships that are vital and important as these appear in his professional practice. If so, he can use whatever he has read or otherwise learned through clinical sources, just as the clinician may learn from the caseworker and the applied sociologist. The data belong to no single discipline.

The Individual Family Member

I should now like to discuss the individual himself, as he reflects family background, so to speak, by lifting him from the context of the family and seeing him primarily in individualistic terms. When the individual has passed through the early phases of family living, and has achieved a self-image, based partly upon seeing his similarities to his father and to his mother and selecting those attributes, such as sex itself and such as aspects of appearance, mentality, feeling, skill, which make him in some ways more like one parent than like the other, he can be said to have identified with either or both parents. He can carry forward half-consciously through the rest of his life a sense of the drama he is enacting. He is in some ways proud and in some ways unappreciative of family background, but basically he knows that he will never escape it. Many children fortunately have a sense that they will never want to escape.

According to the newer concepts and terms so beautifully worked out in recent years by Erik Erikson,[6] the child then has achieved an *identity,* a sense of who he is, what he is, the depths and heights and ranges of his own individuality as it is today, and as it has been and will be as a part of a life continuity. Erikson speaks of realizing how the portrait of a patient's grandfather on the wall gave him a perspective which the verbal interchanges in the consulting room were inadequate to supply. All of us observe the glow, the warmth of identity as someone recounts what the family did on some occasion in the past, and how the speaker himself acted as a sort of front or pivot or representative of the family. One knows that just as the father or mother talked long ago of his or her own boyhood or girlhood, the individual has the sense of a continuing identity, which he also is proud to be able to project forward through the lives of his children and his children's children. The family becomes in such cases more than a pattern of interpersonal relations; it becomes the basic vehicle through which the culture as a whole and basic humanness itself are projected into and concentrated within the structure of an individual personality. The intensive study of the family is never finished until the family in its quintessence is seen looking out through the eyes of an individual whom one intimately observes and learns to understand; and the individual is never understood until the process of family development and its role in the genesis of this particular individuality are understood.

[6] Erik H. Erikson, *Childhood and Society,* W. W. Norton and Company, New York, 1950.

Family Atmospheres

But behind all of these sociological issues there is a new way of looking at families today, especially an awareness of family atmospheres, the tone or spirit of family living, as seen in large trends or in homely details. Slacks, lounge clothes, and slippers, easy chairs, pipes, dogs bringing newspapers—such conceptions of the home contrast with the image of the home as the place of isolation, the castle defended, the place where visitors come on Sundays or in the evening, but where people don't just drop in. There was a period when some resentment was shown of people who came without announcing themselves; perhaps with television shows shared by several families there is a change in the conception of the family. The family atmosphere reflects our conception of the family. New conceptualization changes our practical working analysis. In return, more realistic grappling with family problems changes our concepts; as in Kurt Lewin's "action research," the attempt to *change* interpersonal relations gives a new system for understanding. What we do will not only reflect the world trends of the twentieth century, but will in some measure give direction to these trends. If humanity, democracy, and the spirit of science can be combined in working with families, families may be strengthened in the world arena.

THE FAMILY AS A PSYCHOLOGICAL UNIT[1]

Irene M. Josselyn

Many fairy stories end "and they lived happily ever after." The nucleus of the family is established, and there the writer ends the story. Perhaps he does so because even in the fairy world of his own fantasy he cannot conceive of the details of a happy fulfillment. This possibility is suggested by the fact that so frequently the fairy princess or fairy prince comes from a family that either includes one or more cruel people, or is faced with social situations that require renunciation of personal desires. Our own fantasy must provide the sequel to the story. Even though the authors have avoided the task of completing the story, we ourselves have a dream of what "happily ever after" means. Our fantasies and our dreams serve to fulfill wishes that do not always find their full expression in reality. The wish for the ideal family is rooted in a cultural pattern that has created a psychological need. Dr. Mead points out that "when we survey all known human societies, we find everywhere some form of the family, some set of permanent arrangements by which males assist females in caring for children while they are young."[2]

Out of his prehistoric origins man has ultimately become, for better or for worse, a personality called a "human being." Was it by mere chance that the nuclear family was established in those prehistoric times? Or was it that, in the evolution of the species,

[1] Published in *Social Casework,* October 1953. Presented at the National Conference of Social Work, Cleveland, Ohio, June 1953.

[2] Margaret Mead, *Male and Female,* Wm. Morrow and Company, New York, 1949, p. 188.

some psychological mutation took place which established, as an essential part of psychological survival, the need for family interrelationships? It would be reassuring if we could know that prehistoric man suddenly experienced a new psychological hunger that drove him to gratifications found only in the family structure. If the fact were established that the need for a family was the result of a psychological mutation occurring in prehistoric times, we could then assume that this urge may be distorted or crippled, but that only by very serious attack against it can it be repressed.

Dr. Mead and many others see the family structure not as inherent in the psychological make-up of the human being, in contrast to other animals, but rather as one of the learned patterns of behavior. Dr. Mead points out that the continuance of the family up to the present is not a guarantee that it will always endure. Our generation cannot relax and take the permanence of the family for granted. "We hold our present form of humanity on trust— . . . it is possible to lose it." [3]

In answering Dr. Mead's challenge we might assume a cynical attitude. Is our humanness in its present form worth preserving, or would we rather write a new fairy tale in which we fantasy an entirely different life pattern? To do this would be to venture into fields that would only be confusing. Regardless of its origin, the family has come to have a deep psychological as well as a cultural significance. Thus, it is more to the point for us to assume that our successors will continue to strive to improve the social structure that is familiar to us. In order to do this it is important to understand the role the family plays in our cultural evalution and the factors that either threaten or strengthen its structure. Ideas from many fields of study must be fused: the economic, social, and political significance and vicissitudes of the family must be understood; and the psychological significance of the family must be continually re-evaluated. In the last analysis no study of the family will have validity if it is undertaken by only one discipline. A complete and accurate image of the family will come into being only when the findings of the many isolated studies are integrated. The following material is focused upon only one facet of the total significance of the family—the family as a psychological unit.

[3] *Ibid.*, p. 194.

The significance of the members of the family in the child's maturation process is familiar to all of us. The newborn baby, through his physio-emotional symbiosis with the mother, experiences a sense of well-being and/or frustration which determines how safe he feels in starting on the long road toward adaptation to the external world. In the framework of this early security, firm or precarious as it may be, he gradually learns to master his external world as well as his own internal impulses. He learns to deal with his ambivalent feelings toward the primary members of the family, and in so doing experiences all the gratifications and dangers inherent in his ambivalent responses. He experiences the conflicts of the oedipal period and finds a solution that does not completely destroy the significance of his primary relationships. He gradually finds gratification for his emotional needs in his relationships with persons outside the family; but hopefully he preserves a feeling of basic security in the interpersonal relationships of the more intimate group. He struggles with his adolescent conflicts, and he attempts to establish himself as an independent adult. He rebels against the bonds that hold him to his primary infantile love objects, hopefully, with the knowledge that while those bonds are weakened, they cannot be broken. He reaches adulthood to find that those bonds are now part of himself. They are no longer something to struggle against, but are part of his cultural heritage and will determine to some extent his own ability to become the nucleus of a new family.

This description of psychological development does not touch upon the meaning of the family unit but only upon the meaning of the individual family members to a particular person. It implies the significance of the child's relationship to his mother, his father, and his siblings. It provides, in a sense, a description of an individual tree in the forest and the effect upon it of the adjacent trees. It does not describe the forest as a whole. Yet the forest as a whole undoubtedly has an effect upon the growth of the individual tree that is different from the specific effect of each tree. Similarly, an analysis of the interpersonal relationships between child and mother, child and father, and child and siblings only partially reveals the significance of the family. The intermeshing of these multiple relationships creates a structure that has meaning over and above the meaning of each of its parts.

Significance of Emotional Atmosphere

Common expressions bring into sharp focus the universality of the value vested in the family. When a person says, "The family was all together for Christmas," he is not only speaking in a verbally economical way that avoids listing each individual, but he is also conveying the idea of the existence of a unit to which he has reacted positively or negatively, depending upon his past experiences with that unit. The absence of the unit arouses the feeling that something is missing. "We never had a family life" carries the implication of a nostalgic wish for something in addition to the primary relationships with parents and siblings. The single person in a strange city is more lonesome on family holidays than he is from day to day. The holiday festivals arouse the longing for something without which life is not complete. When a person says, "That place is like a second home to me," he is conveying much more than the fact that he has found a place in which to sleep and eat. His statement implies a feeling of "family" and "at-homeness" that only emotional interrelationships can provide. When a true family does not exist, the individual often creates one. He will speak of his "family" even if it is an atypical constellation made up of foster parents, distant relatives, or, in some instances, merely close friends.

The significance of the family structure for the individual is difficult to define. In part it provides an "emotional atmosphere." In spite of the fact that analogies usually are inadequate, I should like to attempt one. Physiologically food is necessary for body growth. For optimum growth certain elements are essential—carbohydrates, proteins, fats, minerals, and vitamins. All these constituents must be combined to produce energy and adequate structural growth. Chemical interaction cannot occur without the presence of oxygen. These foods can be compared, in our analogy, with the emotional food the child receives through his interpersonal relationships with his father, mother, and siblings; the oxygen in the air can be equated with the emotional atmosphere created by the family. Oxygen is an essential in the physical metabolic process of life. Just as inadequate oxygen results in only partial combustion, so psychological metabolism is incomplete without healthy emotional elements in the family atmosphere. Partial psychological utilization of one-to-one relationships can occur in a depleted family atmosphere, but psychological maturation will remain incomplete.

The family unit plays a significant part in ego development and the maintenance of ego strength. It offers a definitive structure as a framework for the ego, and thereby represents a reality relatively more predictable than the less intimate reality beyond the home. Furthermore, the family is a little world bound together by a more compact interlacing of personal relationships than occurs in the outside world. As a constituent as well as an occupant of this structure, the individual experiences an extension of his own ego. He is not only his "self" but also a part of a closely interlaced whole from which he draws increased strength.

The dissolution of a family unit, irrespective of the cause, in some instances results in real ego disaster in an individual. For example, the death of an essential member of the family may result in the complete breakdown of the family structure. Although each person may share his grief with the other family members, the sharing may be done in panic and with little strength gained from it. In other instances, a death may bring about a closer interlacing of the remaining members. Each individual, in the latter case, strengthened by this intermeshing, is able to deal with his grief without ego disintegration. Often an adult will say, "In spite of my father's death when I was a small child, my mother kept the home together." If the child-mother relationship were the only factor that offered security, there would be no need for the use of the word "home."

The special significance of the family as an entity should probably be borne in mind when we evaluate the resistance on the part of husband, wife, or children to a dissolution of a marriage. Although it is true that significant neurotic factors hold many marriages together, there are many instances in which the anxiety created by the disruption of the general atmosphere, even when that atmosphere is unhealthy, acts as an additional cohesive factor. When a woman says, "I don't like to break up the family," she may be expressing not only her neurosis but also an unconscious recognition of the importance of the family atmosphere, even though it may be an atmosphere filled with noxious gases. Breaking up the family may destroy the ego boundaries of the individual and the integration of the family unit.

The significance of the family atmosphere can be illustrated by its effect upon the early mother-child relationship. While the capacity for "motherhood" is inherent in the feminine psyche, it is not effectively mobilized until the woman has the biological experience of becoming a mother. In the one-to-one relationship between mother and infant not only does the child gain security, but the mother experiences the gratifications of motherhood. Through the fact of being a biological mother the woman becomes a mother in a psychological sense. This psychological metabolism is most successful, however, in an atmosphere that provides other psychological chemicals. The changes in the woman take place most successfully when there are parallel changes in her husband. He is also undergoing a psychological modification. Whereas he has formerly been a husband, a businessman, a sportsman, and so forth, he now becomes a father. Through a parallel change in both husband and wife, a new relationship evolves, and a true family is born. In this new husband-wife relationship, the child's own psychological metabolism is fostered. In addition to the primary importance of the mother-child relationship, the intra-family relationships come to have great significance in the creation of the family atmosphere. If this atmosphere is healthful, the mother will not only be a more adequate mother, but the family will also become a source of safety and confidence. The family unit, itself, becomes, in a less specific way, a "mother."

Enhancement of the Maturation Process

The family unit provides the child with rich and broad sources of security. The experience of being part of this unit not only gives the child the feeling of safety in the world beyond his relationship with his mother, but also encourages him to relinquish his dependence on her in favor of the more mature dependence upon the family. If he is to accomplish this, the family milieu must be safe enough so that protection by the mother is not frighteningly urgent. Later he will be able to accept multiple relationships beyond the family group. The overprotective mother may subtly prevent the child from making this transfer of some of his feelings from her to the family group, and may thereby deprive him of this intermediate step in forming relationships with the wider social group. The family thus retains throughout life the symbolic meaning of the mother; it becomes a token of security but free of the limiting bonds of the intimate mother-child dependent relationship.

The family unit also plays a part in the outcome of the child's struggles with his ambivalent feelings toward primary love objects. On the one hand, a child who successfully works out his ambivalent feelings toward his mother does not necessarily transfer that solution to his other interpersonal relationships. Within the family constellation, he is not only ambivalent toward his mother, but also ambivalent toward all other members of the family. He finds a pattern of solution that involves many relationships. More significantly, he works out these ambivalent feelings in the framework of the interrelationships in the family. He senses the approval and disapproval, the love and the rejection, of the total group, as well as the more intimate response of the parent figure.

From another standpoint, the child appears to want not only the love of the person toward whom his ambivalent feelings are directed but also acceptance in the family unit. A scene familiar in many homes is one where a child becomes angry at his mother and expresses his anger in a temper tantrum directed toward all the members of the family. The mother removes him from the family circle, taking him into a room alone, where she calms him down and reassures him of her understanding and her love. He nestles in her arms, apparently content at first to be re-established in a favorable position with her. Suddenly he sits up and asks, "Can I go back now?", apparently feeling an urge to be a part of the total family again rather than to preserve his isolated one-to-one relationship with his mother. The pull is not toward the activities in which the other members are participating, for when he returns to the living-room, where the others are reading, he quietly takes a picture book to look at without disturbing the others.

The interrelationships among siblings in the family offer another example of the role of the family in the social maturation process. It has long been recognized that an only child has a difficult problem when he faces the outside world where he is suddenly forced to deal with sibling relationships with his own age group. It is assumed that his problem is inevitable because, until the only child leaves his family, he faces no real competition. Although this problem is somewhat less severe when the child has early social experiences with other children, as for example, in a nursery school, these experiences do not provide a complete solution. As the only child approaches the latency period in his psychological development, he has two opposing needs: he wishes to continue the security of being the center of the child universe in his family; he also has an urge to establish himself as part of the peer group. The child who has siblings has a better chance of coping with this more diluted but significant emotional experience.

Sibling relationships are apt to be described in the negative. It is pointed out that the child resents the presence of another child; that he resents the need to share his parents with another; that he finally reaches a truce in his battle with this problem when he relinquishes his own need for priority. A sibling relationship is not, however, typically so negative. Usually a child loves as well as hates his sibling. It is partially true that love is manifested, and the underlying hostility is hidden, in order to deceive the parents. It is questionable, however, that the wish to deceive the parent wholly accounts for this profession of affection. Love in itself is a valuable and gratifying human experience. It provides more positive rewards than simply the avoidance of punishment. The positive aspects of the relationship between siblings add to the child's feeling of security in the world.

Furthermore, the parents' love for each of their children is not only frustrating to the child, but is also reassuring. It indicates the elasticity of the parents' capacity to love and suggests that, in the atmosphere of the family, there is adequate nutritional love for all. This was interestingly illustrated in the case of a 3-year-old child who, with the birth of a sibling, developed severe anxiety and marked hostility toward the baby. The parents, in an attempt to avoid this sibling jealousy, had made elaborate plans to have the baby cared for without parental intervention. A nurse took over the complete responsibility for the new baby as soon as it came home from the hospital. The parents continued their relationship with the older child as if the baby did not exist. In spite of this, the older child showed alarming hostility toward the baby, to the point that the baby's life was actually in danger. The obvious explanation for the situation would seem to be the inability of the older child to accept the presence of the new baby. Particularly did this seem true inasmuch as this child who had formerly given every evidence of being unusally secure was now showing great anxiety about her own relationship with her parents. She could not tolerate having her mother out of her sight and reverted to many infantile patterns of behavior. In the course of therapy the fallacy of this explanation became apparent. This child was not merely jealous of the sibling; she was frightened at the parents' failure to behave as its parents. She wished to destroy the baby as a favor to the parents, who would thus be relieved of their responsibility and perhaps would have, at least, the capacity to love her. The evidence of the parents' rejection of the baby frightened her. It meant that these parents whom she had evaluated as loving were actually incapable of loving children. She had been living in a fool's paradise, believing in parental love which she now feared was a mirage. When the nurse was discharged and the new baby was included as a member of the family, the child's anxiety lessened sharply. She continued to show normal jealousy of the new baby's relationship with the mother, but her healthy ambivalence toward the baby was manifest. She changed from what appeared to be a seriously emotionally ill child to a child dealing realistically with the problem of adapting to a family unit. It would appear that in spite of every evidence of a secure parent-child relationship this child was frightened by the absence of something more encompassing. She was deprived of the reassurance given by a family constellation.

The family unit also plays an important role in the ultimate resolution of the oedipal triangle by providing an additional outlet for the libidinal energy that cannot be expressed in its primitive form. Some of the libidinal energy is partially sublimated in a love for the family as a group rather than merely for the individuals in the family. This represents, in the author's opinion, the first step in the desexualization of the primary relationship, a desexualization which predates the child's turning toward the peer group, and which is essential for the resolution of the oedipal conflict. From this experience the child gains a sense of the future family of which he will be the nucleus. This new family will not only make possible, ultimately, the expression of his sexual urges, but will also provide him with the sublimations that will make his marriage both a gratifying sexual experience and an experience enriched by the asexual aspects of family love.

As the child enters the latency period, his energies are largely invested in adapting himself to his social group. It is obvious that the one-to-one relationships in the home still remain the foundation upon which the latency child struggles to build his social world. But there are indications that, over and above the one-to-one relationships, the family as a group has significance for him. How often a child who is having difficulties in his social adjustment will leave his playmates and return to his home to read, to watch television, or to play with his own toys! He may make no particular demands upon the individual members of the family. His behavior suggests that the family atmosphere of his own home has a specific meaning to him. It offers him security over and above the security offered by any individual in the family. Through adolescence and adulthood this same impulse to return home continues. It is a rare adult who travels endlessly without moments of wishing to return to the home which serves, symbolically, as the container in which the family atmosphere is found.

Changing Roles of the Family Members

Defining the atmosphere of the family is so difficult that any attempt to do so may appear somewhat artificial. Yet the word "family" has a significant place in the psychological matrix of each of us. For this reason it would seem important to preserve the family unit in as constructive a form as possible. Preservation of the family as a unit requires that the role of none of its component parts—father, mother, children—be allowed to atrophy. The family unit as a separate entity develops only as the individual family members become a part of it. In its final form it is crippled or enriched in accordance with the crippling or enrichment of each member. The continual changes in our culture are having an effect on all members of the family and will ultimately affect the pattern of the family unit. Many examples can be cited to illustrate these changes. Three instances are of particular importance: the role of the man as father, the woman as mother, and the child as a family member.

The impact of culture on the role of the man as father will affect the modifications that will occur in the structure of the family. Dr. Therese Benedek [4] has described the change that is occurring in relationship to the man's economic and authoritative role in our culture. In the past the father was the acknowledged head of the family, as well as its economic center. One of the many considerations that contribute to modifying his authoritative role is his absence from the home during most of the family's waking hours. Since he is not present to control the family himself, he

[4] Therese Benedek, "The Emotional Structure of the Family," *The Family: Its Function and Destiny*, Ruth Nanda Anshen (ed.), Harper and Brothers, New York, 1949, pp. 202–225.

has had to relegate control of the children to the mother. Also newer theories of psychological development have contributed to change in his role. As the ideal maturation pattern for our culture has begun to be defined, stress has been placed upon the significance of the mother in early childhood. The father is too often considered of secondary importance, and he is in danger of becoming the "forgotten man."

The mother used to feel quite justified in saying to the recalcitrant child, "Wait until your father gets home." Now she is urged to handle her own disciplinary problems and to avoid adding to the child's fear of the father. The child is more often reminded that the father will come home tired and must be protected from additional strain. The middle-class father is encouraged to believe that he performs his duty to his children by providing adequate income and, ideally, a suburban home. The latter aspect is of real psychosocial significance. Suburban living tends increasingly to remove the father from the family group. Longer commuting time shortens his hours at home and necessitates staying in town "for business." Even if he is available to the child, he is encouraged to be the child's playmate, not his parent. He must not be feared, and to avoid being feared he must be as innocuous as a compliant toy.

In certain sub-cultural groups still another pattern for the father is becoming more clearly defined, in which the father shares with the mother the maternal care of the child and often assumes some of the burdens of housekeeping. The value of relief to the fatigued mother is obvious. The care the father gives is also significant in giving the child the concept of a father, not as an ogre, but as a gentle, helpful, and comforting person. One should hesitate to condemn this family relationship, but students of the family should be alert to some possible inherent drawbacks in it. It may tend to make the father a substitute for the mother rather than giving him the complementary role that is necessary if we believe that the future healthy development of the present culture is dependent, in part, upon the conservation of a bisexual society that encompasses more than sexuality itself. The father should represent a masculine figure, giving a feeling of warm protection not by sheltering the child but by attacking dangers aggressively. His role is not an imitation of, but is complementary to, the role of the mother. The "mom" role of the mother has come to be recognized as a real block to the fulfillment of the present concept of maturity. There may be as much danger in the possibility that the father will lose his role in dropping out of the family by default as in the "moms" taking over. The role of the father in the psychological development of the individual is recognized, but we must re-evaluate the role of the father as a constituent part of the family unit.

The role of the woman in our culture is also undergoing changes. The impact of these changes can be traced in sympathetically written scientific treatises as well as in the vitriolic attacks found in such recent books as *Modern Woman: The Lost Sex* [5] and *The Second Sex*.[6] The change can be explained in terms of shifts in our mores, in our educational policy, in our economic patterns, or in our psychological approach. Regardless of the explanation given, we cannot deny that a new role for woman is gradually evolving. The question of how the change in the role of the woman will affect her place in the family unit cannot yet be answered with certainty. It seems apparent, however, that the cultural goal cannot be reached unless the role of the woman in the family unit is defined not only in terms of her meeting the child's needs for a mother, but equally in terms of how the mother can fulfill herself as a person in the family milieu. If she can function economically and politically as readily as a man, if her whole domestic life is simplified by a world of gadgets, if her young children are cared for in day nurseries or nursery schools, and if educators later discourage her from playing a part in the education of her children, will her role in the family atrophy? If it does, our social structure will change radically because the family unit, as we know it now, will be gone.

The child also has assumed a new role in the family structure. Not long ago, he was an unimportant component of the family—to be seen and not heard. More recently, the child has been looked upon as an individual for whose enrichment the family exists. Present thinking suggests that the child's role in the family, a role that is different from a self-focused role, is also important. He is not only a recipient, but also, within his capacity, a participant in the family unit. Failure to be part of a family unit may result in the child's growing up with a limited concept of what family

[5] Marynia L. F. Farnham and Ferdinand Lundberg, *Modern Woman: The Lost Sex,* Harper and Brothers, New York, 1947.

[6] Simone de Beauvoir, *The Second Sex,* Alfred A. Knopf, New York, 1953.

life means—not because of emotional immaturity, but because he lacked this fundamental experience.

The appropriate roles of father, mother, and child, as well as of many other persons in the family, cannot easily be delineated. Our culture will not become progressively enriched, however, by reverting to earlier, less confusing patterns. Psychological growth will be dwarfed if we attempt to reinstate the patterns of "the good old days." New patterns must be found for meeting the new situations that now exist.

Summary

The family is the product of the interrelationships of several people with varied needs and varied potentialities. While considerable headway has been made in understanding the needs of the individual members of the family, there is a danger that the other side of the coin will be overlooked. The family is as much a part of the individual as the individual is a part of the family. Unless concern for the individual is balanced by concern for the family group, emotional starvation will result, not because of the absence of emotional food, but because of the absence of the atmosphere that is required for the utilization of the food.

The family can be defined politically, economically, and sociologically. It needs also to be studied psychologically. Not the individual but the family is the smallest unit of our social structure. The family can be analyzed by studying its individual parts, but the findings must be synthesized before it can be understood as a unit. Much of the consideration of the psychology of the family is focused upon the effect of the family on the individual rather than on the effect of the individual on the family unit. If the family unit is anthropomorphized, perhaps we can better study its bisexual and asexual drives, its loves and its aggressions. The neuroses and the psychoses of the unit rather than the neuroses and psychoses of its component parts can then be understood. By studying family pathology we can determine what constitutes family health. Until this is done, there remains the danger that noxious gases will replace the necessary oxygen of which the healthy family atmosphere ideally must be predominantly composed.

Part II
Casework Practice

THE LOGIC OF DIAGNOSIS [1]

Louis J. Lehrman

DIAGNOSIS HAS BEEN DEFINED by Gordon Hamilton as "the thought process directed to the nature of the problem and its causes. . . ." [2] In further discussion, she adds:

> Findings are the raw materials of diagnosis, but they are not diagnosis. Facts and inferences are not the same. It is important to be able to distinguish findings from diagnosis, just as it is important to distinguish diagnosis from treatment. Findings are the analyzed breakdown of the essential factors in a case. They may be listed separately or grouped under headings, as in the conventional diagnostic summary; diagnosis, however, requires the synthesis or interpretation of these factors to give the psychosocial meaning of the case as a whole. While in a logical way one would say that first one gathers data, then derives from these data certain significant items (findings), which when configurated give one the meaning (diagnosis) of a case, actually the inferential process is continuous and one can see fragmentary interpretative thinking related to an incident, an interview, or even a piece of behavior or attitude within a single episode.[3]

Two distinct, yet related, processes seem to be involved in Miss Hamilton's formulations: (1) a diagnostic thought process or mode of reasoning; (2) a diagnostic scientific method in which, within a matrix of other operations, the thought process in question is deeply embedded.

In the material that follows I shall attempt to set forth (1) the exact nature of the diagnostic mode of reasoning and (2) in a general way, the sequential steps in the diagnostic scientific method. To accomplish these tasks, however, it will first be neces-

[1] Published in *Social Casework*, May 1954.

[2] Gordon Hamilton, *Theory and Practice of Social Case Work* (2d ed., rev.), Columbia University Press, New York, 1951, p. 214.

[3] *Ibid.*, p. 225.

sary to review the thought processes or modes of reasoning known as deduction and induction.

Deduction is a mediate form of reasoning in which two premises are involved. Thus a typical deductive syllogism assumes the form:

First Premise—Socrates is a man.
Second Premise—Men are mortal.
Conclusion—Therefore Socrates is mortal.

The first premise in deduction sets forth an instance or case of something. The second premise sets forth a rule or generalization which includes the case. The conclusion, which follows not just from one but from both of these premises, establishes a particular. The complete form assumed by the deductive syllogism is thus the following:

Case (First Premise)—Socrates is a man.
Generalization (Second Premise)—Men are mortal.
Particular (Deductive Conclusion)—Therefore Socrates is mortal.

Without the mediate role played by the case, the reasoning in deduction would be incomplete and the particular would not ensue. Once both of the premises have been admitted, however, the deductive conclusion is their necessary and inevitable consequence. It is, indeed, contained in them and hence, in a formal sense, adds nothing to our store of knowledge that was not already there. Although deduction is a basically uncreative reasoning mode, its importance is nonetheless great.

One important use of deduction in social casework is immediately apparent. For example, on receiving a diagnostic statement from a psychiatrist to the effect that the client is a paranoidal schizophrenic, the caseworker is enabled, by means of deduction, to anticipate how the client will act. Schematically, his thought process is as follows:

Case (First Premise)—Mr. Smith is a paranoidal schizophrenic.
Generalization (Second Premise)—Paranoidal schizophrenics are delusional.
Particular (Deductive Conclusion)—Therefore Mr. Smith will be delusional.

Case (First Premise)—Mr. Smith is a paranoidal schizophrenic.
Generalization (Second Premise)—Hallucinations are associated with the delusions of paranoidal schizophrenics.
Particular (Deductive Conclusion)—Therefore Mr. Smith will have hallucinations.

The caseworker would, in fact, form many such deductive syllogisms, their exact number and the degree of his reliance on them depending mainly on his own psychiatric knowledge and the current stage in the scientific development of psychiatry.

Induction is also a mediate form of reasoning. The two premises in induction, however, are the case and the particular. The conclusion is the generalization. A typical inductive syllogism assumes the form:

Case (First Premise)—Socrates is a man.
Particular (Second Premise)—Socrates is mortal.
Generalization (Inductive Conclusion)—There is therefore a probability that men are mortal.

The conclusion in induction, as generations of logicians have pointed out, is no longer a mere re-wording of its premises, but a new idea which, though it is suggested by these premises, actually goes beyond them. Induction is thus a creative reasoning mode by means of which the store of man's knowledge may be gradually increased. The conclusion in induction, moreover, is no longer certain, but is only probable. Inductive conclusions remain constantly in need of continued examination, and, if possible, of reinforcement.

By developing a chain of related inductive syllogisms, the probability of an originally weak inductive generalization may be progressively increased. The proposition that men are mortal, for example, has become elevated to the status of a reliable scientific law by means of some such inductive chain as the following:

Case (First Premise)—Socrates was a man.
Particular (Second Premise)—Socrates was mortal.
Generalization (Inductive Conclusion)—There is therefore a probability that men are mortal.

Case (First Premise)—Napoleon was a man.
Particular (Second Premise)—Napoleon was mortal.
Generalization (Inductive Conclusion)—It is now more probable that men are mortal.

Case (First Premise)—Frankin D. Roosevelt was a man.
Particular (Second Premise)—Franklin D. Roosevelt was mortal.
Generalization (Inductive Conclusion)—It is now highly probable that men are mortal.

The total process by means of which such inductive chains are constructed includes, in addition to the core logical process of induction proper, a number of other operations, such as observation or fact-gathering, identification, verification, deduction, prediction, and test. The process as a whole constitutes what might be called the *inductive* scientific method. Its sequential steps have frequently been described.[4] Its goal is the establishment of ever better-founded inductive generalizations, that is, scientific laws.

A third form of mediate reasoning remains; one that proceeds from a particular and a generalization as premises to a case as conclusion. This, it seems to me, is precisely the thought process or mode of reasoning implied in Miss Hamilton's formulations. In a course of lectures in the philosophy of science given at Brown University in 1931, the American logician Curt Ducasse referred to it as the diagnostic reasoning mode.

The diagnostic reasoning mode has received almost no attention in the standard textbooks of logic. The main reason for this may be the common but mistaken tendency to regard deduction as reasoning from the general to the particular and induction as reasoning from the particular to the general. Though these definitions are correct as far as they go, they are actually incomplete, and therefore misleading, inasmuch as they leave out the essential role played by the case or instance in both deduction and induction. When the role played by the case or instance is ignored, no third form of mediate reasoning seems possible. Ducasse, so far as I know, was the first and only logician to point this out. Schematically, thc diagnostic reasoning mode has the form:

Particular (First Premise)—Socrates is mortal.
Generalization (Second Premise)—Men are mortal.
Case (Diagnostic Conclusion)—There is therefore a probability that Socrates is a man.

Diagnosis, like induction, is a creative reasoning mode. Its conclusion is not formally contained in its premises, but, merely resting on them as evidence, extrapolates beyond them. As in induction, therefore, its conclusion is never certain, but only

[4] See John S. Mill, *A System of Logic,* Harper, New York, 1848; W. S. Jevons, *Elementary Lessons in Logic,* Macmillan and Company, New York, 1894; Morris R. Cohen and Ernest Nagel, *An Introduction to Logic and Scientific Method,* Harcourt, Brace and Company, New York, 1934; Roy W. Sellars, *The Essentials of Logic,* Houghton Mifflin Company, Boston, 1917; "Method (Scientific)," *Encyclopedia of the Social Sciences,* The Macmillan Company, New York, 1937.

probable; also, the probability of an originally weak diagnostic conclusion may be strengthened, this time by means of a chain of related *diagnostic* syllogisms.

The diagnostic proposition that Socrates was a man was raised to the status of an almost certain scientific conclusion by means of some such diagnostic chain as the following:

Particular (First Premise)—Socrates was mortal.
Generalization (Second Premise)—Men are mortal.
Case (Diagnostic Conclusion)—There is therefore a probability that Socrates was a man.

Particular (First Premise)—Socrates had the power of speech.
Generalization (Second Premise)—Men have the power of speech.
Case (Diagnostic Conclusion)—It is now more probable that Socrates was a man.

Particular (First Premise)—Socrates was introspective.
Generalization (Second Premise)—Men are introspective.
Case (Diagnostic Conclusion)—It is now highly probable that Socrates was a man.

The caseworker, to complete his psychosocial diagnosis, proceeds in a similar manner to establish the psychiatric normality of his unemployed client. When such are the facts, he constructs the following diagnostic chain:

Particular (First Premise)—Mr. Roe's behavior is appropriate.
Generalization (Second Premise)—The behavior of psychiatrically normal individuals is appropriate.
Case (Diagnostic Conclusion)—There is therefore a probability that Mr. Roe is psychiatrically normal.

Particular (First Premise)—Mr. Roe is realistic and sees his situation as it actually is.
Generalization (Second Premise)—Psychiatrically normal individuals are realistic and see their situations as they actually are.
Case (Diagnostic Conclusion)—It is now more probable that Mr. Roe is psychiatrically normal.

Particular (First Premise)—Mr. Roe's behavior is flexible.
Generalization (Second Premise)—The behavior of psychiatrically normal individuals is flexible.
Case (Diagnostic Conclusion)—It is now even more probable that Mr. Roe is psychiatrically normal.

Particular (First Premise)—Mr. Roe responds to rational appeals and to consequences and learns from experience.
Generalization (Second Premise)—Psychiatrically normal individuals respond to rational appeals and to consequences and learn from experience.

Case (Diagnostic Conclusion)—It is now highly probable that Mr. Roe is psychiatrically normal.

Problems in differential diagnosis inevitably arise during the course of constructing such diagnostic chains. A problem in differential diagnosis arises when the known particulars in a given situation lend themselves equally to interpretation in the light of two or more generalizations. Thus, in the case of the creature called Socrates, it was just as probable, as long as the one particular in our possession was that of his mortality, that he was a horse or a dog as a man, since horses and dogs, no less than men, are mortal. Only as additional particulars are gathered and reviewed in the light of additional generalizations, does it gradually become possible to make a scientific selection from among the varying diagnostic hypotheses contained in an original list of diagnostic conclusions.

The following is a commonplace example of diagnostic reasoning, containing the essence of differential diagnosis:

Compound Particular (First Premise)—The unregistered letter that was carefully mailed to Mr. Brown requesting a reply was neither answered nor returned.

Compound Generalization (Second Premise)—Unregistered letters that are carefully mailed to incorrect addresses are not received, and therefore are not answered; however, neither are they always returned.

Case (Diagnostic Conclusion)—There is therefore a probability that we are dealing here with a case or instance of our having mailed the letter to an incorrect address where the addressee never lived.

Compound Particular (First Premise)—The unregistered letter that was carefully mailed to Mr. Brown requesting a reply was neither answered nor returned.

Compound Generalization (Second Premise)—Unregistered letters that are carefully mailed to correct addresses are generally received, and therefore are not returned; however, even though answers are requested, they are not always forthcoming.

Case (Diagnostic Conclusion)—There is therefore an equal probability, having no other evidence, that we are dealing here with a case or instance of our having mailed the letter to a correct address where the addressee does or did live.

To select scientifically between these two hypotheses, one would employ the device of sending a registered letter.[5]

[5] A great deal of the experientially derived social knowledge that caseworkers possess and employ is difficult to express in the form of generalizations. Lawyers have a similar problem. Certainly the kind of reasoning that lawyers frequently employ and denominate as reasoning from circumstantial or indirect evidence is "diagnostic" in its essence. Mary Richmond recognized this process and mentioned it in *Social Diagnosis,* Russell Sage Foundation, New York, 1917.

The process of selection in differential diagnosis is generally a double one. It was not only because Socrates had the particulars of speech and introspection that we decided that he was a man (diagnosis by positive evidence or inclusion), but also because he had neither four legs, nor a tail, nor a mane (diagnosis by negative evidence or exclusion).

The deductive reasoning mode always plays a role in the construction of diagnostic chains.[6] A caseworker, therefore, armed with a sufficient number of generalizations, might, on the basis of an original observation that his client was irresponsible, reason diagnostically-deductively as follows:

Particular (First Premise)—Mr. Jones is irresponsible.
Generalization (Second Premise)—Psychopaths are irresponsible.
Case (Diagnostic Conclusion)—There is therefore a probability that Mr. Jones is a psychopath.

Case (First Premise)—But if Mr. Jones is a psychopath,
Generalization (Second Premise)—Then, since psychopaths are impulsive,
Particular (Deductive Conclusion)—Mr. Jones will be impulsive.

Assuming that objective study, guided in this way, disclosed that Mr. Jones *was* impulsive, the caseworker would then be ready to forge another link in his diagnostic chain, as follows:

Particular (First Premise)—Mr. Jones is impulsive.
Generalization (Second Premise)—Psychopaths are impulsive.
Case (Diagnostic Conclusion)—It is now more probable that Mr. Jones is a psychopath.

Case (First Premise)—But again, if Mr. Jones is a pyschopath (as we now have more reason to believe),
Generalization (Second Premise)—Then, since psychopaths have practically no capacity for object love,
Particular (Deductive Conclusion)—Mr. Jones will have practically no capacity for object love.

In this way he would slowly or rapidly, intuitively or consciously, separately or collectively, cover the entire range of known psychopathic behavioral manifestations. Finally, to complete his diagnosis, he would include development and causation.

Both deduction and diagnosis, as modes of reasoning, depend on the generalizations provided by induction and the inductive scientific method. As a consequence, our deductive conclusions, how-

[6] Deduction plays a similar role in the construction of inductive syllogistic chains.

ever validly they may follow from their premises, are, at best, but probable. Our diagnostic conclusions, by the same token, are multiply probable, that is, probable on a plurality of levels for a number of reasons.

Even the simplest diagnostic conclusion is probable on at least three levels: (1) the level of probability resulting from the uncertainty inherent in the observational process by means of which the particular is gathered; (2) the level of probability introduced by the uncertainty attaching to the inductive generalization diagnostically employed to interpret the particular; (3) the level of probability contributed by the extrapolative nature of the diagnostic reasoning process itself.

To those of us who may be rendered restless or incompetent by such a state of affairs, it is necessary to point out that all three uncertainties can, with care, be progressively reduced, and that it is the task of the scientifically trained social caseworker (or metallurgist or physician) to do so. Hans Reichenbach, the scientific philosopher, once said to a faculty group made up of various professions at the University of California, "This is our world—let us take it as it is, let us live in it, let us attempt to shape it as best we can. No higher recognition can be awarded to a man than is expressed in the judgment that, whatever difficulties faced him, he always did his best." [7] I can think of no truer remark with which to bolster the pride and self-confidence of social caseworkers.

In every field, the total diagnostic chain-building process constitutes, in the true sense of the term, a scientific method, even though the goal of this method is not the construction of a new inductive generalization, but the formulation of a sound and highly probable diagnostic conclusion. It is thus a *diagnostic* scientific method.

Steps in the Diagnostic Method

As in the case of the inductive scientific method, the diagnostic scientific method also includes, in addition to its core logical operation of diagnosis proper, certain standard additional operations—namely, observation or fact-gathering, verification, deduction, prediction, and test. The sequential steps in the diagnostic scientific

[7] Hans Reichenbach, *Philosophy and Physics*, University of California Press, Berkeley and Los Angeles, 1948, p. 13.

method, particularly as it operates in social casework, are roughly as follows:

1. *Initial Exploration.* The diagnostic scientific method in social casework begins with an exploration of the specific problems identified by the client and covers such items as nature, duration, extent, emotional concerns, and referral circumstances. To start with the client's problems as the client sees them is the necessary first step in the diagnostic scientific method in social casework, although the center of interest must subsequently shift to the objective nature of those problems. Internal verifications play a major role during this stage of study.

2. *Horizontal Exploration.* The diagnostic scientific method moves into a horizontal or bird's-eye survey of the main aspects of the client's total life situation. Such standard items as the client's family composition, present employment and employment history, education, intellectual level, physical health, past and present income, mode of management, intrafamilial relationships, relationship established with the caseworker, and so on, are panoramically investigated. Such a gross and somewhat standardized broad view makes it possible for the rest of the investigative process to be, as Josephine Tey once said in a novel, ". . . like coming down from above in a plane. First the lie of the country, then the details of farms and gardens, and then the close-up of the house so that the thing [is] whole in [the] mind from the beginning, and the [subsequent] details [need] merely to be pointed on a picture already etched." [8] External as well as internal verifications assume importance during this stage of study.

3. *Initial Structuring of the Data.* The particulars thus secured are carefully charted under appropriate headings, and the degree to which they have or have not been factually verified is indicated.

4. *Formulating the Diagnostic Hypotheses.* The particulars as charted are reviewed in the light of generalizations for the purpose of formulating the various diagnostic hypotheses that may be elicited from them. The list of diagnostic hypotheses in a recent case, for example, included loss of employment due to neurotic breakdown on the part of a psychiatrically normal individual subjected to extremely traumatic current circumstances; loss of employment due to neurotic breakdown on the part of a basically

[8] Josephine Tey, *Brat Farrar,* The Macmillan Company, New York, 1950.

psychoneurotic individual; loss of employment on the part of a psychopathic individual due to a combination of overt acting-out and an unconscious need for punishment.

5. *Designing the Vertical Study Plan.* The fact-controlled, theory-controlled diagnostic possibilities are again reviewed in the light of theory, this time for the purpose of designing the next stage in study. Thus, in connection with each diagnostic hypothesis, the caseworker formulates a special set of questions. For example, he says, "If my client is psychiatrically normal and his present loss of employment and his neurotic breakdown are mainly due to extremely unfavorable current circumstances, I should, according to my professional heritage of tested generalizations, find that his life performance was competent just prior to the current circumstances. I should also find that his infancy and childhood, barring a therapeutic intervention, were relatively free from highly traumatic experiences. To confirm or exclude the diagnostic hypothesis in question, I must examine, therefore, not only his present life circumstances, but also his previous functioning and circumstances."

6. *Vertical Exploration.* The caseworker's carefully conceived vertical study plan is then carried out. Carrying it out is not a routine or a simple operation, but is, on the contrary, a highly dynamic and intensely interpersonal one. Problems in tempo and order inevitably occur, since the worker does not wish to engage his client in matters that are relatively alien to him at the moment, to pace him too rapidly, to obstruct his spontaneity unnecessarily, or to miss any opportunity to gain relevant data. Other complex problems arise. Minor resistances frequently have to be overcome, and major ones, though noted, must be permitted to remain. Similarly, transferences and counter-transferences often have to be dealt with, as do special problems created by the continued need for external and internal verifications. Still other forms of study-centered help usually have to be rendered. Finally, although the caseworker has entered this stage of study with a careful plan, he must continue to keep both his heart and his mind alert to the nature of the new information he is receiving, continually formulating additional hypotheses and questions and adding them to his vertical study plan. Frederic Wertham[9] describes psychiatry as, among other things, an art of listening. Social casework is

[9] Frederic Wertham, *Dark Legend,* Doubleday and Company, Garden City, New York, 1949.

also a sensitive listening art. At no time is this more apparent than during this highly dynamic, increasingly individualized, carefully planned and yet relatively free-flowing vertical study stage.

7. *Final Structuring of the Data.* To facilitate the further diagnostic reasoning that must now occur, the social-psychological-physiological data that have been accumulated up to this point are again charted.

8. *Formulating the Tentative Diagnosis.* The particulars as now charted are again reviewed in the light of theory or generalizations, this time for the dual purpose of weeding out those diagnostic hypotheses that were originally suggested by the initial and horizontal data, but that now fail to agree with the total data (diagnosis by exclusion), and of retaining those that do agree (diagnosis by inclusion). If more than one diagnostic hypothesis remains, the task of differential diagnosis is incomplete. Further "verticalization" of study must then be undertaken (if necessary through the use of special tests and consultation), until but a single diagnostic hypothesis remains. This final diagnostic hypothesis, methodically established by means of both positive and negative evidence, then becomes the tentative diagnosis on the basis of which the caseworker may now plan and venture definitive treatment. The use of the term "tentative" is based on the sound methodological principle that no diagnostic conclusion is final until its theoretical consequences, deductively derived, have been tested and proved in definitive treatment.

At times, of course, the available professional knowledge is insufficient to enable the caseworker to complete the task of differential diagnosis. (A similar situation frequently occurs in medicine and psychiatry.) On such occasions, the worker, left with two or three tentative diagnoses, must design a number of definitive treatment plans simultaneously, to be carried out either conjointly or consecutively.

The terms "initial," "horizontal," and "vertical," as used above, bear no direct relation to time. Thus, during the initial stage of study, the client, in presenting his current problem, may include a portion of his past. During the horizontal stage of study the caseworker ranges panoramically over both the past and the present. During the vertical stage of study, on the other hand, the problems in differential diagnosis that have emerged may at times require that the worker concentrate almost entirely on the present.

Nor do the terms necessarily relate to dynamic depth. Having once ascertained that the client is schizophrenically delusional and having discovered enough about the manifest content and reality ramifications of the delusions to design an appropriate "supportive treatment" plan,[10] the caseworker finds it neither necessary nor permissible—nor does he possess the techniques—to examine them further in terms of their dynamic depth.

These terms have mainly a methodological significance, and refer essentially to those sequential stages in the progressive search for particulars on the basis of which the problems in differential diagnosis that inherently characterize and govern the diagnostic scientific method are first created and then resolved.

Demands of the Method

Are the demands of the diagnostic mode of reasoning and the diagnostic scientific method beyond the scope of the average social worker? It would be misleading to minimize the undeniable intellectual difficulties they do entail. Yet the fact remains that logic and scientific method, however complex their upper reaches may become, are in essence but extensions and refinements of ordinary thought and ordinary orderly procedure. As such they are native to normal human beings who, in fact, use them naturally and constantly. The following example may serve to make this clear.

The diagnostician involved was 5 years old. Her attention, in strolling along the street with her father, was attracted by an elderly woman who was leading two dogs. The dogs were of a type she had never seen. Silently sizing them up in what we might call her horizontal stage of study, she noticed that they looked almost exactly alike, but that one was bigger than the other. Apparently fascinated by this sole apparent difference, and after submitting her findings to a kind of diagnostic review in the light of the few generalizations her limited life experience had as yet provided her, she suddenly turned to her father and said, "Daddy, the big one was born before the little one." Then, after pausing a moment for further reflection, she added, "Or else he eats more and sleeps more." These were, in our terminology, her diagnostic hypotheses.

With our greater command of theory accumulated during the

[10] Lucille N. Austin, "Trends in Differential Treatment in Social Casework," *Social Casework,* Vol. XXIX, No. 6 (1948), p. 206.

course of our longer lives and formal educations, our own lists would of course be longer, but the basic logic and essential process would be the same. Had she, in addition, stopped to ask questions of the owner of the dogs, as children so often do, her vertical exploration would have begun. Do we not too often underestimate the conscious and preconscious capacities of our students and workers to reason diagnostically and to employ a scientific method?

The specific form assumed by the diagnostic scientific method will vary from field to field, and from content to content. Thus, the special form employed by an analytical chemist will differ from that employed by a physician. This variable element is not unique in the diagnostic method but, as students of induction have long since pointed out, is also present in the inductive scientific method.[11] Nor do such variations destroy the essential unity of the diagnostic scientific method as a separate and distinct methodological entity.

How does the social caseworker translate his knowledge and understanding of an adequate diagnosis into a definitive treatment plan? A number of writers have dealt with various aspects of this important question.[12] Here, it is sufficient to say that understanding both the categorical and the individual social-psychological-physiological implications of a diagnosis is half the battle in planning definitive treatment; and that the process by which a scientifically trained social caseworker translates such understanding into a concrete and definitive casework treatment plan is no more mysterious than the one by which a doctor, or a metallurgist, translates his scientific diagnosis into a definitive medical, or metallurgical, plan. In all three instances the success or failure of the plan may lend further credence to, or lead to the revision of, the inductive generalizations on which it was based. Treatment of whatever

[11] See Robert B. Lindsay and Henry Margenau, *Foundations of Physics,* John Wiley and Sons, New York, 1936; and F. S. C. Northrop, *The Logic of the Sciences and Humanities,* The Macmillan Company, New York, 1947.

[12] Gordon Hamilton, *Psychotherapy in Child Guidance,* Columbia University Press, New York, 1947.

Lucille N. Austin, *op. cit.,* pp. 203–211.

Florence Hollis, "The Relationship Between Psychosocial Diagnosis and Treatment," *Social Casework,* Vol. XXXII, No. 2 (1951), pp. 67–81.

Fritz Schmidl, "Casework Treatment of the Psychotic Client," mimeographed report published by the Veterans Administration, Regional Office, Seattle, Washington, October 25, 1949.

Eleanor E. Cockerill, Louis J. Lehrman, Patricia Sacks, and Isabel Stamm, *A Conceptual Framework for Social Casework,* University of Pittsburgh Press, Pittsburgh, 1952.

kind, and however carefully it may be planned, involves a degree of rational risk. Casework treatment is no exception.

The English mathematician and philosopher W. K. Clifford once wisely remarked that a truth arrived at by scientific thought cannot be ideally contemplated as being without error, but that we may act upon it without fear.[13] This observation seems particularly apt when applied to the diagnostic truths that can be arrived at in social casework through careful use of the diagnostic scientific method.

[13] Paraphrased from a reference in "Science, Cytology and Society," by C. L. Huskins, in the October 1951 issue of *American Scientist,* p. 689.

THE DYNAMIC USE OF THE EGO FUNCTIONS IN CASEWORK PRACTICE[1]

Othilda Krug

In recent years ego psychology has held the interest of many workers in the helping professions. By some, it is viewed as dramatically new and different and as promising an almost magical solution to the complexities of psychological and social treatment. In actuality its principles did not emerge as a sudden discovery, but rather are the product of a gradual evolution in man's quest to know about himself and his world.

Early leaders in the field of social work recognized the need to help people with their personal as well as with their social problems. Their first methods, primarily those of environmental modi-

[1] Published in *Social Casework,* December 1955. Presented at the Annual Mid-winter Professional Meeting of the Boston University School of Social Work Alumni Association in February 1955.

fication, were often found to be limited in their usefulness for attaining improved social adjustment and, therefore, were frustrating. Thus social workers were quick to accept and apply the newer insights into the functioning of the total personality which were developing in dynamic psychiatry and psychoanalysis.

In contrast to social work, which initially dealt chiefly with external reality factors in inidividual maladjustment, dynamic psychiatry and psychoanalysis originally concentrated on the unconscious aspects of the personality, that is, on the internal biological and psychological energies. Although Freud's early work is best known as the psychology of the unconscious, even in his early writings he referred to the conscious aspect of the mind as the ego, a repressing force, in conflict with the unconscious instinctual forces. Academic psychologists had previously dealt with a circumscribed sphere of ego psychology in their description of the intellectual faculties and other functions of the conscious mind.

An earlier elaboration of ego psychology was just not feasible. It was only when the methods of psychoanalysis led to an understanding of the nature of the instinctual energies that the ego's methods of handling them could be thoroughly investigated. Later, psychoanalysis broadened its field of inquiry and undertook to explore the ways in which inner drives are expressed externally, in both direct and disguised patterns.

The greater awareness by psychiatrists of social and cultural forces as dynamic causative factors in personality disturbance led also to the inclusion of these forces as factors in a comprehensive treatment plan. From social casework, dynamic psychiatry learned certain environmental and educational techniques for supplementing and modifying the classical method of psychoanalysis. At the same time social work was aided by the new ego psychology to overcome obstacles it had encountered in its direct treatment efforts, and it thus could progress to the formulation of more meaningful principles and skills of diagnostic casework practice. Beginning at opposite poles of emphasis, social work and psychiatry, each maintaining its basic orientation, its specific discipline of training, and its own distinctive treatment methods, have met in a broad overlapping zone of mutual interest and helpfulness concerning the interaction of individual suffering and social disharmony.

Functions of the Ego

In a sense, ego psychology is the common meeting ground for the first explorers of the deeply buried personality strata and for the early social topographers and "manipulators." Similarly, the ego is the bridge of communication between the unconscious and external reality. The dynamic concept of the total personality was first described by Freud in *The Ego and the Id.*[2] The three dynamic processes of the mind have been given the shorthand terms of the ego, the id, and their mutual offspring, the superego. They are not static structures nor do they completely represent specific functions of separate areas of the brain. All three have both conscious and unconscious aspects. The id refers to those inherited, instinctual, chaotic energies generated in the basic biological processes. Although predominantly unconscious, some of these instinctual energies regularly appear in consciousness as physiological and psychological tensions. Others are made accessible to consciousness only by psychoanalysis. Many conscious experiences are, for the sake of economy, relegated to the preconscious; others, under the pressure of external fear or internal anxiety, are banished indefinitely into the unconscious.

The ego governs the continuous two-way traffic between the id and reality. Its over-all function is to maintain the dynamic equilibrium of the personality which is constantly being threatened from both within and without. As the central core of the personality, it has a double perceptive function. On the one hand, it perceives internal stimuli as physiological needs; on the other, it perceives external stimuli from the environment which set the conditions for gratifying these needs. Through its integrative function it balances the internal against the external demands as a basis for its executive function in finding, selecting, and learning the methods of adaptation. The learning of effective behavior patterns proceeds partly by trial, which results in some errors but in many more successes; by repetition, which tends to fix the successful methods; and especially by identification. In its executive function, and as the center of motor control, the ego is responsible for co-ordinated, goal-directed, voluntary behavior of such a nature as to permit optimal inner gratification within the social requirements.

[2] Sigmund Freud, *The Ego and the Id,* International Psychoanalytical Library, No. 12, Hogarth Press, London, 1950.

In the well-integrated ego this is accomplished economically, without anxiety or guilt, and with a minimal expenditure of energy, thus freeing additional energy for preserving and enjoying life, for further learning and growth, and for mastering new life situations.

A mature ego, however, does not spring full-blown from the biological processes. At birth, the infant's organization is wholly on a biological level, and the personality is predominantly unorganized id from which the ego is gradually differentiated. The only trace of ego function in the newborn infant consists of some sensory perception which can be inferred from the signs of his acute discomfort when external stimulation is excessive and from the apparent alleviation of inner psychological tensions, such as those produced by hunger. The integrative and executive functions of the ego are practically nil; the infant can relieve tensions only by random movements and automatic reflex behavior. Moreover, he cannot distinguish external from internal perceptions; he does not differentiate the outside world from himself. Oblivious to reality, he strives to regain the nirvana of the unconditional intra-uterine pleasure of fetal life which temporarily he attains by magically hallucinating previous satisfactions. Then gradually he feels omnipotently gratified in response to his magical gestures, thoughts, and utterances. But since life inevitably involves some discomfort and tension which actually are relieved repetitively from the outside, he begins to recognize the alternately depriving and satisfying environment, especially the mother, as separate from himself. If the period of waiting is not too long, he trustingly postpones his pleasure and acquires an increasing capacity to tolerate some frustration. Thus, the basic step in ego growth consists of the gradual relinquishment of the pleasure principle in favor of the reality principle, and the slow movement from autism to a symbiotic object relationship.

During the next five years, the specific characteristics of the personality grow out of the child's many experiences with others. From those close to him he learns a great deal about the world around him; about himself, including the parts of his body and their functions; and about methods of relating to others. He learns through identification, by introjecting or incorporating certain qualities or attitudes from objects, animals, or people, and by projecting his own characteristics onto persons and objects in the outside world. To help in meeting new and different emotional situations emerging from continued physical and intellectual growth, he turns again to his parents who previously had satisfied all his needs. Generally, they can grant his wishes during this period when he still strives for some primary libidinal comfort but also aggressively seeks the secondary libidinal satisfactions of growth and achievement. In regard to certain muscular and genital strivings, however, which would be destructive to others if expressed directly, he encounters active parental resistance and suppression. He becomes fearful about his personal safety and about losing the parents' continued love and help in growing up. To avoid the tensions of consciously inhibiting the tabooed wishes, he incorporates the parental prohibitions and accepts their particular prescriptions for substitute gratifications.

Through this process of making the parental standards his own, the child reaches another important milestone in ego development —the emergence of the superego. His conscious fears and the original painful conflict between the ego and reality are internalized and are experienced as anxiety and as a conflict between the superego and the id. The active unconscious rejection of the forbidden id impulses—just before they reach consciousness—under the aegis of the superego anxiety, is the process of repression. Although some repression is necessary for healthy ego growth, not even the most rigid superego can completely repress the basically worthwhile and persistent life energies. The superego, in alliance with the ego, works in the service of both the id and reality and synthesizes their demands into socially approved gratifications.

Normally, throughout the formative years such compromises between the id and society should be established for all the forbidden impulses. For example, the infant's narcissism should be converted into some interest in others, and his possessiveness into some ability to share. His enjoyment in messiness should give way to some degree of cleanliness, his exhibitionism to some modesty, and his cruelty to some sympathy for others. His destructive aggressiveness should be channeled into fantasy, play, and constructive activities; his sexual curiosity into learning at school; and his early dependent, aggressive, and oedipal rivalries into appropriate companionability and group relationships. This early process of socialization is achieved through the ego's establishment of various types of direct and defensive executive functions.

As the child moves through the several developmental stages, additional qualities of ego strength are gained through the mastery of various functions. In the latency period he gains confidence as he develops a range of new skills; and in adolescence he achieves an even greater sense of self-suffiicency as his concept of his personal, sexual, and social identity becomes crystallized.

When the adolescent finally emerges into young adulthood, his dependency and oedipal striving become integrated so that the ego is further strengthened. A reasonable degree of self-sufficiency includes an ability to accept appropriate help. A more objective appreciation of his parents enables the individual to experience a new kind of love and esteem for them. A valid self-respect and enjoyment of his own sex and of his actual abilities as a person replace earlier attitudes of inferiority and shame or of superiority and false pride. A conscious ego-ideal rather than a rigid infantile superego allows him to test reality and to take initiative and responsibility. The self-discipline of working toward desirable goals, despite certain frustrations, is balanced with some immediate pleasure. Childhood insecurities and inhibitions yield to a capacity for loving others and for intimately enjoying reciprocal give-and-take relationships with others—in work, in play, in sexual relations, and so on. The ultimate integration of ego strength is characterized by the achievement of personal integrity which frees the individual's energies for creative interest, and for loving, taking care of, and contributing toward the growth of his children and others.

To understand the ego in all its ramifications from birth to maturity embodies the aggregate of psychodynamic knowledge. Freud believed that there are inner resistances to learning about the ego just as there are resistances to the analysis of the unconscious and to previous scientific developments. For example, the Copernican theory that man's earth is not the center of the universe dealt a narcissistic blow to man, and the Darwinian theory of animal descent in its devaluation of his body was even more shattering to his pride. To defend himself against these insults, man responded, as a reaction formation, by increasing his technical knowledge about the world and by developing medical mastery of his body. Freud's discovery that man does not consciously control all his behavior was a similar injury; and the technique of psychonalysis was developed for the purpose of bringing the unconscious under the control of the conscious. But to understand the ego, especially the unconscious part of it, was even more difficult, for not only was the ego required to perform the function of observing itself, but it also had to examine illogical guilt and anxiety and inappropriate infantile behavior. The resistances involved in this undertaking have been likened to the final and greatest resistances encountered in personal psychoanalysis, the analysis of narcissism. The refinement of treatment methods, based on ego psychology, may be the means of mastering this final blow to man's self-esteem.

General Application of Principles

The successful application of ego psychology in any treatment process depends on a comprehensive understanding both of psychodynamic principles and of specific individual psychopathology. Ego psychology, therefore, offers no easy, quick, routine method of treatment, but its application requires skillful and flexible planning based on a complete psychosocial diagnosis, that is, on knowing "through and through" the total person in his environment.

A diagnostic formulation entails a careful appraisal of ego functioning; of the ego's basic integrative capacity, its strength and flexibility; of the effectiveness of its defenses against anxiety; and of the efficiency of its mechanisms in affording realistic instinctual expression. Ego functioning must be weighed against both the nature and strength of the internal drives and against the actual environmental challenge. In all maladjustment, the ego fails to co-ordinate harmoniously the diverse inner needs with each other and with external conditions.

Sometimes the degree of environmental stress plays a significant part in ego dysfunction, and occasionally even the well-integrated person cannot cope with the excessive strain of exceptionally difficult life circumstances. More frequently, if the person has been confronted with only the ordinary vicissitudes of life, breakdown is the result of certain weaknesses in the ego itself. Physical and intellectual frailties may impair the ego's functional capacity, but usually the nature of childhood experiences and the quality and consistency of parental attitudes lay the foundation for the ego's later efficiency in mastering its problems. The particular configuration of ego mechanisms that evolve from experience (the personality structure) determines the ego's threshold of vulnerability to specific situations.

The failure of the ego to master an actual conflict with reality is the first step in ego disintegration. The frustration thus experienced leads the ego to attempt to find a substitute satisfaction. often by regression to some previously gratifying behavior. The concomitant return of the old, but inappropriate, feelings and anxieties about the parents constitutes a revival of the primary infantile or internal neurotic conflict between the ego and the id. In the attempt to relieve the anxieties of the internal conflict, the ego then resorts to various combinations of defense mechanisms that are psychopathologic in nature since they too fail in the integrative task. When severe ego weakness and deep regression are present, the id may be victor over both the ego and reality; this victory is manifested in psychotic symptoms. Neurotic symptoms provide only partial and disguised instinctual expression. Since the infantile superego demands also some punishment for any instinctual satisfaction, the symptoms also cause frustration and conscious suffering. These frustrations, in turn, create a secondary conflict with reality. The use of energy in attempting to deal with all these conflicts exhausts and impoverishes the ego, and the resulting lack of enjoyment and of drive for living adds further to its ineffectiveness in coping with life. However, the stronger this secondary dissatisfaction, the greater will be the motivation for help. If, on the other hand, the regressive symptoms bring greater gains, such as conflict-free dependency satisfactions, then there is marked resistance to treatment.

This type of psychodynamic understanding comprises, in its specific application, the total clinical, dynamic, and genetic diagnosis. A clinical dynamic diagnostic evaluation is a current cross-sectional formulation of the total presenting problem and situation. It includes an assessment of the area and degree of the individual's disability, of his environmental stresses, and of the particular ego mechanisms that he uses in current relationships to others, including the therapist. It takes into account the expressed reasons and unexpressed motivations for seeking help, as well as any recent life experiences that may have precipitated the current problems. The ego's potential strength is evaluated from the history of previous school, work, personal, and social adjustments under ordinary and under critical conditions.

Establishing a total working diagnosis involves skillful interviewing by the therapist in order to create a therapeutic relationship and to permit observation of the individual's dynamic interplay with the therapist. Such interplay contains certain realistic aspects of the situation as well as illogical displacements from the past. Establishing a diagnosis also involves a gradual co-ordination of pertinent historical data concerning the emotional responses to past events and the patterns of reaction to developmental experiences. This leads to the construction of a longitudinal and genetic diagnosis which can greatly facilitate a meaningful utilization of current ego patterns toward the goal of their modification for a better adjustment.

All procedures for the effective treatment of psychosocial problems should be based on such comprehensive diagnostic thinking. This is obviously necessary for treatment methods directed toward a reintegration of the personality and toward establishing healthier ego mechanisms—that is, when the unconscious is actively explored, when resistances and conflicts are resolved, and when the therapist works directly *with the transference.* Such diagnostic thinking is also essential in treatment directed toward the improvement of adaptive patterns, when the focus is on conscious attitudes and on the reality situation, and when the therapist works with the defenses *within the relationship.* Actually the latter method is frequently more difficult, often calling for greater skill and art, and always requiring continuous accurate diagnostic understanding to give therapeutic purpose and direction to the empathy of the relationship.

In working, on the conscious level, to help an individual achieve a more harmonious balance of his ego defenses, the therapist must respect the significance of the defenses in the total economy of the personality. At all times the positive aspects of the defenses, as well as the individual's basic abilities and strength, should be supported and encouraged. In fact, the prognosis is poor unless the therapist can accept warmly the deepest layers of the personality, the value and basic decency of the inherent energies and drives toward maturity, which lie beneath the inappropriate surface manifestations of anxiety. The undesirable mechanisms are redirected into more constructive channels through some clarification and education, but the precipitous removal of inept patterns is avoided lest overwhelming anxiety be aroused. Accentuating the positives and capitalizing on the negatives constitute a manipulation of the healthy, in relation to the unhealthy, defenses which can lead to their mutually enhancing rearrangement for more harmonious adaptation.

The dynamic force for achieving this goal is the therapeutic relationship which develops out of the individual's realistic desire for help and the therapist's mature interest in being of service. The illogical transference attitudes are not interpreted by the therapist, but an understanding of some of the attitudes that inevitably develop can be used in providing a therapeutic experience for the adult person. A therapeutic transference relationship is not fostered when the therapist repeats the mistakes of parents, when he attempts to meet the individual's excessive infantile wishes and needs or when he rejects his legitimate unmet strivings and their currently appropriate satisfactions. For example, the therapist's diagnostic understanding of an individual with a conflict around dependency enables him to support the individual's actual needs for dependency and to stimulate his potentials for growth, thereby helping him achieve a new balance. But in affording the adult a new relationship the therapist does not take a role or play some dramatic, artificial part. As an interested, relatively mature person, free of excessive counter-transference attitudes, the therapist offers empathy and spontaneous rseponses appropriate to the person's needs and different from those of his past. The relationship is therapeutic when it becomes a corrective emotional experience for the individual. By failing to meet his illogical expectations, it counteracts the harmful influence of unhealthy parental attitudes and frees the individual for more appropriate behavior.

Application in Casework

The dynamic use of the functions of the ego in casework practice is illustrated in the treatment of a 24-year-old housewife who sought help from the Family Service of Cincinnati and Hamilton County for her marital problem and her difficulty in managing her 3-year-old daughter, who was not yet toilet-trained. Although Mrs. M focused chiefly on her own problems during the nine months of treatment, she originally sought help following a vacation with her sister, whose children behaved entirely differently from her own.

Mrs. M was a tall, striking, well-groomed blond woman who looked like a model or show girl. She was the youngest of five children and seven years younger than the next older child. She had been told repeatedly by her mother that she had been conceived only to save her parents' difficult marriage, which finally had culminated in divorce three years before. Her mother, a rigid, controlling person, had constantly complained about her suffering at the hands of her alcoholic husband, a handsome, charming man whose behavior always caused Mrs. M much shame and embarrassment. Feeling that she had never belonged within her family group, Mrs. M had participated actively in dramatic programs but felt hurt when her father never attended. After one year of high school and attendance at a special business school, she became a typist in an institution where she lived because of her unpleasant home. This was the happiest time of her life.

She married early in her pregnancy after a stormy three-year courtship during which Mr. M had constantly belittled and ignored her. She described Mr. M as pleasant, brilliant, and ambitious in his work in a civil-service position. Although they were well suited sexually, she said she always felt inferior to him and belittled by him as her mother had been by her father. She wondered if she demanded too much from him, compared him to her father, and frequently confused the two. Often referring to her daughter as "it," and as one year older than she actually was, she emphasized her own repugnance to the child's soiling and described, at great length, the stools and the problems around toilet-training. With guilt, she told of frequently sending the "noisy, aggressive, though otherwise normal" child to the paternal great-grandmother who had reared Mr. M after his own parents' divorce. Mrs. M found herself yelling at her daughter as her own mother had yelled at her children. She constantly likened her feelings to those of her child's but contrasted her own conforming behavior toward her mother with her daughter's aggressiveness. In the early interviews Mrs. M emphasized her inadequacies and faults, her desire to be liked, and her constant expectation of being rebuffed, mistreated, and hurt. Her relationships indicated that she continuously set up situations in which she would be depreciated and rejected. She, too, had problems with elimination. She had many rigid patterns of performance, excellent abilities in sewing and designing and in making the most of her appearance. There were indications of good relationships with her siblings and some friends.

After the first thirteen interviews, a psychiatric consultation was utilized to clarify further the clinical, dynamic, and genetic diagnosis as a guide in planning continued treatment. The predominant picture was that of a severe masochistic neurotic character disorder. The unresolved conflicts at both the pregenital and oedipal developmental levels, with resultant lack of personality organization, were similar to those observed frequently in adolescents. The defense mechanisms utilized to handle these various conflicts permeated Mrs. M's entire life adjustment. Inasmuch as her behavior patterns and almost all her relationships were determined illogically by previous life experiences, they represented a repetition compulsion. Of genetic significance were Mrs. M's early feelings of being unloved and worthless. She felt that she came into existence only to preserve her parents' marriage, that she deserved no basic pleasures for her own sake, and that she had to conform and achieve only for her parents' sake.

In her relationships both with her husband and others, Mrs. M demonstrated the repetitive pattern of her masochism—her self-depreciation and her need to suffer even to the point of eliciting mistreatment through provocative behavior. Her masochism as well as her conforming behavior represented defenses against the anxiety engendered by her marked hostility toward her parents. The mechanism of identification was also significant in determining her behavior. She was identified with her daughter in expecting and encouraging her to be conforming and much more grown up than she was emotionally ready to be. She also had made a hostile identification with her mother's masochism and attitudes toward children. Her attractiveness and good grooming were overcompensatory and served as a compulsive defense in response to her own soiling tendencies and her concept of women as dirty and inferior. Her interest in dramatics and the meticulous care of her body also served as sublimations for her narcissism and exhibitionism and constituted practically the only channels available to her for counteracting her deep feelings of unworthiness as a person.

In the relationship with the caseworker, Mrs. M was eager to please but she also tested the worker's acceptance of her through provocative, depreciatory attitudes. Her strengths included a good capacity to relate to others in more positive ways and a real desire for change based on her recognition that life could be different. In adolescence, she had moved away from home to improve her life situation, and she had sought help from the agency after observing her sister's happier family. Early in the contact she indicated a capacity to take responsibility for her own involvement in the family problem.

The casework treatment aimed principally to provide her with a supportive relationship, with some use of the technique of clarification. The worker helped Mrs. M acquire more self-regard by pointing out her many strengths and abilities when Mrs. M emphasized all her deficiencies. The worker did not accept Mrs. M's evaluation that events had been as devastating as Mrs. M had described them. She offered direct suggestions about housekeeping and other feminine activities, and did not accept Mrs. M's rigid patterns as desirable for everyone. As a relaxed, accepting, mature woman, the worker provided a healthier pattern of femininity for Mrs. M and gave her permission to enjoy being a woman and to have more meaningful and enjoyable relationships. Mrs. M indicated some surprise in finding the worker's attitudes so different from those of other women—her acceptance, her lack of defensiveness, and her encouragement. She showed almost childlike pleasure in gaining approval for something she had done well.

With growing confidence in herself and in the worker, Mrs. M began to express some hostility by verbalizing her irritation and annoyance about the disheveled appearance of the worker's desk and her casual, "not-too-clean" shoes. In many of Mrs. M's comments she expressed a depreciating attitude toward Negroes. It seemed especially meaningful to Mrs. M that the worker, who was a Negro, was not threatened but remained accepting and giving, as she clarified Mrs. M's misconception that outward appearances are of major importance. Because Mrs. M herself was so aware that she tended to confuse her father with her husband, she was further helped to understand that, as two separate persons, they would not necessarily behave toward her in the same way. The worker helped her to see that in some ways she expected belittling behavior from her husband, had elicited it, and at times had had a distorted view of it.

As Mrs. M gained further security about her own worth and adequacy, even in the face of her hostile, depreciatory attitudes toward the worker, there was increasing evidence of her improved relationships with her husband and daughter. Her greater relaxation with the child was reflected in her daughter's improved behavior, the absence of soiling, and comfortable acceptance of toilet-training. She was pleasantly surprised when the child expressed her love, and she spoke warmly of how much fun children can be. She showed increasing ability to relate to the positive qualities of her husband, less provocative behavior, and greater capacity to enjoy his companionship. She brought family pictures, expressed happiness at her sister's wedding, and felt more like a member of her original family than ever before. She felt different about her mother's handling of her father; she no longer thought that her mother bowed down to him, and even began to think that there were two sides to her parents' problems. She spoke humorously of her past upsets over everyday family problems, and compared them to her current relaxed attitudes when similar things occurred. She gradually felt that she had less need for the worker's help as a mutual plan for spacing appointments and eventually terminating treatment was discussed. Approximately one year after termination she was eager to inform the worker about her pleasure in her current pregnancy and about the family's progress, which included her continued improvement, her daughter's good adjustment in kindergarten, and her husband's promotion at work which would better the family's living conditions.

In this casework treatment, the therapeutic relationship provided the client with a truly corrective experience, through the support of her strengths, and helped to clarify some of her inappropriate defenses. The change in Mrs. M was effected within the transference relationship but without interpretation or deep insight. It is an example of the effectiveness of casework treatment on the ego-reality level when the principles of ego psychology are utilized.

THE DIAGNOSIS OF NEUROTIC MARITAL INTERACTION [1]

Nathan W. Ackerman

THIS PAPER is concerned with the means for evaluating the mental health of marital relationships. Within this context special emphasis is placed on the search for appropriate criteria for the psychosocial diagnosis of neurotic marital relationships. The mental health of family relationships is, in the main, an expression of social process. Unhealthy marital relationships, widespread as they are, are significant not only for themselves, but as the epitome and the very core of disintegrative trends in family life as a whole, and as forerunners of emotional illness in the offspring of such unions.

The rate of divorce has now reached a point where there is one divorce for every three or four marriages. Even when marital conflict does not culminate in legal divorce, the disurbance often reaches such a critical point as to bring about an "emotional divorce" of the parents. The day-by-day experience of psychotherapists, educators, and spiritual advisers affirms this as a crucial mental health problem in regard to both therapy and prevention.

We live in an age of social crisis. We have reason to believe that the intrinsic value conflicts of our changing culture have a direct bearing on the fate of family life and family relationships. It requires no great stretch of the imagination to realize that the survival or destruction of our kind of civilization will depend in no small part on how these value conflicts are resolved and what happens concurrently to the mental health of the family. It is the clear and

[1] Published in *Social Casework*, April 1954. Presented on October 21, 1953, as one in the lecture series sponsored by the Psychiatric Forum Group in New York.

present threat to our cherished values in family living which challenges us. The threat is a large one and it hits home, literally. Our anxiety is for ourselves, and this impels us to take a stand on the issues involved.

Naturally, it would be our wish to apply the dynamic insights of psychoanalysis to the mental health problems of marital relationships and family life. We must admit, however, that up to the present our scientific concepts are not yet adequate to the task, though we are making progress in this direction. We can readily discern some of the relevant developments in the behavior sciences: the emphasis on multidisciplinary research, the joining of hands of psychoanalysis and the social sciences, the increased influence of the anthropological principle of relativity of behavior, the effort to move beyond Freud in linking the phenomena of biological maturation with the processes of social participation, the effort to correlate ego-dynamics with social interaction, the rediscovery of the ancient principle that behavior is determined not only by a person's view of his past, but also by his view of the future, and so on. In a recent lecture, Dr. Frieda Fromm-Reichmann made the statement that we are on the eve of a revolution in the development of our understanding of the principles of human behavior and the principles of psychotherapy.

Of particular importance is the need to evaluate pathology of individual personality not in isolation, but within the frame of the psychosocial structure of the family, and to establish the specific dynamic relations of personality and family roles. Only as we can correctly merge the dynamics of individual and group behavior does it begin to be possible to deal effectively with the mental health problems of family and marital relationships.

For several years I have been engaged in the study of the problems of family diagnosis. Naturally, a central aspect of this study is the development of criteria for the diagnosis of marital interaction. In this research on family diagnosis, our particular interest has been the exploration of the relation of emerging emotional disturbance in a young child to the group dynamics of family life. Toward this end, the child, though a distinct unit in the biological sense, is viewed not as an intact, separate individual but rather as a functional expression of the social interaction processes that characterize the given family. At each stage of development we explore the child's interaction with mother, with father, with parents as a couple; we explore further the relation of personality to the marital and parental roles and, finally, the family as an integrated social unit. We attempt then to relate these data specifically to the patterns of child rearing and child pathology.

The nature of this research requires a conceptual frame within which it is possible to interrelate the dynamics of the individual with the dynamics of the group—that is, to correlate intrapsychic processes with interpersonal ones, the phenomena of individual personality with the phenomena of family role—and finally to relate these partial processes to the psychosocial dynamics of the family as a whole. In accordance with this scheme, we have investigated thus far forty families, in which child and parent have been or still are in therapy. In the course of this study, it has been necessary to evaluate systematically the marital relationhip, its history, its path of motivation, and the past and current pattern of marital interaction. The long-term goal is to build a conceptual framework for psychosocial diagnosis of the family, and also of marital and parental role function. In this context it is self-evident that the issues of mental health must be considered both at the individual and group levels.

In approaching the problems of diagnosis of marital relationships, we are concerned with the concept of diagnosis not as a mere label, but as a definitive evaluation that absorbs within itself the dynamics and the etiology of the disorder. In the mental health field, diagnosis and therapy are two facets of an essentially unitary process: diagnosis has meaning only in the context of devising a plan of action. When we seek to define what has gone wrong we are already embarked on the path of applying appropriate corrective action, a therapeutic program. Precisely because of the affinity and interdependence of diagnosis and therapy, it is poor practice to apply therapy in the absence of rigorous standards of diagnostic formulation.

Of first importance is the clear-cut recognition of the general category into which this problem falls. In undertaking to diagnose marital relationships, we are not concerned in the first instance with the autonomous functions and pathology of individual personalities, but rather with the dynamics of the relationship, that is, with the reciprocal role functions that define the relations of husband and wife.

A relationship represents more than the sum of the personalities that make it up. The whole is greater than the sum of its parts.

A marital relationship, like a chemical compound, has unique properties of its own over and above the characteristics of the elements that merge to form the compound. A new level of organization creates new qualities. A marital relationship is therefore an entity, new and different, but, again like a chemical compound, its properties, while unique, preserve a specific dynamic relation to the elements that have joined in its creation. This is another way of saying that the psychological principles that govern the behavior of an individual and those that govern the behavior of a relationship are not the same, that we cannot directly extrapolate from our knowledge of indivdual personality to behavior of a relationship or a group, that the psychological processes involved at the relationship or group level must be viewed in a different dimension because a different level of biosocial organization is implicated. The dynamics of the two situations, individual and group, are therefore not interchangeable, and the integrative processes appropriate to the one level of biosocial organization cannot be imposed upon the other.

By way of pointing more sharply to the nature of our problem, let us consider the mental health implications of some common empirical observations. The outcome in mental health terms of a particular marriage relationship is not contingent exclusively on the character of the neuroses of the individual partners. The ultimate effects on mental health are determined rather by the dynamic part that neurotic conflict plays in the complex process of integration of the personalities of the partners into the reciprocal roles of husband and wife. The factors that shape this process are multiple; we shall discuss them at a later point. In some instances neurotic conflict destroys the marriage; in others, it seems to save the marriage. It is common knowledge that the neurosis of one marital partner often complements that of the other. Sometimes the traits of one partner reinforce in the other healthy defenses against neurotic conflict, so that its destructive effects are highly mitigated. Sometimes this form of "complementarity" decompensates and the marital relationship progressively disintegrates. The bad marriages that neurotic persons often make are notorious, but what enables some to make good ones? The wonder is not so much that one neurotic marries another one but rather that some neurotics marry partners who enable them to strengthen themselves against neurotic regression and also support them so that they can function as reasonably good parents.

The potentially hopeful aspect of this whole problem is that some neurotics, despite traumatic childhoods, make fine marriages and fine parents. Neurosis in individual personality, therefore, is not the sole factor that predetermines the fate of marriage, family life, and the new crop of children. Were it so, there would be little hope for the world. The saving grace is that character can and does change after the crucial childhood years. If we are motivated to rehabilitate the mental health of a disturbed marital relationship, we must take into account not only the neurotic core of behavior but also the malleable aspects of character in both partners, the factor of realistic strength in their personalities, the residually healthy ego tendencies, the positive qualities of the marital relationship and of the family life, and the motivation of both partners for change; all these are needed to counterbalance neurotic tendencies.

The Salient Factors in Marital Disturbance

Disturbances of marital relationship are characterized by two salient elements: (1) failure of reciprocity of satisfactions and (2) conflict. The conflict usually bears a specific relation to the failure of reciprocity in the relationship. With our present inadequate knowledge, it is easier to spot the more obviously pathological marital relationships than it is to be definitive regarding the standards of "normal" or "healthy" marital interaction. Yet the goal of progress in scientific understanding of such problems requires a continuing effort to achieve an explicit formulation of "healthy" marital interaction, elusive and changing as this may be in our culture. We hope that from the criteria for evaluating the dynamics of marital interaction which are here considered, we can evolve a useful operational definition for a healthy marital relationship.

For clinicians, conflict in marital relationships presents a knotty problem. The relevant factors are multiple and of a complex nature; they overlap and interact to such an extent that a clear and communicable definition of the problem is difficult to achieve. Our task is to reduce the salient issues to a clear-cut formulation, but this is more easily said than done.

In marital disorders conflict may be overt or covert, real or unreal, conscious or unconscious, in varying mixtures. The conflict between the partners, moreover, bears a special relationship to the structure of intrapsychic conflict in each partner. The very first question to arise is: What part of the conflict is real, what part unreal and determined by neurotic perception and motivation? Further, how does the unreal part secondarily distort the relatively more real aspects of marital interaction? Regarding that level of the interaction which is relatively realistic, all that is needed is accurate awareness of it, and a plan of action appropriate to this awareness. One cannot psychoanalyze realistic components of experience. The unreal part, structured by neurotic interaction, calls for a different program—definitive diagnostic evaluation and suitable psychotherapeutic correction.

In the first instance, then, it is important to see the neurotic pattern of marital interaction in the context of total interaction. Although it is easy to detect the more pathological types of neurotic marital relationships, the task of evaluating the mental health significance of specific patterns of neurotic interaction in the context of the total relationship and the prevailing social realities is a complex one. The effects of neurotic motivation may be variably diffuse or localized both in individual personality and in a relationhip. Just as, in the individual, some areas of adaptive functioning may be heavily disabled and other areas relatively conflict-free and less disabled, so, in a relationship, some levels of interaction may be critically impaired while other are relatively conflict-free and less impaired.

It is common observation, however, that neurotic disturbance of a marital relationship is rarely, if ever, the creation of just one of the partners. In marital pairs ambivalently bound in neurotic love and neurotic competition, when one partner exhibits pathological anxiety responses, the other usually does too. Being immature and unready for full heterosexual union, the partners tend to parentify each other. Seeking the love and protection of a parent figure in the marital partner, each pushes the relationship toward the needed form of child-parent relationship. In this context, the marital relationship is forced to assume a compensatory and curative function for the anxiety-provoking features of the original child-parent experience. In so far as the marital relationship is coerced into satisfying conflicted and regressed childhood needs, or compensating for the lack of fulfillment, the relationship is burdened with an extra and an inappropriate psychic load. It should be remembered, however, that some marriage relationships are so patterned as to bear this extra load with a minimum of damage to mental health.

In any case, a clinician faced with such a relationship problem must make some ticklish decisions. Should one or both of the partners receive psychotherapy? If both, should the two therapies be initiated at the same time or staggered? Should the two partners be treated by the same or different therapists? If by different therapists, can the therapeutic efforts be co-ordinated? If only one partner is to be treated, which one? And by what kind of psychotherapist? By what criteria do clinicians currently draw such judgments? If we speak with candor, we cannot but admit that at present such judgments are arrived at either intuitively, or with a relatively crude assay of the relevant facts, rather than with an ordered diagnostic formulation both of the facts and of the dynamic relations between them. Clearly, the latter is an ideal toward which we must strive.

Once psychotherapy is initiated, whatever the criteria, there are further problems. It is hardly possible with present knowledge to predict with any real confidence the effects of psychotherapy of one or both partners on the marital relationship itself. As any practicing therapist knows, such predictions are hazardous and are apt to be wrong as often as they are right. This empirical observation in and of itself attests strongly to the inadequacy of present-day criteria for both the diagnosis and therapy of marital disorders. The actual results of psychotherapy from our standpoint are extremely variable. Sometimes the psychotherapy of individual partners ameliorates the disturbance in the marital relationship. Sometimes it has little or no effect; sometimes, and this is quite striking, as one partner gets better the other gets worse, and the relationhip suffers further damage accordingly. In a seeming paradox, the increased health and strength of one partner become an added menace to the other. As one partner matures and becomes sexually more adequate, the other gets depressed and shows signs of regression. This unfortunate result is more likely to occur when the psychotherapy of one of the partners is oriented to an abstract goal of cure of individual neurosis without regard to the complex factors that control the emotional balance between the partners. It is unreal to treat neurotic tendencies in a marital partner as if he existed in a social vacuum. The interdependence and reciprocity of the roles of husband and wife should be remembered. Any effect on the one partner will always influence the behavior of the other.

The hopeful assumption that therapeutic resolution of neurotic anxiety in one or both partners will mitigate the marital disorder proves on occasion to be unwarranted. Some of the reasons for this are clear; neurotic anxiety, although a significant etiological factor, is but one among the many that determine the fate of such a relationship. The causal factors lie partly in the pathology of the individual personalities, partly in the special characteristics of the relationship itself; the relationship is multiply determined in a variety of ways—by the compatibility of temperament, goals, values, and interests, by the quality of empathy and communication, by lines of identification, by reciprocity of emotional and sexual need, by the contingencies of ancillary relationships and of social events, and so on.

Finally, there is a specific factor deriving from the vicissitudes of the psychotherapeutic experience itself which is difficult to appraise. It matters considerably whether the patient's presenting complaint is his neurotic disability or conflict in the marital relationship. What the patient asks to be cured of is of no small importance since this affects his motivation for change. The effects of therapy are in part the result of who practices it and how it is practiced. The primary focus of classical forms of psychotherapy, especially psychoanalytic therapy, has been the internal economy of the individual personality, even though the therapy uses relationship process as its medium. The inner orientation to self and to neurotically conflicted personal needs receives the primary emphasis, rather than the processes of social interaction. Although the orientation to self affects orientation to other persons, and vice versa, there is by no means a one-to-one correlation between the two. This involves the elusive problem of the dynamic interplay of individual and group experience, many facets of which are not yet clearly understood. It is apparent, then, that the extent to which disturbance in a marital relationship is alleviated by individual psychotherapy of one or both partners varies with many factors: the nature of the pathology of the relationship; the secondary effects of ancillary relationships; the psychosocial status of the family as a whole and each marital partner's corresponding adaptation; and, finally, the nature of the pathology and psychotherapy of each partner and whether the therapy of the one partner is effectively coordinated with the therapy of the other.

A corrective approach to marital disturbance cannot, therefore, be a simple undertaking. It is a question of the therapy of "husbanding and wifing," rather than straight therapy for an individual neurosis. I have stressed some of the complexities of the therapeutic challenge because, as already indicated, diagnosis has meaning only in the context of devising a plan of action.

It is clear, then, that marital disorders belong in the sphere of social psychopathology. A marital relationship is something beyond the sum of the personalities that make it up. The relationship itself tends to influence and change each partner, and this in turn influences the relationship anew. In confronting this special problem we shift our traditional focus of interest as psychiatrists from the pathology of the individual psyche to the pathology of a human relationship as a social unit. We have to admit, accordingly, that the efficacy of our diagnostic and therapeutic tools for dealing with the pathology of relationships and groups lags behind our ability to deal with the intrapsychic disorders of the individual.

This raises an interesting problem of definition: Does the term "neurotic" as it refers to marital interaction have precisely the same connotation as the term "neurotic" when it applies to fixed forms of conflict within the individual psyche? I might offer several definitions of neurosis to illustrate the point. For example: Oberndorf [2] defines a neurosis as "a compromise formation showing itself repetitively in thinking (mentally) or performance (bodily), caused by a preponderant intrapsychic conflict, and the compromise is incapacitating and ineffectual, i.e., the compromise does not accomplish what it sets out to do." Freud has described the structure of a neurosis as resulting from chronic repression of a specific internal conflict between id and superego, where the repressed instinctual impulses are displaced, disguised, and reappear in the form of disabling symptoms. Is conflict between persons to be conceived in the same terms as conflict within a person? Is neurotic interaction in a marital pair to be conceived as having dynamic connotations identical with neurosis in the individual psyche? Even when we take full cognizance of the principle that neurosis in the

[2] Clarence P. Oberndorf, M.D., "Diagnostic and Etiological Concepts in the Neuroses," *Current Problems in Psychiatric Diagnosis,* Paul H. Hoch, M.D., and Joseph Zubin (eds.), Grune & Stratton, New York, 1953.

individual psyche implies a particular set of propensities in interpersonal adaptation, we must nevertheless phenomenologically draw the distinction that conflict between people, real or neurotic, is not identical with conflict within the individual psyche, although they overlap. The proof of the pudding is readily available in empirical observations which unequivocally demonstrate that a given individual with a fixed neurosis will interact in significantly different ways with different partners. For example, a psychoneurotic male with strong castration fears may be totally impotent with his wife, and strong as a bull with another woman. In other words, though he is affected by or, we might say, enjoys the same neurosis in both relationships, as a person he is differently integrated in the two situations, and the psychosocial consequences of neurotic conflict are correspondingly different.

Neurotic interaction, therefore, is a a new dynamic entity, not to be defined merely as the sum of the neuroses of the two individuals who join in the relationship. Hence, we must proceed with an attempt to discern those criteria that would enable us to diagnose the specific characteristics of neurotic interaction. If we agree to the proposition, however, that neurotic interaction is a part, perhaps a central part but nevertheless a part, of total interaction, it is necessary first to hypothesize criteria appropriate for evaluating the total process of marital interaction and then to differentiate the neurotic component of that interaction.

Criteria for Evaluating Marital Interaction

We present now a series of such criteria for evaluating total marital relationship interaction and offer some hypotheses for the dynamic interplay between individual personality and marital role. We shall then, finally, differentiate the specific criteria pertinent to the discernment of the neurotic component of marital interaction.

Marital Relationship

I. Goals, Motives, Value Orientation
- A. Explicit and implicit
- B. Real and unreal
- C. Conscious and unconscious
- D. Clear and confused
- E. Stable and unstable
- F. Consistent and conflicting

II. Performance
- A. Personal interaction of partners
  - 1. Past interaction
    - a. General pattern of interaction
      - (1) During courtship
      - (2) After marriage, but before children
      - (3) After children (Use criteria listed under current interaction.)
  - 2. Current interaction
    - a. General pattern of interaction
    - b. Compatibility: specify as follows
      - (1) Nonsexual aspects of love
        - (a) Emotional. Capacity for affection and tender intimacy, capacity for sympathy, communication, identification, mutual support, common interests, other binding factors
        - (b) Social and economic. Social aspects of marital relationship, balance of authority, companionship, mutual activities, sharing of economic resources and problems, and division of labor
      - (2) Sexual aspects
        Sexual satisfaction or frustration: specific maladjustments, conflicts, and anxieties
      - (3) Family aspects
        Parental—the interdependence and reciprocity of parental functions
    - c. Conflict (Specify pattern, intensity, degree of spread, controlled or "acted out." Differentiate areas for functioning most involved—emotional, social, sexual, and so on.)
    - d. Complementarity (Differentiate positive and negative and defensive complementarity.)
      - (1) Mutual support
        - (a) As husband and wife
        - (b) As father and mother
        - (c) Sharing of pleasure
        - (d) Sharing of responsibility
        - (e) Sharing of authority
    - e. Specific trends toward isolation, disintegration, or regression
- B. Interaction of partners as couple with external environment—
  With extended family, friends, community groups, culture patterns

III. Achievement (measured against an ideal conception of "healthy" interaction in our culture)
- A. Fulfillment of goals and motivations
  - 1. For relationship
  - 2. For each partner
- B. Relation between goals and actual performance
  - 1. Relative approximation or discrepancy
- C. Complementarity (positive or negative)
  - 1. Mutual support as husband and wife
  - 2. Mutual support as father and mother

3. Sharing of pleasure
4. Sharing of responsibility
5. Sharing of authority

D. Specific conflict
E. Specific trends toward isolation, disintegration, or regression

IV. Dynamic Interrelations of Individual Personality Structure and Family Role
A. Individual personality structure
1. Symptoms of character structure of husband (psychiatric diagnosis)
2. Symptoms of character structure of wife (psychiatric diagnosis)

B. Dynamics of integration of personality into family role (husband and wife, father and mother)
1. Goals for relationship
2. Perceptive image of the relationship
3. Self-image projected into the relationship
4. Personal need and conflict projected into the relationship
5. Patterns of emotional control of the relationship
6. Patterns of control of anxiety—specific defenses

C. Interdependence and reciprocal interaction of family roles
D. The effects of ancillary roles, in own family, as children of own parents, as employee, friend, member of the community, and so on

V. Specific Neurotic Component in Interaction
A. Specific pattern of neurotic interaction
B. Intensity and depth
C. Spread of involvement
D. Degree of deviation from healthy marital interaction
E. Failure of personality of each partner to integrate into family role
F. Degree of symbiosis in the pathology of the relationship
G. Specify the pathology of the relationship in the following terms:
1. Unreal, inappropriate goals and motives for the relationship
2. The distortions of perception of the relationship
3. The conflicted, confused images of self projected into the relationship
4. The specific neurotic needs and conflicts involved
5. The pathological techniques for control of the relationship
6. The pathological mechanisms of control of anxiety

VI. The Consequences of Neurotic Interaction, Evaluated in Terms of Impaired Achievement. Specify the effects on:
A. Compatibility: emotional, social, sexual, and so on
B. Conflict
C. Patterns of complementarity
D. Trends toward isolation, disintegration, or regression

VII. Specific Patterns of Compensation (Restitution)
A. Increased tolerance or support of immature or regressed emotional needs in the other partner
B. Increased tolerance of distorted perceptions of the relationship; tolerance of irrational projections, one partner on the other
C. Tolerance of inappropriate (irrational) patterns of control of relationship

D. Tolerance and reinforcement of pathological defenses against anxiety. Or in each of the above categories, effective control of the neurotic tendencies of one partner by the other, or the facilitation of healthier forms of defense

When the specific component of neurotic interaction has been differentiated, a careful estimate of the balance between the pathology and the residual health of the relationship is of the utmost clinical importance. The following questions might be helpful in making such an estimate:

1. Appraisal of the damage to the relationship, resulting from neurotic interaction: (a) Does it threaten to engulf all major aspects of the marital interaction, or are its effects relatively localized? (b) Do the conflicted urges, irrational projections, and inappropriate rigid defenses of one partner threaten to overwhelm the other partner? (c) Are there clear signs of a push toward isolation, disintegration, or regression in the relationship?

2. Appraisal of the residual health of the relationship: (a) What areas of marital interaction and shared functioning are least damaged? (b) What is their importance relative to the critically impaired areas? (c) What degree of mutual trust and acceptance prevails despite the existence of neurotic conflict? (d) What is the motivation for reconstruction of the relationship in each partner?

A careful survey of more than forty disordered marital relationships in which the above concepts and criteria were applied leads to the following tentative conclusions:

1. The variety of pattern of neurotic marital interaction is large; the intensity, depth of pathology, and spread of involvement are equally variable; and in accordance with this, the relative balance between the degree of spread of the neurotic interaction and the residual components of health in the marital interaction covers a wide range.

2. Neurotic marital interaction as it affects total marital interaction must be evaluated both quantitatively and qualitatively.

3. The neurotic involvement is by no means uniform for the various areas of functioning of relationship—emotional, social, sexual, economic, and so on.

Some varied patterns observed are:

1. The neurotic interaction covers all or most areas; there are mutual frustration and conflict, and relatively total disablement of the relationship.

2. The neurotic interaction covers chiefly the sexual area, and there is reasonable compatibility in other areas.

3. The neurotic interaction covers the the emotional and social areas, but the sexual area is least impaired; that is, sexual compatibility is high, but complementarity is not effectively preserved in other areas.

4. Complementarity in emotional, social, and other areas is high, and sex adaptation, though objectively poor, is minimized in its importance.

5. Traditional sex roles are reversed and there is high negative complementarity (mutual buttressing of defenses).

6. There is severe mutual marital isolation, damaging all areas of shared functioning.

7. Interaction as husband and wife is unhealthy, but there is mutual devotion to parental family roles, in which complementarity is high.

8. Interaction as husband and wife is unhealthy, but there is mutual devotion to conformity with standards; in this the community complementarity is high.

In a general sense the theoretically pure types of marital interaction may be hypothesized as follows:

1. Marital relationships in which there is negligible integration of the partners in the marital role. Each partner narcissistically preserves his premarital individuality, largely untouched by the requirements of the marital bond.

2. The individualities of each partner are mainly subordinated to the requirements of the marital role.

3. The individualities of each partner are mainly subordinated to the requirements of the parental role.

4. The individualities of each partner are mainly subordinated to the requirements of successful conformity to the culture pattern of the surrounding community.

If one estimates in this manner the assets and liabilities with regard to the mental health of a marital relationship, it begins to be possible to institute a realistic program of therapy. One may then erect goals for the psychotherapy of husband and wife in the context of a clear awareness of the reciprocity of the marital roles, rather than operating psychotherapeutically with an abstract goal of cure of neurosis in one individual partner, while giving insufficient attention to the features of the total marital relationship.

One must take into account, too, what is residually healthy in the personality of each partner, and the positive factors preserved in the relationship over and above the content of its neurotic component. Adequate diagnosis of the marital relationship makes it possible not only to focus therapy on the damaged areas of functioning but also to reinforce and strengthen the relatively healthy areas of functioning, and this tends to fortify the whole relationship.

Through a discriminating application of such criteria, it becomes possible to provide appropriate answers to the questions originally posed: Should one or both partners receive psychotherapy? By the same or different therapist? At the same time or different times? And by what kind of therapist?

Finally, we might assay the difficult task of erecting a model for a healthy marital relationship on the basis of these criteria. Presumably, such a relationship would be characterized by a relatively clear awareness of goals, positive in emphasis rather than defensive; these goals, reasonably shared by both partners, would be relatively realistic, stable, and flexible. There would be a modicum of compatibility in the main areas of shared experience—the emotional, social, sexual, economic, and parental areas. Conflict would not be excessive, would be under control, and would have mainly a realistic, rather than an irrational, content. There would be empathic tolerance of differences based on mutual understanding and equality; also tolerance of any residual immaturities of need which may be present in either partner. There would be reasonable sharing of pleasure, responsibility, and authority. There would be reasonable fulfillment of goals both for the relationship and for the further development of each partner as an individual. Each would be as much concerned for the welfare and development of the partner as for the self. Where differences exist, the mutual, unreserved acceptance of each partner by the other would make of these differences a stimulus for growth, both for the relationship and for each partner as an individual, rather than a basis for conflict or isolation. Actually, performance in marriage would reasonably approximate goals. There would be a relatively high complementarity on a positive basis as husband and wife and as father and mother. There would be no significant trend toward isolation, disintegration, or regression.

INTAKE AND SOME ROLE CONSIDERATIONS [1]

Helen Harris Perlman

THIS PAPER MIGHT BE given an alternate title, "The Case of the Third Man," for it came about because of my concern with this person. The present title is derived from a proposition I am offering for discussion and testing by caseworkers, as a possible approach to the "third man" problem.

People in trouble in some aspect of their daily living appear at the door of the social agency or clinic and present themselves and their problems. They are recognized as needing the help these agencies are equipped to give. They are given some promise of held or at least of further attention. Two thirds of them return for a second interview. One third do not return. Of every three persons given the time, attention, and beginning casework help at the agency's intake desk, one drops out before the second interview.

This is a troubling situation. It is troubling from several points of view. Most obvious is the economic waste. The intake process, even if it is one interview, absorbs time, money, and the energies of the casework, supervisory, and clerical staff members. That one third of such expenditures should be fruitless is a discomforting fact, and one that we are rightly embarrassed to reveal even to our most loyal supporters.

But there is a more serious loss involved. It is the loss of the chance to give casework help not only where it is manifestly needed but at the moment in time when both stress and motivation are high enough to push a person to reach out for help. It is the loss of the moment of white heat, when change and even prevention through casework help may be most achievable.

[1] Published in *Social Casework,* April 1960. Presented at a meeting of the Chicago Chapter, National Association of Social Workers, Chicago, October 1959.

A person who brings himself, or is brought, to a social agency is a person in a critical moment of living. His problem may have arisen suddenly or it may be an old, long-festering one, suddenly come to a head. This person puts on his shoes and goes to open the agency door because he has come to a point where he can no longer tolerate, or others can no longer tolerate, the strain of his problem. Even the unwilling applicant—who has been forced into the agency by the volition of someone else—experiences this first encounter with the social agency as potentially crucial, although his problem is not one that he brings but one with which the agency confronts him.

Every applicant, then, is at a point of mobilization to get (or to avoid) help. In this mobilization of himself in relation to his problem and the agency lies the dynamic potential for a shift in his adaptive-protective mechanisms. Since high discomfort cannot be sustained without defensive moves to regain stability, and since stability may be gained by poor adaptation as well as constructive adaptation, the effective or ineffective intervention by the case-worker affects the direction the applicant's balancing efforts will take. Thus, this moment or hour that we call "intake" is a critical one in the life of the person applying for help. Moreover, it is often the case that not only does the applicant "feel" his problem to be a crisis but it actually is one. The forces creating his problem may have come to a point where one or a series of breakdowns and maladaptations may occur in his life situation unless effective intervention takes place. (Parenthetically, since the subject cannot be dealt with here, the case placed on a waiting list is never quite the same case when it is finally taken on for service as it was at the point of application.) Social workers are increasingly concerned with the idea of prevention. Here, in the intake phase of casework, is a potent opportunity to do preventive work. This is the opportunity we lose or waste when the applicant who needs help fails to take it.

Reasons for "the Third Man"

A number of recent studies concerned with the problem of dropouts have attempted to analyze possible reasons for them.[2]

[2] Leonard S. Kogan, "The Short-Term Case in a Family Agency," Part III, *Social Casework,* Vol. XXXVIII, No. 7 (1957), pp. 366–374. This study reveals

A recurrent explanation, reported by Dr. Shyne, is this: the applicant's understanding and expectations of the agency were not clear. This explanation, stated in two different ways, appears again in the caseworkers' study reported by Miss Stark. One explanation is that "the misconception that all clients have some knowledge and acceptance of the purposes of social agencies created barriers between caseworker and client." The other is that the caseworker operated in an unproductive way because of "certain misconceptions of the role of the client and caseworker." These explanations seem to have a vital bearing on the problem of dropouts. They point to poor communication between the applicant and the caseworker due to faulty perception or actual misconception of the reciprocal expectations involved in a client's help-taking and a caseworker's help-giving.

It must, of course, be noted that other possible reasons for dropouts are also suggested in these studies. None of them, however, has been less explored than this idea: that the applicant may not have any real understanding of what he is applying *for* or *to,* that his expectations may be quite at odds with the reality he encounters; that, on the other side, the caseworker may be assuming that what he asks, does, and proposes make complete sense to the applicant because they are so manifestly sensible to *him.* One cannot overlook the fact that many subtle factors and also simple ones, known and unknown, operate to make for dropouts after intake. But here, plainly before us, is an explanation that says, in a common-

that, of the people applying to the Community Service Society of New York who are accepted for service following an intake interview, about one third do not return.

Lilian Ripple, "Motivation, Capacity, and Opportunity as Related to the Use of Casework Service: Theoretical Base and Plan of Study," *Social Service Review,* Vol. XXIX, No. 2 (1955), pp. 172–193. Sampling for this study in two Chicago family agencies, the Family Service Bureau of the United Charities and the Jewish Family and Community Service, agencies selected in part because of their high standards of practice, reveals a dropout rate of approximately one third of the clients who were expected to return for a second interview.

Ann W. Shyne, "What Research Tells Us About Short-Term Cases in Family Agencies," *Social Casework,* Vol. XXXVIII, No. 5 (1957), pp. 223–231. This article summarizes a number of studies done on cases that continue and those that discontinue, in an effort to understand the causes of dropouts. The one-third dropout rate was characteristic in sixty-four member agencies of the Family Service Association of America.

Frances B. Stark, "Barriers to Client-Worker Communication at Intake," *Social Casework,* Vol. XL, No. 4 (1959), pp. 177–183. This article is of particular interest because it is a self-study by caseworkers of their own experience with cases at intake. Of twenty clients judged to be motivated to seek help only seven were "successfully engaged in contact." The article deals with possible reasons for the loss of almost two thirds of the applicants.

sense way, that an applicant's continuance or discontinuance with an agency beyond the point of intake may be affected by the understanding and agreements between applicant and caseworker about what in the way of service and behavior is wanted, expected, and realizable. This proposition, it seems to me, deserves to be tested as one possible approach to the problem of the third man.

The Aim of the Beginning Phase

Elsewhere I have proposed that the aim of the beginning phase in casework (and this phase may be completed in one interview, although it usually requires more) is "to engage this client with his problem and his will to do something about it in a working relationship with this agency, its intentions and special means of helpfulness." [3] The focus implied is somewhat different from the position taken by some other casework writers who consider the initial phase of the casework process to be chiefly a study or exploratory phase.[4] In the latter, emphasis is placed on the caseworker's gaining as much understanding as possible about the nature of the problem and of the person who carries it. In the former, the major emphasis is on the caseworker's active effort to *engage the applicant in wanting to use the help the agency can offer him.*

It goes without saying that the caseworker must first have elicited enough of the nature of the problem to be sure that it falls within the agency's purview. Doing this properly means that the caseworker has not only asked for certain information but has responded to it with warmth and intelligent concern; has not only observed the behavior of the applicant but has drawn some inferences from it to guide the "what" and "how" of his reciprocal behavior. But when this much has been done, the essential next step is to bring the applicant into a working agreement or a "compact" with the agency. If an applicant for casework help has been brought to the point where he indicates verbally or in other explicit ways that he sees and partially understands the agency's place in relation to his problem and that he is willing to try its ways of getting at the

[3] Helen Harris Perlman, *Social Casework: A Problem-solving Process,* University of Chicago Press, 1957, p. 113.

[4] See, for example, the statement on "The Study Phase," in *Method and Process in Social Casework—Report of a Staff Committee, Community Service Society of New York,* Family Service Assocation of America, New York, 1958, p. 9; and Frances H. Scherz, "Intake: Concept and Process," *Social Casework,* Vol. XXXIII, No. 6 (1952), pp. 233–240.

problem, then the caseworker has a "client." Then he may "study," "explore," "understand," as far and as deeply as necessary. But unless this compact is reached, the applicant may never come again no matter how splendid the exploratory study.

This suggests, then, that my original formulation can be condensed into this idea: the aim of the beginning phase of casework is to help an "applicant" to undertake the role of "client."

Applicant, Client, and Role

Immediately the terms within this condensation—"applicant," "client," and "role"—must be defined. An "applicant" is one who makes a request for something he wants. The person who comes to the social agency or clinic is an "applicant"; he is not yet a "client."

According to Webster, a "client" is "one who employs the services of any profession or business." Mary Richmond first made consistent use of this term in social work. "Those with whom social case workers are dealing are called by many names. . . . One word will be used for all, usually, in this volume—the word 'client.' Its history is one of advancement from low estate to higher. First it meant 'a suitor, a dependent.' Later it meant 'one who listens to advice,' and later still 'one who employs professional service of any kind.' "[5] What Miss Richmond indicated is that the concept of client in our profession as in others has undergone an evolution from that of being a recipient of another's largesse and protection, as in the days of the Roman patrons, to that of being one who has undertaken to use a service. It is "undertaking to use a service" which marks the role of client as different from that of applicant. Thus, certain understandings must evolve between caseworker and applicant before the latter becomes a client.

"Role" is a word that carries a considerable freightage of meaning and emotion in social work today. As it is being used here it means a person's organized pattern or modes of behaving, fashioned by the status or functions he carries in relation to one or more other persons. Such a behavior pattern is selected, shaped, and colored by several dynamic factors: (1) the person's needs and drives—what he wants, consciously and unconsciously; (2) the person's ideas of the mutual obligations and expectations that have been invested (by

[5] Mary E. Richmond, *Social Diagnosis,* Russell Sage Foundation, New York, 1917, p. 38.

custom, tradition, convention) in the particular status and functions he undertakes; (3) the compatibility or conflict between the person's conceptions of obligations and expectations and those held by the other person(s) with whom he is in reciprocation.

One can say, then, that any person who wants something of another person or organization—job, scholarship, counsel, membership, service, or grant—assumes the role of an applicant. In the applicant role, one behaves not only in line with his particular personality organization but also in such ways as he feels or believes are called for in a petitioner, and also in relation to his perception and ideas of the circumstances and functions of the person and place to which he applies. The applicant's ideas about what he wants, what he can get, and his expectations of what the potential grantor will do and require of him (in money, gratitude, promises, behavior) may be vague and half-formed, totally erroneous, or quite correct. A person's behavior as an applicant will be heavily determined by these ideas and expectations.

The role of client, too, is given dimension and color by a person's ideas and expectations of what "undertaking to use the services" of a professional person involves. Becoming a client of a lawyer, an architect, or a broker means not simply that one brings a problem-to-be-solved or a goal-to-be-gained and asks for help with it. Beyond this, it involves a working agreement or compact arrived at between applicant and helper. This agreement or compact includes some exchange of mutual understandings about what the applicant wants and expects of the helper and what the helper can or cannot, will or will not, do about the problem-to-be-worked. It includes agreements about "who does what" and "where we go from here"—of joint and separate tasks, and of next steps. This process constitutes, in essence, a definition of reciprocal roles and aims arrived at by a professional helper and the applicant who decides to become a client—tentative and limited though this definition must be. It follows that the caseworker does not have a client, whether at intake or later, until he and the applicant have come to some rudimentary agreements about their relationship to one another and to the problem.

If the caseworker assumes from the first that an "applicant" is already a "client," he tends, I believe, to take for granted that the applicant has achieved certain understandings, perceptions, and commitments which the latter may not have come near to reaching. What the worker says and does will be subject to the applicant's misconceptions or partial apprehensions and, therefore, barriers to communication will arise. Perhaps this is why we lose the third man.

The proposition I suggest for testing is this: What an applicant will do in the intake phase of a case is heavily conditioned by his conception of what is expected of him and what he may expect, in return, from the caseworker and agency—in short, *by his conception of his and the caseworker's roles in relation to the problem he brings.* If this is so, the process of intake must have as one primary purpose the clarification of at least preliminary ideas and expectations of reciprocal roles and working relationships. When these are accepted by the applicant and the caseworker, the applicant then becomes a client.

I do not know precisely how to go about testing this proposition. Case records do not typically contain the data from which it can be studied. For the moment I can only put it forward for some consideration.

The Applicant's Perceptions

It is rather remarkable how little attention we have paid to this question of who and what the applicant has presumed the caseworker and agency to be. We ourselves have been so immersed in our functions and skills, and so sure about our helping intents and services, that we have quite lost sight of the possibility that the person who faces us across the desk may have very little idea of any of these. On the other hand, he may have many ideas about all of these, and all of them may be seriously mistaken. Sometimes as the applicant presents himself and his story with one part of his mind, considerable mental juggling is going on, unspoken, in another part of his mind, in his effort to determine just who and what this potential helper is or can be to him. The name of the agency to which the applicant brings his problem tells him only in the most general way what the agency is for. What it actually can do for him, how it will do it, where he "comes in" or where he "gets off"—of these he has little comprehension or often much misapprehension. If the setting is one to which the person has applied for one kind of service—for example, medical or psychiatric —and he is then sent to the social service division, his perception may be further confused.

One does not need to examine the perceptions of applicants in order to know how little general understanding there is of the role of the social caseworker. Every caseworker knows persons who have been active in supporting and developing casework agencies not only by money but by hard work and interest, who may even be board members of his agency, but who show by questions or comments that they have only the vaguest idea of what casework services actually entail. These are interested, even devoted, people. Many of them have had considerably more education and greater access to interpretation of casework services than have most applicants. In the light of our chagrin that at times even members of our own families display appalling ignorance of what it is we do, and who we are as caseworkers, is it not interesting that we assume that a person coming to us because of his troubles perceives us accurately, and understands our function and role? We even assume that the applicant, following this supposedly correct perception, has the capacity to adapt, unaided, to the requirements of the part he must play if he is to be a client.

The recent professional literature is replete with self-exhortations to understand the culture and class membership of our individual clients. Perceptions and role expectations are undoubtedly conditioned by these social factors. Yet we have taken small account of them in the intake process and have tended to proceed as if each applicant's perception and ideas of us, and of himself in relation to us, is like every other applicant's. We have paid little attention to the problem of who and what he thinks we are or can be to him.

One of the truest ways by which to know the feelings and necessary defenses of another person was taught us in our professional infancy: step into the other's shoes. It is not even necessary to imagine being an applicant to a social agency. Imagine you are making an application for a job. (There is an immediate difference here from an application for help because the person who is looking for a job is offering, at the very least, potential competence; an applicant for social service usually begins from a position of failure with the problem for which he seeks help.) Watch what you are doing and feeling as you apply for the job. You will be telling an interviewer what you want, why you want it, and what you have to offer. Simultaneously you will be trying to assess what this place and person are like; you will wonder if you are telling and asking too much or too little; you will be trying to "size up" what the employer's expectations are. If they are not explicitly stated, you will ask questions to find out what will be expected of you and what you can expect in return—what the reciprocal obligations and rights are. If you are not so bold as to ask them, you will remain uneasy and dissatisfied, plagued by doubts as to whether you want to commit yourself to these vague unknowns. It is in the latter position that the applicant to a social agency so often finds himself. Since he is usually under greater stress than an employment applicant, since he knows less about "the company" to which he is applying, since he offers only "trouble" and not competence, and often feels he is asking for "something for nothing," he is not at all free to ask the questions that we can imagine we would ask.

The more one thinks about this, the more surprising it is that most of the applicants to agencies actually do continue past the first interview. Two possible reasons suggest themselves. One is that need for help is so great or is felt so keenly that the applicant clings to the promise of agency concern and on-going attention. As Charlotte Towle has put it, "The needful man is not a free man." The other reason may be that the caseworker's warmth and actual demonstration of helpfulness, by manner, attitudes, and indications of understanding and know-how, provide the necessary security for going on. Yet even here, there remains the question of what the applicant conceives to be his part in relation to that of the caseworker. Perhaps the phenomena of participation, of dependency, and of transference are related to this question.[6]

The Client Role

In this discussion, we are primarily concerned with those applicants who "discontinue" and with what we can do to help those who need help to undertake the role of client. Regardless of the

[6] See "Some Cultural Aspects of Transference and Countertransference," John P. Spiegel, M.D., *Science and Psychoanalysis, Vol. II, Individual and Familial Dynamics,* Jules H. Masserman, M.D., (ed.), Grune & Stratton, New York, 1959, pp. 160–182.

profession that is offering the service, the client role has these components:

1. Help is sought in some area of difficulty or in moving toward some goal.

2. It is expected that the helper has a willingness to help and the necessary expertness.

3. It is expected that, either at once or within a reasonably short time, some counsel, guidance, tangible means, or promises will be given by which the problem may be solved or the goals achieved.

4. It is expected that some "payment" will be required for the service given; this payment is often money, but when it is, and certainly when it is not, the applicant anticipates (if he is part of our Western give-and-take, take-and-give culture) that there will be certain reciprocal obligations.

5. It is expected that some agreement or understanding will be reached between the applicant and his professional helper as to their on-going roles and direction.

The applicant for casework service is faced with some added complications. He does not choose his helper, the person he meets at intake. Therefore he may be even more involved in trying to make out the nature of his helper than he would be if beforehand he had chosen to go to Dr. Jones or Lawyer Smith or Caseworker Doe. He does not usually pay in money for the service he asks. (Fee-paying clients in social work constitute a small minority.) This circumstance makes him especially uncertain about what he is supposed to put into the venture, or where his obligations begin and his expectations end.

To induct an applicant into the role of client involves our giving thoughtful and imaginative consideration to the conditions and expectations outlined above. To bring a person who needs and wants help to the point where he perceives what help is available for his problem, what possibilities, limits, and conditions are involved, what he may expect and what may be expected of him as a participant, and then to come to mutual agreement as to where and how he and the caseworker can move ahead—this, I believe, is to help a person consciously to undertake to become a client. He may still, of course, choose not to become one, since what has been suggested is no magic formula. It is only a proposition, based on everyday understanding of people in our culture, that offers a possible bridge between the person who wants and needs help and the institutions set up to give it.[7]

The question of *how* roles are to be clarified and operating agreements are to be reached is a subject that cannot be dealt with here. Despite space limits, however, two things must be said. We must still begin where the applicant is. He is involved in a problem and is under stress. Therefore, our first effort must be to help him tell his trouble and what he wants, and simultaneously to elicit and respond to the expressive and defensive emotions which both the problem and the application excite. Only when this matter has been given the caseworker's attentive, compassionate understanding can discussion be held about what the applicant wants or thinks he can get in coming to the agency; what the caseworker and agency realistically are and can do in relation to his particular problem; and what their mutual expectations are. It is in this discussion that misapprehensions, unrealistic expectations, confusions, fears, and immediate mutual goals are clarified. Only then can the applicant say, by his explicit or tacit agreements or his behavior, "I will be your client."

It cannot be overemphasized that this kind of discussion is in no sense the final paragraph of an interview. It is in no sense a tidy summing up of the "rules of play," so to speak. An applicant's conception of his and the caseworker's roles may be charged with emotion; his ideas of what he wants and how he is to get it may also be so charged. Because the caseworker is rarely able to offer a packaged solution to the problem, there are inevitable frustrations involved which the applicant must be helped to face and try to bear. In brief, there are emotional involvements as well as ideas to which the caseworker must relate and with which he must deal in offering casework help.

Summary

I have tried here to state a problem and to present a proposition by which the problem may be better understood and coped with.

[7] It is of interest that some psychiatrists are giving attention to this same problem: role clarity between patient and doctor. In Karl Menninger's recent book, *Theory of Psychoanalytic Technique*, (Basic Books, New York, 1958) developed from his teaching sessions with young psychiatrists, he presents at some length the idea that the psychiatrist and his potential patient must, at the beginning of their relationship, come to a "contract" of agreement about their mutual roles and obligations.

My argument is simply this: If the caseworker conceives of intake as a "study" or "exploratory process" and the applicant conceives of it as a help-getting experience, the two participants will have a hard time understanding one another. If the caseworker conceives of the applicant as his "client," that is, a person who is ready to use his services, and the applicant conceives of himself and the caseworker in who-knows-what ways, they will have a hard time communicating with one another. If some preliminary and partial agreements and expectations about reciprocal roles are not clarified at intake, the applicant may still continue with the agency, but he is likely to have confused or even unrealistic expectations which may affect the ensuing course of relationship and treatment. Or he may not return at all.

In recent years, it has been the fashion for a writer to conclude his paper by suggesting that "only further research will tell us" whether or not the proposition he has put forth has value. I shall not place this burden on the overloaded shoulders of social work researchers. It must be placed, I think, on the overloaded shoulders of social caseworkers. Only practice will tell; only actual try-outs, and assessments of those try-outs, will say whether, in fact, this proposition offers a way to solve the troublesome problem of that "intake" which becomes instead a "dropout."

A FRAMEWORK FOR UNDERSTANDING FAMILY DYNAMICS [1]

Viola W. Weiss and Russell R. Monroe

Part I

THE FAMILY has become an important focus of study in an increasing number of disciplines. Since the family is a universal institution, it is of utmost interest to the fields of sociology and anthropology. In recent years medicine has recognized the importance of family functioning to the extent that a number of medical schools include either a single course or an educational sequence designed to teach the relationship between illness and total family functioning. The social caseworker, particularly if he is employed in a family agency, has always focused his attention on the family as a unit. For a time an emphasis on depth psychology diverted the caseworker into a preoccupation with the individual client, although he never totally overlooked the presence of other family members. It seems to us, however, that since Frances Scherz wrote, "In a family agency the family constellation is the focus of study and treatment," [2] a greater concentration of thought and study has been applied to the processes within the family. Social workers, psychiatrists, sociologists, and anthropologists, working separately and together, have engaged in studies of the family and of the relationship of the individual to other family members. Much of this material was synthesized at the jointly sponsored interdisciplinary conference held by the Family Service Association of America and

[1] Published in *Social Casework,* January and February 1959.
[2] Frances H. Scherz, "What Is Family-Centered Casework?," *Social Casework,* Vol. XXXIV, No. 8 (1953), p. 343.

the Elizabeth McCormick Memorial Fund in October 1957.[3] At this meeting Dr. M. Robert Gomberg pointed out that "no diagnostic or conceptual system exists which describes, assesses, or classifies the family configuration."[4] The paper presented here is the result of our study of this problem in the Family Service Society of New Orleans.

Even though the casework goal is to treat the family as a whole, the caseworker has characteristically attempted to achieve it by working with only one family member. Sometimes this type of treatment is sufficient, but frequently casework efforts are blocked by forces within the family that are beyond the client's control. Thus, the caseworker needs a specific theoretical framework within which family dynamics may be properly understood. It is only through such understanding that the caseworker can logically plan treatment that focuses on the family as a unit rather than on the individual members. A framework of knowledge of the family's dynamics should lead the worker to decide whether more than one member of the family needs to be treated and, if so, whether one caseworker or several should undertake the therapy. It should pinpoint the areas of conflict, as well as suggest realistic casework goals. With this understanding, the caseworker should be able to predict what individual changes will upset family equilibrium and what changes will stabilize it. The caseworker should be able to recognize distortions in the reporting of various family members, which, in turn, may necessitate his making home visits in order to observe family interaction directly. Finally, this framework should suggest a simple and concise way in which family dynamics may be interpreted to clients.

The purpose of the present paper is to suggest a framework, a specially designed outline, which may facilitate the caseworker's focus on family, rather than on individual, dynamics and assist him in accumulating and organizing pertinent data in a meaningful way. The worker must understand not only the behavior patterns and conflicts of individual family members, but also the relationships between them, that is, the organization of these members in terms of what each member contributes to the family unit and what the family unit contributes to the individual. It is also important for the worker to observe and to understand the

[3] "Family Casework in the Interest of Children," *Social Casework,* Vol. XXXIX, Nos. 2–3 (1958).
[4] *Ibid.,* p. 73.

relationship of the family as a unit to the larger community. The interplay of social, cultural, physical, and psychological forces that are largely responsible for family disequilibrium must be identified. The cultural and sub-cultural value systems, as well as individual family values, should be given particular attention. Understanding them is a special problem because even the professional person often is consciously unaware of the value systems within his own culture and may be unfamiliar with normal sub-cultural variations. Without this knowledge, it is difficult to decide what is normal or average for a family, what is variant but successful, and what is deviant or pathological.[5]

The caseworker must have access to some broad generalizations and new concepts regarding family dynamics if he is to draw effective understanding from these extensive data. A review of the literature in 1955 revealed certain attempts in this direction, notably articles by Dr. Nathan Ackerman[6] on the criteria for evaluating marital interaction. Subsequently, there have been several additional articles by the same author and by others.[7] This present attempt, however, is not so much one of formulating concepts for a family "diagnosis" or nosology as of formulating an outline of family dynamics which will be useful in planning casework treatment. As the Committee on the Family of the Group for the Advancement of Psychiatry pointed out: "To change the object of inquiry from the individual to the family, however, means the employment of different methods of observation and of different conceptual tools. . . . The family is a fairly well-defined, organized entity with a life history and dynamic principles of its own."[8]

[5] On the subject of this sub-cultural variation, we found two books particularly suited for the social worker: John Sirjamaki, *The American Family in the Twentieth Century,* Harvard University Press, Cambridge, Massachusetts, 1953; Earl L. Koos, *Families in Trouble,* Kings Crown Press, New York, 1946.

[6] Nathan W. Ackerman, M.D., "The Diagnosis of Neurotic Marital Interaction," pp. 148–162 of this volume, reprinted from *Social Casework,* April 1954; and Nathan W. Ackerman, M.D., "Interpersonal Disturbances in the Family," *Psychiatry,* Vol. XVII, No. 4 (1954), pp. 359–368.

[7] Nathan W. Ackerman, M.D., and Marjorie L. Behrens, "A Study of Family Diagnosis," *American Journal of Orthopsychiatry,* Vol. XXVI, No. 1 (1956), pp. 66–78; Nathan W. Ackerman, M.D., "Mental Health and the Family in the Current World Crisis," *Journal of Jewish Communal Service,* Vol. XXXIV, No. 1 (1957), pp. 58–72; and "Toward an Integrative Therapy of the Family," *American Journal af Psychiatry,* Vol. CXIV, No. 8 (1958), pp. 727–733; M. Robert Gomberg, "Family-Oriented Treatment of Marital Problems," pp. 198–212 of this volume, reprinted from *Social Casework,* January 1956.

[8] Committee on the Family of the Group for the Advancement of Psychiatry, "Integration and Conflict in Family Behavior," Report No. 27, 1954, p. 1.

It seemed to us that such psychoanalytic concepts as "the unconscious," "repression," "introjection," "ambivalence," and so on are less useful in explaining family dynamics than they are in understanding the individual. When, however, more emphasis is placed on sociologic concepts, particularly those of "transaction" and "social role," data can be organized in a concise and simple enough manner to make such an outline practical in the daily work of a family agency. The authors are particularly indebted to Dr. John Spiegel for the use of these concepts in the more familiar therapeutic setting.[9] Spiegel also emphasizes that the usual psychodynamic terminology is inadequate in describing family dynamics. As he points out, the term "unconscious," when applied to the family, sounds [10] "too planned and too much under the control of one or more persons." He goes on to say that within the family, "Much of what occurs in the way of behavior is not under the control of any one person or even set of persons but is rather the upshot of complicated processes beyond the ken of anyone involved. Something in the group process itself takes over as a steering mechanism and brings about results which no one anticipates or wants, whether consciously or unconsciously."

Concepts for Organizing Family Dynamics

What concepts, then, will be useful in organizing an understandable framework for family dynamics? We believe that the motivational framework which deals with behavior in terms of goals and the methods of obtaining these goals is as useful in describing a family as in describing an individual. We also feel that the concept of adaptation—that is, family survival or integration in a given cultural milieu—should be the yardstick for determining what is normal and what is pathologically deviant. The adaptational concept is flexible enough to allow for variant but successful family patterns in a given culture. Another concept, borrowed from biology, is that of the "hierarchy of organization." Any organization (in this case, the family) must be considered both in terms of the lower organization which makes up its component parts, that is, the individual, and of the higher organization—the rela-

[9] John P. Spiegel, M.D., "The Social Roles of Doctor and Patient in Psychoanalysis and Psychotherapy," *Psychiatry,* Vol. XVII, No. 4 (1954), p. 369.

[10] John P. Spiegel, M.D., "The Resolution of Role Conflict Within the Family," *Psychiatry,* Vol. XX, No. 1 (1957), p. 2.

tionship of the family unit to the extended social system with the cultural values existing at a particular time and in a particular locale. As previously mentioned, we feel that the concepts of "social role" and "transactional field" are especially helpful.

Transaction

Transaction, as defined by Dewey and Bentley,[11] refers to a reciprocal, reverberating process, which occurs in any system of action or behavior. Such a system includes a two-phase, cyclical exchange, which is largely self-regulating and self-correcting. This seems to be a more useful concept than the more familiar one of interaction. Interaction implies the action of one person and the response of the other, while transaction encompasses a continuing exchange of communication between the individuals in a given field; there is a constant feedback which modifies the subsequent response of each individual. The following serves as an example of this transactional process.

The husband, a college teacher, returns home from giving a particularly successful and rewarding lecture that has been stimulating to his students. The questions and the enthusiasm of the students have elevated his self-esteem. He feels important and enters the house exuberantly, grabs his wife and kisses her, and in a very pleasant but authoritative way demands his dinner. She responds warmly to the embrace and says, "Sit down, dear. It will be ready in a few minutes." At the dinner table the wife cautiously and a little hesitantly reveals to her husband that she must go out this evening, so that he will have to stay home and baby-sit. The explanation given is that her job as a recreational director demands that she interview parents of prospective members. He protests and rather affectionately states that he was hoping that he could be with her this evening. However, she is firm and insists that she must leave him on this particular night. The husband now becomes angry and tries to assert his authority as head of the house, particularly since his self-esteem had been elevated because of the response in his classroom. He insists that he is too tired to bathe the children and put them to bed. The wife returns his anger, replying, "Well, if you would get your Ph.D. and make

[11] John Dewey and Arthur F. Bentley, *Knowing and the Known*, Beacon Press, Boston, 1949.

enough money to support us properly, I wouldn't have to go out at night to work!" By thus reducing his status as a man, she effectively overcomes his resistance, and he rather meekly acquiesces. Now she becomes the dominant person within the family (the breadwinner), while the husband passively takes over the mother role of bathing the children, putting them to bed, and staying home while his wife is out working. It is this kind of process that is meant when one speaks of a reverberating, cyclical exchange, which is self-regulating and self-correcting.

Social Role

As one can see, this process is dependent upon communication between the individuals in the transactional field. One of the most useful ways of describing this communication is in terms of the concept "social role." For example, in the illustration above the husband first plays the role of "successful teacher," and then the role of "the head of the household." However, in response to this wife's degradation of his role as the breadwinner, he shifts and assumes the role of the passive, feminine mother as his wife demands that she take over the roles of head of the house and breadwinner. By "role" is meant a description of behavior from the point of view of the social situation—the role being governed by inner motivational forces and outer cultural value orientations. For instance, the man in this family rather willingly acquiesces to accept the mother role because of inner motivational forces. It is also probably true that there are certain cultural forces in middle-class American life which tend to force the man into the mother role more often than in other cultures. Roles can be either consciously or unconsciously assumed. In this case the husband, while consciously rejecting the feminine role, unconsciously often assumes it.

Roles also can be assigned, accepted, or declined.[12] This wife, for example, assigned the role of mother to the husband. He tried to decline it but after her derogatory statements ultimately accepted it. Roles also can be described as implicit or explicit. Explicitly this wife accepted her role as wife and mother but implicitly was always rebelling against it, and her rebellion was nonverbally conveyed to her husband. Thus, the stability of a trans-

[12] Ralph Linton, *The Study of Man*, Appleton-Century, New York, 1936.

actional field depends upon a certain complementarity of role; equilibrium exists with high complementarity, and disequilibrium results from low complementarity. In the husband-wife transaction described above, high complementarity existed as long as the wife accepted her role as affectionate marriage partner and housekeeper. As soon as she asserted her demands by being the breadwinner, however, disequilibrium in the transactional field resulted, and equilibrium was re-established only by the husband's acquiescence to become the passive, feminine mother and even wife while the wife took over the role of husband and breadwinner.

The attempt at re-establishing equilibrium in a transactional process that is threatened by disintegration is called by Spiegel "re-equilibration." At times, a distorted or inappropriate complementarity may be established in order to maintain the transactional field. The role reversal in the husband-wife relationship is an example of this. Although these sociological concepts show some similarity to concepts in individual psychology, such as symptom formation, defenses, or reparative moves, it seems to us that the sociologic concepts are more useful.

It is obvious that an individual is constantly playing many social roles in his everyday life. In the occupational field he may be a school teacher; in the family, a husband, father, or son; in the economic sphere, a consumer; in the community, a leader. As with any concepts borrowed from other fields, there is relatively slow acceptance of transaction and social role in the practical science of human behavior. Since they are new, they may be difficult to understand at first; but it is hoped that their use in casework will be clarified to some degree by the examples that follow later in this report.

Devising an Outline

After members of the staff of our agency had reviewed the literature on cultural and sub-cultural value orientations and had engaged in considerable discussion of these new sociologic concepts with the psychiatric consultant, it was decided that an attempt would be made to construct an outline of family dynamics which would be useful in the family agency setting. A committee of the staff first met in December, 1955, and slowly evolved an outline which was presented to the total staff and psychiatric consultant for further revision. It was then used in a study of a number of families; in the fall of 1957 a final revision was made. This outline subsequently has been used in preparing case summaries for psychiatric consultation, in organizing the worker's thinking in preparation for supervisory conferences, in preparing case material for presentation to total staff, and, in some instances, it forms the basis for the case record.

Outline for Family Dynamics

I. Family Identifying Data
- A. List of persons in household by family role, name, and age
- B. Relatives out of home (similar data to above)
- C. Significant family dates, e.g., marriages, divorces, births, deaths
- D. Social and economic facts: race, religion, occupation and income, school level of children and adults, military status, housing and neighborhood, cultural background, group affiliations, contacts with other social agencies

II. Agency Contacts
- A. Date of initial contact or contacts
- B. By whom referred, reason for referral, relationship of referring person to family
- C. Family member who initiated contact, reason for contact
- D. Length and frequency of contact of each person being seen, how many caseworkers are involved, locale of contacts (home or office)

III. Current Social and Psychological Situation
- A. Pertinent elaboration of identifying data; physical descriptions of family members, home, and neighborhood; cultural patterns
- B. Family functioning, including:
  1. Housekeeping and living arrangements
  2. Eating and food preparation
  3. Money handling
  4. Discipline
  5. Recreation
  6. Family routines and rituals, if any
  7. Family values
- C. Description of each client in terms of:
  1. Problem as client sees it, verbalized feelings about problems
  2. Client's current life adjustment, including work, family, health, and recreation
  3. Nature of important relationships in client's life, including feelings about these persons
  4. Symptoms

5. Evaluation of client by other family members
6. Client-worker relationship, including worker's observations

D. If information is available and pertinent, similar descriptions of other family members

IV. Social History
A. History of each parent
B. Family history

V. Present Transactions
A. Cultural description of family from point of view of community, including an evaluation of identifying data
B. Degree and kinds of environmental stresses upon family and their effects upon family integration; the precipitating stress
C. Nature and degree of cultural and subcultural conflicts, if any, in terms of:
1. Differences of cultural values within family
2. Members' acceptance of family values
D. Characteristic handling of social roles by family members:
1. Roles accepted, rejected, and so on
2. Complementarity of roles or refusal to accept complementarity, giving reasons
3. Disparity between explicit (conscious) roles and implicit (unconscious) roles
4. Evaluation of failures to accept social roles
a. Internal stress (inner conflict)
b. External stress (not permitted to play role)
5. Cuturally inappropriate roles
6. Evaluation of individual's role playing by other family members
7. Deviations from characteristic handling of roles
8. Attempts at re-equilibration
E. Dominance pattern:
1. Stability or fluctuation
2. Rebellion against hierarchy of dominance
F. Family goals:
1. Common goals, if any
2. Appropriateness of goals
3. Success in achievement
4. Willingness of members to sacrifice personal satisfaction to family goal
G. Degree and kinds of satisfactions family provides to individual members

VI. Historical Perspective of Family Transactions

VII. Psychodynamics of Individual Members
A. Characterological descriptions:
1. Main and subsidiary traits and/or outstanding symptoms
2. Areas of inhibition and substitutes for inhibited areas

B. Basic conflicts
C. Developmental dynamics
D. Diagnosis

VIII. Family Treatment
A. Casework goals for family as unit:
1. What various members want agency to provide
2. Prediction of optimal family adjustment to be expected through casework treatment:
a. Modifications of individual behavior necessary to attain goal
b. Effect of behavioral modifications upon family transactions
c. Problems modifications might create in family equilibrium
B. Casework techniques needed to achieve modifications:
1. How many clients, how many workers, in what settings
2. Specific techniques to be employed and degree of their use, e.g., guidance, exploitation of defenses, insight
3. Timing of various techniques

Elaboration of Outline

The broad outlines of Sections I, II, III, and IV need little elaboration because of their similarity to a dynamic, psychological evaluation of an individual. Yet there are some important differences. Since the family as an entity is not able to express itself directly to the caseworker as does the individual client, the family must be evaluated primarily in terms of what its component units (individual clients) report. For this reason, there is an emphasis on an evaluation by several members of the family of the home situation, family problems, attitudes toward other family members (Section III, C and D). Also, the family cannot be viewed in its entirety in the agency's office; hence, it may be necessary to make a home visit to view the family in its usual setting in order to observe its cultural patterns and its relationship to the community. It is often true that the family's verbalized or conscious attitude may be quite different from that revealed by direct observations of the neighborhood in which it lives, its type of house, furnishings, relationships with the neighbors, and so on (Section III A).

The subheadings included under family functioning (Section III, B) provide a framework for describing family behavior. This information gives us the data by which to judge whether the family is functioning efficiently or whether there is an extravagant use of physical and psychic energy in everyday living. Do the beds get made, the children get bathed, the meals get prepared automatically?

Or is every action fraught with conflict and indecision? That is, are the typical social roles accepted automatically? Such automatic assumption of roles in the family may be considered the equivalent of the ego functioning in an individual.[13] This section should delineate whether the problems are limited to one area—for instance, the discipline of the children—or whether they invade the entire family structure. It is from this information that an evaluation of the social roles will be made.

At first glance, family values (Section III, B, 7) may seem to belong more properly to present transactions (Section V). In this section, however, we mean the value system of the family as expressed in the family's behavior and verbalized sentiments. These values affect to a considerable degree family cohesion and family attainments. For example, one family may put great stress upon academic achievement in striving upward toward social betterment. Another family may emphasize accumulation of material possessions to the same end. Some families are strongly identified either positively or negatively with their national background, their race, or their religious denomination, while other families live alone and appear to have no group identification. Some families value masculinity, some femininity. Some deny sexual differences. To understand the family as a unit, it is also important to know whether there is a family cohesiveness in these beliefs. This evaluation is as important as evaluating what the family does, and may be considered comparable to the "ego ideal" of individual psychology. These data are essential for evaluating the family under family goals (Section V, F), as well as determining the degree and kinds of satisfaction the family provides for the individual members.

It is the intent in the first four sections of the outline to provide a comprehensive and dynamic description of the family as it is presently constituted. The rest of the outline provides a system for evaluating the data collected (Sections V, VI, and VII) and criteria for planning treatment for the family unit (Section VIII). The evaluative and treatment planning sections of the outline are perhaps less familiar to many caseworkers than are the earlier sections. In Part II we shall discuss the evaluative and treatment sections, using an illustrative family history.

[13] Helen Harris Perlman, "The Basic Structure of the Casework Process," *The Social Service Review,* Vol. XXVII, No. 3 (1953), pp. 308–315.

Part II

In Part I, concepts found useful in understanding family dynamics, particularly the concepts "transaction" and "social role," were discussed. The necessity for recognizing and understanding cultural and sub-cultural value orientations was emphasized. An outline for organizing and evaluating family data was proposed, and Sections I–IV of this outline were discussed in terms of what data are unique in understanding the family, in comparison with the data necessary for an individual psychodynamic formulation. In Part II, the sections on family transactions and casework planning are emphasized. Since these are the evaluative sections of the outline and lean heavily on sociologic concepts, they require extensive explanation. For clarification, the discussion is focused on an illustrative family history. The outline is followed more rigidly in this presentation than is necessary in its day-to-day use.

This is a white Protestant family consisting of Mr. and Mrs. L, parents in their middle thirties, and three sons, ranging in age from 6-year-old John to a 14-month-old boy. The father teaches at a small college, and the mother contributes to the family income by working week ends and during summer vacations as director of a teen-age social program for the children of wealthy parents. Mr. L takes over all housekeeping and child-care chores while his wife works. The presenting complaint was the intolerable behavior of John, who was described by the mother as demanding, overdependent, fearful, and chronically dissatisfied. She used almost the same words in describing her husband. She felt that both of them were intelligent but ineffectual. The 3-year-old child was considered intellectually slower than John but lovable. He had no problems save a dislike for all foods except sweets and peanut butter. The youngest was no problem because he was "just a baby." Almost from the beginning Mrs. L spent as much time discussing her marital problems as she devoted to her son's difficulties. She was also full of bitter complaints that her older brother had inherited the family business, although she felt as competent as he to run it. Mr. L described many difficulties at work, complaining of the poor academic standards of the college; and, although he minimized the danger, apparently his job was in jeopardy. Both Mr. and Mrs. L were seen by the same caseworker while, at the recommendation of a child guidance clinic, John was seen by a different worker.

Present Transactions

Cultural Description: Again we wish to emphasize that this is an evaluation, not of the individual members of the family, but of the family as a unit. Section V of the outline may be compared to a characterological description of the individual. The family under consideration, for instance, may be considered quite deviant, although not unsuccessful. The family lives in a lower-middle-class subdivision, yet is upper middle class from the educational point of view, since both adults are college graduates, and the husband, who has had postgraduate education, is now functioning as a professor.[14] Most of the people in the neighborhood have not had education beyond high school. There is further discrepancy, not unusual in our present culture, in that the family has less earned income than its neighbors. The income is supplemented, however, by gifts of money received from Mrs. L's mother. The family is isolated from its immediate neighborhood and, in fact, isolated from other social groups as a family unit because of the aloofness of Mr. L, although his wife participates in women's activities—garden clubs and so forth—with a group of women of similar educational status but of much higher economic status. Thus, it would seem that the family appears to the community as deviant but successful, since the community accepts the fact that professors are intellectuals and are expected to be eccentric and poor.

Environmental Stresses: It is important to identify those external stresses more or less beyond the control either of the family as a unit or of the individual family members and to evaluate their impact upon the family's functioning. These stresses may or may not lead to agency contact. In this family the outstanding environmental stress, the father's small salary, was chronic; and the family had worked out certain techniques to accommodate to it. The one external stress which might have precipitated seeking outside help was the fact that John, who had long been a problem to the family, was now ready for school and thus took the family's problem into the community. Hence, there was a real community pressure on the family to modify the child's behavior. This demand threatened the family's integration, because the parents ran the risk of being exposed as failures and also because the father's passive acceptance

[14] For purposes of uniformity, Serjamaki's system of five classes is used: upper class, upper middle class, lower middle class, working class, lower class.

of, and perhaps even identification with, the problem son, might deter modification of the boy's behavior. However, as we shall see later, it is likely that the mother's internal conflicts were more influential in precipitating her contact with the agency than any specific external forces.

Cultural Conflicts: The social and economic mobility of our present culture often leads to cultural conflicts between generations. Frequently such conflicts occur between Americanized children and Old World immigrant parents. Even more often there are more subtle conflicts between sub-cultural values within the same generation. It was this sub-cultural conflict between husband and wife that became one of the central problems within the L family. In her earlier years, Mrs. L's internal conflicts and the influence of a minister prompted her to accept a missionary set of values; this complemented the value system of her husband, whose childhood culture pattern was determined by a semirural, inhibited, Calvinistic sub-group in which individuality was prized more than conformity. The result was that both were willing to rebel against the dominant cultural value system of their adult environment. However, shortly before agency contact, Mrs. L, as she had in her teens, began to vacillate between these self-sacrificing, altruistic attitudes and those of her parents, which were typical of the urban, merchant group who valued competitiveness, ambition, vigorous action, and economic success, while depreciating intellectuality.

Characteristic Handling of Social Roles: In this part of the outline a number of relatively new concepts, for example, social role, are utilized in understanding the family transaction. Of primary interest is how the various members handle ascribed social roles. By ascribed roles we mean those social roles such as wife, father, daughter, which are assigned to the individual by cultural forces regardless of innate ability. These roles are differentiated from achieved roles [15] in that personal choice and ability determine the latter; for example, doctor, foreman, senator. In this family, Mrs. L is less successful in her ascribed roles—mother, daughter, and wife—than she is in the achieved roles of community leader and wage earner. On the job she assumes responsibility, carries it through, and administers the program efficiently and imaginatively.

[15] Talcott Parsons, *The Social System,* Free Press, Glencoe, Ill., 1951, p. 64. "Achievement-oriented roles are those which place the accent on the performances of the incumbent, ascribed roles, on qualities or attributes independent of specifically expected performances."

She is active and receives recognition and approval for her activities in the garden club, faculty wives' club, and church. However, in the ascribed role of mother, although she is successful in handling the mechanical aspects of child care, she is chronically resentful and punishing, particularly in regard to her oldest, rebellious son. There seems to be a constant battle for control between mother and son, which suggests that the unconscious role in relation to John is more that of a sister and thus that a competitive sibling relationship exists. It is also clear that, while consciously feeling she is an adult, Mrs. L implicitly maintains a dependent child relationship with her own mother. Similarly, Mrs. L meets the minimal requirements of the housekeeper role, but her total lack of pleasure in the performance of this role suggests that she sees it as a prerequisite to being allowed the greater satisfaction of performing the role of community leader. Although she functions adequately as a sexual partner, her handling of the wife role cannot be considered successful because of her derogatory attitude toward her husband. Since this is so characteristically a part of her competitive attitude toward her brother, it is suggested that implicitly the relationship between husband and wife is one of brother and sister. Thus, Mrs. L demonstrates that the failure to handle social roles may be the result of conflicts between explicit and implicit roles, the latter representing unconscious motivations.

Mr. L fails to some degree in both ascribed and achieved roles, since both are affected by his aloofness. When he is at home, he usually keeps busy reading, correcting papers, occasionally watching television, or working in the garden. When his wife plans to be away from home, she assigns to him the role of mother, which he usually assumes without overt protest. His easy assumption of the mother role suggests, along with his passivity, an implicit acceptance of it. As a husband, Mr. L is "considerate" and gently affectionate; yet his inability to compete and thus to provide financially leads to his failure as protector and as a source of dependency gratifications. Combined with a covert condescension toward Mrs. L's social activities, these attitudes interfere markedly with his handling of the husband role. He is most successful in the achieved role of teacher, in which his patience and kindliness are real assets and in which he displays qualities of imagination and ingenuity not apparent in his other roles. However, he again fails as a colleague, withdrawing from both peers and superiors because of repressed chronic resentment against authoritative figures, with a suggestion that at work he implicitly plays the role of little boy seeking preferential treatment from parental figures.

In the eyes of both parents, John fails in his role as son. His mother objects mainly to his "babyish" behavior of whining, nagging for attention, and refusal to dress himself; his father complains of his messiness and deplorable table manners. Thus, both parents assign to him a more mature role than he is chronologically capable of assuming. His reaction to their demands, becoming even more whiny and fussy and occasionally enuretic, suggests that, implicitly—and perhaps to some extent explicitly—he is playing the role of younger child or even baby. This reaction is reinforced by the open admiration of both parents for the "cuteness" of the next younger sibling. On the other hand, in play situations John implicitly assumes the role of mother, playing only with younger children and bossily assuming the leader role, often inappropriately inventing impossibly intricate games which he insists his playmates perform by his rules.

Thus, it is clear that, to deepen understanding of the family, it is important to evaluate role performance and to distinguish between implicit and explicit roles. When marked disparities exist between implicit and explicit roles, conflict is inevitable. It is also important to establish where and in what circumstances complementarity between various roles exists. Assumption of even inappropriate roles can result in family equilibrium, if complementarity exists and if the roles are not so culturally inappropriate that community displeasure is brought to bear on the family. For instance, Mr. L sometimes assumes the mother role while his wife is assuming the father role by being gainfully employed. As this open role reversal occurs only on week ends, the cultural inappropriateness is not marked; and, since this reversal also meets the emotional needs of the parents, family equilibrium is maintained. If Mr. L were to spend most of his time at home while Mrs. L became the principal wage earner, the family as a unit would be so culturally deviant that conflicts would be precipitated. However, the internal problems of each parent would make such a total role-reversal highly unlikely, since both Mr. and Mrs. L are ambivalent about sexual identification and have some guilt in regard to the assumption of the inappropriate social role. Apparently there is no complementarity in transaction between the parents and oldest son. Thus, there is constant disequilibrium and no constructive attempt at re-equilibration. This transaction has become the primary problem and the reason for the family's seeking help. The highest degree of complementarity seems to exist in the transactions occurring between each parent and persons outside the family. Mrs. L's performance in her role as club president is welcomed and appreciated by her more passive women friends. Mr. L's achievement in the role of teacher is valued by his students and respected by the dean.

Dominance Pattern: In any organized system, such as the family, there is a hierarchy of organization with a dominance pattern. This pattern often is culturally determined. However, it is often based on intrafamilial relationships determined by personality, economic dependence, or physical coercion.[16] Despite the fact that in the United States today there is a characteristic leveling of status differentiation in family roles, the usual hierarchy of dominance is considered to be father, mother, and children in chronological order. This pattern is not always followed, however. Mother, for example, may be dominant in certain areas, such as handling money, while father is still considered to be head of the household. In some families the dominance pattern is inconsistent, with dominance shifting from one person to another. Such inconsistency usually represents some conflict in family transactions. However, a general acceptance by family members of the dominance pattern will result in equilibrium, even when the pattern is quite deviant. In the L family there is a fairly consistent dominance pattern of mother, father, John, younger children. The father accepts this pattern, but John openly rebels against it and, by his coercive demands, vies for the dominant role himself. John's refusal to accept a subordinate role is implicitly encouraged by the parents' wanting him to be a grownup; at the same time it threatens their own position in the family.

Family Goals: If the family is a unit, there should be some identifiable common goal which must be evaluated as to its appropriateness in terms of the capabilities of the various members of the family as well as in terms of outside forces which may be beyond the control of the family itself. Initially, the L family's goals were those of a self-sacrificing, altruistic, missionary family, dedicated to edu-

[16] Earl L. Koos, *Families in Trouble,* Kings Crown Press, New York, 1946, p. 48.

cation and rejecting the more materialistic, competitive aspects which were prominent in the wife's background. The fact that both husband and wife are of superior intelligence and educational background made this a feasible and relatively appropriate goal, except that the underlying motivation was probably neurotic in both instances—the wife rebelling against her family mores and the husband shunning aggressive competition. This goal was successfully achieved in that the family overcame the earlier tribulations of postgraduate education with all of its required sacrifices, since both Mr. and Mrs. L apparently were willing to sacrifice personal gratification for this common goal. If family integration is to be maintained, the family as a unit must provide satisfactions to the individuals which outweigh the sacrifices the individual makes for the family good. However, when Mrs. L renounced some of her missionary zeal soon after her father's death, dissatisfaction with family goals ensued. The present family goal is less clear. Mrs. L wants a higher economic status and wider social relationships for the family, but Mr. L derides these goals. Mrs. L is not only willing to work for her goals but pushes her husband to achieve them, while Mr. L is not willing to work for them and denies their value.

Satisfactions Family Provides to Individual Members: As the economic and educational functions of the family dwindle almost to the vanishing point, the family as a source of gratification of personal needs becomes more important. Therefore, in understanding the family as a unit, this function of the family must not be overlooked. Despite the open and covert conflicts, the L family provides considerable satisfactions to its members. The parents have a real depth of tender feeling for each other, and the children were all wanted by both parents. In addition, Mrs. L's strength, though often expressed in hostile ways, provides both her husband and John with some gratification of their dependency needs. Mr. L's gentleness and somewhat absent-minded kindness give Mrs. L the tenderness she feels she never had from her own parents. As illustrated earlier, neurotic needs are also met, but the positive values that this family has should not be underestimated. The family as an entity provides a haven, a place in which the individual members can be free to express their true feelings, even if this expression results in dissension.

Historical Perspective of Family Transactions

One can interpret changes in family integration in terms of a longitudinal or historical view of the family as a unit. For instance, as earlier described, several years before the L family came to the agency there was a much higher degree of complementarity and therefore more family equilibrium. During the period when Mr. L was a graduate student, he was not expected either by the culture or by his wife to earn or to compete in society at large. The wife's working at that time was culturally accepted; she, herself, saw her working as a temporary measure. Both husband and wife were still playing the roles of dependent children, since her father was contributing to their support. John was still too young to be able to act out his rebellion. The change occurred when the maternal grandfather died. His death cut off financial support and forced Mr. L to take a teaching job before he had fully completed his academic work. The grandfather's death also created a change in Mrs. L's internal problems.

Psychodynamics of Individual Members

Basic to understanding the family unit is an awareness of the intrapsychic life of each of the family members. In several of the earlier sections reference has been made to the internal problems of the family members as related to their place in the family. It seems valuable to identify, as is done in Section VII of the outline, the more uniquely individual problems of each person. It has already been mentioned that Mrs. L has some masculine, aggressive strivings, probably based on intense sibling competition and her own rebelliousness toward the control of her parents. Apparently she was also denying incestuous impulses in selecting a husband so different from her father and cultural values so different from those of her own family. In the past, guilt attached to these impulses kept her involved in a vacillating, ingratiating, rebellious, and dependent relationship with her parents. The death of her father liberated her from this defensive reaction formation, with the result that she began to demand more material gratification from her husband and thus disturbed the previously established family equilibrium. Clinically, Mrs. L appears to be having a neurotic, depressive reaction superimposed on a passive-aggressive personality.

Mr. L's passivity and his unconscious wishes to be a woman have also previously been suggested. His most pressing internal problem seems to be a sense of inadequacy accompanied by intense guilt, which is expressed in a fear of competition, a fear of success, and an aversion to pleasure. A clinical diagnosis of obsessive neurosis based on a passive-dependent personality was made. The child guidance clinic found John to be a passive, insecure boy, who lacks a healthy self-concept and who denies both his dependency needs and his aggressive impulses, expressing them only indirectly by projection upon the next younger brother. He attempts to deny his feelings of inadequacy and to compensate for them by using intellectualization. It was suggested that his anxiety is interfering with productive use of his superior intellectual capacity. Some compulsiveness was also noted.

Family Treatment

Casework Goals: The ultimate purpose of any attempt to understand family dynamics is to provide an effective guide to the methods most suitable for helping the family achieve a higher state of equilibrium, a state that will provide maximum satisfaction to the individual members while maintaining the unity of the family group. Thus, it is necessary to consider treatment plans in relation both to the welfare of the individuals in the family and to the common good. Section VIII of the outline is concerned with the formulation of treatment goals and techniques.

The L family sought help ostensibly because of difficulties with their rebellious son—a valid and important problem. From the family dynamics it is obvious, however, that this problem is secondary to the over-all family disintegration which began when Mrs. L started to express disappointment in her husband and thus her anticipated disappointment in family achievement. Mr. L recognized that he and his wife had problems with the oldest son. He was unaware, however, that his neurotic acceptance of the role reversals within the family created a family problem. The conflict, as he saw it, centered on his failure to progress satisfactorily in the professional area, a failure resulting from personal inhibitions and character deviations of long standing which, as our formulation of family dynamics indicates, were aggravated by his inappropriate role within the family. Despite these negative factors, the high intelligence of both parents and the shared desire for help suggested a promise of future stability as well as the potentiality for family achievement. Nevertheless, the well-established neurotic traits in both Mr. and Mrs. L make one cautious in establishing high family goals to be achieved through casework methods alone. This consideration suggests that, if casework could induce family stability, further psychiatric help for one or both parents might be indicated.

For instance, to expect that Mr. L's personality would change sufficiently so that he could assume the social role of provider, as it was assumed by Mrs. L's father and which Mrs. L now seemed to expect, would be unrealistic on two accounts. Mr. L's masochistic passivity could be resolved only by prolonged psychoanalytic treatment, which he at this time is neither willing nor able to accept. Also, Mr. L has already invested considerable time and money in acquiring advanced education and seems to have natural abilities in this area, despite his inhibitions and failure to complete his Ph.D. thesis. On the other hand, Mrs. L's recent demand that the family be more like her parental family was probably the result of a maturing process, despite its immediate adverse effect, since she was renouncing her own defensive masochism and reaction formation. If this is so, it would seem possible that she could give up this materialistic competitiveness and drop her need to play the role of sibling with her husband and son, or the role of the masculine provider, if her husband could obtain status in her eyes. He could most easily acomplish this goal, not through business competitiveness, but by the social prestige of a Ph.D. degree and being a professor in an academic atmosphere, such as a small college town, where these accomplishments would give social status. Also, shifting from a lower-middle-class housing development in a large metropolitan community to a small college town would reduce some of the community pressures disturbing the family equilibrium.

Through casework treatment Mr. L might be helped to see that women are not necessarily dangerous or depreciating and that his own professional achievement did not have to mean destroying either his siblings or his father. He could then give up the role of the angry little boy who rebels because he isn't the favorite. Whether or not he can do this will depend to a large extent on Mrs. L's realization that her own unconscious need to degrade her husband defeats her conscious aspirations for the family.

Such changes in the individuals' behavior patterns, unless appropriately timed, would only reinforce the present distortions in role playing and enhance the present disequilibrium. It is important to guard against one partner's beginning to change before the other is capable of tolerating this new behavior. If Mrs. L, for example, begins to relinquish the dominant role in the family before Mr. L has sufficient strength to assume part of it, her extreme disappointment in him will return and will probably result in more open, critical attacks upon him. Such behavior on her part will drive him further into his characteristic withdrawal. Since Mr. L's attempts to reinstate himself in his wife's favor are of the same type that succeeded in his son-mother transaction, that is, to do more housework, his customary attempt at re-equilibration would only demonstrate again to his wife his inadequacy as a male and thus reinforce her earlier pattern of taking over the male role within the family.

On the other hand, assertiveness on Mr. L's part, before Mrs. L realizes her sibling competitiveness and resentment of the female role, would only stir up a highly competitive sibling relationship with threatening retaliation, the very thing that the husband fears and tries to avoid by remaining passively rebellious. It can be anticipated that the more normal assumption of the male-female roles by the parents would provide a better climate in which John could mature and should also help him to work out a more satisfactory identification. If the sibling transactions between the parents and between John and his mother disappear, the parents' expectations of John will be more appropriate for his chronological age.

Casework Techniques: Because timing is such a vital matter in planning treatment for this family, so that changes in the individuals will not induce a further lack of complementarity in their social roles, it seems best to have one caseworker for both Mr. and Mrs. L. One worker will be more sensitive to the changes in the transactional process between the marital partners. Since paranoid patterns are not predominant in the personality structure of either Mr. or Mrs. L, it is to be expected that both can establish a meaningful and trustful relationship with the same worker. Another indication for the use of one worker is the fact that both clients are strongly motivated to maintain the marriage; therefore, the problem of the worker's taking sides with one or the other client will not be a great threat to family integration. There will be advantages in having a female worker who, throughout the relationship, can demonstrate to Mrs. L that a woman can accept her role without anger and resentment and demonstrate to Mr. L that women are not a threat to his masculinity. Support will be necessary for both, as neither now feels he is getting adequate support from the other. Encouraging them to be introspective about their feelings will be important if it is accompanied by at least superficial insight. Use of confrontation will help Mrs. L to realize that she degrades her husband and will not let him assume the role that she consciously expects of him, while Mr. L must see that he is reacting to his wife as he did in the son-mother transaction—placating the wife by helping her with the housework. He must realize that his wife can accept him as a strong male and will actually be more giving rather than retaliating if he plays this role. Use of clarification should help Mrs. L develop insight into the confusion in her feelings toward her son and her husband, as well as into how these feelings are intertwined, and also into the confusion in her feelings between brother and husband, and how they, too, are intertwined. When Mr. and Mrs. L are ready to accept John as the little boy that he really is, actual guidance regarding the appropriate expectations for a child of his chronological age must be given.

It seems necessary for John to have a separate worker, since he now feels that his parents are either unreliable (father) or dangerously destructive (mother). Without his own worker there would be a danger of identifying the caseworker with either one or the other parent. Expression of his feelings, particularly the angry feelings, without danger of retaliation is important, as is the development of pride in his role as the oldest child and a growing emulation of father—particularly as Mr. L becomes stronger and can handle mother.

Conclusion

This outline for organizing data to clarify family dynamics has gradually evolved from experience in applying variations of the outline to families under casework treatment in a family service agency. It is realized that such an outline will have to be continuously revised on the basis of experience and with the further development of the concepts of social role and transaction as applied to the practical science of human behavior. For instance, recently Dr. Spiegel has elaborated a number of new concepts for describing disequilibrium in a transactional process and attempts at re-equilibration, using such concepts as cognitive, goal, allocative, instrumental, and cultural discrepancies, and dividing re-equilibration procedures into two large groups, those of "role induction" and those of "role modification." [17] Other workers in the fields of sociology, psychiatry, anthropology, and social work will have other contributions, and eventually we shall need to integrate them conceptually. In the meantime those of us in the helping professions must learn to select those concepts which are of most use to us and to incorporate them, a few at a time, into our practice.

[17] John P. Spiegel, M.D., "The Resolution of Role Conflict Within the Family," *Psychiatry*, Vol. XX, No. 1 (1957), pp. 1–16.

FAMILY-ORIENTED TREATMENT OF MARITAL PROBLEMS [1]

M. Robert Gomberg

A THOROUGH PRESENTATION of the treatment process in work with marital problems in a family agency would require an examination of such basic casework assumptions and concepts as the need to understand character structure, personality development, and the dynamics of interpersonal relations, as well as the relation of these psychological factors to psychosocial diagnosis, to the casework method, and to differentiated treatment goals. Obviously it is not possible to present so comprehensive a review in this paper. Our

[1] Published in *Social Casework*, January 1956. Based on a paper presented as one in a lecture series sponsored by the Psychiatric Forum Group in New York.

purpose is to discuss the special aspects of "family-oriented" treatment of marital problems in a family agency.

Family diagnosis and family-oriented treatment, by definition, throw the spotlight on the interaction between the significant members of a family; in a marital problem, on the interaction between husband and wife. Although a sound clinical understanding of each partner is essential, it is equally important that the relationship between the partners be understood. This interaction should be viewed as a vital phenomenon, crucial to the marital adjustment and therefore crucial in treatment.

Only recently have we focused attention on the interaction in a crucial relationship, such as marriage, and recognized it as a separate factor—something beyond the intrapsychic phenomena of the individual personalities involved. It is interesting to note the development of the literature on the subject, through which a common thread seems to run.[2]

In essence, this literature stresses that new knowledge must be added to the existing body of knowledge about personality development, motivation, change, treatment techniques, and so on. It also suggests a need to reconsider, and possibly to correct, certain assumptions on which we have based our practice. If this impression is correct, what assumptions require re-evaluation and revision? The basic one, we believe, is that the quality of a marital relationship is only a by-product of the degree of health or disturbance in the personalities of the two partners.

From the traditional position, the marital relation is viewed on a one-dimensional screen, showing only the healthy and/or neurotic behavior of each partner but leaving out the "new compound" formed by the interaction between the two personalities. This view does not show a second dimension—the use that each partner makes

[2] M. Robert Gomberg and Frances T. Levinson (eds.), *Diagnosis and Process in Family Counseling—Evolving Concepts through Practice,* Family Service Association of America, New York, 1951.

Nathan W. Ackerman, M.D., "The Diagnosis of Neurotic Marital Interaction," pp. 148–162 of this volume. Reprinted from *Social Casework,* April 1954.

Sidney Berkowitz, "Some Specific Techniques of Psychosocial Diagnosis and Treatment in Family Casework," *Social Casework,* Vol. XXXVI, No. 9 (1955), pp. 399–406.

Bela Mittelmann, M.D., "Simultaneous Treatment of Both Parents and Their Child," in *Specialized Techniques in Psychotherapy,* Gustav Bychowski, M.D., and J. Louise Despert, M.D. (eds.), Basic Books, New York, 1952, pp. 103–118.

Otto Pollak, "Relationships between Social Science and Child Guidance Practice," *American Sociological Review,* Vol. XVI, No. 1 (1951), pp. 61–67.

of the other. Because the constructive and destructive elements of the interaction between the partners are omitted, we do not get a true picture of the real "balance" or "equilibrium" that has been attained in the marriage.

Clinically, the addition of this new compound has two implications: first, a prerequisite to a "good" marriage and a "good" family is not necessarily two neurosis-free individuals, however desirable such health may be; second, it is possible to achieve substantial improvement in conflicted marital relationships without working through all the neurotic elements in each partner's personality.

Caseworkers in family agencies, working closely with psychiatrists over a considerable period of time, have been developing techniques for this type of treatment. The treatment of marital problems represents a substantial part of the case load of all family agencies.[3]

It is important to underscore that selection of the family for marital counseling or casework treatment must be made on a sound diagnostic basis. Many marital conflicts are symptomatic of pathological disturbances that contraindicate casework help. When possible, these disturbed persons are referred for psychiatric treatment. However, for a large number of families, casework—with psychiatric diagnosis and consultation as needed—is an appropriate treatment. The goal of casework is not to bring about character change or to treat the pathological processes. Casework deals with the adaptive functions of the ego. When the marital partners have sufficient ego strength or maturity, when the interaction between them is sufficiently constructive—despite certain disruptive forces at work—casework is able to build on the strengths within the family Gestalt.[4]

Dr. Jules V. Coleman describes casework method and goals in the following way:

> In psychoanalytic terminology, casework is a method of psychological treatment concerned with the reality aspects of ego functioning. Its purpose is to stimulate the automatic organizational and integrational impulses of the ego in dealing with reality problems. It does so by resolving specific conflict responses through interpretation with concurrent emotional support. In its therapeutic

[3] In the Jewish Family Service of New York, of some 3,500 families that received extended casework service in 1954, more than a third came for help with a conflicted marital relationship.

[4] Sidney L. Green, M.D., "Psychoanalytic Contributions to Casework Treatment of Marital Problems," *Social Casework*, Vol. XXXV, No. 10 (1954), pp. 419–423.

attitude, it attempts to create an optimal transference situation, i.e., a positive relationship, and to maintain it, through focus on current material and reality-oriented interpretation, and by avoiding dependence stimulation. It interprets preconscious material, helping to bring out what the client is trying to say but cannot make clear because of anxiety, and also attempts through interpretation to clear up and to allow the client to dispense with the presenting screen of distortion and misconception.[5]

Casework treatment of marital problems must be based on sound diagnosis; moreover, the diagnosis must be adapted to a particular treatment purpose and method. To arrive at a psychosocial diagnosis in a marital problem, therefore, we need: (1) a clear clinical picture of the separate personalities; (2) a psychological evaluation of the relationship; (3) an assessment of the degree of readiness of the persons to use help, and of the influence of social, cultural, and economic factors.

In summarizing the factors to be considered in evaluating a marital relationship for purposes of rehabilitation, Dr. Ackerman states:

If we are motivated to rehabilitate the mental health of a disturbed marital relationship, we must take into account not only the neurotic core of behavior but also the malleable aspects of character in both partners, the factor of realistic strength in their personalities, the residually healthy ego tendencies, the positive qualities of the marital relationship and of the family life, and the motivation of both partners for change; all these are needed to counterbalance neurotic tendencies.[6]

In order to illuminate the casework treatment process in marital problems, we shall present the B case in some detail. It illustrates (1) concurrent treatment of both husband and wife; (2) the complementary nature of the personality problems of the two clients and the negative and constructive elements in their interaction; (3) the conflict between unresolved personal problems stemming from earlier family life and the counteracting personality strengths and healthy ego drives.

Presenting Problem

Mrs. B, 28, an attractive young school teacher, applied to the agency for help with her marital problem. She knew something

[5] "Psychotherapeutic Principles in Casework Interviewing," presented at the Annual Meeting of the American Psychiatric Association, Cincinnati, Ohio, May 11, 1951.

[6] Ackerman, *op. cit.*, p. 152.

about the services of the agency. She felt that her situation was reaching a point of desperation and that she needed help. She had been married for three years and had known her husband for three years prior to the marriage. During the years of courtship and engagement the relationship had "matured and developed" and she had looked forward to marriage. She thought of her husband as strong, reliable, and intelligent. Their difficulties began about a year and a half before application.

She reported that she and her husband had bitter quarrels and arguments, followed by long periods of angry silence on his part. As she narrowed the area of her complaints, she spoke of his overcautious and methodical behavior. Although these traits had not offended her earlier, she now found herself growing increasingly tense and exasperated by them. She described herself as "spontaneous, outgoing, vivacious." Their differences kept them in perpetual conflict, and the satisfactions in their marriage seemed to have drained off. Their sexual relationship had become less satisfactory, and the many values and satisfactions that she had known earlier seemed to have slipped through her fingers. She said she could not see how they could continue their life together unless some change took place.

Her behavior, as first observed in the interview, seemed to be diametrically opposed to her husband's behavior as she described it. She seemed impulsive and highly emotional. The caseworker noted, however, that there seemed to be an over-determination in her enthusiasms. Even in the interview she laughed too hard and cried too hard. She seemed to play each emotion to the hilt; thus, in her own way she lacked the very spontaneity that she felt she missed in her husband.

Mrs. B was seen for a period of about two months before her husband began his treatment experience. Treatment continued for both of them then for one year.

Mrs. B's Patterns

Mrs. B came from a lower-middle-income family. Her father was in business and the family had always known modest economic security. Both her father and mother had some educational background and considerable interest in cultural activities, particularly in the arts. Mrs. B was the older of two children; she had a brother four years her junior. Mrs. B spoke of her family as a warm, closely knit unit, with many interests in common. The family had always been proud of her good scholastic record and her many social successes. She reported that their relatives were envious of their closeness.

The reported family closeness and family feeling seemed to be a significant factor in the personality development of this young woman. Actually, when we began to examine more closely the mother-daughter relationship, the father-daughter relationship, the sibling relationship, she reported a great many anxiety-producing experiences which might be assumed to have had an impairing effect on her personality development. An appraisal of only these unilateral relationships and their potentially harmful effects would lead to the conclusion that this girl's ego had been seriously impaired. We therefore had to account for the relatively high degree of personality development that she had achieved. It became clear, as we looked more closely, that within each of these separate relationships there had been certain supportive and constructive elements. Even more important, it was also evident that there had been nurturing qualities in the total family interaction that had contributed to her growth.

Mrs. B described her mother as an attractive, intelligent, but a highly self-centered and complaining woman. She had been hypochondriacal since Mrs. B's childhood. Her mother had told Mrs. B that she, the mother, had almost died at the time Mrs. B was born. Her mother had always seemed to respond with both enthusiastic interest and subtle rivalry to Mrs. B's activities; she expressed happiness about her daughter's many social advantages but at the same time talked about her own impoverished early life.

Two points are of interest. First, Mrs. B had been successful in her social life and in school. She always had had several close friends and a great many acquaintances, and took a leadership role. She had been a good student through grade school, high school, and college. She had enjoyed these experiences and gained a great deal from them. At the same time she was aware of a sense of guilt toward her mother. Quite early she had developed a feeling that somehow these pleasurable experiences by right belonged to her mother, who had been deprived of gratifications in her own youth. Thus, even as Mrs. B participated in them, enjoyed them in part, found success in them, and gained the approval of her peers and elders, a feeling lurked in the background that, by accepting these experiences for herself, she was continuing her mother's deprivations. It became clear that the so-called "spontaneity and impulsiveness" were essentially parts of a reaction formation; by plunging into experiences, she could not be charged with deliberately having chosen activities that "properly" belonged to her mother. Her mother's partially encouraging attitude about these experiences and Mrs. B's own satisfaction in them served to further her growth and development. But since the mother's attitude also engendered hostility and guilt, which Mrs. B had had to repress, her natural maturational process had been blocked and her self-image and values had become distorted.

Mrs. B reported that her father was a mild, passive person who was completely controlled by his wife. It was only after considerable discussion that Mrs. B was able to describe to the worker—or to admit to herself—the extent of her own positive feeling for him. She had deep affection for him and had been deeply disappointed in him. Very early in life she found that she could not rely on him. When she got into any kind of difficulty with her mother, even though she sensed that her father sided with her, she could never count on his support. There was a sense of something clandestine in her relationship to him. He never emerged as a strong parental figure within the home. She said, "Men are nice but you really can't rely on them."

A marked duality in her feeling and experience was also evident when she discussed her young brother. On the one hand, she described a warm, close relationship with him, recognizing the inevitable sibling rivalry and fighting, and telling amusing stories of her annoyance at him during her teen-age years. On the other hand, she told of her feeling that he had displaced her in her parents' favor, especially the mother's. The brother, like herself, had been an excellent student, winning many honors in both high school and college. He is currently successful in his professional career, and they continue to have frequent contacts.

One of the things that became clear was that Mrs. B's feelings about her family—her resentment at being displaced by her brother and at the mother's marked preference for the brother, her guilt in relation to her mother, her disappointment about the unreliable quality of her father's affection—had impelled her, very early in life, to woo people and to try to gain affection, admiration, and love at any price. She continued to try to recapture the feeling of "coming first." Her efforts to attract people now were not only motivated by a desire to fulfill natural affectional drives, but were also motivated by, and were accompanied with, anxiety and guilt. Because of her repressed resentment, hostility, and guilt, her efforts to attract interest and admiration, even when successful, were only partially satisfying and provided only limited growth-inducing experiences.

This pattern continued into adulthood. The over-all picture of this woman, at the time she sought help, was of one who was respected and admired by her friends and colleagues. There was no question but that these attainments gave her some satisfaction and that they strengthened the healthy aspects of her personality. On the other hand, it was equally clear that there was an imbalance between the energy that she expended in these pursuits and the amount of inner security and gratification she achieved from them.

Mr. B's Patterns

Mr. B, 30, is a chemist, and the only son of a rather well-to-do family. His father is a successful attorney. Mr. B described his family as a "close" one. Mr. B's father was a "family man," went to ball games and movies with his son, and so on. He was a very exacting taskmaster—a perfectionist when it came to such matters as cleanliness, morals, marks and achievement in school. Mr. B's mother was an ambitious, driving woman with many dreams about her son's future achievements.

Even in his earliest years, Mr. B sensed that he must produce "honors" if he was to find a secure place in the family, that he would be loved and judged according to his achievements. Being successful in school, in sports, and in his relationships with other youngsters therefore became of greater importance to him than finding personal gratifications in his activities. He was a good student, a fine athlete, and a successful member of clubs. These achievements obviously brought certain gratifications, but he paid for them on the altar of his parents' demands. They represented a security offering, a means of holding on to a precarious tie to their affections. Whatever he did, therefore, was under the closest surveillance, and he always had a feeling that "something more" was expected of him.

In spite of the exacting pressures placed upon Mr. B by his

parents, he undoubtedly received considerable love from both of them. His relatively mature adjustment indicated that many of his growth needs had been met. It was clear, however, that he felt a degree of uneasiness and uncertainty that was out of keeping with his capacities and achievements. He moved slowly and cautiously into new experiences; he calculated all risks; he wanted to know what he was getting into and what the chances were of succeeding. However, he was never immoblized. He was able to take on responsibility for decisions and to follow through on them.

Mrs. B had been attracted to Mr. B because of his steady, well-organized approach to life. His steadiness, which represented something that she lacked in herself, compensated for her own impulsiveness. Mr. B, in turn, was attracted to Mrs. B's outgoing, spontaneous qualities. Their respective patterns were not only defenses but were actually strong capacities that had been integrated into their respective egos and had been consolidated by reality successes. During their courtship and in the early years of their marriage, Mr. B relied heavily on Mrs. B's social ease. She broke the ground, made new relationships. With this preparation he found it much easier to communicate with people and to participate in social events. Conversely, Mrs. B found that his steadiness served as a check against "going too far."

Treatment of Mrs. B

In all therapy one must be alert to the defensive component in patterns of behavior, but not at the expense of overlooking the constructive values and ego strengths represented in them. In casework treatment, we attempt to draw upon and build upon the healthy aspects of the ego and to enlarge the scope and flexibility of the ego's functioning. An understanding of the negative component helps us to determine what should be handled directly and worked on in treatment and what should be avoided.

A thematic pattern emerged from Mrs. B's description of her various experiences with her husband. His behavior embarrassed her, and she then became anxious and hostile. It was usually some event involving other people that precipitated a crisis. Mrs. B was inclined to concur with opinions expressed by their friends, while Mr. B tended to raise questions. Later, when they were alone, she would go over the incident and reproach him for alienating people and losing their friends. In these disagreements she grew bitter and hostile and lost control of herself; he first argued and then withdrew into a sullen silence, and often went into another room to work. His silences infuriated her and at the same time made her increasingly anxious.

As Mrs. B grew more secure in the treatment relationship, she was able to admit that she was not in essential disagreement with her husband. It became clear that she became anxious about the attitude of her friends—that she feared losing the approval of the group.

In this first phase of treatment, Mrs. B began to recognize that she had been projecting blame onto her husband and had been creating conflict situations with him because of the anxiety she experienced in her social relationships. Her irritation at her husband subsided somewhat and she began to question her own attitudes. Why did she feel so insecure with a group? Recalling that this had not been true in the past, she became interested in the cause of her unhappiness and anxiety. She thought that her quarreling with her husband had begun about a year and a half earlier.

At this point—about two months after Mrs. B had sought help—Mr. B entered into treatment with the same worker. Before he began treatment, Mrs. B had been responsive to the worker and she seemed to be making progress in handling her relationship with her husband. Shortly after he began contact, Mrs. B's attitude toward the worker changed and the marital relationship seemed to become more strained. There was an angry edge to her voice in the interviews, and she again began to build up indictments against her husband. She was easily "hurt" by comments from the worker which previously she had accepted with interest and thoughtfulness.

After a few weeks the worker brought these changes in Mrs. B's attitude to her attention. At first Mrs. B protested but when the worker suggested that her shift in feeling might offer clues to understanding the reasons for her anxiety, she acknowledged that she had been aware of disappointment in the treatment and of anger at the worker.

During this period of treatment, the worker was supportive and reassuring, while at the same time he endeavored to clarify her feelings. The entrance of her husband into the treatment situation was the turning point in Mrs. B's own treatment. Before he became involved, Mrs. B was reliving the experience of the exclusive interest of a kind, protective, and guiding parent, symbolized in the worker. Mr. B's involvement threatened this exclusive interest, and Mrs. B re-experienced the feelings she had had in early life when her brother arrived on the scene and displaced her in her parents' affection. At this point, the worker became the symbol of the father who had never backed her and who had "deserted" her. The fear of being "pushed out" made her behave as though she had been. In trying to help Mrs. B see these connections, the worker kept the discussion on a reality-testing level. He pointed out that his attitude had not shifted and that he was still interested in helping her work out a better marital relationship. She was able to see how anxiety had distorted the reality situation and prevented her from expressing her real feelings.

This experience led her to re-examine a number of important factors in her use of herself. She recognized that she reacted in the same way in relation to her husband and her friends. She became aware, too, that she had tried to gain the worker's approval—had followed her pattern of wanting to be liked at any cost. As the relationship with the worker continued, Mrs. B discovered through having her attitudes and feelings accepted by the worker that security does not depend upon gaining another's approval. The experience of being able to agree or differ with what the worker said, without jeopardizing the relationship, had important therapeutic value.

As Mrs. B continued to examine her fear of being displaced and its connection with her marital difficulties, she became aware that the serious disagreements occurred after she and her husband began to talk seriously of having a child. Previously, they had spoken rather generally about having a family "when they were ready." She recalled that she had taken the position that she was the one who wanted the child and increasingly accused her husband of a lack of enthusiasm, while he had insisted that he really wanted a child. During treatment, she came to realize that she wanted a child—partly because "it was expected of her" and partly because she genuinely wanted one—and yet, at the same time, had considerable fear about having one.

Here again, on a reality-oriented basis, the worker helped her examine and clarify her feelings about having a child. With genuine relief she faced her own ambivalence. She realized that she had built up an image of herself as a person whose social role and position would include motherhood; she could not permit herself to have doubts about her readiness or wish to have a child. After expressing her unreadiness for this experience, she was able to move on to an examination of the reasons for her fears. Anxiety about having a child stemmed largely from the birth of her brother and her sense of being displaced by him.

Mrs. B reported that she and her husband discussed the things they talked about with the worker, and that, as a result, they seemed to be closer together; their social as well as their sexual relationship had greatly improved.

Throughout treatment, the worker kept the focus clearly on the marital relationship, and endeavored to relate Mrs. B's present attitudes and feelings about the past to the current conflict. She began to realize that her hostile and repudiating behavior against her husband stemmed not only from his pressure on her to have a child but also from her fear that, within her new family, she might again be displaced by a child. The fear of being rejected or displaced spilled over into many of her significant relationships—with her husband, with friends, and with the worker. As she attempted to protect herself against this anxiety, the unhealthy component of her "spontaneity" had come into exaggerated play. As a result, her husband's conservative and deliberative behavior had increased her anxiety. His failure to operate in line with her own defenses represented a threat to her. (In marital problems we frequently find the Pygmalion motif, where one partner seems to wish to remake the other person's personality; in reality he needs the marital partner to serve as a bulwark to strengthen his own defenses and sees the mate less as a separate person than as an extension of himself.)

Throughout the treatment of Mrs. B, we worked with feelings and attitudes that were readily accessible to her—her fear of rejection and displacement, her unreadiness to have a child, and her inability to face and acknowledge this feeling. In much of the material that she produced about her relationship to her father, mother, and brother, there were evidences of the unconscious oedipal conflict. These were never dealt with, as such. Mrs. B was helped to see that she had some justification for her resentments and that she had exaggerated her feeling of being unloved.

Treatment of Mr. B

Limitations of space do not permit a detailed review of the contact with Mr. B. A few points, however, will be mentioned. When he first came into treatment, he responded in the manner of a good and co-operative son. He stated that he was prepared to do anything to improve his relationship with his wife. He confirmed her picture of their courtship and the first year and a half of their marriage. In the early phase of treatment, he stated that he did not know why the problem had developed or what his wife wanted of him; she examined every statement he made, and no matter what he did it came out wrong. It seemed evident that her behavior had reawakened his earlier experience of having someone constantly expecting something of him and his own feeling of never being quite able to live up to these expectations. He was completely unaware of the extent to which he resorted to punitive and retaliatory behavior. He was unable to acknowledge, even to himself, that her provocative behavior had engendered resentment and hostility in him. Later he gradually recognized that his tendency to withdraw from a discussion with his wife was an indirect way of punishing her. Mr. B also came to recognize that his feelings were colored by his earlier experiences in his parental home.

As Mr. B was helped to clarify his own feelings and to distinguish between his "real" difficulties with his wife and his displaced resentments, he became more effective and helpful in the marital relationship and more tolerant of Mrs. B's upsets. He recognized the extent to which his own behavior, at least in part, had contributed to the difficulties between them, even if this was unrelated to the accusations that his wife made against him. Instead of just trying to understand what was wanted of him and then trying to produce it, he became more protective of his wife. Another significant factor was the improvement in their sexual relationship. Because of Mr. B's tendency to let his wife take the lead in many things, he had permitted the frequency of intercourse to drop off during the time Mrs. B had been upset. Mr. B was encouraged to assume more initiative, which he did. His greater ability to tolerate and to understand her disturbed feelings, together with his ability to become more assertive, led to improvement in the sexual aspect of their relationship.

Although Mr. B complained mildly about his wife's need to be active socially, it was apparent that he left all decisions about their activities to her. As he began to understand something of his dependency on her, he began to assume more responsibility for participating in the choice of activities. Mr. B was a less disturbed person than his wife. If a crisis in their relationship had not developed, he doubtless would have been comfortable in his usual way of functioning. The crisis and the treatment that followed served not only to place the marriage on a more effective basis, but to increase Mr. B's own self-understanding and maturation.

Evaluation

Mr. and Mrs. B were seen over a period of a year; Mrs. B had fifty interviews and Mr. B forty-one. At the end of treatment, both seemed to be functioning on a level that seemed to meet their respective needs. Each probably had certain unresolved, unconscious, neurotic problems, but each seemed to be drawing on the respective strengths of the other. In the two years following termination of treatment, they were seen twice for follow-up interviews at intervals of one year. There was evidence that they had maintained and increased the growth achieved in treatment. Mrs. B had had a child; when they were last seen, the child, a girl, was a year old. Both Mr. and Mrs. B reported a sense of well-being and stability in their family relationship.

Conclusion

This brief comment on concurrent treatment is pertinent: We believe that it is advisable that treatment, whenever possible, be made available to both partners in the reciprocal relationship of marriage. A number of technical questions require further exploration, such as the proper timing for involving the second partner, and whether one or two workers should carry the case. Although experience demonstrates that, by and large, both partners should be involved, there are times when this procedure is contraindicated. At present, we lean toward one worker's seeing both partners unless there are sound indications to the contrary. Technically, this procedure is more difficult and complicated, but has many advantages; in the case reported in this paper, Mrs. B's reaction to her husband's involvement in treatment with the same worker had important therapeutic value. When two workers carry the case, close collaboration between the workers is necessary.

The casework treatment of marital problems must be based on a psychosocial understanding of the two partners as individuals and of the interactive relationship between them which functions as a "third force."

The interaction of the personality traits and defensive patterns of the two marital partners takes place in many areas of their interrelationships and operates in both complementary and antipodal ways. The degree of marital balance that results is not necessarily identical with the degree of emotional health that the individual partners have achieved.

In casework with marital problems the arena for treatment of each individual is the adaptive functioning of the ego. Casework treatment enlists the ego's capacity for motility and object relationship to the fullest extent possible. Not least among the assets to draw on is the individual's ego-ideal of positive family life and of harmonious marital relationships.

FAMILY INTERACTION: ITS SIGNIFICANCE FOR DIAGNOSIS AND TREATMENT [1]

Frances Levinson Beatman

OUR INCREASED understanding of family interaction is itself a result of an interactive process—the interaction of various disciplines concerned with understanding man, his family, and his social

[1] Published in *Social Casework,* March 1957. Presented at the Biennial Meeting of the Family Service Association of America in Cincinnati, November 15, 1956.

setting, as these are influenced by physical, psychological, social, and cultural forces. From this interdisciplinary process, in which social workers are participants, is emerging a new frame of reference which includes not only an appreciation of these diverse influences in the development of personality but also an understanding of their dynamics in family interaction and behavior as family members move from one role to another and from one set of cultural influences to another.

Family interaction is an all-inclusive term for a multifunctional, multidimensional operation. Research may make it possible for us to extract from among the many interactive processes in family life a significant few that will serve to describe and classify a total family operation. Research is already being undertaken toward the development of a system of family diagnosis. The increased knowledge that will result should enable us not only to identify the stage in a family's life at which conflict instead of growth became predominant, but also to evaluate more quickly those interactive processes that give a positive direction to the family's functioning and those that promote family disturbance.

Acquiring a thorough understanding of family interaction at any stage in a family's development is a difficult process. It rests upon an ability to isolate the theme or motif in the family's relationships. Discovering this theme is the end result of sifting processes which bring to the fore the dominant intra-familial relationships and reveal their influence upon the development of the family members and upon their extra-familial relationships.

Although the emphasis in this paper is on the interactive processes within a family and their relationship to diagnosis and treatment, these processes do not exist in a vacuum. They are bounded on two sides by crucial phenomena that have causal implications in their own right. On the one side, the social and cultural forces that shape the mores and values of a people play a significant role; on the other are the unconscious psychic forces that are motivating factors in human behavior. In addition, diagnosis must include an individual appraisal of the personality, character structure, defenses, and pathology of each family member in order that the worker may understand the persons who are interacting in the family drama. The examination of the interactive processes is not a substitute for individual appraisal. Rather, it affords an enlarged view of personalities in action which enables us to understand how different personalities combine, either to offset in some degree individual neurotic tendencies or to intensify and aggravate such tendencies.

Interactive Patterns

In focusing on the subsequent thesis of this paper I shall concentrate primarily on the second of the complex of factors that includes (1) the individual internal, (2) the interactive interpersonal, and (3) the social cultural. This emphasis is not intended to minimize the significance of the other two aspects, but has been selected as the focus of this discussion. This three-fold complex is the frame of reference for understanding the individual's role concepts and identifications, his cultural orientations, his self-image, and his capacity to estimate and respond to day-by-day expectations and responsibilities in an appropriate manner. These pattern the diversified tendencies which can combine in an interactive process to create either family disturbance or family equilibrium.

The internal pattern of a family develops as each member tries to manipulate the various family relationships into a reservoir for the gratification of his own needs. Each member thus determines the alignments, negative and positive, that can be used to meet his needs, support his defenses, and give plausibility to his behavior as he carries his familial and extra-familial roles.

The family's internal resources provide one means of meeting and gratifying the needs of its members; jobs, school, friendships, or membership organizations also provide experiences through which the family member may secure emotional support that will aid him to function in a positive manner. Conversely, if the family's interactive patterns produce or maintain conflict, they may negatively influence the person's ability to function in his extra-familial roles and may produce a state in which the tension created spreads to other functional areas and his symptoms increase.

The caseworker's concern with the client's extra-familial experiences is similar to his concern with the intra-familial relationships. Diagnostically, both types of experience furnish data for understanding the personality in operation, and for practical purposes they both afford opportunities for corrective and constructive experience, in which each can be used to supplement the ego satisfactions and growth possibilities of the other.

One may learn about the personality dynamics and interactive patterns in a particular family through analyzing any one of a number of possibilities, such as family structure, family operation, or the manifestations of value orientation. Analysis of any of these would need to incorporate the influence of every other aspect of family life and would bring into play with varying emphasis all the same considerations.

Family Roles

Let us use as an as example the family roles through which the intra-familial relationships and business are conducted. Our social and cultural mores establish certain responsibilities and activities in line with specific family roles, and broadly define the various role relationships within the family group. To the broad social concept of role responsibility are added the individual's conscious estimate of the significance of a particular aspect of his role responsibility and the underlying unconscious motivations for his estimate. If a man says, "I want to earn just enough to support my family and spend the rest of my time on my hobbies," one needs to know what he is trying to express. Is he saying that he has never felt adequate in assuming adult responsibilities and is afraid to test his ability to succeed? Is he saying that women have never let him succeed and that he does not anticipate anything different from his dominating, forceful wife? Or is he saying that he has ambitions for himself as a novelist and that his plan has been carefully evaluated, is reality-oriented, and can be carried out within his family's standards and attitudes?

One also needs to determine his wife's concept of her role in relation to her husband as well as her concept of his role in relation to her. Is she a self-sacrificing woman whose needs are met by proving her ability to manage on little, and whose estimate of herself is enhanced by backing a future novelist? Or has she had a lifetime of inadequate men and does her husband's attitude and her recognition of its motivation produce a nagging, hostile relationship?

The man's concept of his role responsibility, his motivations, and his awareness of these in arriving at his role concept, the amount of support he receives from his wife, and the interactive relationship resulting from a sense of togetherness or separateness on this issue, influence his relationship to his job and his use of that job relationship to control the family and gratify his needs.

Interactions

One sees here the interaction of two personalities—their differing or shared concepts of the man's role in relation to the level of family income, and the woman's role in meeting the man's needs and supporting his dreams. The interaction can result either in the support by each of the other or in heightened tension and retaliatory behavior.

The family disturbance serves as the frame of reference within which one may seek to understand this criss-cross of influences and motivations. Family interaction affords us significant diagnostic material in this process.

As one looks at the clinical and dynamic diagnosis of each individual family member in combination with all the others, the diversified tendencies that operate to create family disturbances and those that tend to attain or reinstate family balance become evident. The interplay of the unconscious attitudes and emotions of the family members, while they may be producing a sadomasochistic relationship, may be meeting and supporting essential personality needs in each and making possible more adequate individual functioning. The ways in which family members carry their roles may have traits that would individually be considered liabilities, for example, a dependent man and a domineering woman. However, in the interaction of two particular individuals, the combined functioning may be mutually supportive and of benefit to the children.

The caseworker is concerned with isolating those family conflicts that are creating family imbalance and producing family pathology. Casework diagnosis must be centered on the impact of these various processes on the family's organization and operation, and the treatment plan is concerned with those changes in the family relationships, in the use of the environment, or in the perception of the problem that will reduce tension and symptomatology for the family as a group.

A family disturbance may be stimulated by some change in the family constellation that requires a change in family organization and the interactive patterns. The disturbance may be precipitated by such things as the natural growth of a family member, a reality change in the family constellation, or a new external influence. A demand is put upon the family to reorganize its relationships and interactive system. If the family cannot incorporate this new demand and effect a new balance, the pressure is felt within the family, in the extra-familial activity of one or more members, or in both areas.

Case Illustration

The R family illustrates these points.

Mrs. R, aged 42, came to the agency when her 14-year-old son, Richard, received a failing grade in English. Mrs. R had long been trying to deal with Richard's poor social and familial relationships, and this final blow threw her into a panic. She described him as having few friends or sustained interests. Although he had good intelligence, he did not use it. He was immature; he constantly baited his father and was demanding of his mother. He was well informed on politics and current events, read scientific literature, and had a few scientific hobbies. Mrs. R thought that he got along well with his few friends. When she and her husband were home he just moped around the house waiting to be pushed into doing "something." Prodded long enough, he would complete one of his chores or his school assignments.

Mrs. R came to the agency with a feeling of desperation. It took courage to risk exposing the fact that she had a problem that she could not handle. She said that she believed in getting professional help, but her presentation was calculated to show that everything that she could be expected to do had already been done. She spoke defensively of their constant efforts to help Richard behave more maturely and appropriately for his age. Among other efforts, they had joined a community club and sent him to carefully selected camps. They had made sacrifices in an effort to help Richard find more friends and some interest or social activity suitable for his age.

As Mrs. R described Richard's behavior, she was visibly tense. Although she emphasized her intelligence, thoughtfulness, and generosity as a mother, her tone indicated that Richard's very existence bewildered and embarrassed her.

In speaking of Mr. R's relationship to Richard, Mrs. R spoke as if she were describing a sibling relationship. There was a sharp conflict between Mr. and Mrs. R over methods of handling Richard; Mr. R objected to Mrs. R's indulgence of, and domination by, the boy. Their previously good marital relationship was being negatively affected, and she felt guilty about this and also about her inability to devote herself to her job in her usual way. The repercussions of the family situation were also distracting her husband on his job. Mrs. R was an economist and Mr. R worked in the field of industrial research.

Mrs. R blamed Richard for her loneliness and unhappiness, as well as for her impaired relationship with her husband. Only when speaking of her two younger children was Mrs. R spontaneous, warm, and witty. At times Richard competed with the other children, but on the whole his relationship with them was not bad.

Mrs. R had spoken to the school counselor, who was surprised at her worry about Richard's scholastic achievement. He had never been outstanding in school, but had been responsive, had accepted responsibility, and was liked by his classmates.

Individual Backgrounds

Mrs. R was the eldest daughter of a demanding, immature, well-educated woman and an ambitious, shrewd, well-spoken businessman who impressed his family as a gentle person interested only in catering to and protecting them. Early in life Mrs. R became her father's partner in meeting the family's financial problems. Together they formed an alliance to protect the mother from "worry" about household and family matters. The mother reacted to pressure by becoming ill and demanding much attention and care. She also needed gratification of many social and physical requirements lest she become "ill"—requirements that were, by other standards, luxuries. The father was driven to provide for his wife on the expected level, and Mrs. R not only helped him to do so but continued this pattern even when he no longer needed her help.

On the surface Mrs. R's family was a closely knit group. They did things together, had many interests in common, protected each other, and never exposed any family problems to the outside world. Mrs. R, as the oldest child, often set the tone and carried responsibility. The father presumably made all the decisions about money, but the mother actually controlled expenditures by her tantrums or sick headaches. Mrs. R indulged her mother, considering her weak and inefficient. Mrs. R also protected her father, appreciating his hard work and his efforts to provide well for his family. She tried to make top grades at school, had friends, particularly successful and intelligent ones, and played an aggressive role in relationships.

Mr. R, the eldest of three boys, had been born into a middle-class family whose standards were quite fixed. His mother placed great emphasis on running an efficient home, and especially on serving good food. She also manipulated family relationships so that the father was an ineffectual figure and the three sons respected and glorified her. Mr. R was his "mama's boy" and took over all her standards of housekeeping, family relationships, and the "smooth front" to be maintained for the outside. His mother's brothers, financially successful, treated the family handsomely and gave the same deference to Mrs. R, Sr., that she demanded from her own family; and she, in turn, gave them more status than she did her own husband.

Mr. R was a conforming member of a conforming family. He did the right things at the right times and caused no one any difficulty. The one area in which he defied his mother was in rejecting her marriage choices for him. At the age of 27 he became engaged to Mrs. R, a "career woman" whose standards and goals were different from those of his own family.

Marital Interaction

Mr. R and Mrs. R were married when he was 27 and she was 24. They had known each other for a year. Mrs. R had done a good deal of manipulating at the beginning of their friendship in arranging for them to continue their meeting through mutual friends. Each participated in the intellectual and cultural interests of the other. Mr. R sought in his marriage a partner on whom he could lean and whose own personality needs would safeguard him from too much exposure to his feelings of inadequacy. He had identified with his mother, and had participated with her in maintaining his father's make-believe role as head of the family, while he competed with his father for her love. His dependency needs were great and although in social situations they were met without hazard, in his job situations his need to cling and to be fed was increasingly evident. His relationship with an employer who wanted him to act independently and without constantly being "patted on the back" was inevitably conflicted.

In the marriage Mr. R was able to express his male authority by insistence that his own home be run as his mother's had been. He took responsibility for handling the finances. His insatiable hunger was disguised under the cap of being fashionably epicurean. His need to cling and be cared for was met by his wife's long-standing masochism and inability to feel accepted and necessary unless she was actively doing something for the other person. His constant whimpering about his bosses, threats of job loss, and switches of job were due partially to his own inability to win promotion, and partially to his wife's unconscious need to maintain his inadequacy. Her role in this was to give a great deal of weight to his complaints and to reinforce his wish to run away.

Mr. R supported Mrs. R's defenses by permitting her need to dominate and control to be expressed in a maternal attitude toward him, by not interfering with her job ambitions, and by accepting as feminine her inability to handle money and her need to keep up with the Joneses.

In everyday matters their relationship was easy—they talked freely to each other; carried their prescribed roles in relation to each other; enjoyed entertaining, reading, gossiping; and had a common understanding of the front one showed the world. They worked well together on household responsibility, and each allowed the other some areas of authority and competence.

Their sexual relationship was satisfactory. Mrs. R was the more affectionate of the two. When, after four years of marriage, they had decided to have a child, Mrs. R had not conceived immediately. The decision to have a child had been precipitated by "Pearl Harbor"—and Mrs. R's inability to conceive immediately had threatened the possibility of a draft exemption for Mr. R. After a few months she had become depressed, uninterested in her home and social relationships. Following minor surgery she had been able to become pregnant. Mr. R and his family had been extremely pleased, and for the first time Mrs. R had been treated by all with extreme care and protection. She had been anxious during the pregnancy and visibly depressed over the slightest discomfort. Mr. R had resented her behavior and had been concerned lest his reactions and demands further depress her. She had become intolerant of his many hypochondriacal manifestations during this period and had resented his competitiveness with her in relation to illness and the need for attention.

Influence of the Child

Richard's birth was normal, but Mrs. R was so exhausted by her anticipated delivery and her anxiety about his normalcy that, many years later, speaking of the pregnancy and birth created tension in her. Mr. R apparently was able to accept Richard for the baby he was and took his development as a matter of course. From the very beginning Mrs. R kept looking for indications of his intelligence.

Mrs. R returned to work shortly after Richard's birth, and he was subjected to a series of maids, each chosen for her emphasis upon routine and cleanliness. Richard was a little slower in walking and talking than neighboring children of similar age. Mrs. R began to talk to Mr. R of her worry about his slow progress, to the exclusion of any other subject. In the beginning he tried to reason with her, but he finally gave up and just listened or yelled.

Although Mrs. R shared with her husband the physical care of Richard, she tended to push him out of a relationship with the child. As Richard grew older and showed his high intelligence and his ability to get along with children, though he was shyer than most, she continued to be anxious about him and his development. She felt that she alone understood him completely. She dictated his relationship to his father and fostered Mr. R's irritability with him.

Although she had talked for a number of years about another child, Mrs. R had put it off until Richard was seven years old. The second pregnancy, and a subsequent one that was unplanned, were both normal, as were the births. She had not been anxious about these pregnancies, and these children had never taken possession of her as Richard had.

Mrs. R's maternal relationship to Mr. R now took a secondary place. Prior to Richard's birth, Mr. R's immaturity, his anxiety about his role in relation to job and friends, had been quieted by Mrs. R's protectiveness. Mrs. R's questions about her own femininity and desirability had been quieted by Mr. R's obvious need to support her superior intellectual abilities, her job success, and the façade of being in a "social whirl." The interactive relationship mutually supported their defenses, reduced the impact of stress situations, and enhanced their work ability and social use of themselves.

With the advent of Richard, Mrs. R was placed in a conflicted role. She had been able to sublimate her guilt-provoking, hostile, aggressive drives toward her mother, whom she tried to replace in her father's affection. She was helpful to her father and condescendingly helpful to her mother. Thus she had created an ego image of self-sacrificing involvement in other people's needs and her own superiority. In order to maintain this image of superiority she needed to surround herself with inferiors who depended upon her, made her feel kind and important. With Richard, where all her need had full reign, she could really set the price. He must never outgrow his dependency. As long as Richard did not grow in an emotional sense, her real feelings of worthlessness and inferiority could be quieted. Since her becoming a mother had been precipitated by her protectiveness of her husband, and since her concept of the mother role entitled her to be pampered, Mrs. R put new demands upon her husband—demands to "be cared for," to be allowed to whimper and to expect special consideration.

Mr. R, because of his negative identification with his father, conceived the father's role as one in which one is pushed aside. The respect accorded the father comes from a "make-believe" atmosphere in which one is only theoretically head of a family, but actually is considered as not amounting to much and an outsider in the mutual admiration between mother and sons. To both Mr. and Mrs. R, Richard was constant evidence of Mr. R's weakness. Neither one was deluded about the basic reason for conception—to avoid military service, which might expose Mr. R's weakness and his need for a protected, pampering setting. Thus the pregnancy had produced conflict in both Mr. and Mrs. R about their respective roles and future relationship. It threatened Mr. R by putting on him the responsibility for parental behavior and by the possible loss of Mrs. R's attention. Her illness during pregnancy had aroused guilt and annoyance in Mr. R, which he was quite ready to direct toward Richard as hostility and rejection. Mrs. R's narcissism and continuing drive to prove herself demanded a superior child. Her guilt and hostility in reaction to this slow, shy child, plus her continuing to work, were converted into overprotectiveness and a seclusive relationship with him. The interaction between Mr. and Mrs. R now changed. Their relationship was less supportive, although Mrs. R continued to be the dominating personality.

The Developed Interactive Patterns

By the time Richard was 14, further changes were taking place in the marital relationship, and his relationships with his parents had become firmly established. His relationships with his school friends and the younger children in the family were good when his parents were not around. His relationship with school teachers had been fair in the past, but recently he had started to ignore their requests or assignments. His recent school failure had been a final blow to Mrs. R. He held the power to show the world that she had produced a less than perfect child.

The interaction in this family had shifted from the kind that offered support to the family members to one that exposed the defenses of the parents and brought forth an increasingly hostile use of each of these three people by the others. Richard had violated his parents' social standard through school failure. Since he had secured part of Mrs. R's attention and time which Mr. R previously had received, the relationship between Mr. R and Richard became one of sibling rivalry, which made him unavailable to the boy. Since Richard could not gain his father's acceptance, he would at least be rejected for actual behavior rather than for what he represented to the father.

Richard developed into a youngster whose few happy moments were spent away from his parents. In the home he competed with his father for Mrs. R's attention. He had learned that holding her attention meant being negative toward his father, whining, and inadequate. Not only was he a problem, but he did not follow their code that the outside world must never see the internal family situation. Richard's expectation of rejection was now being converted by his parents' attitude into a pattern that invited it. The high intellectual standards of Mrs. R were compromised by her marriage. Her silent questioning of her child's inheritance from his father was felt by both the father and son.

The interactive patterns that were now evident offered clues to the appropriate treatment. Before Mrs. R could lend herself to helping Richard or could improve her relationship with Mr. R, she would have to have some of her own needs met. Since she was the key factor in permitting positive relationships within the family, treatment must first be directed to meeting her needs. From the family pattern it was evident that most of the weight of responsibility had been carried by Mrs. R, who, at best, had serious question about her own likableness and value. The worker must begin by supporting her adequacies—the values of her intellect, her professional ability, her capacity for assuming responsibility, and her generosity. Her healthy defenses would need to be supported and strengthened if there were to be any shift in her neurotic defenses. The latter were expressed by her seeking ego strength from the outside to such a degree that she lost her self-identity. She could be a career woman or a vain, fun-hunting female; weak like her mother and husband, or a perfectionistic housewife like her mother-in-law. With more appreciation of herself, and an appreciation of her assets, she would have less drive to have Richard carry for her the burden of her own self-questioning. She could then relate with less hostility to Mr. R and restore to him some of the support so essential to his carrying his job role and relating to masculine authority.

Because there was so little available for Richard in the family, the worker had to turn to other possibilities. Knowing the significance to Mrs. R of school success and intellectual achievement, the worker turned to the school as the first avenue of help for Richard. The goal was to help Richard attain some satisfactions, assume some responsibility, and gain social credits that go with success. In a co-operative plan the school began to use Richard for assembly talks, in working with younger children on science projects, and in the drama group, where his store of knowledge and his intelligence could be used. In each of these experiences Richard was free to perform according to his interest and ability without having to be graded on his performance. Although he whined and complained to the faculty about the younger children and the amount of work entailed, he was sweet with the children, bossy in an acceptable fashion, and considerate of the less able. He did extra work in English, which gave him an opportunity to assume responsibility for his own activity, in this instance making up for his lack of work earlier in the year. The school also encouraged his participation in neighborhood sports activity. Richard would be able to use these experiences for his own positive purposes, rather than to please his parents.

Although the worker is planning to have a more intensive contact with Mr. R, this is not yet timely. It is highly questionable whether Mrs. R can permit a contact with Mr. R while she is so threatened in her own relationship. Her masochistic needs will direct her back to meeting Mr. R's needs should Richard continue to show less response to her manipulation. If she is less threatened by Richard's behavior, and more positive about her own role in and out of the family, she will have less need to show up Mr. R through her fluctuations between extravagant purchases and masochistic self-sacrifices. Mrs. R's narcissistic needs can be transferred to her job if she has less guilt about working and therefore less need to make it a source of stress rather than pleasure.

Conclusion

The dynamics of the interactive pattern must always be understood if we are to formulate a sound diagnosis and plan appropriate treatment. The pattern of family interaction determines where the first treatment focus should be—whether on the marital relationship itself, on the members' extra-familial roles, or on their individual personality problems. Correction can come from any one, or any combination, of the components influencing the interactive pattern—psychological, emotional, social, and cultural.

In order to determine where the worker's and the client's energies can best be directed, we need to know how the psychological, social, and cultural components of the interactive pattern are operating to create the problem, or to maintain it, and what resources can be used to restore or initiate more adequate family functioning.

CULTURAL AND SOCIO-PSYCHOLOGICAL CONSIDERATIONS IN WORK WITH THE AGED [1]

Maurice E. Linden

Learn Cyrnus, learn to bear an easy mind;
Accommodate your humor to mankind
And human nature; take it as you find.
A mixture of ingredients good and bad—
Such are we all, the best that can be had.
The best are found defective, and the rest,
For common use, are equal to the best.
Suppose it had been otherwise decreed;
How could the business of the world proceed?
—Theognis (of Megara), circa 600 B.C.[2]

THERE IS MUCH appeal in a fatalistic and passive philosophy that takes human nature as it is found. Perhaps it is the role of the philosopher and of scholars, who merely record the parade of reality, to be uninvolved observers. How enviable is the position of those secure watchers who take note of man's social evolution and move with its tides, but who utilize their perceptiveness merely to describe man—not to change him. Such an attitude toward mankind is a luxury, a comforting isolationism, of which there can be no partaking by those who would relieve man's suffering, correct his mistakes, and plan for him an improved future.

[1] Published in *Social Casework,* November 1959. Presented at the Biennial Meeting of the Family Service Association of America, Washington, D.C., April 2, 1959.

[2] Quoted in Will Durant, *The Story of Civilization, Part II, The Life of Greece,* Simon and Schuster, New York, 1939, p. 95.

The student of human behavior and the worker devoted to reducing human misery can hardly be unaffected by the awesome statistical picture of the aged in today's civilization. If the worker in the professional therapeutic disciplines is unmoved by exposure to the cold majesty of figures alone, certainly his interest and attention *are* aroused by a desire to reduce the daily pressure upon his service headquarters occasioned by throngs of hapless oldsters and their distraught families seeking solutions to human-relationship problems.

Some Facts About Aging

There are today about 15,500,000 persons who are 65 years of age or older in the United States. They represent an increase of over 400 per cent since the turn of the century, a period during which the total population increased about 130 per cent. A quarter of a million older people are treated in mental institutions annually. Nearly a half million live in nursing homes and homes for the aged. It has been estimated that, at any one time, approximately 10 per cent of the total number of older citizens have mental problems severe enough to make institutional care appropriate. If only half of these were actually hospitalized in psychiatric beds, they would occupy all the institutional space available for all diagnostic entities of all age groups throughout the country.

Of all the aged in nursing homes, more than half are at times confused, disoriented, and incoherent. Fewer than half of the nursing-home group can walk unassisted. Two thirds have a circulatory disorder.

Most of the aged have marginal or sub-marginal incomes. Three fifths of all persons 65 years of age and over have no income at all, or less than $1,000 a year. It is estimated that probably about 30 per cent of all aged citizens are in an abject dependency state. About 10 per cent of the aged are seldom or never seen by their children. Approximately 11 per cent are cared for by a single or widowed daughter. Living grandmothers outnumber grandfathers by two to one, the majority of the former coming from the maternal side of families.[3]

[3] Since no validated statistics in these general areas are available for the entire United States or even large population groups, the figures given here are

The 65-years-and-over group now constitutes nearly 9 per cent of the population. By 1975, trends remaining unchanged, the aged will number in the neighborhood of 23,000,000 and will comprise nearly 12 per cent of the total population. Whereas in 1900 in the United States the average age at death was 49 years, and the average age today is approximately 70, it is estimated that by the year 2000 people in this country will have a better than even chance of reaching age 82. It is further noted by physiologists that the human machinery is so designed and engineered by nature that, were it not for interfering diseases, abnormalities, and accidents, man should be able to reach age 125.

To demonstrate the fact that longevity is a modern phenomenon, mathematicians have estimated that of all people who have ever reached 65 years of age or older since the dawn of mankind, one-quarter are living today.

Social Change and Aging

Clearly, these elder citizens are a massive social force regarding whom it is not fair to say that their needs are similar to or identical with those found in all age groups. Certainly, like all mankind, the elderly need the standard physical, social, emotional, and spiritual supplies that are indispensable to civilization. But the comparison stops there.

The inexorable and continuous changes that affect the environment of all living things are a particularly vivid reality in human societies. Eternal alterations in the social matrix of living require eternal adaptation and readaptation. It is this process that taxes the aging most severely.

Although all progress is change, not all change is progress. As a rule, the aging have found within themselves and the surrounding culture the most expeditious means of adaptation to the progressive elements of living. But they are the ones who are more apt to react

assumptions based on extrapolations of Ruth Albrecht's findings in a moderate-sized midwestern community.

Ruth Albrecht, "Social Roles in the Prevention of Senility," *Journal of Gerontology,* Vol. VI, No. 4 (1951), pp. 380–386; "Intergeneration Parent Patterns," *Journal of Home Economics,* Vol. XLVI, No. 1 (1954), pp. 29–32; "Relationships of Older Parents with Their Children," *Marriage and Family Living,* Vol. XVI, No. 1 (1954), pp. 32–35; "The Parental Responsibilities of Grandparents," *ibid.,* No. 3 (1954), pp. 201–204; "Relationships of Older People with Their Own Parents," *ibid.,* Vol. XV, No. 4 (1953) pp. 296–298; "Social Factors in the Health of Older People," *Geriatrics,* Vol. VIII, No. 2 (1953), pp. 106–110.

unfavorably to social retrogression and to the less attractive psychological features of humanity. Their persevering efforts to maintain a status quo comprised of the best aspects of living according to their own lights tend to meet with failure as insuperable changes take place inside and around them. The elderly are thus in a special class—a class which, with respect to the culture, appears variously to be composed of shapers, products, fugitives, and outcasts.

The aging have been described as a quasi-minority group with most of the disadvantages accruing thereto. To be sure, a great many older people do not fit into the grimmer picturization of aging. A fair number of them are leaders in almost every field of human enterprise. It is said that older women, as a group, are the progressively great repository of the nation's financial wealth. Undoubtedly a significant number of aged citizens reach life's terminus having experienced few inconveniences along the way.

Yet anyone who seeks a broad overview of the course of growing up in our culture must at least be stimulated, and probably disturbed, by the evidence of family and social upheaval and change during recent centuries, the outcome of which constitutes our current social milieu. I am convinced that juvenile delinquency, the problems of aging, alcoholism, part of the increase in mental illness, the high accident rate, suicide, even important aspects of international tension and strife, as a few examples, are all related to one thing—family life with all its conceivable implications.

The Family

For the purposes of comparison, let us consider briefly family structure and relationship in an important era in human history—stoic Rome (508–202 B.C.). Will Durant's [4] description portrays the patriarchal family as the most basic and characteristic Roman institution. The father's power was nearly absolute and controlled the life, death, and sale into slavery of his own children. Only the father enjoyed any rights before the law in the early republic. The application of his rights by the *paterfamilias* was subject to modification, to a degree, by custom, public opinion, the clan council, the praetorian law, and his own human sensibilities. The effect of the paternal rights, to quote Durant, "was to cement the unity

[4] Will Durant, *The Story of Civilization, Part III, Caesar and Christ,* Simon and Schuster, New York, 1944, pp. 56–84.

of the family as the basis of Roman morals and government and to establish a discipline that hardened the Roman character into stoic strength. They were harsher in the letter than in the practice; the most extreme of them was seldom used, the rest seldom abused. They did not bar a natural deep *pietas,* or reverential affection, between parents and children." We are told that the epitaphs on Roman tombs were as tender as those of Greece or our own.

We learn further that the Roman matron was an honored mistress who superintended the servants but made it a point to relegate to herself alone the nursing of her children. Durant tells us, "The children rewarded her patient motherhood with profound love and respect; and her husband seldom allowed his legal mastery to cloud his devotion."

In the miniature society of the Roman *familia,* under the domination of a virtual male monarch, the child grew up "in piety and obedience, to form the sturdy citizen of an invincible state. . . . the child was taught by the eloquent silence of example that the undying fire in the hearth was the sign and substance of the Goddess Vesta, the sacred flame that symbolized the life and continuity of the family; which therefore must never be extinguished but must be tended with 'religious' care and fed with a portion of each meal. . . ." Everywhere around the child were mementos "warning him not to stray away from the ways of his ancestors, and reminding him that the family was composed not merely of those individuals that lived in his moment, but also of those that had once been, or would some day be members of it in the flesh, therefore forming part of it in its spiritual multitude and timeless unity."

Making allowances for author Durant's rapturous value judgments, and my own enthusiasm as testified by the selection of these passages, a case still can be readily made for a mutual interrelationship among patriarchy, tradition-boundness, close family ties, strong ego development, and elder veneration.

Those of us who deal every day with the human results of various forms of family breakdown cannot avoid the feeling that, at least in the family life our professional work encounters, there are glaring psychological omissions as well as affective distortions which appear to be the yield of a general family departure from ancient time-tested formulas.

Today's family, on the average, is very different from that of the stoic Roman period; this is especially true of the less favored socioeconomic classes in which a looseness of family ties is not uncommon. For a variety of reasons, people today marry at an early age. This means that there are more living generations and that families have become elongated. One increasingly finds parents in their late teens or very early twenties, grandparents in their forties, and great-grandparents in their later fifties and early sixties. But in today's world the elongated living family is not necessarily an elongated unity.

The immense mobility of our society, the perpetually changing personality of each neighborhood, the diminishing communications between separated generations, the fervid change of fads and fashions, unresolved vindictive and petulant attitudes between generations, overdetermined drives toward independence, and an often exaggerated social striving for individualism, have driven wedges of social distance between the various family levels.

Family life today is increasingly subjected to the diluting and fragmenting effects of urban life. Persons at the younger age levels are apt to find a greater degree of mutual support among their peer groups than they do in their vertical relationships with elders. Such reinforcement from their youthful confreres, readily available in the populous city, drives the young to seek counsel about the tribulations of living from those outside the family. The young advise each other outside the home and convert the family household into an arena for argumentation, invidious debate, and open defiance. The stability of family life is thus constantly threatened. Under such circumstances the leadership of the elders, already greatly reduced by factors presently to be discussed, becomes a hollow and impotent authority that is preserved in maudlin sentimentality but not in practice.

In the course of growth from birth through life, the natural hostility between the generations can actually contribute to each individual's personal maturation. In childhood, drives for autonomy, efforts at self-mastery, sexual and romantic urges and fantasies, needs to satisfy curiosity, the seeking for self-expression and self-assertion, strivings to structure a personal identity, the reaching for social success, and indeed a myriad of manifestations of a longing for independence, create inter-generational conflict. Such conflict is not without its solutions.

Whenever parental leadership is affectionate, firm, just, understanding, and stable, inter-generational conflict progressively yields to a reconciliation with the parental image. Some fortunate individuals achieve this happy psychological goal and become, in turn, secure personalities capable of assuming the parental leadership role. My own clinical observations, however, lead me to conclude that a very large number of individuals retain throughout life a relatively unmodified attitude of rebelliousness against the elders. This is generally an unconscious force that militates against the complete maturation of developing persons. The widespread characterological immaturity thus generated may well become a sub-cultural trait incompatible with social maturation.

Not only is this process a vicious and self-perpetuating cycle generation after generation; perhaps more significant, it contributes to the social and emotional insecurity of the aging who are, after all, subject to the same group of forces. Clinical experience with older patients and clients frequently reveals that they are the later targets for their own developmental attitudes.

The unconscious defiance, petulance, aggression, hostility, vengefulness, and sulkiness against the elders, maintained in a state of fairly successful repression through the middle periods of life, tend to escape from repression in the later years and are then turned against the host-elder himself. The elder's position of authority is strained and depleted by the sense of his own guilt and inadequacy perpetuated from childhood. In paraphrase it may be said that the victorious crown of seniority sits uneasily on the head of him who senses his own unworthiness.

Cultural Rejection of the Aging and the Aged

Western cultures, particularly that of the United States, seem to create out of the later stages of life a kind of anticlimactic superfluousness which may be thought of as the outliving of usefulness. This phenomenon arises from several factors. Certainly it is an outgrowth of a culture's orientation to youthfulness, in which the bulk of the values of social living are consigned to one end of the life cycle.

A rejecting attitude toward elders also arises out of the shortsighted and self-centered comprehensions of young people. It is the immaturity of the young, aided and abetted by the permissiveness of their elders, that imposes upon the young a "here and now" philosophy of life which looks upon the later years at best as a nebulous ambiguity and at worst as a delayed prelude to the morgue.

The feeling of having outlived one's usefulness is frequently an artificially induced reaction. Mandatory retirement is a recent development; to many it means mandatory withdrawal from productive activity long before biophysiological events require it. Certainly many individuals welcome retirement and enjoy the freedom of unscheduled living for several years thereafter. Even so, there can come a time when inactivity and lack of social status are heavy psychological burdens.

The feeling of stagnation so often occasioned by retirement may lead to a sense of social dependency. To be sure, only the mentally defective, some neurotics, the psychologically regressed, and the infantile can enjoy a parasitic existence in which one is dependent upon the charity and generosity of others.

In addition, our often fickle, work- and achievement-oriented society is hypocritical in its munificence relative to retirement. Amidst fanfare contrived to disguise its ulterior attitudes, society tends to reward loyalty and durable industriousness with the promise of Eden-like paradise, only to turn its back upon the idle of its own creation. While it forces inactivity, isolation, and dependency upon many older people, society fails to make appropriate preparations for the new and pressing needs brought by retirement. Usually both the individual and his community are blameworthy for such lack of preparedness. Moreover, facilities for productive and creative participation and activity for older people are scarce.

Cultural Exclusion

A large number of people subtly reject the aged. One reason for this attitude is that the aged are a reminder of death. Since each human being is aware of his own eventual demise, and since death is an unknown factor in his thoughts, some degree of fear of it is nearly universal. What a person fears he prefers not to think about; hence the rejection and denial of the reality of aging. Aging becomes symbolic of man's mortality and is similarly warded off, denied, and avoided.

Psychiatric clinical experience also reveals that, despite all the denial and apparent disregard for aging, younger people think of older persons as the representatives of wisdom and mature judgment. The youngster, whose instincts and ambitions tend to be strong, sees the aging as unwelcome potential critics, who, *in loco parentis,* stand as external symbols of conscience. Thus, in the deeper recesses of young minds, older people are ascribed demigod-like qualities. Their mere presence may be evocative of guilt—as well as serving as a dampening agent to silly, erratic, original, and explosive childish enthusiasm.

Undoubtedly another reason for excluding the aged in modern society is their reduced tempo of living. In the stepped-up pace of modern living, the slow and cautious elderly are commonly treated impatiently by the mass of arrogant and madly rushing people whose hurry is more a symptom of internal psychological tensions than it is an appropriate response to external needs. Hence, the elderly are forced into a state of cultural isolation.

When the aged discover that they are isolated, they search for needed psychological supplies—affection, acceptance, recognition, and participation, only to find that the surrounding environment has grown dispassionate, disinterested, and preoccupied. Friends and loved ones have either moved away or died. Thus the circle of social contacts has grown small and the opportunities for emotional and intellectual interchange have diminished. Loneliness and lonesomeness become the lot of many older people thus beset by a cruel reality.

Changes in and after the Middle Years

The most important physiological and psychological events that take place in the middle years are menopause in the woman and climacterium in the man. The cessation of menses coupled with the rigors of "change of life" often constitutes a serious threat to the woman's psychological well-being. The fairly abrupt termination of the child-bearing period, particularly when childbearing and family rearing have been the major goals in the woman's life, tends to undermine personality and to promote a sense of life's bleakness and meaninglessness. When a woman's major goal is suddenly neutralized, she may develop a feeling of lost femininity. Often this brings about the need for compensatory modes of behaving.

If the woman has successfully overcome the initial feeling of melancholy she may employ two other devices. The first is the development of defense mechanisms of projection, usually directed against the husband. She may become sexually frigid, and may develop a paranoid perception of the husband as oversexed and interested in straying from marital fidelity. A lack of trust emerges because of the husband's imagined faithlessness. Since such fantasies tend to become exaggerated into delusions, the husband's efforts to counteract such notions with logic and reason are doomed to failure, and extremely strained relationships may develop between the marital pair.

A second response to the threat of menopause is for the woman to develop exaggerated notions about her own femininity. Such a woman may become flirtatious and coquettish while dressing in immodest clothing designed to accentuate her feminine charms. Frequently, there is an increase in sexual interest paralleled by a tendency toward impulsive infidelity.

The threat of the male climacterium, which promises to reduce the insistence of the sexual drives, may also be accompanied by a transitory increase in sexual interest—a "last fling" effort at sexual acting out. This is particularly likely to occur when the man's wife has become sexually frigid because of her psychological attitude toward menopause. In both instances, behavior may assume such proportions as to promote extra-marital acting out which has a profound guilt-producing effect. Such guilt may doggedly pursue the marital pair into later periods of aging and interfere with household tranquillity as each spouse alternately accuses and defends himself against the other. Guilty and hostile feelings of this type, whether based on reality or on fantasy, are particularly prone to enter into fantasy and delusion formations in the mental disorders of later life, especially those that begin with depression.

After the children have matured and have left the household, and when a greater amount of leisure time is available to the head of a family, there is often an additional psychological complication —the discovery that the breadwinner's daily employment has for many years been the means of sublimating deep neurotic complexes. Frequently the man discovers that his daily work has been instrumental in dissipating his neurotic drives and energies; his fellow employees have been the targets for some of his deeper hostilities and defense mechanisms. Since he is now faced with an increasing amount of leisure and more time at home, he may redirect his neurotic impulses into domestic activities and relationships. Thus, the stability of his marriage becomes severely threatened after several decades of apparent success.

Projected Future of the Elongated Family

Some students of family life believe that the future of the elongated family can be bright. The studies of Dr. Ruth Albrecht, which were mentioned earlier, give several reasons for this belief, which are paraphrased briefly here:

1. Studies in a midwestern community revealed that a disproportionately large number of mothers tended to prevent the emancipation of their children for an excessive period following adolescence. Fathers were more apt to release their children to the process of maturation. Dr. Albrecht suggests that when parents have to care for their own antecedents they will be more likely to free their own children for independence. Moreover, grandparents will assist young married couples in rearing their youngsters; in turn, as the children grow up and leave the household, the now middle-aged parents can direct their attention to their own aging parents.

2. Younger individuals can discover the meaning of aging through association with older people and through experiencing the cultural impact on the various stages of life.

3. More people can have the privilege of knowing oldsters. The immigration of large numbers of young persons into this country before the first World War denied them the opportunity of witnessing their own parents' aging, since the latter frequently had been left in Europe. When more generations are alive, aging becomes a part of social living and is witnessed by the young who will thus, theoretically, be more able to incorporate the concept of aging into their total living experience.

There are signs, too, that the future of the aging population can also be bright—improved pension plans, better patterns of retirement, preretirement counseling, the retention of physical health well into old age, educational opportunities for adults, and increasing public and professional attention to the needs of the aging.

There is abundant evidence that responsible civic leaders and governmental officials are concentrating their efforts upon the problems and needs of an aging population. Certainly, good programs will come out of well-documented studies and research. Yet I believe the picture is not nearly so bright as some would have us think. Those who pay attention only to the favorable aspects of cultural development often overlook the changes in family leadership that have taken place during recent centuries—changes that militate against adequate solutions to the problems of the aging.

Social Revolution and Changes in Family Leadership

A host of popular writers have taken issue with the viewpoint I shall present. Nevertheless, there is now an abundant scientific literature that convincingly documents the effect upon family life occasioned by the two-centuries-old Industrial Revolution.

Industrialization and concomitant social change have succeeded progressively in (1) reversing the parental roles of the sexes, (2) reducing parental authority, (3) fragmenting family life, and (4) aiding in the development of inept autonomy in children. More significant than urbanization has been the progressive emancipation of women.

The "release" of the woman from the home to industry afforded her two advantages: (1) a new social role with greater personal independence combined with social "rights" approximately equal to those enjoyed by the man, and (2) additional protection under the chivalric laws and practices. The increased social activity of the female is paralleled by a progressive diminution in male dominance which has come about partly through the neutralization of male aggressiveness by female aggressiveness and partly through male default. The default of the male may be viewed socially as renunciation of leadership, as a reaction to frustration; psychologically it is a renunciation of masculine aggressiveness that permits the latent passivity in the male to become ascendant.

The outcome of these shifts is a progressive exchange of leadership roles between the parents. The father withdraws to a position of relatively uninvolved isolation within the family or assumes a position almost analogous to his own children's, subordinate to the mother. The mother assumes dominance, decision-making, and control functions, in part because of inter-sexual conflict, in part to fill the gap left by the father.

In normal development the boy identifies with his father while retaining his mother as the ideal image of the heterosexual love object. Similarly, the girl identifies with her mother and idealizes the image of the father. When parental roles have become reversed, the boy's alliance with the father means unconscious identification with a passive role embodied in the masculine form; he selects as love object the maternal image replete with aggressiveness and dominance. The girl identifies with the aggressive and dominant mother, while her love object is the passive father. This is a considerable oversimplification of all the actual forces at work, but it does demonstrate the way in which role reversal is perpetuated from generation to generation as well as the way in which unconscious homosexual conflict is precipitated and propagated.

Concurrent with the psychological changes hypothesized above, family life during the past century has witnessed a revolutionary alteration in the social position of children. Child labor laws, welfare programs, alterations in school systems, pediatric practices and public education, mental health movements, and general social emancipation have progressively removed so many of the nineteenth-century restrictions on children that the twentieth century has come to be known as the "century of the child." [5] Certainly, there are very desirable features in the social reforms that have enabled the child to come into his own. Yet social agencies report a widespread "paralysis" among parents in their efforts to rear and discipline their children. It may well be that many of the natural inclinations of parents have been inhibited by new social principles designed to aid children. The social pendular swing apparently has been so great that children sense the ineffectualness of their parents and develop an excess of autonomy. While the parents look to the counseling professions for help in rearing their young, the latter escape from family control to a new-found freedom of self-direction.

Conclusion

Why are the above observations included in a treatise on aging? Because the neuroticism that develops out of unconscious psychosexual conflict and the secondary leadership position of the elders emerge as etiological factors in the production of psychological breakdown in the aging. Even in instances where frank emotional disturbance does not develop, the powerlessness and lack of authority of the elders may yield an impotent elder generation, a bewildered middle generation, and an arrogant and mis-

[5] United Nations, *Comparative Survey of Juvenile Delinqency, Part I, North America,* United Nations Department of Economic and Social Affairs, New York, 1958, p. 108.

directed younger generation. The system cultivates itself and guarantees a continuing and growing problem.

The solution to this problem is not at hand. Great social reforms are enormously difficult. Yet it would seem that a restoration of family leadership containing elements of the father as patriarch and the mother as "honored matron" of the household are needed for dignified elderhood and good character development in the young.

In the meantime, we must approach the problem piecemeal, case by case, in the hope that here and there in our therapies and family counseling our Lilliputian efforts may succeed in promoting social mutations toward normality. All the while we shall be concerned with the second industrial revolution, automation; will it bring solutions or new problems?

PREVENTING DEPENDENCY PATTERNS IN CHRONICALLY ILL CHILDREN [1]

Jessie P. Dowling

Rehabilitation of adults who have been disabled from childhood is difficult when they have not had enough help during the significant stages of growth and development to prepare them for independent living within the limitations of disability. Those who have worked with such individuals believe that the problems inherent in being handicapped must be dealt with sometime before adolescence is past if successful rehabilitation is to be realized. Much attention has therefore been given to reaching the disabled

[1] Published in *Social Casework*, October 1960.

child and his family as soon as possible, in order to provide him with the optimum opportunity to become an independent adult.

Ideally, help in these situations should be given over a long period of time, during which all available resources are brought into use. In many instances, casework help to these children and their families may be available only for short time, or under other limited circumstances, such as during a period of hospitalization. The question arises whether anything of lasting value can be accomplished within these limitations and, if so, how the social worker and others can best use the opportunity to help the child build toward independence in adulthood.

The author, with the attending physician and nursing personnel, had an opportunity to study this problem at the Clinical Center, National Institutes of Health, where a group of male patients with hemophilia were the subject of medical research studies in hematology for varying lengths of time over a period of two years. There were twelve patients altogether, ranging in age from 5 years through 32. Specifically, there were four adults, from 21 to 32, three adolescents, 13, 14, and 15, and five children, two aged 5, one aged 6, one aged 7, and one aged 8. All these patients suffered from severe manifestations of hemophilia. Although our observations were limited to this relatively small group, all with one disease, we felt that what we learned may be of use to others working with chronically ill children.

Nature of Hemophilia

For an understanding of this particular disorder, some knowledge of its special features is necessary. Hemophilia, like other disorders of long-term nature, has many emotional implications for the victim and his family. It is a hereditary, sex-linked disorder transmitted from the mother to the male child. It can be severely or mildly disabling. With careful medical supervision and proper education, however, its victims can be enabled to live useful, productive lives. In simple terms, the victim has a defect in the blood-clotting mechanism and is subject to both internal and surface hemorrhages. These hemorrhages may be induced by trauma or may occur spontaneously. The episodes vary in duration and severity, and may involve much pain, particularly if joints or other internal areas are involved. Various forms of permanent crippling from hemophiliac arthritis may result.

From the time of diagnosis it is necessary to protect the child from any trauma, even slight bumping, bruising, or cutting, which may produce hemorrhage. The mother, who must provide protection by denial of many of the normal, vigorous experiences of physical growth and development, may, because of guilt feelings or other factors, find it difficult to distinguish the necessary protective measures from unnecessary ones. Further, even if she can recognize these distinctions, and feels free enough herself to risk giving the child as much freedom as possible, she may still be unable to carry out a day-to-day program in which the child is helped to distinguish frustration based on the realities of his disease from maternal rejection.

The habit of managing the protection by herself, or with the help of other adult members of the family, may become so ingrained that the mother fails entirely to engage her child in understanding and participating as age and stage indicate he might. Thus, the child accepts the mother's surveillance as an inevitable and invariable external condition, experiences no sense of participation with the mother in providing controls, and remains dependent upon the mother and other adult figures to set behavior limits for him. In short, the many realities of restricted living, imposed in the interest of his survival, may entirely defeat the child in his striving toward independence.

Observations in Adults

In our hospital, interest in a treatment approach that aimed at prevention of what otherwise seemed an inevitable developmental sequence in the children was stimulated by the observations, by the nursing, medical, and social work staff, of the dependency shown by adult patients in the research unit. These observations led to grave concern on the part of the staff for finding ways to help the children under our care avoid the development of such patterns. The fact that it was possible to observe in the adults the behavior that resulted from failure to give them help as children is illustrated by a striking example. One of the doctors had had a trying day with an adult patient who was making unreasonable demands, pitting doctor and nurse against each other, and threatening to leave the hospital. The doctor finally exasperatedly remarked, "There's Jimmie Oliver twenty years from now." Jimmie was a hemophiliac, aged 6, who was a favorite of the staff. The genuine disbelief of the staff (although the doctor had probably touched on the heart of the matter) was merely further proof of the necessity of finding ways to help avert the development of the same dependency patterns if it were possible.

The adult patients in the group had certain common characteristics dramatically exemplifying the passive-dependent personality, which frequently results when a child is born with a genetically determined handicapping disease. This was a rather carefully selected group of patients, even for hemophiliacs, since we had to have patients who were able to stay a long time in the hospital for research purposes. This group was able to do so because all were single, and were only tenuously involved in heterosexual relationships, if at all. None was vigorously engaged in education or employment, although three of them were active cases with their state vocational rehabilitation agencies and interrupted their courses of training to come to the hospital for studies. None had completed a course of training, and they seemed to view their contacts with the vocational agencies as interminable. Therefore, they had no skill or trade at this point, and had never had steady long-term employment, although all had had some jobs at various times for short periods. (It must be remembered that these patients had severe hemophilia and actually had long periods of acute illness, necessitating hospitalization. Even a person strongly motivated toward independence could be seriously discouraged and hampered by these circumstances.)

In the hospital the staff regarded this group as "troublesome" patients. Having missed in varying degrees the opportunity to internalize controls and develop self-reliance, the patients used the hospital setting in the same way they had habitually used the family, the vocational rehabilitation agencies, and others. They seemed to expect that, because of long and painful suffering through no fault of their own, compensation by having their demands met was due them, regardless of hospital routines and discipline. Staff members often referred to the adult patients as "grown-up little boys." While showing deep resentment and hostility about hospital restrictions, these patients nevertheless often provoked the imposition of the restrictions they abhorred.

Because narcotics are often necessary in the treatment of hemophiliac bleeding, there is always the possibility of addiction. These adults had had long experience in hospitals, and the matter of administration of drugs had become a familiar battleground for them. During bleeding episodes, the patient's chronic, persistent pain, which he knows from past experience cannot be wholly alleviated even by narcotics, erodes his ability to understand and co-operate in his own treatment. The desire for immediate relief overrides all other considerations, and patients, although they know there is no possibility of complete release from pain, may still plead for excessive medication. Moreover, they are sophisticated about the time-spacing involved in medication, and tend to accuse the staff of negligence if the medication schedule is not strictly observed. After recovery from the episodes, when drugs were no longer needed, they were likely to persist in feeling unfairly treated. Casework sessions devoted to helping them vent their resentful feelings frequently seemed to afford little relief. They talked about having had to learn to use "watchdog" tactics in regard to their medication and often continued to feel resentful toward the staff members they considered responsible. Sometimes it seemed they could perceive the caseworker only as a possible accomplice in forcing the staff to comply with their demands.

None of these four patients seemed eager to leave the hospital setting although they would threaten to leave if their demands were not met. When offered the choice of discharge, however, they elected to stay and give the hospital "one more chance." They rarely showed impatience about getting out of the hospital in order to resume a more satisfactory and vigorous way of living.

Observations in Children

Beginning counterparts of adult reactions were fairly discernible in the children, although there were differences in the expressions of dependency. All appeared to be passive, quiet, and initially eager to please the staff with superficially conforming, obedient, rather seductive behavior. The younger the child, the more obedient. These children, of all the children in the hospital, tended to be favorites of the staff, and were described as "good" and "well behaved." Rebelliousness in general was manifest only in the adolescents, and this was likely to take the more passive forms of sullenness, refusal to eat certain foods, forgetting to "sign out," and minor clashes with the less powerful members of the nursing staff. "Mischievousness" in the younger children was confined to "cuteness" and what they termed "only pretending" to disobey or rebel, followed quickly by conciliatory behavior. All were plainly expectant of a continuation in the hospital of the world of "don'ts" to which they were accustomed in the home environment. When restrictions by staff were not immediately forthcoming, their behavior became increasingly provocative. There was evidence in some children of the beginning of compulsive behavior in extreme cleanliness, frequent hair-combing, and hand-washing. This compulsive behavior has been described by Anna Freud as a reaction to the controls exerted by the mother, in her overzealous vigilance about the child's health, to guard against imaginary dangerous contact.[2]

The children failed to form strong initial attachments to any one staff member, but seemed impartially friendly and amenable. The younger ones, even after several weeks, were confused about individual staff members' names and appeared to view staff in terms of their functions rather than as individuals. The smaller ones who had had long periods of hospitalization and little consistent experience in family life actually were confused about the sex of the persons involved, and sometimes called male doctors "she," and female nurses "he." To them "he" and "she" seemed to be synonymous terms with which to speak about individuals.

All the young children were fearful of medical procedures, whether benign or hurtful. Some of the younger ones cried, screamed, and were upset both before and after blood-drawing and other procedures, although their apprehension lessened as they adapted to the hospital. The pre-adolescents and adolescents usually assumed stoically indifferent attitudes toward painful procedures and were able to admit to hurt and anger only after the staff had undertaken considerable work with them. This attitude was sometimes observed in the younger children also, particularly after they became identified with the older boys and wished to imitate them.

Most of the children seemed abnormally afraid of punishment for the most minor infractions, and these fears diminished slowly,

[2] Anna Freud, "The Role of Bodily Illness in the Mental Life of Children," in *The Psychoanalytic Study of the Child,* Vol. VII, International Universities Press, New York, 1952, pp. 69–81.

even in a ward atmosphere that was permissive, reasonable, and kindly. It was fairly clear that they associated their disease with badness. It was not always clear at what level the associations were made, but the manifestations were varied. Because from early infancy they had been subject to sudden emergent hospitalizations, they seemed to assume this experience meant rejection for having been bad. Later, in experiencing the mother's controls against injury, they had undoubtedly been told that if they were bad they would get hurt. The acute pain the hemophiliac suffers upon injury may mean to the child only further evidence of the dire consequences of bad behavior. In the hospital they would protect themselves from discovery of "badness" by failing to report accidents when they happened, and denying, even after bruises and bleeding occurred, any knowledge of the cause. Among even the youngest children there was a group protectiveness about reporting accidents, and nobody would tell on anybody else, although on other matters a child was quite likely to tattle on another to gain favor.

Therapeutic Approaches

Although there were many aspects of casework service to this group of children and adults which might be reported, this paper deals with the specific areas of the children's exaggerated dependency in the hospital setting and our efforts to help them develop self-reliance in the management of their illness.

Of the five children and three adolescents to whom we gave special attention, two children and one 14-year-old adolescent stayed over a year in the hospital, and three others—one child and two adolescents aged 15 and 13—were here for two to three months. Other children came and went, staying short periods for diagnostic studies only, and no casework service was attempted with them, except to make whatever appraisal was possible of the family situation and to refer them for further help in their communities if this was feasible.

The three children who stayed longest were over 400 miles from home. In two instances, the caseworker saw the mother only once, for a brief interview, on her only visit to the hospital. The mother of the third child was available only every two to three months for brief interviews. Therefore, with the children who were most accessible over the longest period, we had to find a way of helping without the usual concomitant help to the mother, at the same time that we used all possible means to keep the ties between child and home strong and alive in order to mitigate some of the effects of separation. We were aware that the hospital could in no way substitute for the home, and that our services, at best, were simply extensions of the home.[3] We tried to help the child understand that he was hospitalized for reasons other than rejection by his parents. We also needed to relieve the parents' guilt, in the contacts we had by letter and personal interview, about their decision to submit the child to long-term research studies far from home.

Although we had to deal with the problem of separation of child and parents, we did not have to assume that all the effects were deleterious. For instance, this was one of many hospitalizations these children had experienced. From early infancy they had been subjected to sudden, unexplainable separations from their mothers. Bowlby, Anna Freud, and others have amply described the pathogenic processes leading to personality disturbances as the result of such separations.[4] Feelings about all these hospitalizations had never been resolved, and the children seemed resigned to the inevitable, but they still struggled to find substitute satisfactions in the hospital. They typified the "institutional child" who develops a facility for superficial relationships with a variety of staff members, with no deep attachments to any one individual. While the damaging effects of separation were evident in all the children, a positive factor to capitalize on was that the intensity of the struggle between mother and child over his control was diminished by the separation. However, substitute maternal, as well as paternal, figures were always present and were utilized as such. Therefore, the child conceivably had a chance in this benign climate to change his perception that controls always come from without, and to learn that he had a part in the management of his illness.

We concentrated our efforts in four main areas: (1) helping the child understand his illness in practical, realistic terms; (2) building ego strength by helping him separate his fantasies of badness and low esteem from the facts of his illness which required restrictions and the application of painful procedures; (3) dealing with the

[3] For a discussion of this subject see Anna Freud and Dorothy T. Burlingham, *War and Children,* International Universities Press, New York, 1943, pp. 185–186.

[4] John Bowlby, M.D., *Maternal Care and Mental Health,* Monograph Series No. 2, World Health Organization, Geneva, 1951, pp. 15–51, 121–122; Anna Freud and Dorothy T. Burlingham, *op. cit.*

child's expectations of endless control from without and helping him participate in his own management; and, finally, (4) furnishing a climate within the hospital in which the child could test out feelings of greater freedom within a benign, permissive setting rather than one that was overprotective and controlling.

1. Understanding of the Illness

First of all, none of the children seemed to have a clear idea about his illness from the standpoint of objective, factual information. Except for the youngest ones, most of them knew the name of the illness, and also knew its effects by bitter experience. Beyond that were much confusion and ignorance. Besides not having whatever knowledge might be appropriate for their age and stage of development, they had not previously experienced shared discussions with their doctors in which they were free to express themselves and ask questions. Our physician, therefore, initially gave the children this opportunity, and in repeated contacts most of them developed a great deal of curiosity and interest in the illness itself. This seemed to lessen their preoccupation with themselves as sick people, and some became quite sophisticated in their understanding. For instance, they were overheard telling others such things as, "We don't have blood like other people's . . . it won't clot. . . ." After these initial discussions the channels were always open for the children to ask questions and in turn receive information.

2. Ego Integration

In general, these children had low self-esteem because of the fantasies of rejection and badness, and of their having seen over and over again their families' disturbing reactions to the crises caused by their bleeding episodes. They tended to feel they were a burden and a disrupting influence, and their conforming, passive behavior was their way of assuring love and attention—as if they needed love to compensate them for the times when they had suffered because they had been "bad" and had upset family routines.

As in any casework approach, we used techniques to build self-esteem, but we particularly emphasized the matter of self-esteem in its relationship to the illness. We verbalized for the younger children that their illness had nothing whatever to do with their being good or bad. We demonstrated, by our consistent concern for them and through regular contacts, that they were important as people. We let them know that their getting sick made us feel concern only because it hurt them, and not because of anything wrong they may have done. We told them many times over that they were in the hospital solely because they were sick and because we and their parents wanted to help them stay well. We endeavored to maintain home ties by helping the children write letters and make telephone calls. We wrote to the parents ourselves, and we helped the children, in letters home, to ask parents' advice and comment about all possible matters, in order to encourage in the children a sense of the parents' participation and active interest. We tried to diminish the feelings of desertion by making as tangible as possible their contacts with home.

The social worker's office became to them a place where they could talk about their troubles and have greater latitude in expressing and acting out aggressive feelings than was possible on the nursing unit. Some of the children found it hard to believe that the social worker was really interested in how they felt and in what upset them in the hospital. They were initially suspicious and doubted that we would not tell others if they said something "bad" about the hospital.

During several interviews, Jimmie, a 6-year-old who was probably the most conforming of the group, remained suspicious and aloof. When he was finally convinced he could trust me, he revealed that he was angry at being denied iced tea with his lunch, which he always had at home. We arranged for him to have it, though he later rejected it because he found he did not like it, after all. From that point, however, he was able to let us know more about his dissatisfactions and discontents, becoming convinced that we were interested in helping him say what he wanted instead of just restricting him. Part of the problem was helping him understand that even though he could not always have what he wanted, we were interested in him and cared about him and his needs. He went through a long phase of asking us over and over if we really, truly did like him; gradually he gave up the need to do this.

A significant instance of the staff's approach to the feeling of badness was the physician's treatment of accidents when medical attention was necessary. Because the children were so fearful of being caught "being bad" and causing a bleeding episode, the physician treated the accidents in a studiedly matter-of-fact way, emphasizing that boys will be boys, and that he expected that accidents would sometimes happen. He further expressed his feeling that he was glad he was there to take care of the children when they did have accidents. As a consequence, it became less and less necessary for them to protect themselves from reporting, and they began to do it with much less anxiety and more forthrightness.

In carrying out medical procedures, the doctor devoted much time and effort to engaging the child's participation and letting him know he understood how much the treatment hurt. With the younger children he played out the blood-drawing by letting them imitate the process with a stuffed animal and toy needle. These techniques were so successful that he became known as the doctor who did not hurt. (There were times when others carried out the procedures.)

The physician spent time with the children at periods when no medical procedures were involved, so that they could associate him with pleasant as well as unpleasant experiences. He also took them on visits to the laboratory where they could see, if not understand, what went on behind the scenes.

3. Expectations of Control from Without

It was fundamental to help these children learn that not only were they capable of exercising control in their own behalf, but it was expected of them. The plan was difficult to execute. Like the mothers of the children, the staff members experienced much anxiety about the amount of permissiveness—where to let the child begin his own controls and the degree of latitude in general in relation to running, jumping, climbing, and wrestling in which the children spontaneously engaged.

The first step was a frank discussion between the children and the doctor in which he informed them that we all were going to help them learn to take care of themselves as much as they could. As a precaution the staff would always be there to protect them whenever necessary and to keep them from going too far if they were unable to handle a situation themselves. He let them know that it would take a long time for them to learn by themselves about running and jumping and such things, and that while they were learning we would always be there to help them.

This talk was followed by sessions in the social worker's office, sometimes with the social worker alone, and sometimes with the doctor present. The casework aim in these early sessions was to let the child explore the boundaries of his freedom to act (verbalizing was important, too, of course) and to test out at what points we would interfere. Jimmie gives a striking illustration of how this exploration and testing were done. After I had explained to him the use of the social worker's office and how we would work together on his learning new things for himself, he was doubtful about whether he really would be permitted the freedom of verbalizing his anger. In the following sessions, he seemed frantically uncontrolled. He raced around the office shouting, hitting the desk resoundingly with books and other objects. He made unintelligible, loud, fantastic sounds into the dictaphone, he wildly shot the ping-pong gun, and pounded uncontrollably on the child's work bench. One day, after twenty minutes of this, he stopped, looked at me slyly, and asked if I had a headache. Thus began a discussion revealing the fact that his mother always got a headache when he behaved aggressively. Therefore, he was asking me if I would recreate the home environment by doing as his mother did.

Jimmie did considerably more testing of me after this episode, but his behavior never again was so wildly uncontrolled. He often arrived bounding and shouting, but when this behavior was met with calmness, he settled down to using constructively all the things he had formerly used so violently. He set up a target for the ping-pong gun and concentrated on developing his skill. He delighted in using the dictaphone to "say letters" to me about his dissatisfactions, and requested me to answer them in the same manner. A letter frequently asked, "Do you really, truly like me?" Sometimes, however, he delighted in spending a whole record in a cacophony of sounds, apparently representing every kind of oral aggression he could allow himself.

Other children developed less dramatically than Jimmie. However, we can say that, in general, the mere verbalization, with the resulting opportunity to test the granting of greater freedom along with the expectation of greater responsibility, had salutary results in the instances in which there was sufficient time and opportunity for the child to respond.

4. Hospital Atmosphere

The nurses had realistic difficulties in modifying the unit climate to provide full opportunity for testing. First of all, the children were not on a pediatrics unit, but were housed on a unit with adult patients, not only other hemophiliacs but also a considerable number of adults with severe bone disease. Therefore, nursing skills had to be adapted almost individual by individual, and the staff was constantly faced with the task of balancing the needs of this heterogeneous group, so that neither children nor adults felt that one group had to sacrifice too much for the other. The children were permitted to run, jump, and bound within carefully explained limits, and were punished with the removal of privileges if they exceeded the limits beyond which injury to themselves or others might result. However, the children were given ample opportunity to understand the limits. Punishment for exceeding limits was handled with discretion and imagination, along with adequate explanations of the reasons for punishment. Each child was helped to feel that he was a participant in the meting out of punishment and not merely the victim of an adult imposition.

In this atmosphere we soon had tangible proof of the development of self-reliance by the children. There was marked contrast between their initial habits of reporting each other's infractions to the staff, and the later exercise of warnings and controls over each other.

The nursing staff had primary responsibility for this phase of treatment. There were staff meetings and other types of conferences, however, including at regular times the doctor, social worker, recreation worker, occupational therapist, teachers, and others. Through these media common goals of treatment of the children were arrived at, periodically evaluated, and modified or continued as indicated.

Summary

Conclusions must be modest because of the limited opportunity to work with these children, in terms of the duration of their stay in the hospital, the unavailability of the parents for intensive casework, and the possibility that patterns already well established prior to hospitalization might very well be resumed upon their discharge to the same environment. We used whatever opportunities we had to explain to the parents what we were attempting, but had no further opportunity to help them integrate and work out different behavior patterns possibly more appropriate to the children's needs. Nevertheless we did observe growth in the children in the areas described. They developed realistic understanding of their illness and a sense of participation with their doctor; self-esteem increased as feelings of badness diminished; controls on their own behavior were strengthened and management of the illness grew simpler. Finally, they all had the concrete experience of living in an atmosphere in which adults took a concerned, kindly, limiting but not controlling, interest in their welfare. Follow-up of the lasting results of this attempt is not possible at this time, but the study suggests an interesting complementary area of investigation.

CONTROL AND VALUES IN SOCIAL WORK TREATMENT [1]

Irving Weisman and Jacob Chwast

SOCIAL WORK TREATMENT, whether casework or group work, is one of society's alternative ways of exercising social control of persons who manifest deviant behavior, although such services are not usually regarded in this way. Society uses other control methods such as reward and approval, open criticism, corporal punishment, and enforcement of segregation. These forms of control are clearly recognizable, which is not true of control through treatment. A treatment service, the purpose of which is to enhance an individual's social functioning, nevertheless contains an element of control. This article will present, in a simplied form, some of the complex inter-

[1] Published in *Social Casework,* November 1960.

relationships between treatment and the control elements inherent in the treatment situation.

In this paper the term "control" will be used to include the entire range of pressures, both external and internal, that lead the individual to function in adaptive ways. External or social controls consist of both formal sanctions governing human actions, as embodied in laws, and less obvious informal sanctions. The informal sanctions are transmitted by parental and cultural approval or disapproval.

The survival of any society is dependent on a system of organization that enables its members to carry out certain tasks. A system of social organization must therefore produce in individuals a pattern of behavior which, in broad terms, conforms with the standards sanctioned by the total group. Individuals, from one generation to another, who are reared in a particular social system therefore come to regard the existing practices as natural and right, since these are the customs and ways of their parents and ancestors. Moral, ethical, and spiritual values become attached to the customs and, in consequence, are considered sacred and inviolable.[2]

In both the theory of social psychology, with its concept of socialization, and the theory of psychiatry, with its concept of growth and development, there is recognition that the society and culture to which the individual belongs play a major part in shaping his behavior and personality. There is also agreement that the individual incorporates the beliefs and attitudes of his culture by use of certain psychological mechanisms. For example, Gillin and Gillin observe that through the use of the mechanism of identification, a psychoanalytic concept, the child absorbs not only the norms and values of the parent but also those of the society.[3] Fenichel notes: "Originally the child certainly had the wish to do the things the parents do; his aim was an identification with the parents' activities. . . . The standards and ideals of the parents are an essential part of their personality. If children want to identify themselves with the parents, they also want to identify with their standards and ideals."[4] The net effect of this process of identification is to bring about socially acceptable behavior on the part of the child.

[2] Robert E. Lee Faris, *Social Disorganization,* Ronald Press, New York, 1948, p. 18.

[3] J. L. Gillin and J. P. Gillin, *Cultural Sociology,* Macmillan Co., New York, 1948.

[4] Otto Fenichel, M.D., *The Psychoanalytic Theory of Neurosis,* W. W. Norton & Co., New York, 1945, p. 102.

Control in Social Work Treatment

Social work agencies that provide various types of treatment services generally deal with individuals whose behavior deviates in some way from society's expectations. These individuals have some difficulty, either psychologically or interpersonally, in functioning in their milieu. The goal of treatment, in a democratic society, clearly is not that of helping such individuals achieve conformity for the sake of conformity. Rather, the goal is to help them make some modifications in their patterns of living, primarily in the area of their particular problem of social dysfunctioning. The areas of dysfunctioning that become the focus of treatment are those in which the consequences of the individual's behavior are damaging to himself or to others. The above definition of the treatment goal is somewhat narrower than others that are sometimes offered. Whether treatment goals are defined narrowly or broadly, they always involve normative concepts and, therefore, some element of social control. This is true even when social control factors are not made explicit in the formulation of treatment objectives. For example, certain control elements are implicit in Hamilton's listing of objectives: preventing social breakdown, conserving strength, restoring social functioning, making life experience more comfortable and compensating, creating opportunities for growth and development, and increased self-direction and social contribution.[5]

The social control function in casework has been elucidated by Taylor, who discusses the control implicit in such goals as strengthening family life, building wholesome community life, improving interpersonal relationships, and so forth. He points out that such verbs as "mould," "restore," "shape," "better," "improve," "help," "encourage," "assist," "develop," "relieve," "solve," and "resolve" are used repeatedly in agency reports. He states: "By its very institutional structure and function, the casework agency is normative, evaluative, and judgmental." [6]

A corollary to the premise stated above is that the social worker, in his interactions with clients in a treatment relationship, inevitably functions as a social control agent whether he intends to do so

[5] Gordon Hamilton, *Theory and Practice of Social Case Work* (2d ed., rev.), Columbia University Press, New York, 1951, p. 239.
[6] Robert K. Taylor, "The Social Control Function in Casework," *Social Casework,* Vol. XXXIX, No. 1 (1958), pp. 17–21.

or not. A particularly thorny problem that arises is whether the worker is aware of the degree to which he reflects, both implicitly and explicitly, the norms and standards of his own culture and social class.

Social workers, as well as other persons in the helping professions, tend to subscribe to types of behavior, and to think of them as universal standards. It would be more appropriate, however, to regard these so-called "universals" with skepticism, since they are not absolutes. For example, Harris observes that in our society we implicitly accept certain concepts of the rights of man and of his place in the universe but that these concepts do not obtain in all cultures.[7] Social workers, from their knowledge and personal experience, are likely to have certain concepts about the feelings of parents toward their children, expecting the parents to be tender toward their offspring and protective of the young. These assumptions may not apply equally in this society or in others, since the family serves a number of social, economic, and biological functions in addition to child rearing. These functions are weighted differently by different groups, but we tend to expect the family to meet the needs of the individual for companionship and self-fulfillment while it serves basic social, economic, and biological functions.

As indicated earlier, if members of a particular society are to live together with some cohesion and unity, even when the society permits considerable individual differences and sub-group variations, some degree of conformity is demanded of its members. All societies, obviously, make some allowance for such variations and differences. To maintain cohesion, however, each society develops a system of social control; the controls serve to encourage approved patterns of behavior among the members and also to deal with violators. Greenwood points out that social work treatment is ". . . concerned with action and change; it therefore belongs among the controlling agencies of society . . . social workers, by virtue of their technical knowledge and community-sanctioned status, possess a form of power which they exercise to reach certain ends." He notes that the aim of the practitioner is unlike that of the social scientist, whose aim is to describe the social world accurately. He states that

[7] Dale B. Harris, "Values and Standards in Educational Activities, 1. Parent Education and Personal Values," *Social Casework*, Vol. XXXIX, No. 2–3 (1958), pp. 159–167.

the "practitioner's chief end is the effective *control* of that world, and to this all knowledge is subordinated." [8]

It seems clear that the control element in social work practice is fundamentally related to its professional value system which embodies certain concepts of individual and community well-being. The question of professional values, of course, raises a number of philosophical issues that cannot be dealt with here. It should be remembered, however, that values represent idealized objectives of human behavior, and that controls, whether exerted by society or by the individual, represent ways of enforcing these values. Thus, a value is the abstract ideal of what is expected of the individual while a control is a social or psychological process by which the ideal is achieved and enforced.

The use of control, as a method of treatment, has generally been frowned upon by the helping professions. Such avoidance of control may in part be a reaction to damage, real or assumed, that has been suffered by clients, or by therapists themselves, at the hands of domineering fathers, castrating mothers, stern teachers, brutal policemen, or punitive judges. Unhappily, this reaction has tended to divert the attention of social workers from this phenomenon and only recently has there been an effort to study objectively the place of social and personal controls in the treatment process. Another unfortunate effect of such reaction was the creation of an artificial antipodality between treatment and control measures. In consequence, the potential, and sometimes crucial, usefulness of various controls for certain clients was often unrecognized and the social worker was thereby robbed of a tool which, if properly used, could be effective in furthering the aims of treatment.

Relationship Between Inner and Outer Controls

The informal controls, obviously, have great power in influencing the behavior of the individual, particularly in his early years when he is absorbing standards from the significant adults in his life. As the standards become internalized, they form an enduring inner self-control system. Even in later years, the process of identification and internalization continues. It would seem that the formal con-

[8] Ernest Greenwood, "Social Science and Social Work: A Theory of Their Relationship," *Social Service Review*, Vol. XXIX, No. 1 (1955), pp. 24–25.

trols, expressed in legal sanctions, are generally less effective in modifying behavior; such sanctions appear to be less powerful in producing long-term positive results. This statement should not be taken to mean, however, that there is not need for externally imposed controls for certain individuals at particular times, or even for many individuals at some time in their lives.

The need for external controls through probation or institutionalization is being increasingly recognized by agencies dealing with persons with character disorders and other types of personality disturbances whose behavior creates danger to themselves or others. Attempts to treat such individuals without the support of some formal control have been relatively unsuccessful. Even in the treatment of other types of clients, the need to set firm, clear demands is often indicated, since such firmness may constitute an ego-supportive experience.[9] Often a crucial treatment problem, in any setting, is to find a way of working with a client within a framework of personal and social controls and still allow room for spontaneity and creativity.

The following brief reports, based on cases treated in various settings, may serve to illustrate the types of control used in the treatment relationship.

John, a gang member, mentioned with obvious discomfort that trouble was brewing on his block. He said that a "rumble" was scheduled over the week end. The worker, observing the boy's distress in the face of real danger, suggested that he stay close to home. He also told John that he would take necessary steps to alert the appropriate authorities to try to prevent the clash. Although such advice and activity on behalf of the client may not technically be "control," the worker was clearly directive and his action was based on social values. In this instance, the worker offered physical protection to the client and also endeavored to relieve anxiety.

On a visit to the furnished room of Mrs. C, whose adolescent son Morton was home for a three-day visit from his foster-care placement, the worker saw only one bed. It was quite evident that Mrs. C and the boy were sharing the bed without being aware of or concerned about the inappropriateness of this arrange-

[9] Jacob Chwast, "The Significance of Control in the Treatment of the Antisocial Person," *Archives of Criminal Psychodynamics,* Vol. II, No. 4 (1957); Dale G. Hardman, "Authority in Casework—A Bread-and-Butter Theory," *NPPA Journal,* Vol. V, No. 3 (1959), pp. 249–255; Calvin F. Settlage, "The Value of Limits in Child Rearing," *Children,* Vol. V, No. 5 (1958), pp. 175–178.

ment. The worker diplomatically suggested that other sleeping arrangements might be more comfortable and thereupon helped Mrs. C to obtain a cot temporarily. This kind of intervention obviously does not deal with the basic problem but it nevertheless is educational. Such direct action by the worker is based on clinical understanding and social values.

Arlene, aged 4½, clouted Mary with a block in the nursery school. As the teacher comforted Mary, Arlene hit George with the same block and then, becoming even more excited, dumped all the toys from the shelf. The worker, who happened to pass by, took Arlene by the hand and led her from the scene to a nearby office, where she soon quieted down sufficiently to return to the group. When no control was provided, Arlene's acting-out behavior continued, which heightened her anxiety and led to further assaults. When control was asserted, both her anxiety and her aggression abated.

Jane, a well-developed girl of 15 from an underprivileged background, was having difficulty both at home and at school. She truanted from school and stayed out late, often not returning home until three or four in the morning. She associated with friends of whom her family disapproved. Finally, after she had stayed out all night, her father took her to court where she was adjudged delinquent and placed on probation. The probation officer found her defensive, uncommunicative, and suspicious. During the course of the contact, it became apparent that Jane's difficulty with her parents and other authority figures was of long standing. The probation officer structured the probationary relationship with her; he informed her in a nonpunitive manner that she could not be permitted to stay out all night. He further explained that such conduct was dangerous and that he felt concerned for her welfare. He pointed out that such actions on her part would necessitate a court hearing, which most probably would be followed by a remand to a detention home. Subsequently, Jane stayed out overnight without permission. This was reported to the probation officer who brought her into court and, in her presence, recommended detention. When the probation officer visited Jane at the shelter, she became communicative for the first time. She told him she was not angry, for he had "leveled" with her and told her exactly what would happen. After this experience, Jane entered into a sustained treatment relationship.

Value Conflicts

In applying controls, the worker must exercise considerable caution. There is risk that the worker, under the guise of promoting necessary adaptations in certain areas of the client's functioning, may attempt to enforce the standards and values of the dominant social group. He may, as a result, intrude into areas of functioning that do not present problems to the client or that are not indicative of possible damaging consequence to the client or others in his milieu. Such intrusion may have the effect of making the treatment relationship an instrument of social control rather than a helping tool; the client's problems may thereby be added to rather than unraveled.

The imposition of certain dominant cultural values is likely to result in a serious lack of communication and rapport between the worker and client, in the establishment of treatment goals inappropriate to the client's needs, and in a treatment approach that contains a strong element of pressure on the client to conform to a particular pattern of behavior. The worker, for example, may unconsciously impose his own middle-class values on the client in relation to education, job selection, courting, and so forth. He may proceed on the assumption that these values are "universals" and are, therefore, equally appropriate for the client and for himself. The following case illustrates this point.

Henry, a 16-year-old delinquent of normal intelligence, came from an underprivileged family and neighborhood. During the course of treatment, he raised the question about quitting school to obtain a job as a shipping clerk in a small factory. Henry's plan evoked, in the middle-class worker, considerable concern, because the boy's academic record showed clearly that he had capacity for a higher level of education. The worker believed that a more appropriate vocational goal would lie in the direction of a skilled occupation, such as that of a dental mechanic or a draftsman. It seemed to him that for the boy to enter a less skilled type of employment would be a tragic waste of potential capacity. Henry, however, was not interested in entering into a long-range educational program, especially since neither his family nor his friends gave him any encouragement along these lines. His father, a longshoreman, with irregular work, had to feed four other children. Also, Henry's mother complained about lack of money. The family expected a boy of 16 to go to work, and their expectation was no different from that of the neighborhood.

It is clear that a conflict in value systems existed between the worker and the client. Although the full implications of the conflict could only be understood by careful analysis of the case, which will not be attempted here, it is obvious that such a conflict created a problem in treatment. The problem might have been avoided if the worker had adhered more closely to the original aim of treatment—to check the boy's delinquent tendencies. If he had been in conflict about leaving school, further exploration of his feelings about the step would, of course, have been appropriate. Henry, however, considered the contemplated job entirely compatible with his personal and social expectations and viewed it as a source of immediate satisfaction. An unskilled vocation was not ego-alien to the boy even though it was to the worker. The worker's value-laden perception of the boy's potentialities and of an appropriate vocational choice gave rise to difficulties in treatment. Such difficulties often arise when the worker and the client, because of different cultural backgrounds and social experiences, do not share the same set of aspirations and goals.

The social worker's middle-class orientation may become conspicuously evident when he deals with problems of aggressiveness and sexuality. To a lesser degree, it may be evident when he deals with such matters as social behavior, patterns of family living, privacy, personal hygiene and appearance, recreational outlets, and education and vocational aspirations. Also, a client's attitude toward his own or another person's possessions and property may be at variance from that of the worker.

In setting goals for treatment, the worker should endeavor to evaluate the appropriateness of his value-laden concepts of desirable behavior and adequate social functioning. If the worker makes the error of considering his own values "universals," his treatment efforts are not likely to succeed. The worker should endeavor to understand the client's values, recognizing that relatively few standards can be validly applied to all members of society. Failure to recognize relative personal and cultural patterns, in fact, can only defeat the purpose of helping persons to attain self-fulfillment in a democratic sense. Also, it may produce unanticipated negative consequences in the treatment process, including new conflicts, increased tension, heightened resistance and, perhaps, a withdrawal from the relationship.

A treatment relationship that does not take into account the client's value system may become a form of coercion and pressure. The coercive element is most likely to appear when the worker deals with persons who do not readily share his own aspirations and whose experiences in day-by-day living are different in character. We do not mean to suggest that social workers must give up their personal and professional values, but only that they recognize that the client's values must also be considered if treatment is to be planned sensibly. Without such consideration, there can be little empathy with the client and little chance of effective treatment.

Another problem in treatment stems from the fact that social workers at times are so permissive and nonjudgmental that they may seem to the client not to stand for anything. When treatment proceeds on this basis, the worker does not provide the client with a sound basis for identification. He may also fail to demonstrate his concern for the client and to offer him the protective care that he may need. This kind of approach is probably the result of the worker's wish to avoid playing an undesirably dominating role. It is not our purpose, here, to appraise the value of a directive or non-directive approach in relation to various treatment situations. We should like to note, however, that the worker must come to accept his role as an enabling person, willing to take responsibility to help the client achieve both self-fulfillment and self-control. There would seem little question, therefore, that the social worker should make clear to the client, at points consonant with the developing relationship, that he subscribes to these principles of a democratic society. Among other things, the worker must make clear that he stands for the rights of others, for lawful procedures, and for solutions by reason and justice rather than by force or trickery. While standing for these values, he must endeavor not to put burdens on the client that will threaten the treatment relationship and create barriers to its forward movement.

The worker should ask himself whether he is trying to make the client a "nice person"—one who is honest, orderly, punctual, industrious, and reliable. Although these values are unquestionably desirable for promoting the welfare of society as a whole—and perhaps of the particular client—he must ask what meaning they have for the client. Are these values meaningful to the client at this time and in his own milieu? Also, to what extent must the client modify these values? Can the worker and his agency accept such modifications? May the demands placed upon the client be tantamount to expecting him to relinquish his sub-group identification? If modifications cannot be made in line with the client's perceptions and needs, treatment success will be diminished.

Value and Controls as They Influence Treatment

It must be quite clear by now that, in the implicit and explicit use of values, social workers are essentially imposing controls on the client. In treatment, we must continually ask ourselves whether the client can be, or should be, helped to incorporate certain values into his own functioning. If we expect him to develop inner controls, the values cannot be alien to him. We know, psychodynamically, that social approval is an important factor in the incorporation of values. Social approval includes the worker's approval, which can be a powerful dynamic when experienced by the client.

In social treatment, there is a crucial need to select an appropriate value focus from a wide range of possibilities. This selection can have real meaning only if it is made on the basis of differential diagnosis. The latter must take into account personal and social data, including a delineation of areas of difficulty and potential or overt danger to the client or to others.

This kind of value focus and its implementation in the treatment process may provide the worker with a foundation for helping clients build healthy internal controls. Such controls, when based on both the client's values and the values implicit in our own social structure, permit a real expression of an individual's potentialities in our democratic society.

AN OUTLINE FOR STUDY OF SOCIAL AUTHORITY FACTORS IN CASEWORK [1]

Elliot Studt

In a recent class in advanced casework, where a parole case was under study, the students formulated alternative propositions about the nature of casework in an authoritative setting. Several students believed that the correct formulation would be, "Casework services are provided in spite of the authority which the caseworker must exercise by the nature of his job." Others suggested that it would be more accurate to say, "Casework services are given in and through the exercise of the authority inherent in the job." In a recent article, "The Function of Contact in Psychotherapy with Offenders," [2] the authors make the point that the psychotherapist who is not part of the legal structure must establish with the offender this separation from legal structure in order to achieve a therapeutic relationship. These are random illustrations of the variety of current ideas about authority and helping which are assumed by many caseworkers to imply that professional help to offenders, directed toward change of attitudes and behavior, is best offered outside the "authoritative agency." [3]

[1] Published in *Social Casework,* June 1954.

[2] By Melitta Schmideberg, M.D., and Jack Sokol, in *Social Casework,* Vol. XXXIV, No. 9 (1953), pp. 385–392.

[3] Both S. A. Szurek and Erich Fromm have defined the word "authoritarian" in such a way that the term "authoritative" would seem more appropriate for application to social agencies. S. A. Szurek ("Emotional Factors in the Use of Authority," in Ethel L. Ginsburg, ed., *Public Health Is People,* Commonwealth Fund, New York, 1950, pp. 212–213) uses the term "authoritative" when the authority relationship is "democratic" or legitimate and is exercised for the welfare of the subordinate; and applies the term "authoritarian" to situations that involve "coercive power" or the exploitation of the subordinate individual by the dominant individual. See also Erich Fromm, *Escape from Freedom,*

Since most of the literature dealing with psychological treatment of offenders has been written by persons outside the formal legal structure, or adjunctive to it, there has been little professional examination of the problems and skills of the caseworker who does carry direct legal responsibility for the offender. Up to this point, the profession has, in general, disposed of questions concerning authority in the casework process by using two propositions: (1) that casework is practiced most freely and satisfyingly in a setting where authority plays the least "handicapping" role; and (2) that in any case where authority factors enter into the relationship, a comfortable attitude on the part of the caseworker toward authority is, in general, all that is required to achieve skillful use of such authority factors. Since there are elements of authority in every agency that offers social services, a more precise development of theory concerning the relationships between helping and authority might be considered a useful contribution of the total body of casework theory.

Discussion of authority factors in the casework process is frequently unclear because the word "authority" itself is left undefined. Two definitions of authority from related disciplines may be clarifying: one referring to the sociological base from which stem formal authority structures; the other formulating the psychological factors that enter into all authority relationships.

A useful definition of authority, derived from sociological analysis, is found in *Power and Society,* by Lasswell and Kaplan,[4] where a series of definitions of the significant words "influence," "power," and "authority" is offered. According to this formulation, *influence* is the generic term, defined as "value position and potential," and its exercise "consists in affecting the policies of others than the self." *Power* is only one—but one of the most important—of the operative values on which influence relations are based. It is defined as "participation in the making of decisions," with emphasis on the fact that power is that form of influence relation which involves effective control over the policy of others. *Authority* is defined as "formal power," "expected and legitimate," or that use of power which has been legitimized in the institutional structure of society.

Farrar and Rinehart, New York, 1941, pp. 164–165, for a similar distinction between "rational authority" and the "inhibiting authority" characteristic of the "authoritarian personality."

[4] Harold D. Lasswell and Abraham Kaplan, *Power and Society,* Yale University Press, New Haven, 1950. See pp. 71, 75, 133.

These authors recognize that a psychological factor enters into operations by persons within such formal structure:

> Authority is thus the expected and legitimate possession of power. . . . To say that a person has authority is to say not that he actually has power but that the political formula assigns him power, and that those who adhere to the formula expect him to have power and regard his exercise of it as just and proper. . . . Thus ascription of authority always involves a reference to persons accepting it as such. . . . Authority is in this sense "subjective"; its existence depends on someone's think-so. . . .[5]

Thus, authority, for the purpose of sociological analysis, is power assigned to a position, and exercised by the individual in that position as he participates in the making of decisions by others. It requires both the delegation of that power to the position according to legitimate means and the acknowledgment by the individual toward whom the authority is exercised that such exercise of power is "just and proper."

Authority Relationships in the Social Agency

Translating these sociological definitions into terms that may be useful in understanding authority relationships in social agencies, we find that power over community resources has been delegated to social agencies to which persons in need of such resources turn; and that authority within the agencies has been assigned to personnel known as caseworkers, who are therefore able to participate effectively in the decisions of clients through the exercise of this formal and legitimate power. Many agencies employ for these positions of authority only those individuals who have, following a period of professional preparation, demonstrated skill and responsibility in the exercise of influence in the lives of those in need. In such instances the authority of expertness, formally recognized through the professional structure of education and experience, coincides with the authority delegated to the position in the agency and is the basis for selection of persons to fill these positions. Every agency, private or public, professionally staffed or not, represents the community-sponsored organization of resources and the resulting delegation of authority to official persons who administer these resources to clients, and who thus exercise formally sanctioned influence over the lives of others.

[5] *Ibid.*, p. 133.

Since casework involves not only the distribution of community resources through socially recognized channels but also the use of interpersonal relations in order to help clients use such resources, we need, for the purposes of social work theory, a psychological definition of authority as well as one drawn from sociological analysis. Erich Fromm has defined authority as "an interpersonal relation in which one person looks upon another as somebody superior to him." [6] It is this acknowledged superiority of one over the other which always appears in a psychological authority relationship—for example, in the teacher-student relationship—that Fromm selects as "the condition for the helping of the person subjected to the authority." [7] All the authority relations included in the definition by Lasswell and Kaplan involve this psychological factor to a certain extent; not all the relationships in which Fromm's "authority" appears are also formally recognized and supported in social structure. However, most of the authority relationships with which social workers deal, such as parent-child, teacher-student, and caseworker-client relationships, are socially recognized and operate within a framework of institutionalized authority relationships.

Social work has long recognized the fact that helping by means of the casework relationship depends upon the acknowledgment by the client that the caseworker is superior to himself for the *purposes of the problem at hand,* and so is able to help. Out of unsatisfying experiences with the impotence of formal authority alone to effect significant changes in the lives of human beings, caseworkers developed the doctrine of the crucial importance of the *voluntary* request for help, since the client, by this act, gives the caseworker the right to help. A formal authority relationship has always been able to secure certain external conformities in behavior depending on the client's need to secure services. But a more meaningful influence relationship is achieved only when the client genuinely joins with the caseworker in dealing with a commonly acknowledged problem, and gives to the caseworker temporary leadership responsibilities in this process. The caseworker accepts the temporary dependency implied in this relationship and attempts to encourage in the client whatever capacities for solving the problem exist within him. In this process the particular authority relation-

[6] Fromm, *op. cit.,* p. 164.
[7] *Ibid.,* p. 165.

ship moves toward dissolution as the client becomes stronger and more able to deal independently with his situation.

An analysis of authority factors in casework, therefore, reveals both social and psychological aspects. Every casework relationship starts with a formal authority relationship. The caseworker is unknown to the client, but is brought together with him by reason of the caseworker's position in an agency to which has been delegated the community's power to help. In each case, and in any social agency, the formal authority relationship must become a relationship of psychological authority if the client is to be helped. It may be said that, in the casework relationship, whenever the psychological aspects of the authority relation develop strongly, the formal, social authority aspects, although still present and effective, become secondary; and the casework process emerges as a particular, highly skilled form of the exercise of influence.

It is possible to order all the social services within which casework is appropriately practiced along a continuum that suggests the specific patterning of the social and psychological authority relationships in each. Variations in patterns along the continuum depend on three interrelated variables: the source of the reality pressures bringing the client to the agency; the extent of responsibility for dealing with the problem assumed by the community; and the difficulty with which the caseworker establishes the psychological authority essential for helping.

At one end of this continuum are found such services as the private family agency and the out-patient psychiatric clinic. In these agencies, the source of pressure that brings the client for help tends to be the psychological suffering caused by stress of problems and maladjustments. The authority of the caseworker depends primarily on professional expertness that is recognized both by the agency in employing him and by the client in seeking this particular kind of help. The casework relationship begins with a degree of psychological readiness on the part of the client to acknowledge the helping authority of the caseworker. In such agencies the client generally remains within the relationship only if he experiences help.

In agencies such as Travelers Aid societies and medical social service departments, the stress that brings the client for help is often related to external emergencies which bother him but which he seldom perceives as suffering produced by an inner problem.

In such agencies the client's acceptance of authority rests heavily on his experience of a reality situation in which he lacks the ability to help himself. In the medical agency the authority of the doctor, who is given great prestige in our society, may influence the patient to perceive the caseworker also as an authority person capable of helping him.

The stress of economic need, a particularly severe external reality pressure, is the effective cause that brings the client to the public welfare agency. In response to this kind of need the community has established public agencies within which the power of the community to relieve need is delegated by law to officials who administer the eligibility requirements in providing services. A century ago, clients receiving such help were assigned a semi-wardship status in relation to the community, with certain restrictions, such as denial of the right to vote to persons on the relief rolls, and community assumption of the right to make disposition of children whose parents could not support them. Such widespread authority over the lives of the economically dependent is no longer part of our public assistance programs, although in relation to the economic aspects of the client's life the authority is unmistakable. A further extension of explicit authority exercised by the community over a particular aspect of the client's life is seen in the public health services, from which individuals with certain illnesses, such as venereal diseases and tuberculosis, must accept medical services and the concomitant restrictions whether they desire them or not.

A more comprehensive assertion of community authority in relation to the life of the client is observed in those agencies in which the client is a ward of the state. In many child welfare services the caseworker is responsible for overseeing and approving all the basic life provisions for such wards. The protective care provided for the mentally deficient and mentally ill wards of the community asserts the right and duty of the community both to provide for and to control certain individuals who may be dangerous to themselves or to others. In these agencies the client enters the casework relationship without voluntary request and is held within it by means of the social authority delegated to the caseworker. Securing the client's acceptance of the caseworker's psychological as well as social authority is necessary in these situations and may be easy or difficult depending on many factors.

In the correctional agencies of the community the authority laid upon the agency includes not only responsibility to care for persons who have been made wards of the state by reason of criminal behavior, but also the responsibility to protect the community from further destructive behavior. The workers in such agencies become "supervisors" of legally determined offenders, participating in legal, quasi-parental relationships with persons who have been assigned a restricted and minority type of status in society. These workers are expected both to administer the restrictions assigned by the community to offenders and to help the offenders modify attitudes and behavior in the direction of "adjustment." In this relationship the client participates without regard to his desire and often against his will. He is held in the relationship by a legal obligation, regardless of real need or psychological readiness. In such casework relationships the task of turning the formal authority relationship into a psychologically useful influence relationship is difficult but is of primary importance. Since in this form of casework service the effect of social authority factors on the casework process is particularly clear, an examination of the problems met in such casework, and the skills to be developed in relation to these problems, may offer clues to the therapeutic use of such authority in any setting.

Social Authority in Correctional Agencies

The social authority relationships in the correctional agency are established by law. The legally determined offender is assigned a restricted supervised status with associated obligations which must be fulfilled if he is to return to normal status in the community. Agencies are created to administer these restrictions and to provide services that will help the offender avoid further delinquent actions. The personnel of these agencies accept legal responsibility to "supervise" the general life adjustment of these wards of the community. Probation and parole officers are those government employees who accept this legal responsibility for supervision over offenders who are permitted to remain in the community. It is obvious, therefore, that it is not possible to speak of the practice of casework by the probation and parole officer "in spite of his exercise of control." Either he can give help within the framework of his agency's assigned function, or he is not properly termed a caseworker.

If a job such as probation or parole is to be studied as casework, it is clear that the services offered in the discharge of its primary functions must be related to the needs of those who are served. Although the restricted status assigned to the offender, with the associated supervision, is legally determined by the community in reaction to an offense, it is often only a formal acknowledgment of a real need in the client for someone outside himself to assume more responsibility for him than is provided for in the normal, unrestricted status accorded a free member of the community.

On the basis of our knowledge of human growth we readily accept the principle that authority, in the sense of loving, effective participation by the more mature and responsible individual in the decisions of the less mature, is essential at all stages of development, particularly at the early, formative stages and in times of unusual stress. Clients who come to the correctional agency have usually experienced special stress and are often persons who, by personality structure, are poorly fitted to handle stressful situations. The correctional case load is largely composed of persons who cannot easily tolerate tension and who have low thresholds for its discharge, who are singularly inept in manipulating their available resources for the purpose of getting normal satisfactions, and who are only tenuously related to the normal group structure of society. The correctional caseworker observes continually in his work his client's ability to damage his own life through producing emergencies, engaging in guerrilla warfare with all representatives of authority, and alternating between acted-out expressions of hostility and dependency. For a large number of these persons the provision of a supervisory individual in their lives seems to be a particularly appropriate response to the needs they are expressing.

Scientific study of the personality types that appear most frequently in correctional agency case loads has been sporadic and is not yet fully developed. Characteristically, these persons do not themselves seek help and so have usually not been reached by those treatment services where individualized study is a usual function. Many of them are known only to the correctional agencies, which are chronically understaffed and limited in resources for research. It is clear, however, that proportionally few classically neurotic individuals and few who are clearly psychotic are to be found in case loads composed of caught and convicted offenders. The central core of the case load consists of those individuals who are variously classified as "acting-out personalities," "delinquent personalities," "anti-social characters," or psychopaths. Much more needs to be understood about the personality needs represented by such persons and the treatment skills that are required. In general we do know that these individuals tend to be persons who need external help in maintaining socially acceptable behavior as well as in mobilizing resources to deal with their problems. Like children, they tend to require in their lives some sponsoring person who has a legal right to provide these necessary services for them. Like children, also, many of them can use a period of supported dependency for their continued growth.

In the correctional case load, even those individuals whose personalities may be relatively well organized need certain services best provided by one who represents the authority of the community. For instance, most offenders require some help in adjusting to the experience of being labeled an offender. The experiences that offenders undergo in arrest, detention, and court hearing often intensify their tendency to withdraw from participation in the normal community, and so separate them still further from the normal group controls provided by the community. The community, perhaps unconsciously recognizing the potential danger to mental health in hostile separation from community life, has created in probation or parole a formal relationship between the offender and its representative, thus keeping him within the reach of influence and providing a bridge to reacceptance on both sides. Also, many legally determined offenders, simply by reason of their restricted status, require, as do many persons in minority status, some mediating person in authority who can effectively mobilize community support for them. Since persons of all kinds and with every sort of need are to be found in correctional case loads, much depends on the caseworker's ability to individualize these persons and their needs and to exercise authority accordingly. The correctional caseworker is responsible for determining the degree of seriousness of the individual offender's problems, how strong the supporting control structure needs to be, and what kinds of social and personal treatment are required. Thus the probation or parole officer, like any other caseworker, makes an individualized approach to persons in his case load in rendering a basic community service that is provided for a designated category of persons with problems.

Casework Functions with Offenders

Making a differential diagnosis of needs and personalities is part of every caseworker's task. The probation or parole officer, however, has certain casework functions that seem particularly dependent upon his legal authority over the offender for their successful discharge: (1) holding the client within a relationship from which he cannot legally withdraw and within which the problems leading to delinquent behavior can be identified and tackled; (2) helping the client digest emotionally the experience of having been classed as an offender; (3) assuming sponsoring responsibility for the client in the re-establishment of normal relationships with the community.

In discharging these three responsibilities, the probation or parole caseworker is attempting to heal a broken social relationship between the offender and his community for the benefit of both. These tasks can be accomplished only by a person who has clear legal responsibility for the welfare of the client, and who is accepted as a responsible authority by both the client and the community.

If we accept the propositions that the services provided in legal supervision of the offender are designed to meet some urgent needs that he is evidencing in his behavior, that certain services cannot be given to him without the legal framework implied in such supervision, and that these services can be properly individualized within the legal requirements, then it is appropriate to study the casework skills by which help is given within such a framework. The social authority factors arising out of such a framework will be seen to affect the casework process and will modify the skills by which help is given. Following is a tentative list of the skill problems met by the professional caseworker who seeks to give psychological help within the supervisory structure of probation or parole.

Problems in Achieving Psychological Authority

1. *Dealing with the characteristic negative transference attitudes which the offender brings to his first contact with the new person in authority and which affect the process of establishing a helping relationship.* These attitudes are, of course, primarily derived from early parental experiences, but in offenders they are found to be distorted and exaggerated by more recent experiences with other representatives of community authority such as police, jailers, judges, and custody personnel in institutions. The offender's ex-

pectations of his new "supervisor" tend to be overwhelmingly negative, while his defenses against entering into a relationship with a person so perceived are strong, ranging from rigid control to fawning conformity. Perhaps the greatest hazard of work with the offender is the ease with which his readiness to perceive the caseworker as hostile, destructive, and magically powerful, and his resulting defense against relationship, render ineffective the worker's efforts to understand and to help.

Everything that Dr. Schmideberg has said [8] about the positive, direct action required on the part of the psychotherapist to establish, in the first interview, a reality relationship that will make communication and helping possible, is equally important for the caseworker who has supervisory responsibility for the client. The difference lies in the fact that the correctional agency caseworker, in making clear his position, will be explicit about just what legal functions he does carry in regard to the client's life. Beyond this difference he will be as active as the psychotherapist in evidencing knowledge of the offender's experiences and culture, in taking initiative to establish a relationship in which feeling can be expressed and to demonstrate that he is a person who can be trusted.

Important professional questions requiring study in connection with this problem include: What are the skills required to establish with the necessary speed this positive reality relationship? Are there individuals who, because of unusually severe difficulties with authority persons, are unable to relate on any basis except a formal one with the caseworker who is responsible for supervising them? If there are such individuals, how can they be recognized and steered to other services for treatment? What are the appropriate treatment goals for the relationship that it is possible to establish between the offender and the social authority figure in his life?

2. *Avoiding a distorted initial psychosocial diagnostic formulation; modifications in the client's behavior due to his experiences with law enforcement and correctional processes immediately preceding his first meeting with the supervising caseworker often occur.* This is a corollary of the first problem but emphasizes the effect of such experiences on psychosocial diagnosis. At whatever stage in the correctional process the caseworker begins with his client, he will find that the experiences preceding this relationship will have had effect not only on the feelings expressed by the client but also on his

[8] *Op. cit.*, p. 388.

behavior and ways of relating. For instance, the parole officer may well find that, during the first six weeks to three months of parole, the client's symptom picture will be so much affected by the preceding period spent in the institution that beginning hypotheses concerning the nature of the client's personality will have to be modified as he becomes "free" psychologically as well as physically. In study of this problem, not only will characteristic distortions of the psychosocial picture resulting from certain kinds of experiences become clear, but the diagnostic value of these for understanding the client's patterns of dealing with authority will be demonstrated.

3. *Handling the increased dependency manifestations in the client's behavior resulting from his quasi-minority status.* This status has been assigned to him and stimulates what may be already severe dependency needs. These dependency strivings are particularly evident in the relationship with his "supervisor."

4. *Relating himself to the varied authorities institutionalized in his agency—judicial, administrative, and treatment—which he must represent to the client.* In working with an individual client, the caseworker may be administering concurrently the orders of the court, the limitations of agency procedures, and the recommendations of the consulting psychiatrist. In the correctional agency, both judicial and administrative authorities set particularly stringent controls on the treatment process because of the weight of responsibility toward the community. As a caseworker, he needs to be able to differentiate with the client between the controls which govern them both and the areas in which he and the client have discretion in developing treatment plans. His own relationship with the authorities inherent in his agency will affect his ability to communicate comfortably with his client as a person in authority.

5. *Using legal procedures and the framework of restrictions as supports for treatment goals and as the content of a socially reeducative process with the client.* This point refers to the little-understood skills involved in such formal processes as writing petitions in such a way that they contribute to the client's acceptance of reality; using the probation investigation so that at the end of the process the client has a better appreciation of his problem; structuring the court hearing experience in such a manner as to maximize its contribution to emotional education; handling parole rules so that they function in a way that brings significant questions for discussion into the relationship with the caseworker.

6. *Working with family members and community agencies from the vantage point of a person in authority in the client's life.* This use of one's position of authority in the client's life for the purpose of encouraging support from other persons is a use of authority to which probation and parole officers must give much attention. The effect of his restricted status on the offender's relationships, and the skills of an added figure in authority in dealing with the normally constituted authorities in the offender's life, need further elucidation as a part of our theory concerning the effect of social authority factors on casework processes.

Throughout his work with the offender, the caseworker in the correctional agency will be concerned to use his socially delegated authority to support and educate his client. While accepting his formal position of authority and using its structure for therapeutic purposes, he will also recognize that formal authority alone never accomplished the casework goal of freeing human beings for richer life. He will, therefore, not deny his position of authority; he will use it in many helpful ways; but he will also seek to build within its framework an experience of psychological authority which will result in a true influence relationship. In studying how an influence relationship may be built within the framework of formal authority, the above listing of points in the basic casework process, where some modification of skill in achieving a position of psychological authority occurs as a result of social authority factors, will be found useful. Since a formal framework of authority exists in all casework relationships, analysis of skill adjustments required in the correctional setting may offer meaningful suggestions about the use of social authority factors wherever they appear.

GROUP THERAPY WITH FATHERS[1]

Emanuel Hallowitz and Bernice Stephens

NINE MEN AND one woman were seated around a conference table on a Monday evening in February.

The woman was saying, ". . . We shall be meeting here weekly; there will be no chairman, no agenda, and there will be no parliamentary procedures. We do not have to observe the rules of polite social exchange here; you can talk whenever you want to and should feel free to interrupt each other."

Mr. Goldberg immediately spoke up, saying, "Look, we're all here for the same reason—because we have problems. I think that the group can be a lot of help to me and to the rest of you. We ought to think about how to begin. It seems to me the best way is to go around the table, with each of us telling what has brought us here." Mr. James cut in: "I'll toss you for the right to speak first."

Thus the first meeting of the Therapy Group for Fathers in the Bronx district began.[2] This preliminary report covers only the first seventeen weekly meetings, which ran from February until early summer of last year.

The purpose of this paper is to show the therapeutic possibilities inherent in discussion groups for adults. In addition, we believe that the content of the discussions throws light on the conflicts,

1 Published in *Social Casework,* April 1959. Presented at the Professional Conference of the Community Service Society of New York, held at the Statler Hilton Hotel, New York, N.Y., November 6 and 7, 1958.

2 Miss Stephens was the therapist for this group and Mr. Hallowitz the supervisor.

confusions, and anxieties that operate in many male clients, and thus the report should contribute to more effective individual work with them in a family agency. Our emphasis, therefore, will be on an analysis of the treatment process as it unfolded in these seventeen sessions.

Our broad objective in this project was to improve the functioning of these men, particularly in their role as father. Specifically, we wanted the men to feel that as fathers they had an important role to play in their families and that they had a significant contribution to make to the welfare of their children. We also wanted the men to develop greater understanding and empathy for the needs and feelings of their children.

Nine fathers were selected for the group. All were white, ranging in age from 35 to 45. Several had not completed high school while two had advanced professional training. The three major faiths were represented.

In two instances the case had not progressed beyond the intake study; in five others the family had been receiving continued service for more than a year but the father had not been seen more than three times; one man had been having bi-weekly interviews and another weekly interviews. In all instances, the wives were having regular weekly contacts.

With one exception, the families were in the middle or lower-middle class. Most of the children were in latency or pre-adolescent periods. Although marital conflict was expressed or implied in all of the cases, the marital relationship seemed sufficiently steady to preclude the danger of separation. In most instances, the families had sought help from the agency because of concern about the children's difficulties. In general, the wives had complained that their husbands were uninterested in the family affairs and left the burden of raising the children to them. Each of the fathers directly or indirectly revealed confusion about his role as father.

Although there were many differences in the functioning of these men as fathers, there was an impressive similarity in their underlying problems. They seemed to be experiencing struggle between their passive and aggressive impulses. It was also apparent that most of the fathers suffered conscious or preconscious guilt about having produced an "imperfect" child.

Initial Reactions

The attitudes expressed by these fathers during their preparation for the group varied considerably. One man was so shy and had so much difficulty talking that neither the caseworker nor the group therapist tried to sustain a full interview with him. He said he had thought the group would discuss the problems their wives were having. On hearing that it was to help fathers, he said, "I'm sure I could use that, too." However, he asked no questions about the group and could verbalize no specific concerns about his children. "Kids are a headache, and I'm sure I'd be interested in anything the men discuss."

Another man first said that he was too busy to come, and that he thought he understood his boy quite well. He believed that if he had time to spend three or four hours a day with him there would be no problem. "Actually," he said, "the problem is really between my boy and my wife." He added that he thought the group would be like a confessional and, for his part, he could confess his sins to himself. He concluded that he would come for a trial, since it was a professional recommendation.

A third man was quite willing to co-operate, but he minimized or denied all the problems, saying that he had an unusally happy family life. He asked how far a father should go in helping his boy to become athletic. He added that experts disagree about this as they do about how to handle infants and, as a result, parents do not know what to believe.

A fourth father said that his boy was not working up to capacity because outsiders had favored his more talented sister. He indicated that the boy was getting better and the problem seemed already solved. He added that coming to the agency had nothing to do with improvement. He expressed interest in attending, however, and said he felt he could be helpful in getting the group started. He thought the men would get bored with discussing problems, and so he offered to organize refreshments and to bring craft materials to sustain their interest.

With this brief background of the men, let us return to the opening meeting. The therapist had indicated that the men could talk about whatever they wished and that they need not follow any rules of procedure. The man sitting next to her attempted to take over as leader, but Mr. James cut in to tell his story.

Throughout the meeting the men talked at great length; there were no silences or lulls and they never once turned to the therapist to watch her reaction or to ask her a question. They did not indicate in any way that they were aware that she was present in the room.

One might say that this was a noble beginning! Here was a group of men eager to talk, to reveal their problems, and to help each other. If, however, we examine the content of their remarks, we begin to sense that there were two dominant themes: (1) they had no need of help for themselves, and (2) each felt competent to help the others. In other words, the nature of the discussion and their rejection of the woman therapist suggest that each was attempting to demonstrate how adequate, how potent, how competent, and above all, how independent he was. This was their first major resistance: they were afraid that their feelings of inadequacy, impotence, and helplessness would be exposed.

Mr. J told the men that he had been coming to the agency because his daughter was "emotional"; the big problem was that she showed no respect. With a good deal of angry feeling, he gave several examples of her behavior. "She gives a snotty answer when told to do something. . . . One of her nasty habits is to stuff herself after finishing a good meal that I work hard to provide for her. . . . She always finds some way to create a disturbance and I can take just so much and then I clout her across the mouth." He then went on to talk about an experience he had had that day on a bus. Some teen-agers were pushing the bus so that it rocked and seemed about to turn over. They had stayed at the doorway, blocking it, and they threw snowballs at other children. He had had to go four blocks past his stop, and when he got home and talked to his wife about coming to the group, he had said that perhaps all children act in this way.

It is obvious that he was telling the group that there might be something wrong with his daughter but not with him and that he could not be blamed for his daughter's difficulties since all children today behave badly. Throughout this first meeting, Mr. J reported that he and his wife had tried everything, that he had done all he could, and yet his daughter was impossible because of her "emotional" problem. At this point, Mr. J did not want help in handling his daughter. Rather, he was trying to convey to the group that the problem lay with his daughter. He was attempting to justify his anger and his wish to hurt the girl, and wanted the group to tell him he was right and to commiserate with him. It is clear that he was disturbed because he could not control his daughter, who, as a woman, should be weaker than he.

Mr. Knight also talked about his problem child, a daughter who was slow and retarded. He commented that most mothers are with their children more than the fathers. He said all of the men in the group seemed to work long hours. He thought the trouble with most children was their mothers, who were either too good to them or too strict.

Mr. Maguire told about the problem he had had with his son, who was a little firebug. The only thing that worked was to give the kid a good "shellacking," which would hold him for a while; the trouble was that a man can forget how strong he is and there was danger that he might hurt the boy. His boy had ear trouble, and if he were hurt, Mr. M would have to pay the doctor's bills. He said nothing bothered the boy, not even being hit; the boy was foxy, knew how to get around his father, and Mr. M could not "find his weakness."

Mr. M's production highlighted the general theme. The feeling of impotence felt by the men at not being able to control their youngsters was graphically stated by Mr. M: "Joe has found my weakness but I cannot find his."

Diagnostically, it is important to note how the other men reacted to such reports. In the early sessions, they tended to minimize the problems that a father presented by calling them "normal," or "typically adolescent," or by saying that "all children are that way." Also, they tried to find quick remedies, usually through use of "gimmicks." Frequently, before a father had a chance to elaborate his concern, the others interrupted to ask "have you tried" this or that. When their suggestions and recommendations were brushed aside by the particular father, they felt frustrated and their anger mounted. They argued and shouted and sometimes pounded the table. It was apparent that their anger and frustrations were out of proportion to the situation and that the experience of having their advice brushed aside stirred up their feelings of impotence and inadequacy. It was also clear that the father who rejected the advice felt misunderstood and that his sense of adequacy was threatened.

Although the men disagreed and argued with each other, they

were actually quite generous in their recognition of the speaker's difficult situation and of his sincere interest in his family. They were aggressive and assertive, but there was little attack or counter-attack.

First Phase of Treatment

In the early sessions, the men continued to talk freely. The frustration they felt at not being able to control the children continued to be highlighted. They asked: "How much should a father do?" "Don't they also have rights?" They continued to place the fault on society, the school, their wives, or the children themselves, and they continued to ignore the therapist.

In spite of the seeming lack of progress, a number of significant things were happening. They were discharging a great deal of anger and relieving feelings of frustration. They were discovering that other men who, to all intents and purposes, were adequate also had troubles; thus their sense of uniqueness and feelings of isolation were breaking down. Many of these men were saying things that they usually suppressed—things that ordinarily bring censure and reproach. Here they were listened to by their peers and a woman in authority, who showed understanding and respect. Such acceptance tended to reduce their guilt.

During this early phase, the therapist was very cautious in her participation. She kept in mind that the transference, while ambivalent, was heavily weighted on the negative side. She was careful not to confirm the men's fear that she would be attacking, depreciating, and controlling like their wives and mothers. She was especially careful not to attempt to puncture their rationalizations, projections, or denials. She was not intent on getting them to admit to their own "part in the problem." She kept in mind that projections and denials are evidence that these fathers cannot tolerate admitting their own contribution to the problem, *particularly* within the framework of a negative transference.

At this stage of treatment, it would be inappropriate even to call attention to their negative feelings toward her. It would seem to these men that she was "seeing through them" and exposing their weakness. Therefore the therapist rarely intervened in the discussion. Her participation was limited almost solely to enabling one individual to communicate with the others and to keeping the discussion going when the group had arrived at an impasse. The aim was to have the men experience the therapist's intervention as helpful, supportive, and relieving of frustration. When the men talked about the shortcomings of the schools, the negative effects of TV, the breakdown of social controls in society, and so forth, the therapist agreed with them but added that "the parent's job is tougher today because of all this."

During this period attempts were made to sensitize the men to the needs of their children. Each such attempt by the therapist, no matter how phrased, was brushed aside. It became evident that the children were symbols of their own failures and inadequacies and, as such, were the objects of their anger. Also any attempt to help them try to understand their youngsters implied incompetence on their part and therefore was viewed as an attack on them. Not until they were "sure" of the therapist and felt less threatened by her could they become somewhat objective and begin to look at their children's needs.

Second Phase of Treatment

The value of the group process, as an aid to our therapeutic endeavors, became clearer at this point. Despite the negative transference to the therapist, the men continued to participate in the group. They gradually drew closer together, identifying with each other on the basis of common interests and common concerns. They expressed a wish that their children would be more on their own and less dependent on them. One father's wish that his son would be more athletic found a responsive echo, since all members seemed to be troubled by the passivity of their children and considered it as a reflection on themselves.

As their mutual identification and mutual support increased, the men felt strengthened and showed greater readiness for participation by the therapist. They were freer in directing questions to her and responded positively to her remarks. It now seemed safe to enable the men to express some of their anger and hostility toward the agency, their caseworker, and the group therapist. The therapist indicated that it was natural for them to have such feelings and that having them did not imply they were inadequate in any way. In these discussions they revealed their anger toward women for not helping them enough and also the reverse—their resentment when help was offered. When they failed to get enough attention, they felt deprived; when help was offered, they believed the woman was attempting to control and dominate them. Their underlying fear was of the phallic mother whose giving had been hostile, controlling, and damaging.

As their anger slowly dissipated, they began to take a somewhat more realistic view of the nature of their difficulties. In the fourth session, one of the men asked if each person felt his problem was less severe since he had learned that other fathers were having similar problems. Also in this session, there were signs of beginning identification with the children; some of the men confided that, as children, they also sat back in school even when they knew the answers. The identification at this point, however, had dual implications. They could now be more sympathetic toward their youngsters, but at the same time they felt increased threat because they saw their own weaknesses in their children. Also, their guilt about their treatment of their children came nearer to the surface.

The therapist highlighted their comments. She pointed out that they were concerned about whether they had caused their children's problems. She said that the group had talked of children, both in the present session and the preceding one, as though they were carbon copies of the parents. The men watched the therapist closely while she was speaking, and Mr. Knight volunteered the remark that the therapist was right—that deep down in their hearts they knew that their children were struggling with the same problems that they themselves had had in the past. The therapist's uncritical attitude, together with the support they received from each other, tended to relieve their guilt, paving the way for healthier identification with their children.

In the sixth session, their positive feeling for the children came more to the fore. The group discussed how to avoid showing favoritism to one child. The men gave examples from their own experience and mentioned that sometimes one child is really more adequate than another. What can a father do if one child gets excellent marks on his report card and the other does not? Gradually, they became aware of the feeling of the second youngster and gained a glimmering of the vicious circle involved in failure and parental disapproval. The group began to talk about looking for things a child can do with some success, and they mentioned that it is not success that is so important but the feeling of accomplishment. The men finally agreed that it was up to them as fathers to find ways for children to accomplish something and achieve some recognition. One father commented, "We must learn to praise the outstanding points of the youngster so we can get off this merry-go-round."

The eighth session was a high point in the group experience and represented the end of the second treatment phase. The related conflicts of dependence versus independence, passivity versus aggression, and impotence versus potency were clearly expressed. The handling of these conflicts, by the therapist and by the group members, resulted in a substantial decrease in the negative transference and a marked reduction in the men's defensiveness. The following examples highlight the process.

Although each man in the group was struggling with essentially the same conflict, they lined up in two opposing sides in this session, each acting as protagonist for one side of the ambivalence. The men who affirmed their wish for independence did so in ways that demonstrated clearly their positive identification with the therapist and the incorporation of some of her attitudes. Others continued to be negative. For example, Mr. Collucci, the man who had complained early that experts never agree, said, with much anger, "We do not get a 'yes' or 'no' answer here and we are left to think out for ourselves what is right and wrong!" Some of the other men immediately took the opposite view, saying that it was neither necessary nor advisable for the expert to say what was right or wrong, that each parent and each child is different; they had been coming here to get some new ideas.

Of particular interest were Mr. Maguire's comments; he had told early of "shellacking" his son Joe and not being able to find his weakness. He said now that one of the things that had happened to him was that he saw his son's problems in a different light; they did not seem so big when compared with the problems of others, and so he had found he was not now pressing the boy so hard. He thought he had expected too much from him; he and his wife no longer made Joe come home at noon but permitted him to have lunch in school. He felt more comfortable now about letting Joe do this and Joe enjoyed it. Also, Joe had a new two-tone jacket which he had wanted to wear with the light side out. Mr. M first had objected because it would get dirty, but instead of "clouting the kid" as he would have done earlier, he had thought about the boy's feelings and had let him wear it the way he wanted. He said he was going to see how this new approach worked out—time would tell. Also, Joe had worked in the garden last week end; Mr. M had expected that Joe would be a nuisance, getting into trouble as usual, but to his surprise the boy had really tried to help. So Mr. M had given him a piece of garden for his own. He is going to let him tend it and grow what he would like there.

Mr. Collucci returned to an argument that he and Mr. Benton had had at the last session. Both their sons had wanted to buy an identical cheap camera. Mr. C had not objected to the purchase even though the boy had a similar camera at home; he thought it was all right for the boy to indulge himself in this way with his own money. Mr. B had not permitted the purchase because he considered the camera trash and he felt a father's job was to teach children the value of money. Mr. C now said that he and Mr. B each had had conviction about his own point of view. He said they both could not be right—there can be only *one* right answer. Mr. B interrupted to say that Mr. C's report was not exactly true. He had had his opinion when the question came up, but after discussing the pros and cons here, he realized that he had not understood everything that was involved. He had been thinking about it during the week, and he now realized that a child has some right to money he earns but that a father must teach him and help him develop judgment. One of the other men pointed out that he too had been doing some thinking about the incident and he thought that both Mr. C and Mr. B learned something from each other. The therapist supported this point, saying that fathers have a role to play in helping a youngster weigh values when he spends his money; when the money belongs to the child, the father, after he has made his educational effort, may need to give the child freedom of choice. The youngster, however, must learn to live with the consequences of his choice. The group seemed to be in agreement about this point of view.

The discussion then returned to whether there should be a "yes" or "no" answer from the expert. The therapist then threw her weight on the healthy side of the ambivalence, appealing to their masculine strivings and, at the same time, endeavoring to allay their fears of domination and castration. She stated that she did have specialized knowledge and experience which she was willing to share with them, but she believed that, as they came to understand their children better and to recognize some of their own interfering attitudes, they themselves would be able to find more effective ways of dealing with their children. Mr. C, who had been most vocal in his wish for specific advice, replied that he believed he already had learned a few things. He had thought more about his situation at home and about his boy and about himself. He believed the discussions had been helpful, but he was not always certain about the right thing to do. The therapist said that there are no "right" answers in the sense of telling people what to do, but that parents, as they become more aware of their own attitudes and understand more about their children, can handle situations more effectively. They themselves can decide how they want to raise their children and what will be best in their families. Mr. C then said the point was becoming clearer to him—that it was *he* who had to make up his own mind about what he would do in his own family. He said, "In a way this is pretty wonderful."

In these excerpts from the group record, we see a number of major dynamics that account for the changes that had been taking place in these families. It is clear that each of the men had begun to think more consciously about his relationship to his children and what he might do to help them and the total family. They became aware that, as fathers, they played an important role in the family.

Third Phase of Treatment

In the following sessions, the men were obviously more relaxed and in better communication with each other. They were more alert and perceptive of each other's attitudes. When one member confronted another with questions about what he might be doing to his youngster, it was done in a kindly, supportive manner. In turn, the father could listen to the others without becoming defensive.

The shift in their orientation to treatment and in their concept of the father's role was evident in a discussion about setting limits for children. The content was quite different from that of early meetings when they had expressed concern about controlling their youngsters, receiving respect, and so forth. Their own conflicts about how passive or how aggressive they should be were now closer to the surface. The former angry tone when they talked about their children was no longer present; instead they spoke with concern and really struggled to understand their youngsters. With the decrease of defensiveness, the anxiety provoked by their children's behavior came to the fore. Since these men had had to struggle so hard to master their own impulses, their controls had been threatened by the free expression of similar impulses in their children.

Their anxiety was decreased through ventilation, mutual support, and particularly by the therapist's attitude. It was further dissipated or brought under control as they gained some understanding of their children's feelings and behavior and as they discovered new ways of responding to them.

The relationship with the therapist became increasingly less ambivalent. They turned to her more frequently for her opinion and were more receptive to her comments. With the shift in the transference, the therapist began to test out their readiness for deeper involvement. For example, in the eleventh session, when it became clear that the other men could not sway Mr. Maguire from his insistence that he would not permit his 14-year-old son to obtain summer employment, the therapist intervened. She explained to the others that Mr. M might not be able to see as many positives in summer jobs as they did because of his own experiences. This comment enabled Mr. M to tell about being forced to work at a young age even though the money was not needed at home. With encouragement from the other men, he elaborated his history. He said he did not know what kind of life the others had lived, but he had had a strict mother. If he had come up to kiss her when he was a boy, she would have slapped him because she would think he was trying to get something out of her. She had refused to spend money on coal, and he had had to keep firewood supplied for the stove. He did everything for his mother, and a younger brother made her life miserable; she had always complained about the latter but, when she died, she left her money to him. Mr. M said he had been pushed around and that was why he felt so bitter.

The other men then also revealed more about themselves. These revelations, within the content of a more positive transference, enabled the men to initiate a discussion of sex. The subject of sex, which came up in the thirteenth session, was first focused on their children. "When should you tell children about the facts of life?" "How much should you tell?" "How should you tell it?" and so forth. In the following session, Mr. Goldberg reported with great satisfaction that he had been able to talk with his young son, who was entering puberty, and they had a "wonderful" discussion. He referred to this experience several times in the next few weeks, indicating that it had been a great achievement for him and had given him considerable satisfaction.

With the therapist's help, they began to move from discussing the facts of sex to sexual feelings and their expression in dirty jokes, dirty words, masturbation, and intercourse. Although there was some intellectualization, much of the discussion had a personal, emotional tone in which their conflicts and conclusions were apparent.

Mr. Knight, the man with the retarded daughter, now spoke about his son, who "had no modesty." When someone spoke to him, he often "felt himself." He put his hand in his pocket and clutched at his penis, especially when he felt shy or nervous. The men exchanged some ideas about this behavior, mentioning that the boy sought comfort; it was like sucking or chewing and fondling a favorite blanket. The therapist recognized that these comments were, in part, rationalizations and made a few comments designed to reduce anxiety. She agreed that certain physical activities were comforting, but noted that as children grow older, masturbation has a different meaning. When boys enter puberty, the sensation in their genitals increases and they have erections and they masturbate. Often they worry about it and feel ashamed and guilty. Mr. K agreed and added that when he was a boy and had "wet dreams," even though he had had no sexual thoughts, he had been embarrassed since he knew his mother would see the sheets. He added that when a person is young he does not understand about these things and he is afraid he may hurt himself or may go crazy. He said that he remembered that the kids said a boy would become "stupid" or a "jerk" if he masturbated.

One man asked, "What should a father do when a son gets an urge? Should he take him to a prostitute?" The question led the men to a discussion of their sexual experiences, particularly while they were in the armed services. Mr. K said that the first thing he did when he was on leave in the army was to go to a prostitute. He was not ashamed, and it seemed physically necessary for him to do so. Some of the other men stated they would have liked to "play around" when they were in the army but were concerned about their wives' finding out or about getting a venereal disease. One man insisted that in the navy they had no "pro kit" and he therefore would not have dared to philander even if he had wanted to.

Out of such discussions, some men gained new information, others became aware that their attitudes were not as universal as they had assumed, and all seemed to experience a degree of relief. The therapist was not unaware of the transference implications; her matter-of-fact attitude about the subject and her acceptance of their revelations seemed to be relieving.

Evaluation

In the last of the seventeen sessions covered in this report, the men did some self-evaluation. Among other things, they said that talking things out was a relief; that this was the only place a man could really talk about his children; that one could not talk with friends or neighbors, for they might think that either the child or the parent was "nuts"; that in the group discussions, even when some idea does not apply to them at the time, they store it up and they can use it later on.

After they had mentioned a number of positives, the therapist indicated there could be negative points as well. Mr. Goldberg said one of the drawbacks was that most of the men had come for a specific answer. After a time they learned that there were no cut-and-dried answers and that they would have to work these out for themselves; he knows now that fathers have to gain more understanding and have to get to know themselves and their children better. The group concurred with Mr. G's evaluation.

Another measure of the effectiveness of this project is the change in functioning of these men. There were nine original members; one withdrew after two sessions and another after ten sessions. An appraisal of the change in functioning of the others was made on the basis of their statements in the group, and on caseworkers' individual interviews with them and with their wives.

Of the seven men who continued, one made only minimal gains, although he stated that he had experienced some relief from anxiety. The other six made improvements in their functioning as fathers. They demonstrated more active interest in the children in their daily lives; they talked more freely and undertook more social activities with them. They showed greater understanding of their children; they permitted and encouraged their sons to be more self-assertive and to engage in masculine activities. The men participated more actively and constructively in the daily management of the children, achieving a better balance between overcontrol and overindulgence. There was a diminution in their tendency to view their children as rivals and to view their wives as enemies. As a result, they were able to support their wives in some areas of daily management. In short, six of the men demonstrated in their daily living a fuller and freer assumption of an appropriate father role.

Mr. Benton perhaps made the most startling change. He was the man with whom neither the caseworker nor the group therapist originally could sustain a full interview. His wife reported that her husband had changed remarkably, especially in his relationship to their two youngsters; he now was more outgoing and did more things with them. Formerly he always reprimanded their son and overlooked their daughter's shortcomings; now he was able to reprimand the daughter if necessary. The group experience had helped her husband understand why she was coming to the agency; he was now more considerate of her difficulties. What pleased her most was that he now talked things over instead of hiding behind his newspaper. During the early sessions of the group, he would not tell her anything about the discussions, even though she "needled" him. Later, he voluntarily brought up the questions, discussing them with her and telling her the point of view he had taken. He told her that he found it a relief to know that other fathers have problems similar to his and that together they could usually find some solution to them. She concluded by saying, "He has become a real father."

Conclusion

The record of these seventeen meetings reveals quite clearly that the group method of treatment enabled these men (despite their early guardedness and resistance) to participate in the discussions and to become emotionally involved to an extent that might not have been possible in individual interviews. As each man perceived that others had similar difficulties, he felt less disturbed about his own failures and those of his child. When a man did not feel able to talk, there were others to carry the ball; but even when he was silent, he could participate through identification with a less fearful member. Also, negative feelings were more freely expressed because of the "safety in numbers." Most important of all, each man received considerable recognition from his peers for his concern about, and his efforts in behalf of, his family.

We should like to call attention to a few of our observations that may have implications for the treatment of fathers, not only in group therapy but in individual treatment.

1. At the beginning of this project, there was question on the part of the wives of these men, and sometimes on our part, about the degree of their interest in their families. It soon became evident, however, that they had deep concern but that, because of their feelings of failure and personal guilt, it was hidden behind their efforts to demonstrate their adequacy. It therefore seems advisable, in the early stage of treatment, to avoid pointing to the part played by the fathers in creating the difficulties; instead, focus should be on the positive contribution that they can make as fathers to their families. It seems wise not to puncture their defenses but, rather, to go along with their rationalizations, projections, and denials, giving them credit for seeking help with the tough job of rearing a family.

2. Because of their inability to control their children, these men felt tremendous anger and frustration since their failure represented a confirmation of their weakness. Beneath their anger were feelings of guilt and anxiety; guilt about having produced an imperfect child and anxiety stemming from the threat to their own controls which they had established with great difficulty.

The fathers, therefore, need ample opportunity to express their angry feelings toward their children; it seems unwise to try to help them see the positives in the early phase of treatment or to question their wish to exercise control over their youngsters. Only after they have discharged some anger are they able to develop sensitivity to their children's needs.

3. The transference factors must be carefully handled because of the strong negative component. Contact with the agency may signify failure to these men. Their negative feelings are likely to be more acute when they must take help from a woman. The negative feelings are further increased when a man comes because of urging on the part of his wife and particularly if she already has

had many contacts with the same caseworker; under such circumstances he fears that the caseworker will be allied with his wife and be controlling, depreciating, and fault-finding—that is, have the same attitudes that he ascribes to his wife.

The fact that these men accepted the offer of help was an indication that the transference was not completely negative. Their ambivalence was apparent in their dependence on the therapist; they felt deprived and unworthy if they did not get attention but, at the same time, they denied their need of help. It seems inadvisable, in the early stage of treatment, to highlight the men's negative feelings toward the therapist since this will confirm their weakness and failings and suggest that the therapist has power "to see through them." As their fears diminish, the positive transference is strengthened and they can then begin to identify with the therapist.

4. Perhaps the most important principle in working with fathers is that we be identified with them. It is the parent who is our client, even though our goal includes helping a troubled child and the family as a whole. Treatment therefore should be designed to restore and to build the father's self-esteem. Attempts should be made in many different ways to affirm his masculinity and competence. Only after he gains some confidence and security can he reveal his concerns and anxieties.

A STUDY OF CASEWORKERS' PERCEPTIONS OF THEIR CLIENTS [1]

David Fanshel

DURING A FOUR-MONTH period early in 1956, the sixty professionally trained staff members of the Family and Childrens Service of Pittsburgh were engaged in filling out a rather imposing research schedule designed for the purpose of *surveying* the agency's casework operations. The schedule was a precoded instrument, almost twenty pages in length, constructed in collaboration with a committee of seven caseworkers. The purpose of the survey was to illuminate some of the social and psychological characteristics of the agency's clients as observed by the caseworkers who had direct contact with them and to relate this information to the clients' patterns of using the agency's service.

This paper presents some of the background, findings, and implications of this research effort: (1) why such a study was undertaken; (2) the basic methodological issues involved in using caseworkers as direct sources of data about clients; (3) some of the substantive research findings, illustrative of the kinds of information that can be obtained in a survey approach to a caseload; (4) the implications of some of the findings for administrative planning and for the development of research programs in social agencies; and (5) future directions for research programs in social agencies using caseworkers as direct sources of judgmental data.

[1] Published in *Social Casework,* December 1958. See David Fanshel, *An Overview of One Agency's Casework Operation,* Family and Childrens Service, Pittsburgh, Pennsylvania, 1958, the full report of this research study on which the present article is based. The study was made possible through a grant made by the Howard Heinz Endowment of Pittsburgh.

The decision to invest time and resources in a broad review of its caseload was made by the agency staff on the basis of two major considerations. First, the staff recognized that the statistical data gathered by the agency gave only the barest kind of information with respect to the characteristics of clients. There was an equal paucity of information about the nature of the professional investment that was required to help the many different kinds of client who come to the agency. In Pittsburgh, as elsewhere in the country, agency statistics had essentially been concerned with the volume of clients as it affected the size of caseloads, the interview count, and the waiting list—a low order of counting procedures. This kind of data was periodically supplemented by various do-it-yourself types of research efforts designed to meet emergent planning needs as well as to supply qualitative information related to staff development. Such research excursions as these most frequently involved obtaining only the general impressions of strategically located caseworkers as key informants. In some instances more formalized written schedules were utilized. The staff felt, however, that these efforts did not provide the kind of information required for sound administration of the casework program. The administrator of the agency was too often in the position of the pilot of a modern airliner attempting to fly by feel rather than by navigational instruments.

A second motivation for the agency's having undertaken this survey was the belief that its new research program would be significantly enhanced if there was first developed a basic body of information about the characteristics of clients coming to the agency and the nature of the service rendered. The diffuseness of thinking shown by caseworkers when asked to suggest suitable research undertakings seemed to be related to their confusion arising out of the fact that the agency was serving such a wide variety of clients who wanted help with such a wide variety of problems.

Choice of Study Method

In this study, the caseworkers were asked to record many simple facts about their clients (for example, source of referral, marital status, problem presented for consideration, and so on). They were also asked to give some admittedly speculative *opinions* regarding the nature of the client's difficulties and his readiness to use casework help. These data were intended to tap the workers' diagnostic skills. We have used the term "opinions" rather than "judgments" because of the desire to differentiate this form of data collection from the kind more frequently used in research in casework settings, that is, the reliance upon expert *judges* who make various ratings of client and worker characteristics based upon the reading of case records.[2] The use of judges has been found to be a valuable source of data in projects which have had a specific research focus. With stringent training procedures, a high degree of reliability can be achieved in the rating of various kinds of complex behavior. The following limitations associated with this procedure, however, were considered when this particular study was contemplated:

1. The use of judges for securing data is an expensive process. The training of judges to standardize judgments is time consuming, as is the process of reading records and recording judgments.

2. The judges are limited by the nature of the recording done by caseworkers. Many of the data required in an overview operation are often not recorded by caseworkers.

3. Although a high degree of reliability can be obtained among judges, there is no evidence to prove that what the caseworker records reflects accurately what has transpired in the casework contact.

For many years, casework records have been regarded as a potential gold mine of information for research purposes. The assumption underlying this particular research excursion was that the *caseworker*—more than the *case record*—was a potential store of treasured information. In the professional training of the caseworker major emphasis is placed on sharpening his skills in the perception of human beings and thus of enhancing his diagnostic understanding. This kind of perception is a crucial element in much of social work practice. Agencies do, in fact, depend upon this skill in the making of various kinds of decisions (for example,

[2] The studies at the Community Service Society of New York, which led to the development of the Movement Scale, and the studies at the Research Center of the University of Chicago are examples of major studies which have relied upon the use of judges to read case material for the purpose of making qualitative ratings of clients and workers. See J. McV. Hunt, Margaret Blenkner, and Leonard S. Kogan, *Testing Results in Social Casework: A Field-Test of the Movement Scale,* Family Service Association of America, New York, 1950. Also, Lilian Ripple, "Motivation, Capacity, and Opportunity as Related to the Use of Casework Service: Theoretical Base and Plan of Study," *Social Service Review,* Vol. XXIX, No. 2 (1955), pp. 172–193.

the decision to place a client on a waiting list, to place an infant with a particular couple for adoption, to place a homemaker in a home, and so forth).

It was felt that there was value in recording, on a systematic basis, a variety of impressionistic observations of the caseworker—for example, the outlook for the case, the insight shown by the client, the client's vulnerability in selected areas at closing. These impressions would then be correlated with the known social attributes of the client (socioeconomic class, race, sex, and so on) as well as with administrative aspects of client behavior (number of interviews sustained with the agency, source of referral, payment of fees, and so on). Although the survey approach is based upon *subjective* impressions of individuals, there is value in recording them if for no other reason than the fact that the subjective orientation of the caseworker may be operative in the individual case. Thus, the finding in this study that 45 per cent of the cases are seen by the caseworker as *unpromising* is significant, particularly when it is found that this rating of the potentiality of cases is predictive of subsequent estimates made by other caseworkers of changes (for example, improvement or lack of improvement) that have taken place in the client's situation.

Substantive Findings

A. *Capacity-to-Communicate:* As part of the attempt to individualize the caseworker's portraiture of the client within the framework of a precoded questionnaire, a 22-item profile was developed. The caseworker was asked to indicate whether each item was "apt to be accurate" or "apt to be inaccurate" in describing the client. The items were chosen on the basis of reading a considerable number of case records and selecting those individual characteristics which appeared to be related to the over-all prognosis of a case. Six items of the profile were used to form a Capacity-to-Communicate Scale (or, possibly a better term would be, a Capacity-for-Meaningful-Communication Scale). It was speculated on an *a priori* basis that these items might be related to a common, unidimensional issue: the ability of the client to communicate *in his role as a client of a casework agency.* The items were intended to tap not only the caseworker's perception of the specific ability of the client to verbalize his ideas and feelings but also the degree to which the individual's acculturation in the role of client permitted the caseworker entry into areas whose exploration was necessary for the solution of his problem. The items and the distribution of the responses for the 538 clients included in the study are as follows:

Item	*Rating*	*Score*	*Per Cent of Caseload*
1. Client tends to be articulate	Accurate (yes)	1	75.0
2. Client is able to verbalize feelings	Accurate (yes)	1	60.9
3. Client seems wrapped up in self	Inaccurate (no)	1	49.7
4. Client tends to disguise hostility	Inaccurate (no)	1	37.1
5. Client tends to compartmentalize problems	Inaccurate (no)	1	28.1
6. Client seems very candid about personal faults	Accurate (yes)	1	23.6

In the distribution of the caseworkers' ratings shown below, it is evident that some of the items are said to describe a majority of the clients while others are less common. Thus, three out of every four clients are said to be articulate (that is, they can engage in normal conversation without any particular handicap) whereas only one in four clients is said to be candid about personal faults. The fact that the six items show a smaller and smaller percentage of clients who show strength in each area mentioned is interesting. Of greater significance is the finding, based upon Guttman Scale analysis, that an internal consistency is evidenced in the ratings of caseworkers. Thus, it appears that all six items seemed to have a bearing on a central issue—the capacity of the client to communicate in a meaningful manner.

The Guttman Scale is one of several scales developed for use in various attitude studies conducted during World War II. The Guttman approach to scalogram analysis hypothesizes that items related to a given attitudinal dimension have an order such that, ideally, ". . . persons who answer a given question favorably all have higher ranks on the scale than persons who answer the same question unfavorably. From a person's rank or scale score we know exactly which items he endorsed." [3] Thus, the fact that the above items are scalable means that the caseworker has located his client's strengths with regard to this dimension. Thus, if the client showed a rarer attribute, such as being "candid about personal faults," he tended to show strength also in the preceding five items. That the

[3] S. A. Stouffer *et al., Measurement and Prediction,* Princeton University Press, Princeton, New Jersey, 1950, p. 9.

discrete perceptions of the caseworker actually showed internal consistency upon analysis is significant [4] and suggests that a professional discipline was operating in ordering the caseworkers' perceptions.

The clients were organized into the following sub-groups for purposes of later cross-tabulation with various client attributes:

	Total Points	*Number*	*Per Cent*
Low communication capacity	0 or 1	138	26
Moderate communication capacity	2 or 3	241	45
High communication capacity	4, 5, or 6	159	29
		538	100

The potential usefulness of the scale for practice must await further replication and refinement. For our sample, the scale served to illuminate several aspects of the phenomena in which we were interested.

There proved to be a significant relationship between the client's score on the Capacity-to-Communicate Scale and the caseworker's judgment regarding the client's potentiality for making use of casework help for the resolution of his problem. Thus, in the following table we see that fewer than one in five clients showing *low* communication capacity are rated as having at least an even chance of resolving their problems through casework help, whereas 31 per cent of those showing *moderate* capacity and 56 per cent of those showing *high* capacity are rated in this fashion. (See Table 1.) This finding has potential significance (if the scale is validated in future research) in that it seems to bear witness to the fact that casework help, as it is now available, is tailored more for the verbal, communicative group than it is for the significantly large group of clients who find difficulty in expressing their feelings and their basic ideas about the problems that bring them to the agency.

Of further interest is the finding that the scores achieved by clients on the Capacity-to-Communicate Scale did *not* discriminate between clients who continued in a casework relationship and those who terminated in an early stage *for the caseload taken as a whole.*

[4] The scale achieves the 90 per cent coefficient of reproducibility, and errors are randomly distributed. However, individual item error does not uniformly stay within the 10 per cent limit of acceptability and thus indicates that the scale is as yet an imperfect instrument and bears further study. A method for IBM tabulation of data was used here to test the scalability of the six items. This method is described in Robert N. Ford, "A Rapid Scoring Procedure for Scaling Attitude Questions," *Public Opinion Quarterly,* Vol. XIV, No. 3 (1950), pp. 507–532.

TABLE 1

CASEWORKERS' RATINGS OF THE POTENTIALITIES OF CASES ACCORDING TO THE CLIENT'S CAPACITY TO COMMUNICATE
(N=538)

	Low Capacity	*Moderate Capacity*	*High Capacity*
Case is promising	7%	15%	26%
Case has even chance	11	16	30
Case is unpromising	63	48	23
Casework judged not particularly appropriate form of help	14	15	18
Caseworker unable to estimate	5	6	3
	100%	100%	100%
Total cases	(138)	(241)	(159)

NOTE: Significant at the .001 level as tested by chi-square.

TABLE 2

MARITAL PROBLEM CASES: NUMBER OF INTERVIEWS COMPLETED WITH PRIMARY CLIENTS ACCORDING TO CLIENT'S CAPACITY TO COMMUNICATE
(N=136)

	Low Capacity	*Moderate Capacity*	*High Capacity*
One interview	35%	54%	41%
Two interviews	31	15	8
Three interviews	17	16	12
Four interviews	4	3	4
Five interviews or more	13	12	35
Total cases	100%	100%	100%
	(37)	(60)	(39)

NOTE: Comparing those clients with fewer than five interviews with those continuing for five or more interviews for high capacity and medium and low capacity (combined), significance level reaches .01.

These scores *did* discriminate, however, between continuers and discontinuers when clients who came with concern in regard to a marital problem were looked at. Table 2 (p. 299) shows that the *high* communication group shows 35 per cent continuing in a treatment relationship compared to 12 per cent and 13 per cent for the *moderate* and the *low* groups, respectively. This would seem to indicate that communication skill has some bearing upon continuance patterns when the problem presented by the client involves an area that requires fairly intensive treatment, such as marital difficulty. It would also suggest that a *high* level of communication skill is a minimal requirement for influencing more complex patterns of client behavior.

B. *Potentiality of Cases:* In the total sample of 538 cases there was the following distribution of caseworker ratings regarding the potentiality of cases as seen in the intake interview:

	Per Cent
Very promising case	3
Somewhat promising case	13
Case has even chance	19
Somewhat unpromising case	22
Very unpromising case	23
Casework not considered particularly appropriate for problem	15
Caseworker unable to make estimate	5
	100

These ratings were associated with the following other facts:

1. Fewer than half of the clients who came to the agency with a marital problem were seen as having at least an even chance of resolving their problem through casework help. Situations involving parent-child conflict were considered significantly more promising. Later analysis showed that these differences in ratings were related to the fact that individuals who came because of concern with parent-child relationships were more positively oriented toward becoming involved in a treatment relationship than those clients who came with a marital problem as the major object of concern.

2. The greater the extent to which personality factors were attributed a causal role in the creation of the problem presented by the client, the less optimistic was the worker about the general prognosis for the case. The amount of insight shown by the client into the nature of his own contribution to his problems was also

closely related to the worker's outlook for the case. Also, the more the problem was attributed to the client's personality functioning (as contrasted with problems whose etiology was attributed to external factors), the more compensatory insight seemed required by the worker in order to rate the case optimistically.

3. There was an association between the socioeconomic class status and the caseworkers' estimates of the potentiality of cases. Thus 28 per cent of the cases in the lower-lower-class group were considered promising or to have at least an even chance. The same was true of 38 per cent of the upper-lower group and 47 per cent of the middle-class group. These ratings appeared to reflect the fact that various class groupings showed different expectations of service, with the lower-lower-class clients showing a greater interest in receiving concrete assistance than the other groupings. There were other factors differentiating the behavior of clients according to their socioeconomic status which may have influenced the caseworkers' general outlook upon cases. For instance, it was found that lower-lower-class clients tended to be agency-referred whereas middle-class clients often came on their own initiative. There were also some suggestive differences in communicative capacity for each stratum of clients.

4. With regard to source of referral or of information about the agency, it was found that clients who returned to the agency after having previously been clients tended to be viewed as having somewhat negative potential. This group also showed the highest dropout rate after the first in-person interview. Referrals by physicians, lawyers, and ministers also had a negative prognosis and a high dropout rate. Clients who were referred by social agencies (44 per cent of the caseload) or who were informed about the agency's services by friends or relatives (19 per cent of the caseload) fell in a middle range as regards the caseworker's prognosis. A group of clients who rated unusually high in the estimate of the staff and who showed the strongest continuance pattern was the relatively small number of clients who had looked up the agency in the classified telephone directory.

5. At termination, there was a greater tendency for the caseworker to report improvement in the cases rated *promising* at intake than in those rated *unpromising*. This relationship held even when one-interview cases were excluded from the analysis on the assumption

that early discontinuance might automatically cause the worker to rate a case as *unpromising*.

C. *Continuance-Discontinuance Patterns:* The number of interviews sustained by a client is one measure of his use of an agency. Although continuation in a casework relationship is not a guarantee that a client will benefit from service, the point is well made by Ripple that "with the exception of a small group of short-term completed service cases . . . continuance is the necessary antecedent to use of service." [5] It seems to be a patent fact that, if an individual comes with a relationship problem and fails to return after the first interview, there is little likelihood that a major impact was made on solving the problem.

Aside from our previously mentioned finding that continuance was associated with the type of problem presented by the client and with the referral source, the following additional facts are of interest:

1. Original client expectations are predictive of continuance patterns. At least seven out of ten of those clients who were seeking some form of concrete assistance or information and referral terminated contact after one interview. On the other hand, two out of three clients who expected to be involved in a substantial treatment relationship continued for three or more interviews.[6] Only a third of the clients who desired the agency to manipulate other members of the family continued for three or more interviews.

2. No significant association was found between the continuance patterns of clients and the attributes of race, sex, and age. There was some association, however, between continuance and the client's

[5] Lilian Ripple, "Factors Associated with Continuance in Casework Service," *Social Work,* Vol. II, No. 1 (1957), p. 87.

[6] The pattern of interview distribution shown for this sample of clients closely approximates the experience reported by the Community Service Society of New York, which reported a study of 360 new cases:

Interviews	*Family and Childrens Service (Pittsburgh)*	*Community Service Society of New York*
One	46%	49%
Two	13	16
Three	9	8
Four	6	4
Five or more	26	23
Total cases	(538)	(360)

See Margaret Blenkner, "Predictive Factors in the Initial Interview in Family Casework," *Social Service Review,* Vol. XXVIII, No. 1 (1954), p. 71.

socioeconomic status. The lower-lower-class clients showed the highest dropout rate. This was related to the heavy demand of this group for concrete services. The upper-lower group showed the same proportion of continuers as the middle-class group but had greater initial turnover.

3. The estimate of the client's mental health status did *not* appear to be related to continuance patterns. On the other hand, the estimate of the amount of insight shown by the client at intake did show a significant correlation with the number of interviews the client was able to sustain.

D. *Mental Health Status:* A relatively simplified classification scheme was utilized in an attempt to locate the clients in our sample as to their mental health status. The five basic categories and their representation in the caseload were as follows:

	Per Cent
Generally asymptomatic, normal	25
Transient situational personality disorder	11
Psychoneurotic disturbance	12
Character disorder	22
Borderline psychosis (3%) and psychosis (1%)	4

The casework staff was able to locate three fourths of the clients in one of these five categories. Another 8 per cent were placed in an undefined category, "Other," which included a number of mentally retarded individuals as well as clients who showed a variety of behavioral difficulties. The remaining 18 per cent of the cases could not be classified because the caseworker felt that the contact did not provide the kind of information that justified making an estimate. Some interesting facts were revealed by an analysis of these judgments, although the categories were admittedly rough-hewn.

1. There was a close association between the caseworker's estimate of the mental health status of a client and his estimate of the potentiality of a case. In relation to clients judged to be normal, only 15 per cent of the cases were seen as *unpromising*. The opinion that the case was "unpromising" was given by the worker in relation to 33 per cent of those clients showing stress due to a transient situation, 53 per cent of those suffering from a psychoneurosis, 68 per cent of those with a character disorder, and 82 per cent of those who were psychotic or borderline. In comparing the psychoneurotic clients with those suffering from a character disorder, it is

to be noted that the proportion of the latter seen as *very unpromising* was twice as great as was true of the former.

The finding of a hierarchical order of mental health classifications as reflected in the worker's prognosis may create the temptation to treat the two global estimates as interchangeable (that is, that the statement that a client is "normal" is just another way of saying his situation is "promising"). Other analyses tend to show that this is an oversimplification of the finding and that actually other ratings associated with mental health status tend to show the caseworker to be more discriminating in the selection of mental health categories.

2. There was a close association between the caseworker's classification of the client's mental health status and the degree to which he saw personality factors operating to create the problem which the client brought for solution. The same close association is found with regard to the amount of insight into the causes of his problem shown by the client.

3. The psychoneurotic client stood out in a singular fashion as expecting to have his problem studied in contrast to the normal client and the individual undergoing a temporary stress situation; the two latter most often expected concrete assistance. The clients seen as suffering from character disorders most often expected some form of concrete assistance or the manipulation of others.

4. Almost 50 per cent of the normal clients and those suffering from an unusual stress situation scored high in communication capacity compared to a fourth of the psychoneurotic group and a fifth of the character-disorder group.

5. There was an interesting variation in the caseworker's predictive judgments for clients included in the several mental health categories concerning their future *vulnerability* in selected areas of living. Thus, the character-disorder group and those suffering from a borderline or full-blown psychosis were seen as having twice the proportion of clients who were vulnerable to chronic economic dependency as the normal group, those undergoing a transient stress situation, and the psychoneurotic group. On the other hand, the character-disorder group was not seen as being particularly vulnerable to suffering mental breakdown, whereas the psychoneurotic group was outstanding in this connection. When the caseworker

was asked to rate the vulnerability of clients to becoming engaged in delinquent or criminal behavior, the character-disorder group was seen as the most vulnerable.

With reference to self-destructive behavior, the psychoneurotic, the character-disorder, and the psychotic groups showed considerable vulnerability. The same held true with respect to the prediction for the client suffering severe disruption of family life, except that in this regard the group showing stress due to a transient situation also appeared quite vulnerable. One interesting finding was that the clients thought to be suffering from a psychoneurotic disturbance were rated as even less vulnerable than the so-called "normal" clients to the hazard of requiring protective or substitute care for their children.

The varying differentiations made by the caseworker in the rating of clients again suggests the fact that a professional discipline was operating to guide his judgments.

Implications of Findings

For Administration: The most significant impression derived from this study is that the direct observations of the caseworkers who have had contact with the clients can form the basis on which meaningful differentiations can be made in relation to the agency caseload. These differentiations can then be used in administrative and research planning. With the type of data available in this study, the administrator was able to locate information which would not otherwise have been available. For example, a public relations committee of the agency was trying to decide the direction of its activity and its emphasis for the coming year. There had been substantial interest in reaching other professional groups. The findings of this study—which indicated that self-referrals were more productive than referrals from professional groups, such as physicians, clergymen, and attorneys—led the committee to emphasize reaching the consumer directly rather than trying to reach the intervening professional person. The committee recognized, however, that there was also a need to do more effective interpretation to professional groups.

For Research: The problem of developing meaningful typologies as a basis for studies of social agency operations is one that concerns many researchers and practitioners alike.[7] This research study confirms the belief that useful typologies will not issue full-blown from some enterprising researcher's brain. Rather, such typologies will be hammered out on the basis of repeated trials in actual research excursions until the most *functionally useful* categories will emerge from the numerous items that have been thrown into the hopper. This is not to say that real creativity in the development of items is not needed. The final carving-out of a useful typology must be based, however, on careful statistical analysis to determine which items show the greatest discriminatory strength in explaining client behavior.

There is a great need for agencies to engage in relatively simple projects involving the systematic recording of the basic phenomena associated with the client's use of service. Once this phenomenology is made quite clear, more sophisticated research projects will readily suggest themselves.

One cannot help going through the analysis of material such as was used in this study without constantly becoming aware of other sources of information that might shed further light upon the casework operation. A few that have occurred to the writer are as follows:

A study of clients' perceptions of what they have experienced at the agency: This material might be gathered at the same time that the caseworker is recording her impressions of what has transpired in the contact. Thus we would have the reports of the two major actors in the system of casework, the client and the worker. These observations could be studied for the divergence and congruence of each actor's perceptions as to what has transpired in the interaction.

A study of the key decisions made by the caseworker in the course of the intake contact with the client: From this study we have seen that the original expectations of clients regarding the service they wish to receive at the agency appears to have a strong conditioning effect upon the future development of the case. They are highly predictive, for instance, of the number of interviews the client is able to sustain. In the face of this, it is of interest to codify all possible worker reactions to the various kinds of expectations presented by the clients. Decision making goes on all the time in social casework, and these choice points in the practice situation are worthy of concentrated research interest.

A study of characteristics of the caseworker as these relate to patterns in the client's use of service: Just as we have examined the social and psychological characteristics of clients and related these to administrative facts, it is possible to

[7] The present lack of adequate typologies in social work is seen by many individuals as one of the major barriers to the development of sound social work research programs. See, for instance: Dorothy Fahs Beck, "Current Research and Study Projects," *Social Casework,* Vol. XXXIX, Nos. 2–3 (1958), pp. 105–113.

do likewise with the social and psychological characteristics of caseworkers. Are there, for example, identifiable traits of caseworkers that are related to patterns of continuance and discontinuance of cases? Perhaps such judgments about caseworkers can be made by having judges view the caseworker's performance through one-way screens.

Conclusion

This study was conducted in a particular agency in a specific geographic area. It is doubtful whether the findings are applicable to other agencies with different populations and their own unique programs. Rather, it is hoped that the material reported here may primarily serve the function of suggesting to other agencies ways of approaching their caseloads for analytical purposes. In addition, no particular brief is held for the specific variables chosen for inclusion in the research schedule. It is hoped that greater experience in this area will result in an improved nomenclature for assessing the activities of caseworkers and for the classification of clients and their problems.

The executive of the agency, Perry B. Hall, has made the following commentary about the agency's experience in this study: "It would appear that this limited experience would at least indicate that an agency can secure full and major participation in research by an operating casework staff if at least three major ingredients are present in the situation: that the research person himself has an obvious identification with casework goals and basic acceptance of the validity of the casework method of helping people; that the administration of the agency indicates in more than words that research has acceptance, status, and a primary place in the agency's concerns; and that the specific piece of research is geared to questions which make sense to the operating staff. Given these three ingredients, it is obvious that many of the research methods must also be adapted to be reasonable and workable to an operating staff. For example, in this instance the lengthy questionnaire was entirely precoded so that while it took thought and judgment it did not take extensive writing time."

Part III
Teaching and Supervision

THE SCIENTIFIC COMPONENT IN THE CASEWORK FIELD CURRICULUM [1]

Samuel Finestone

Some major educational assumptions underlie this discussion. The first, long accepted, is that training in scientific ways of thinking and the attendant development of scientific attitudes are components of professional education for social work.[2] The second, also accepted but not as manifest in educational practice, is that scientific training and development should permeate the entire curriculum; such a goal is appropriate, not only for the research course and the thesis requirement, but for all academic and field work as well. The rationale for this second assumption is that unless the student is given opportunity to develop a scientific orientation in the parts of the curriculum most directly related to practice, he will not be emotionally and intellectually able to integrate such an approach into his total professional outlook. One of the practical implications of this assumption is that field and classroom instructors, as part of their shared responsibility for the content of the field experience, must provide opportunities for the student to acquire the attitudes, knowledge, and skill that characterize the scientific method.

The attainment of this educational objective of providing training in scientific method and attitude requires organic introduction of relevant content into the sequence of field experiences. Just as a scientific approach cannot be effectively taught by encapsulated presentation in the research course, so it cannot be taught by isolated

[1] Published in *Social Casework,* May 1955.

[2] Katherine A. Kendall, "Education for Social Work," *Social Work Journal,* Vol. XXXV, No. 1 (1954), p. 19.

experiences in the field. To be sure, the scientific approach is not sufficient in itself; for casework is art as well as science, calling for skill as well as knowledge. Yet the principle holds that the field instructor in his day-to-day activity should provide opportunity for student experiences favoring skills in and attitudes of scientific inquiry as intrinsic to casework and social work practice.[3] In the planning of field work teaching, simultaneous consideration needs to be given to the student as a learning person, to the development of his casework and social work knowledge and skill, and to the development of a scientific outlook.

It is obviously necessary to set down some specification of the broad term "scientific component." What is meant by this phrase? It is used here with a generic, nontechnical meaning, not in its more narrowly technical sense. The scope of scientific method as a component of field instruction in social casework does not include such technical and specialized aspects as problem formulation for research purposes, research design construction, and methodological technique. It is true that some understanding of these aspects is required of the graduate of a school of social work, but these more specific aspects are dealt with in the research courses and in the project or thesis requirement. What then *is* pertinent for field work?

Specifics of the Scientific Component

From the viewpoint of pertinence to social work education, the scientific component in the field work curriculum encompasses four closely related goals for student learning. The student should be helped (1) to acquire *an attitude favoring scientific inquiry;* (2) to gain some facility in *the discipline of scientific inquiry;* (3) to develop *an ability to think conceptually;* and (4) to link *values of human welfare to the processes of scientific inquiry.* Instead of one diffuse term, we now have four perhaps equally diffuse terms. To make these terms somewhat more meaningful requires some elaboration, however brief, as well as an attempt to apply them specifically and concretely to field work.

An attitude favoring scientific inquiry is based upon awareness and acceptance by educators and students of the fact that much of

[3] See Charlotte Towle, "Some Basic Principles of Social Research in Social Case Work," *Social Service Review,* Vol. XV, No. 1 (1941), pp. 66–80, for a stimulating discussion of similarities in social research and casework.

social work knowledge is fragmentary or untested. Corollary to this acceptance is a curiosity about the unknown or unconfirmed. The desire to discover and test is characterized by concern for evidence and for reliable and valid inferences from evidence. A sense of accountability for one's own inferences or those of others is involved. In the student, this attitude requires, among other things, willingness to face change in his own ideas and in the ideas of others. The attitude is as pertinent in work with individual cases as it is in learning social work theory generally. In the educator, this attitude involves a view of social work as a changing, not a static, profession. Generally, then, this first educational goal may be termed the development of research-mindedness—a problem-solving attitude characterized by independent and critical thinking.

The discipline of scientific inquiry is related to the development of a scientific attitude. Here, we expect to see the attitude manifested in well-established habits of exploration of evidence through interviews, observation, and analysis of pertinent written material. Thoughtfulness in drawing inferences and conscious activity in the testing of inferences are also part of the scientific discipline. The scientific discipline in casework involves examination of phenomena from both qualitative and quantitative points of view. The aim to be achieved is systematic and logical thinking; that is, ability to use the concepts and processes of scientific inquiry in casework practice, and to relate them to agency and community programs and to underlying theory.

The ability to think conceptually is especially bound up with the understanding of underlying theory. The student should be helped to relate empirical knowledge of behavior to general theory, and to relate treatment specifics in particular cases to general principles of treatment. He should learn to identify the particular in the general, and the general in the particular. He should be able to search for and recognize similarities as well as differences in the cases with which he works. He should apply general theory flexibly and he should recognize the developing nature of theory. He should be able to distinguish between value concepts and technical concepts, and to separate value preferences from scientific theories.[4]

[4] See Robert C. Angell, "A Research Basis for Welfare Practice," *Social Work Journal*, Vol. XXXV, No. 4 (1954), pp. 145–148, 169–171. In a section entitled "Three Kinds of Misunderstanding" (pp. 148, 169), Dr. Angell illustrates the presence of value and technical concepts in casework practice.

All this implies the ability to identify, define, and apply pertinent concepts. It would be unrealistic, however, not to recognize that the field as a whole must still identify concepts useful in psychosocial study, diagnosis, evaluation, and treatment, and define them in precise operational terms.[5] Students cannot, of course, be expected to learn more than the field has to offer.

Linking human values to the processes of scientific inquiry involves, in the first place, the incorporation of value assumptions.[6] This goal is included because social work proceeds from a basic assumption that any advance in the welfare of individuals and society is a positive good. This fundamental ethic has implications for developing research-mindedness in students. These values—such as the belief in man's potential ability to understand and control the psychosocial forces affecting him, the desire to find means of preventing as well as of relieving distress, and conviction about social action directed toward progressive mastery of the conditions of life—all influence the selection by social workers of problems for research. These values influence the way in which research-mindedness is taught. On the case level, the interrelationship between scientific inquiry and concern for treatment of individual need should be made clear; on the social level, scientific inquiry and concern for social betterment should be connected. It might be said, also, that the scientific approach, as evidenced in attitude, knowledge, and skill, helps to provide a link between individual treatment and social betterment.

Application to Field Work Training

How is the scientific component of social work, as here described, to be taught in all parts of the curriculum? Particularly, how can the four goals be included as part of field work learning in casework? It must be acknowledged that any attempt to answer the latter question will be largely arbitrary, since there is not a body of experience readily available for analysis. Field work teaching has been technically oriented to emphasize the development of casework understanding and skill and of professional self-awareness necessary to

[5] For a pioneer effort in this direction, see *A Conceptual Framework for Social Casework,* School of Social Work, University of Pittsburgh, 1954.

[6] Eduard C. Lindeman, "Science and Philosophy: Sources of Humanitarian Faith," in *Social Work as Human Relations:* Anniversary Papers of New York School of Social Work and Community Service Society of New York, Columbia University Press, New York, 1949, pp. 207–221.

this process. Recently, emphasis has been put on the contribution that field work can make, by teaching more than narrowly technical matters, to the development of a broad, professional outlook in the student. This new viewpoint has stressed that conceptual learning takes place in the field as well as in the classroom. However, research is not yet embedded in the programs of many agencies, and consequently research experience or the learning of research concepts takes place to only a limited degree. Hence, what is to follow is partly a projection of what we may look for as well as an analysis of what already exists. It is hoped that supervisors will review the points presented here, and test the value and comprehensiveness of the suggestions offered.

Generally speaking, both the content of the cases assigned to students and the content of other field experiences may be useful in the development of a scientific component in social work. Consideration will be given, first, to case assignments; later, to other kinds of field experience.

The Scientific Component in Casework

Casework, with its central emphasis on the basic interrelation of psychosocial study, diagnosis, and treatment, is fully consonant with the premise that activity in each case requires of the practitioner not only skill but a scientific attitude. Each case constitutes a problem to be solved by systematic inquiry, by formulation of hypotheses that tentatively explain the problem, and by a process of testing these hypotheses through treatment. There are, of course, significant differences between a piece of social research per se and the casework process. They are not so great, however, as to nullify the statement that scientific inquiry is part of both.

What happens in casework? An individual or family experiences some breakdown in social functioning resulting in psychosocial disequilibrium. The situation then comes to the attention of a social agency or social service department through a request for help by the troubled individual or by someone else in his behalf. These events lead to systematic exploration, or psychosocial study, of the problems.

The study process has a number of technical elements; we can select a few of the most pertinent for the teaching of scientific skills and attitudes. The very concept of social study, with its emphasis on the necessity for evidence and on the exploration of pertinent facts, is a powerful reinforcement for habits of scientific thinking. Underlying the exploration process, in which the client's concerns and problems are the center of inquiry, are some basic assumptions about the field of attention. Similar assumptions underlie any piece of social research.

In casework the field of attention comprises the psychological, social, and physical facts that are thought to be related to the client's problem. This field of attention exists as a general guide which structures casework inquiry.[7] The student should be helped to understand that while the field of inquiry is relatively constant for any one period in the development of social casework, it is not absolutely so. The field of attention of twenty years ago differed from the current field; the next twenty years similarly will demonstrate differences. Like psychoanalytic concepts, social science concepts have reached a level of formulation where they are becoming increasingly usable,[8] and will tend to widen the psychosocial field of attention. The educational principle involved here is that the student should be helped to understand the range and extent of relevant theory, so that in practice he keeps the entire field in mind. This is not to say that in each case the entire field is covered. Some problems do not need this total inquiry, and the client's readiness to share information at a particular time also affects the scope and timing of exploration. If a student gets the sense of a broad field of attention, is able to apply theory flexibly in practice, and yet is aware that the field of attention changes with developing knowledge, he has mastered an important aspect of scientific thinking.

Some of the specific principles involved in the casework study process lend themselves to the development of a scientific approach. Students should gain an understanding of the conscious and unconscious selectivity and distortion that operate in a client's conflicting statements; thus they should learn early not to accept uncritically what is said or what appear to be facts. This attitude of critical intellectual evaluation is necessarily combined with the caseworker's emotional acceptance of the client and of himself.

[7] See Florence Sytz, "The Unit of Attention in the Case Work Process," *The Family*, Vol. XXVII, No. 4 (1946), pp. 135–139. Miss Sytz traces historically the changing range of content characteristic of the field of inquiry in the diagnostic process.

[8] Herman D. Stein, "Social Science in Social Work Practice and Education," *Social Casework*, Vol. XXXVI, No. 4 (1955), pp. 147–155.

A related principle is that the caseworker should not, directly or subtly, consciously or unconsciously, predetermine the client's responses. Predetermined conclusions, rather than flexibly held alternate hypotheses, lead to the kind of interviewing which does not permit genuine exploration of a client's problem.

Specific facts, whether of an emotional or more tangible nature, are needed before a situation can be understood. Securing sufficient and meaningful information is not only a matter of intellectual alertness, but also requires that the student have emotional freedom, empathy, and ability to relate to clients. Indeed, it is difficult to separate, except for purposes of analysis, the student's emotional and intellectual equipment, his "intuitive" and "scientific" skills.

Psychosocial diagnosis emphasizes the processes of inference from data, as social study emphasizes the processes of collection of data. Diagnostic inference includes two overlapping levels: the descriptive and the causal. On either level, what is aimed at is an ordering of the data obtained through social study into meaningful description and causal relationships. This ordering results in a series of related and tentative hypotheses in each case—hypotheses that are tested out and may shift in the course of treatment. This is, of course, a broad and oversimplified description of what occurs. In an actual case, social study, diagnosis, and treatment overlap to a much greater degree than their descriptions indicate, but it is convenient to separate them in discussion.

In the processes of inference, some "rules of the game" should be observed. One rule is that we must be wary of the seductive appeal of a few favorite explanations, or of a first ingenious hypothesis, which carry a kind of internal conviction as to their power to illuminate and explain what is going on. Unfortunately, the degree of internal conviction does not necessarily correlate with the actual situation.

Diagnostic hunches are valuable, but they need to be exposed to scrutiny in the light of canons of proof. Such required canons of proof may be found in explicit form in social research discussions of principles of data analysis.[9] They have also been, and continue to be, an implicit part of good diagnostic thinking and teaching.

The point can be illustrated by a brief listing of some of these principles. Any inference should be supported by all available

[9] Paul B. Foreman, "The Theory of Case Studies," *Social Forces,* Vol. XXVI, No. 4 (1948), pp. 408–419.

relevant evidence. The existence of contradictory evidence should be carefully noted and its implications thought through, for rejection or refinement of the tentative hypothesis. The simplest hypothesis that fits the facts, rather than an unnecessarily elaborate one, is to be preferred. However, the nature of diagnostic inference requires more than the consideration of one fact at a time. A cumulative or configurational interrelationship of factors is necessary in any thinking about human behavior. In an individual case, if a constellation of factors is presented as the hypothetical cause of stated effects, it is necessary to review the detailed way in which the assumed causal factors actually operate in producing the effects. Not only the association between one fact and another but the dynamic processes that link the two should be made explicit.

To go beyond diagnosis in an individual case to factors that are presumed to operate in a number of cases involves additional considerations.[10] Here we are in the realm of experimental research, with its requirements for representative sampling, and control of relevant variables. To establish cause and effect, there must be a demonstrated relationship greater than that expected by chance. Similarly, causes must be followed by the expected effects to a greater-than-chance degree if the cause-effect relationship is to be accepted as valid.

At our stage of professional development, we are just now beginning to define and test the concepts of psychosocial behavior with which we work. Very often, we have to go ahead with generally accepted concepts without being certain of their experimental verification. At the very least, however, we ought to know what concepts we are utilizing, where the concepts come from, and the state of their verification.

In our consideration of how to teach psychosocial diagnosis in a way that encourages scientific habits, an important postulate should be mentioned: every diagnostic inference in an individual case involves a normative assessment. In other words, no inference can be made without a background of norms, or general expectations of behavior, against which the facts in an individual case are adjudged as typical or deviant.[11] Unless these norms are explicit, inferences in an individual case may be opportunistic and inaccurate. Further,

[10] *Ibid.*

[11] LeRoy M. A. Maeder, M.D., "Diagnostic Criteria—The Concept of Normal and Abnormal," *The Family*, Vol. XXII, No. 6 (1941), pp. 171–179.

the context in which the norms are held to operate should be explicit. Norms that hold for one sub-group may not hold for another. There is another way in which explicit knowledge of norms is helpful in diagnosis. This consists in the recognition that elements that one might expect to be present in a situation are missing. These missing elements are often of considerable significance.

In brief, it may be said that psychosocial diagnosis and a scientific approach are compatible when diagnosis is thought of as a tentative inference or hypothesis, subject to verification and change, and when the processes of inference are checked by criteria of logic.[12]

Is the scientific approach similarly applicable to casework treatment, and can the teaching of casework treatment therefore increase research-mindedness and scientific skills? If treatment is consciously planned on the basis of clear, *written* diagnoses and evaluations, if treatment methods and goals are specified, then it is possible to begin to assess results and, incidentally, to strengthen habits of scientific thinking. The recording of written evidence for diagnostic inference and for treatment planning forms the basis for scientific procedure in treatment.

The end of a case should be marked by careful evaluation of the apparent outcome. Some cautions must be introduced here. Any inference drawn about the connection between the type of treatment and the outcome can only be presumptive. The reasons are that spontaneous progress may be involved, or factors external to treatment may have been operating, or the favorable outcome may be transitory.

If students are helped to develop some sophistication about the limitations in the ex post facto type of inferences characteristic of evaluation of treatment, they will have assimilated an important concept useful in the critical review of research of any kind.[13] The value of follow-up studies to test whether apparent changes in a case situation hold up should find mention in the casework field instruction.

Scientific procedure is part of casework treatment although scientific sophistication alone is not sufficient preparation for professional

[12] The type of logic involved in the drawing of diagnostic inferences is analyzed by Louis J. Lehrman in "The Logic of Diagnosis," pp. 121–134 of this volume. Reprinted from *Social Casework,* May 1954.

[13] For a brief discussion of the logical difficulties in ex post facto inferences, see Robert K. Merton, *Social Theory and Social Structure,* Free Press, Glencoe, Ill., 1949, pp. 90–91.

performance. Casework competence in making a social study and diagnosis involves knowledge of content, psychological capacities of warmth, sensitivity, and object-relatedness, and skill in the disciplined use of oneself.

There are other opportunities for developing research-mindedness through case assignments. Each case is a source of knowledge of social needs and of the adequacy or inadequacy of social resources to meet them.[14] The professional vision of students may be broadened if cases are considered not only in the framework of individual need, but also in the framework of implied social needs and required social action. It is, of course, true that conclusions cannot properly be drawn from inadequate samples, but the habit of recognizing general social need when it exists in individual cases prepares the student for more organized research efforts.

We have indicated that an ability to think conceptually is part of scientific competence. The reason for this emphasis is that it is not possible to build knowledge without the use of general concepts which enable one to see how events within a case are related to one another, and how the various cases are related. Without knowledge of these intra- and inter-case relationships, one's attempts to help people remain on a trial-and-error level, and training remains on an apprentice level. The development of concepts is also essential from the viewpoint of research.

Research that is not related to theory, in the sense of a system of interrelated concepts, does not contribute to general knowledge. It remains on a purely *ad hoc* basis, rather than being used to build on or to refine existing knowledge. Thus, if students are helped to synthesize and generalize within a case and from case to case, and if the concepts employed are made explicit, then scientific ways of thinking in particular, and professional ways of thinking in general, are stimulated. The identification of similar aspects in a variety of contexts and the formulation of the unifying element (the concept) are basic to such learning.

Supervision

The supervisor's basic educational attitudes and approach are intrinsic in the strengthening of the scientific component in the student's learning. Perhaps the most important point to make here is

[14] Charlotte Towle, *op. cit.*

that student supervision should not aim to create disciples. It is true that identification with a professional model plays a large role in student learning, but this identification should be a mature and selective one, with plenty of leeway for critical thinking and independent action by the student.

Operationally, the supervisor should provide opportunity for the student to test out his own ideas. The student should be encouraged to ask, "How do I know I am right?" and to seek answers not solely by recourse to tradition, or authority, or the supervisor's experience, but from his experience in the living relationship with his client and in the light of the information available to him. This involves respect on the part of the supervisor for the student's capacity to think and act independently. Of course, the supervisor also gives answers out of his own experience, but not in a smothering way.

This emphasis on providing the student with opportunity to find out some things for himself may appear to contradict what has been said earlier about the value of teaching general concepts and principles, rather than relying on a purely experiential approach. The important point here is *timing*. Principles and concepts must be taught, but not before the student has had some opportunity to become acquainted with some specifics and particulars. These experiences and associations enable him to see the application of a general principle. Otherwise, teaching of principles becomes doctrinaire, and the student's spontaneity in relationships is impeded.

Generally, if a student is permitted, in the very first months of field work, to make some discoveries of his own, he will begin to see related points. He has enough examples in his own work and in the cases he has discussed in class to identify likenesses. The supervisor can then become increasingly active in accelerating this process of relating specifics to a general concept, or applying a general concept to illuminate a particular situation. The process of learning principles is an uneven one. General principles are often, unfortunately, too general. After the initial period of grasping a principle, the student often faces the need to differentiate its application. He needs time and help before he can handle the differential aspects without losing the principle.

The importance of attitude and timing is also evident in the matter of encouraging the student's concern with logic and proof. Immediate and rigid insistence on logic and proof is likely to inhibit the student's diagnostic hunches, even when they are based on very little. The student has first to be encouraged to think speculatively; after this he may be given training in scientific examination of inferences, in increasingly complex forms. An ultimate aim of supervision from this point of view is the student's harmonious use of emotional and intellectual capacities in the job of helping people.

Other Assignments

The casework agency is an educational resource for the teaching not only of casework skill and knowledge but of many other aspects of social work. Administration, community resources and needs, the place of the agency in community organization, and social work research are some of these generic aspects.

It is important that an atmosphere of interest in scientific inquiry be built up with which the student may readily identify and in which he may readily learn. The agency that carries on some type of research program creates such an atmosphere. The attitude of wanting to discover and test is then more easily transmissible. The student may learn something about the problems that need research, and generate some research interests of his own. Later in his training, he may be oriented to the particular agency studies that are going on, and to the designs and methodologies that are used. All this makes for a kind of broadly integrated learning.

There are other ways in which the imaginative supervisor may stimulate scientific thinking and attitudes. Generally, students fill out statistical reports on their own activities. These statistical reports, presumably, form part of a total agency report. Presumably too, these statistical reports accomplish specific purposes for agency administration by providing knowledge of the volume and type of problems and services given. How much do students usually know of the purpose of these reports? If the student has been given explanation of the purposes of these reports, and the way in which they provide administrative guidance, he has been given valuable exercise in quantitative thinking, as well as some insight into the administrative process. The educational point here is that the student's positive motivation toward helping people can be usefully channeled as he is helped to see the necessary connection between statistics and the efforts of the agency to increase its effectiveness in meeting needs. It may hesitantly be hoped that this kind of supervisory activity may begin to dilute the potency of that occupational phobia, the morbid fear of figures.

It may help the supervisor to know the sequence of research content in the student's academic experience. Many schools give a course in social work research in the latter part of the first year. General considerations of scientific method, a framework for evaluating research, the critical reading of research monographs, and an introduction to selected statistical concepts often constitute the major content of such courses.

In the first half of the second year, students begin to be faced with the problem of selecting a project or thesis topic and developing a preliminary outline. Some schools have developed a seminar to guide the student through this process. After a preliminary outline has been prepared, the student will be reading background material for his project, constructing tools for collecting data, selecting the data for the study, and refining the questions or hypotheses of the study. The last part of the second year is generally the period of major project activity, in which the student collects and analyzes data, and presents his study in written form.

The supervisor and agency can provide educational support throughout the period of project activity. The student at this time is often an anxiously inquiring person, who expends a good deal of emotional energy searching for a project topic. The supervisor's remembrance of times past in his own school experience will help him to recall some of the impact of this period. There are several ways in which the student may be helped in his initial search for a project topic. Students may fit into agency research interests by being helped to formulate one or more topics related to agency research programs. However, the choice of the topic should be the student's own, and he may elect to do a project outside the agency. Nevertheless, there is a powerful motivating effect when the student can see the usefulness of his project topic to the field or to his agency. The supervisor, out of his knowledge of the student's interests and needs, can suggest topics that are likely to be useful to the student. The supervisor can also be helpful in checking the availability of pertinent agency material as sources of data for suggested student projects.

The combination of agency interest in a research program, and of supervisory interest in incorporating the scientific component of social work into field work teaching, provides the basis for a fruitful project experience for the student, whether he elects to do a study within or outside his agency.

Conclusion

On the assumption that a scientific orientation should pervade all parts of the social work curriculum, the potentialities of the casework field placement for contributing to this orientation have been explored. An attempt has been made to translate the assumption into specifics applicable to the development of scientific thinking and attitudes through the field placement in casework. Both specific case assignments and more general social work experiences have been reviewed.

It is apparent that there have been implicit assumptions about the harmony of a scientific orientation and casework competence, whether these are looked at in the equipment of the professionally trained caseworker or in the nature of casework practice. The capacity to perceive and respond to things as they are is as basic for research as it is for casework. Creative imagination, a desire to put knowledge to use, the capacity to move back and forth freely between the generalized abstraction and the empirical particular, the logical, inquiring mind—these qualities, among others, are what we need to encourage in students in order to ensure the continued growth of our profession.

THE INTEGRATION OF CLASS AND FIELD IN PROFESSIONAL EDUCATION [1]

Louis J. Lehrman

SOCIAL WORK IS, at the present time, in the process of becoming a profession. Every scientific art moves, during the course of its transition from the status of a craft to that of a profession, along similar lines of development. To demonstrate the typical steps in this process, I should like to give an illustration from the field of metallurgy, with the help of Charles Lamb and a little imagination.

Eons ago men accidentally discovered, by making a fire out of a certain kind of wood on a certain kind of stone for the purpose of roasting a pig, that a molten liquid resulted which, when it cooled, was hard and malleable. The metal they thus discovered was iron, and they found it useful for making harder, more penetrating spearheads, arrowheads, and axes than they could previously make. For hundreds and perhaps thousands of years they continued to extract iron from the same kind of stone in the same way. They even became expert at it. Through a process of apprenticeship training, they taught others and thus passed on their operations to their sons and their sons' sons. A craft was thus born. The development of this craft marked a turning point in the history of men. Nevertheless, looking back, we note how wasteful, unilluminated, and lacking in precision were those original craft operations.

Later, the descendents of these men learned how to eliminate

[1] Published in *Social Casework,* June 1952. Presented in March 1952, at a Symposium on Education for Social Work at the Mid-Century, sponsored by the School of Social Work of the University of Buffalo, the Buffalo Chapter of the American Association of Social Workers, the Buffalo Council of Social Agencies, and the Social Workers Club of Buffalo.

the pig and even to use other kinds of wood, though whether these discoveries, like the original one, were also accidental, or the result of thoughtful questions thoughtfully posed and even more thoughtfully tested out in practice, I do not presume to guess.

Still later, the concepts and principles that, until then, had lain hidden in the operations, gradually were deduced. Not wood but a reducing agent, it was discovered, was necessary, and not fire but just free energy, since the chemical reaction between the ore of iron and the reducing agent was an endothermic one. The scientific art, or profession in the learned sense, of metallurgy was thus born.

This, roughly, is the line of development through which every scientific art moves during the course of its transition from craft to profession. Its operations at first are rough, approximate, and lacking in economy and precision, and the principles that are inherent in them are unknown. Gradually, however, these inherent principles are identified. At this point the craft is beginning to become a profession. Later, the emerging principles are made even more explicit. They are then refined and tested in further practice. Finally, they are made sufficiently clear and explicit to constitute what, in the scientific sense, is a body of theory. Concepts and principles thus represent the elixir distilled from practice over a period of years. Thereafter, employed to guide and illuminate practice, they make practice more precise and practical. This process is one that never ends: theory continues to guide and illuminate practice; practice continues to lead to the further enrichment, refinement, correction, and revision of theory. The action is mutual, and the professional practitioner characteristically participates in and contributes to both.

A Profession Emerges

Social work is now at that stage in the process of becoming professionalized in which it is concerned about theory. What, we ask, are our concepts and principles? Where and how should we teach them? Or again, how much of our time should we spend teaching concepts and principles as the theoretical shorthand of operations? How much of our time should we spend teaching operations as the exemplifications or concretions of concepts and principles? What relation do these two types of classroom teaching bear to the guidance of the student through his *performance,* illuminated by theory, of the operations in the field? Should any of our time ever be devoted to the teaching of operations craftwise, that is, simply as operations?

Professional education or, speaking more strictly, education for professional performance, characteristically concentrates on the teaching of operations in relation to theory, whether in class, where the student's relation to the operations is purely mental, or in the field, where he is, in addition, expected to perform them. Craft teaching, on the other hand, concerns itself solely with the teaching of the operations simply as operations, that is, out of the context of theory. This is probably the main distinguishing difference between craft training and professional education.

Continuing my analogy to the field of metallurgy, I shall put it this way: We are training metallurgists, not steel-puddlers. Like most analogies, however, this one is not perfect. The social worker, in practice, has to be both metallurgist *and* puddler. When we puddle our steel, however, we do it not as a craftsman would, but with the superior understanding and skill of the professional person, whose competences exceed those of the craftsman. Our operations, in other words, even when they are most manual, are at the same time theory-based and mental.

What is the significance of this in connection with my main topic? In my opinion, it has great significance. First, it means that we who are professional, and particularly those of us who teach, must immediately and openly declare our allegiance to the broad professional proposition that professional practice must proceed from and express a clear set of consistent concepts and principles which (1) are derived from and tested in practice, (2) can be formally expressed, and (3) are communicable and can be taught. No such set of concepts and principles can ever be either complete or perfect.

Second, this means that once having thus declared ourselves professionally, it is incumbent upon all of us, and again particularly upon those of us who teach, to put clearly into words what are our basic concepts and beliefs—ethical and religious, scientific and philosophical, psychological and theraupetic, and so on. A number of agencies and schools are now doing this.

Third, it means that this vast theoretical content, along with illustrative cases, must be organized into four basic "practice" courses, with syllabi, which courses, for purposes of simplification, I should like to refer to simply as Casework I, Casework II, Casework III, and Casework IV. The emphasis in the classroom teaching of these courses would then have to be on the concepts and principles as such, on the manner in which they were derived from old operations, and on the old operations, especially as they are visible in the illustrative cases, as exemplifications or concretions of the designated concepts and principles. The student's classroom relation to the operations will, of course, be mental. What but mental could it be—under any classroom circumstances? But mental, let us remember, means emotional as well as intellectual. How infinitely great the power of the mind has always been to move not only the minds of mature and potentially mature men, but also their hearts! As teachers and as administrators, we must never forget this.

Relation of Class and Field

Toward what end will the student be learning concepts and principles directly, and operations only indirectly (through a kind of intellectual-emotional projection) in class? Obviously toward the end of becoming a beginning professional practitioner. In this phrase all three terms have to be emphasized: beginning, professional, practitioner.

Is the classroom experience enough to accomplish this? Decidedly not! The field experience is no whit less necessary or important. This was made clear by Mary Richmond as long ago as 1917 when she wrote: "Case work cannot be mastered from books or from classroom instruction alone, though both have their place in its mastery." [2]

Concurrently, or on a block basis, the student will also be provided with an experience in the field where, with the help of his supervisor, essentially in her capacity as a field instructor, he will carry a case load of appropriate size. I emphasize the fact that it is essentially in her capacity as a field instructor for the school, and only secondarily in her capacity as a worker or supervisor for the agency, that, consistently with agency function and structure, she will help him to do this.

In the field, the field instructor, we hope, will be no less committed than the classroom teacher to the broad professional proposition that professional practice is theory-based and theory-related.

[2] *Social Diagnosis,* Russell Sage Foundation, New York, 1917, p. 32.

In addition, I assume that she will have been provided by the school with its carefully elaborated classroom syllabi, so that she knows at every point what has already been taken up in class, what has not yet been taken up, and even what will be taught as being untrue, contradictory, or inconsistent. The school should, if possible, also give the field instructor a syllabus for the field work course, detailing, at least roughly, what the student would be expected to learn, under ideal conditions, in the field each semester. Does this sound too ideal? I do not think so if we mean to take the integration of field and class seriously. A few schools are already trying to work out such field syllabi. Moreover, to the extent to which the school supplies the field instructor with criteria, semester by semester, which she is expected to use in evaluating the student, a syllabus has, it seems to me, been implied. The implication in the use of standard criteria supplied by the school is that the field instructor, whether or not the school has given her a syllabus, nevertheless has one. Here, certainly, is a need for greater integration.

With such a field syllabus, plus her realization that her relationship to her student is essentially that of a teacher with a certain amount of ground to cover, the field instructor would be in a much better position to take her place in the school's integrated plan for the student's total education. What is her place?

The task of the field instructor, essentially, is to help the student complete his task of learning theory and practice together and in relation to each other, by focusing with him on the performance of operations, not simply as operations but rather as what we have called here exemplifications or concretions of theory. The classroom teacher, you may remember, focuses on the student's mental rather than "muscular" mastery of operations in relation to theory. It is as these two—the mental and the "muscular" learning—meet and merge, that real professional development takes place.

My purpose has not been to describe the thousand and one ways in which, by performing the operations in the field—with the field instructor there to help him to see them as exemplifications of theory—the student develops in self-awareness and enriches his grasp of both theory and practice. Nor has my purpose been to point out all the ways in which such learning is simultaneously intellectual and emotional.

My purpose has been rather to stick to fundamentals and, by describing the sort of ideal class-field situation that a number of schools are now attempting to approach, to point out that since class and field teaching are both based on theory, the fundamental requirement for integration must therefore be that the theories on which the two are based are the same. Unless they are the same, integration will not exist; nor will any tricks produce it. To discover whether they are the same is, therefore, the first and fundamental requirement. Unfortunately, in many instances, too little effort is made either to determine whether they are, or to make them, the same.

In what I have said so far it may appear that I see instruction in class and field as proceeding not just hand in hand, but in a kind of military lock step every inch of the way. Such a lock step would in actual fact not be possible; nor is it necessary or even desirable. It is impossible because not all the direct explication of theory can possibly take place in class. A certain amount of it has to occur in the field. The field teacher, for example, has to act as a classroom teacher with respect to the specific concepts and principles of her own agency's function, structure, policies, and procedures, regardless of whether or not the general concepts have already been taken up in class. She frequently has to act as a classroom teacher with respect to individual cases, for not every case that every student receives can be anticipated in class. In addition, the different learning patterns and paces of the individual students can be more fully taken into account in the field, where the instruction is more tutorial, than they can be in class. For these reasons alone, such a lock step would be impossible. But there is a fourth and even more fundamental reason: whereas classroom teaching must of necessity confine itself solely to operations in thought, field teaching deals, in addition, with operations as the student himself performs them. This fact inevitably raises problems that are more difficult, more intense, and even somewhat different in kind from those that arise in class. The rhythms, the tempos, and to some extent even the natures of classroom and field teaching must of necessity, therefore, be different.

Nor is it necessary or desirable for instruction in class and field to proceed in lock step. We must assume that the field teacher is not without the capacity both to select cases carefully and to impart directly to her student whatever theoretical knowledge these cases happen to require. In addition, we must also assume that when a case turns out to be too difficult, she will know how to transfer it constructively to a more advanced student or worker, or assume it herself and then use it, if possible, in a classroom manner to help her student.

The most constructive experience it is possible for the student to have is that of participating in two processes having somewhat different natures and rhythms, one dealing with operations mentally and the other dealing with them "muscularly," and then seeing and feeling them move together around a single set of basic underlying concepts and principles. Under no circumstances would it be desirable to rob the student of this exhilarating, constructive experience. Fortunately we cannot; the experience is inevitable.

In what I have said it may also appear that the kind of integration I am talking about can take place only between the student's "practice" courses and the field. This is not true. All the student's courses are involved, particularly those in behavior theory, in culture, in social welfare, in philosophy and social philosophy, and in research.

Achieving Integration

I should like to consider some of the changes in the nature of the relationship between the classroom teacher and the field teacher, which may have to take place in order to achieve this kind of integration. These persons will have to know one another, professionally speaking, more intimately. Do they subscribe equally to the professional proposition that theory and practice are interrelated? Is either one biased, whether in the direction of theory or in the direction of practice? Are their basic theoretical concepts and principles the same? Where differences exist, have they been explored for the purpose of ascertaining whether they are reconcilable or not reconcilable?

How can we promote the kind of basic theoretical agreement between class and field without which, as I have said, integration cannot exist? In addition to the school-prepared statements and syllabi that I have mentioned, it seems to me that the school should also, as often as necessary, be prepared to offer special theoretical courses for the field instructors. Such courses would simply help some to recover—from the depths of what Freud called the preconscious—concepts and principles they once knew consciously, still use constantly, but can no longer identify. To others, much of the material may be new but acceptable. To still others, basic sections may be unacceptable. Even more important would be the provision of workshops where the class and field teachers could get together for the mutual discussion and threshing-out not only of concepts and principles but also of how, when, and where these should be taught. Primarily in class or primarily in the field? When in class and when in the field? For example, should recording be taught primarily in class or primarily in the field? And at what point should the student be expected to start learning how to record in summary instead of process? In addition, more attention should be given in field consultation to the discussion of cases. At present the discussion too often centers exclusively on the student. Agreement on the teaching points in the student's cases is all too often merely assumed.

Another way to promote theoretical agreement between class and field is to have the field keep the school constantly supplied with the best possible cases for classroom teaching. This cannot be stressed too much, particularly since it is important in good classroom teaching not so much to illustrate a principle by means of one case as to provide the student with a group of cases for the illustration of each principle.

Agency and School

In this co-operative effort, what is the agency's role? I must frankly state that I do not see the student's education as consisting of a school part and an agency part, for the former of which the school has responsibility and the latter, the agency. On the contrary, the two parts of the student's education, consisting as they do of class and field, are both the direct responsibilities of the school. The agency's role is adjunctive and co-operative. The agency, both in its own interest and as a professional responsibility, provides the school with the setting and the placement, with the cases (which will of course be carried within agency function and structure and under appropriate safeguards), and, usually, also with the worker or supervisor who, in relation to the student, is to function as the school teacher in the field—the field instructor.

A further question can be raised about the integration of agency and school. If what the school teaches and what the agency believes are incompatible, an untenable situation exists which sooner or later will have to be altered; for in this instance the same person cannot simultaneously serve the school as a field instructor and the agency as a member of the staff. Integration of class and field, which the school owes to every student, cannot be achieved under such circumstances. Nor should the agency be asked to tolerate the carrying of cases—whether by worker or student—according to principles, and in a manner, inconsistent with its own principles and beliefs. Here, perhaps, we have a new principle—which my experience, at least, bears out—that the integration of class and field rests on the integration of agency and school. Sometimes it is not clear whether a disagreement between agency and school actually exists. When this is so, both the school and the agency should act quickly to put their respective beliefs into writing as completely as possible, as a first step in a professional process of school-agency mutual examination.

There are still other ways in which school and agency can co-operate. The schools, for example, should more often offer refresher courses, such as those offered by certain medical schools, and courses calculated to keep agency workers abreast of new developments. The agencies, on the other hand, should offer the faculty members periodic opportunities to practice. Faculty members frequently feel keenly their increasing isolation from practice as the years go on, and their teaching suffers as a result of such isolation. One semester of such practice every second year would, perhaps, not be too much for the agencies and the schools to work together to provide.

In addition, the schools need representatives of the agencies on their advisory committees, and the agencies might similarly use faculty members on their own boards and committees. Finally, I can think of no kind of school-agency co-operation leading toward greater integration than that represented by the symposium at which this paper was presented, and which a school and agencies jointly arranged.

I should like to say one last word about what the agency stands to gain out of lending itself to the kind of integrated class-field professional training program I have tried to describe. In the long run it will gain better beginning workers who, because of their base in theory, will be able to stand on their own feet and do a competent, professional job in practice. What, after all, is more practical than scientific theory? With it, we are giants. We stand on the shoulders of our predecessors and can live a thousand lifetimes in one. Without it we are indeed limited. Professional carry-over, in contrast to the carry-over of a craft, stems primarily from basic understanding of underlying concepts and principles. Because such carry-over is always limited, we can make gains in social work only as we continue to work for improved integration of our programs of professional training.

AN EXPERIMENT IN TEACHING AN INTEGRATED METHODS COURSE [1]

Alfred Kadushin and Quentin F. Schenk

THE RECENT PERIOD in the history of social work has been characterized by a diminution in the strength of sectarian allegiance to particular methods as well as to specializations within the methods. The present-day trend is toward an increasing identification on the part of all persons representing specializations with the total field of social work. A single professional organization, publishing a single professional journal, exemplifies this trend.

Social work education reflects, and in turn reinforces, this development. The Hollis-Taylor report [2] urged the revision of the social work curriculum along more generic lines; this recommendation was adopted by the Council on Social Work Education in the cur-

[1] Published in *Social Casework,* October 1957.

[2] Ernest V. Hollis and Alice L. Taylor, *Social Work Education in the United States,* Columbia University Press, New York, 1951.

riculum policy statement of January, 1952.[3] A review of recent changes in the curriculum of schools of social work indicates that a widespread effort is being made to implement the policy statement.[4] More recently the board of the Council on Social Work Education approved, in principle, the policy that accreditation of specializations be discontinued.[5]

The faculty of the University of Wisconsin School of Social Work, after a lengthy study of its curriculum, adopted a generic program in 1953. As part of that program it was decided that the basic casework and basic group work courses were to be taught as an integrated methods course.[6] Previously all casework students were required to take a basic casework methods course, which met for two hours each week over two semesters; all group work students were required to take the first semester of the basic casework course. Similarly, all group work students were required to take a basic group work methods course of two hours each week over two semesters; all casework students were required to take the first semester of this course.

Since the change in curriculum, a methods course has been given, which replaces both the two-semester basic casework course and the two-semester group work course. Formulation of the general content and approach of any course is a matter of joint faculty planning, but the specific content and approach are left to the individual instructors.[7] The new methods course met twice each week for a total of four hours a week over a period of two semesters. The course was taught jointly by a group work instructor and a casework instructor. Both instructors sat in on every meeting, but

[3] *Curriculum Policy* No. 120, Council on Social Work Education, New York, 1952.

[4] *Social Work Education,* Vol. III, No. 5 (1955).

[5] *Letter from the President,* Council on Social Work Education, New York, Number 11, June, 1956, p. 3.

[6] See Clara A. Kaiser, "Methods of Formulating and Teaching the Conceptual and Scientific Base of Social Work Practice," *Workshop Reports, 1953 Proceedings Annual Program Meeting,* Council on Social Work Education, New York; and Irving Miller, "Concepts and Processes," *Alumni Newsletter,* New York School of Social Work, January, 1952, for reports of other integrated methods courses.

See Dorothy Sumner, "An Experiment with Field Work in Generic Social Work," *Social Casework,* Vol. XXXVII, No. 6 (1956), pp. 288–294, for a discussion of a field work program applying this same approach.

[7] The article describes the experience in teaching this course of one team on the Madison campus of the University. We are indebted to Joseph Soffen, who is a member of a similar team on the Milwaukee campus, for many perceptive ideas regarding the integrated course.

each instructor had primary responsibility for conducting one of the two two-hour sessions each week. The integrated course had some of the characteristics of the two previous parallel courses, since it was taught by two instructors skilled in one or the other of the basic methods and each had the same amount of time as previously to present his material. The crucial difference lay in the fact that the instructors were committed to teach this as a joint course and to move from parallel presentation of material to optimum integration of content.

The following discussion is the itinerary of the journey toward integration.

Course Content

In setting up the new course, the two instructors shared the responsibility for determining the specific content; the syllabus was the result of their joint planning. In general, the material deriving from both casework and group work, which forms the substantive content of this course, falls into three broad categories—material that is homologous, material that is analogous, and material from each method which has very little or no relationship to material from the sibling methods.

The homologous material presented little problem for integration. The bulk of such material is used in the first semester, and it is concerned primarily with the basic concepts and philosophy that are fundamental to all social work and consequently are not the special province of any method.

Thus, both casework and group work record material was selected to teach certain concepts. The listing is illustrative rather than exhaustive.

1. The basic attitudes of the worker in approaching the client —individual or group—are the same. He demonstrates respect, seeks to understand rather than to judge, and communicates an acceptance of the client.

2. A social service cannot achieve optimum effectiveness unless the client—individual or group—has the freedom to make his own decisions and unless he is granted the opportunity for full participation in the decision-making process.

3. Individual behavior is purposive and, in broad terms, the individual acts so as to minimize tensions and maximize satisfactions.

4. Uniqueness as well as likeness characterizes all individuals and all groups.

5. The focus of help is on the client and his needs, whether in a person-to-person relationship or in a group.

6. The caseworker or group worker is an enabler, a catalyst who is charged with the professional responsibility for helping the clients achieve their goals. Since every situation with which social workers are concerned is psychosocial in nature, this may require mobilization of community resources, mobilization of resources inherent in the client, or a combination of the two.

7. The feeling interaction—the professional relationship—between worker and client is the context in which such help is offered, and the worker consciously uses the relationship in accordance with the scientific method, that is, information gathering, diagnosis, and treatment.

8. All social workers operate within the framework of a particular society and a particular agency, and the worker is bound by the precepts of that society and the regulations of that agency.

The integrated course was designed to teach certain basic skills, such as interviewing and recording, as well as basic concepts. These skills are based on general principles and are utilized in all social work settings. The principles can be illustrated through the use of both group work and casework records.

We found as we moved from the first to the second semester that the course content shifted from homologous to analogous material. The two methods—even though they operate from the same basic concepts and philosophical presuppositions—have some differentials, since they are directed toward different situations and utilize different processes.

Clients of both group work and casework agencies make some kind of application, however informal. Following this, the social worker makes some sort of exploration, however unstructured, which attempts to determine, for the agency and client, what acceptable service can be offered. Since many of the concepts about application and intake are analogous for both methods, we presented them in a comparative way. The casework instructor discussed with the class, on the basis of record material, such points as how and why people come to the agency, sources of referral, client reactions to coming to an agency, the worker's responsibilities at intake, the nature of the worker-client relationship at intake, the kinds of information about the client which the agency needs, the kinds of information about the agency which the client needs, questions of eligibility for service, and so forth. The group work instructor then presented record material from his field which raised similar questions about similar problems.

The same teaching method was adopted in presenting the social study component of the helping process. Discussion centered on the kinds of information needed to help the client, the sources of such information, how much needs to be known, how it is obtained, what principles guide the worker in making a social study, and so forth. The study component is perhaps less clearly and less explicitly articulated in group work than in casework, but some type of social study is made and the principles that guide the caseworker are applicable, with some adaptation, to group work. The casework record provides material to illustrate the kinds of physiological, social, and psychodynamic information needed to understand the individual. Similar information about the group members is available in group work records. Knowledge about the previous history and the current situation of the group is as significant for the group worker in planning "treatment" as is knowledge about the history and current situation of the individual for the caseworker. The process involved in diagnosising the needs of a group is similar to the diagnostic process in casework,[8] and it, too, is based on a social study. Background information—such as that presented in courses in human growth and development—from which principles regarding specific cases are deduced, is similar for both methodologies.

The teaching of treatment in the integrated course offered a more complex situation. Treatment in the two methods seems to be less clearly analogous. We have equated programming in group work with treatment in casework. We have defined both processes as the "institution of specific remedial measures in a specific problem situation." The therapeutic atmosphere, which is the *sine qua non* for treatment in casework, develops out of a type of attitudinal approach that has its counterpart in group work. The approach on the part of the worker includes warm acceptance, permissiveness

[8] The recent emphasis on diagnosis of the family configuration permits a teaching transition to diagnosis of a group as an entity. See Nathan W. Ackerman, M.D., and Raymond Sobel, M.D., "Family Diagnosis: An Approach to the Preschool Child," *American Journal of Orthopsychiatry*, Vol. XX, No. 4 (1950), p. 744.

within defined limits, and a noncritical and noncondemnatory attitude. Practitioners in both methods strive for a worker-client, worker-group interaction characterized by rapport, that is, for an easy, relaxed, secure, nonthreatening relationship. Both the worker-client and worker-group relationships are clearly analogous in their structured aspects. Both are designed to meet the client's needs and are time-limited and agency-centered; in both, confidentiality is respected.

In group programming as well as in casework treatment, the worker utilizes supportive techniques. His accepting manner enables the group to discuss anxiety-provoking propositions or plans. Also, program evaluation sessions frequently present opportunity for developing self-awareness, on the part of group members, about their behavior in group interaction. What-would-you-like-to-do and how-would-you-go-about-it planning sessions of programming have many aspects that are analogous to clarification in casework treatment.

Although the treatment-program component of the process suggests many analogies, such as those mentioned above, the specific program skills required by the group worker and the specific advance knowledge of interviewing required by the caseworker have made this area in the course the sector where methodological specificity might require separate sessions for caseworkers and group workers.

Class Organization

Although each instructor assumed primary responsibility for two of the four hours of class meeting each week, both instructors sat in on all sessions. Once the instructors were comfortable with each other, they tended increasingly to comment on each other's presentations and material and to apply points to their particular field of interest. As the teaching team developed confidence in doing this, the class members also engaged in cross-methodological discussions with increasing frequency. Thus a discussion of leadership functions by the group worker led to a discussion of the analogous leadership responsibilities of the caseworker in the interview situation; points mentioned were his responsibility for keeping the process in motion, for sensing the direction in which the client wants to move, for helping him achieve his goals, and for summarizing and recapitulating what had taken place in the interview. A discussion of the differentiation between group work and recreation led into a discussion of the differences between social conversation and the casework interview. A sociometric analysis of group membership was followed by a similar sociometric analysis of the family of a casework client.

A discussion of the casework contact as a protected learning situation, in which clients develop skill in problem-solving, was followed by a discussion of the group situaiton, which provides a protected setting for persons to develop social skills. Such topics as role differentiation, contagion, anchorage, group cohesiveness, group status relationships, problems of consensus in decision-making were all used, at one time or another, as the basis for understanding group behavior and for showing its relatedness to both methods.

The cross-discussion between members of the teaching team was, in itself, an exemplification of the principle of integration. Also, the fact that all assignments to students were joint assignments reinforced the principle. In all instances both casework records and group work records were assigned to all students, and they were asked to answer the same questions regarding each. For example, toward the middle of the first semester, the students were asked to compare a case record and a group record with reference to the similarities and differences in the worker's attitude toward the client.

Since the instructors were not in a position to develop special case records for the course, standard records published by the Family Service Association of America, the American Association of Group Workers, and the Council on Social Work Education were used. In some instances we used various developmental periods of life as the point of contact between the two methods; a case record of an Old Age Assistance client was studied alongside a group record of a "golden-age" club, and the case record of an adolescent alongside a record of an adolescent club. In other instances the psychosocial problem was used as the point of contact. An Aid to Dependent Children application, precipitated by an illegitimate pregnancy, was studied together with a record of group sessions held in a receiving home for unmarried mothers; a family service record, in which illness was a problem, was studied together with a record of a group of children in latency, in which the effects of the disability of several members on group relationships were illustrated.

The social work process has also been used as the point of contact. A casework intake interview was studied alongside an interview with a group of boys who came to an agency to find out what it could offer them.

The selection of a point of contact is a mechanical device which ensures some thematic consistency as the class moves from one session to another. However, the instructors have found from their experience in using records with no apparent similarities that almost any two records can be used side by side, and that they will raise questions and illustrate points that have application to both methods. Our experience confirms the generally held belief that the two methods have many common components.

Student Reaction to the Integrated Course

The integrated course, we believe, has had a number of positive aspects for the student's professional development. It has given him an identification with the social work field rather than with one methodology. It has helped develop a healthy respect for the sibling method and, at the same time, it has vitiated a tendency toward smugness about one's own method. These advantages are illustrated in the student comments that we received in response to class assignments.

Some of the comments were:

> It appears that the same social work methods were used in each of the two cases. Differences are inherent in the setting and not the approach. There are basic similarities in the "tone" or the atmosphere that exists in both cases.
>
> It would seem that the feelings and behavior of the group worker were not really different from the feelings and behavior of the caseworker. Both the caseworker and group worker showed feelings of interest and acceptance. Both reflect helpfulness and understanding.
>
> I think it is of importance to mention that while at first I thought there were wide differences in approach between group work and casework, I found in doing the assignments that I had more difficulty in factoring out differences in approach than similarities.
>
> Analysis of these records demonstrates the fact that one has to be a social worker before becoming either a caseworker or group worker.

Teaching social work methods in an integrated way seemed to be of benefit to both caseworkers and group workers. The opportunity to illustrate basic concepts in different contexts helps to reinforce them and to enrich the student's learning. Charlotte Towle has pointed out that imaginative repetition reinforces learning.[9] Analyzing a process and seeing its application in a setting other than the one in which the student is primarily interested help him develop a more comprehensive understanding of the process. Drill in one method is reinforced by drill, through use of similar material, in the other method.

This method of presentation had the value of exposing the student to the method of secondary interest to him with a minimum of resistance. Previously, casework students who were required to take the group work course grumbled at its supposed lack of relevance to their primary interest. The same was true, in reverse, of the group work students. In the new course, the consistent attempt to relate casework content to the group work setting, and vice versa, enabled the students to recognize explicitly the pertinence of content developed by each field of interest. Thus it was easier to teach group work to caseworkers and casework to group workers.

Evaluation of the course from the point of view of the student supervisors has been less systematic and therefore less explicit. Some pertinent questions were raised, many of which cannot be answered at this time.

Values and Questions

The integrated methods course offered certain advantages, but it also posed some problems.

Since the course covered substantially the same content as had been previously taught in the two traditional courses, the instructors were able to interpret the change to field work supervisors and to the social work community with a minimum of difficulty. Also, the instructors were able to make the change easily, since they utilized familiar material.

The plan to have both instructors present at all sessions helped them develop a more intensive, and hence a more effective, teaching relationship with the student group. The instructors were in contact with the same students, actively engaging in discussions with them, for a total of four hours a week.

[9] See Charlotte Towle, *The Learner in Education for the Professions,* University of Chicago Press, Chicago, 1954, pp. 168–169, for a discussion of "repetition with difference."

This allotment of time permitted flexibility in scheduling content; material could be selected to follow the interest and responsiveness of students rather than to meet the dictates of a rigid outline. If a discussion of group work terminated at a point where a good deal more needed to be said, the second period in the week could be given over to a continuation of the discussion.

Joint teaching, the vehicle through which we endeavored to achieve the integrated course, naturally posed some problems. Such teaching requires that each instructor be sufficiently comfortable in his role so that he can risk facing the possible criticism of a colleague. We found that our self-consciousness and anxiety diminished rapidly and were overcome within a short period of time. This may not always be true, and some instructors may be reluctant to teach a course under these conditions.

Joint teaching requires mutual respect and acceptance between the instructors, not only as people but as representatives of their particular methodologies. If one instructor thinks that his field is intrinsically more important, or should be accorded more prestige, than the other, he will inevitably arouse defensiveness in his colleague and engender conflict in the teaching team. Both instructors must be able to share a session without feeling threatened, and they must be able to exercise conscious control of any narcissistic desire to take over a session taught by a colleague.

In general, our plan was for each instructor to be responsible for alternate sessions. The instructor chairing the session permitted, and even encouraged, interruptions from his colleague. As the course progressed and the instructors gained a feeling of relaxed comfort with each other, they were inclined to comment in each other's sessions with less hesitancy, less diffidence, and fewer apologies. Knowing that the intrusions were acceptable to the other, each spoke up freely, and the discussion moved easily from one method to the other.

The expenditure of staff time, of course, is increased by teaching a course in this manner. Not only is the actual teaching time in the classroom doubled, but additional time is required for preparation and conferences. Both teachers felt obligated to do a considerable amount of reading of the literature of the less familiar methodology. They believed that only in this way could they be sensitized to possible homologies, analogies, and differences.

A rule was rigidly enforced to the effect that each session should be followed by a conference, however brief, for the purpose of reviewing the session just ended. Sometimes there was little to say; oftener it happened that, when they met, there was a good deal that required saying. As a by-product of these meetings, the instructors came to know each other better, and this understanding affected, in a positive manner, their relationship during the class sessions.

The conviction of the instructors of the value of the integration course posed a problem in itself, since they tended originally to be overdetermined in their efforts to assert it. They tended to force legitimate differences into the shape of apparent similarity. It took them some time to accept the idea that legitimate differences can be freely recognized where they do indeed exist, without jeopardizing the orientation of such a course. For example, one discussion involved the criterion that a dyad relationship is a group, and effort was made to show that the worker-client relationship was therefore a group in the same sense that the term is used in group work.

Other problems in teaching such a course are inherent in the current level of development of the profession. Both instructors had to reorient their thinking, based on their own experience in professional education, in undertaking to teach the course; their training had been oriented toward emphasis on specifics. In the social work field generally there is a feeling, however muted, that sharp differences exist between the two methods. The bulk of the literature—the only literature that we can make available to students —reflects a specialized rather than an integrated point of view. As noted above, record material specifically designed to meet the needs of such a course is not readily available.

Conclusion

We have not yet achieved a fully integrated course. In the continuum of progressing from parallel courses to a truly integrated course, we now stand beyond center toward the integrated end.

In our opinion, integration of the basic methods course is not only possible, but desirable. It is to be hoped that the field will continue to identify homologous, analogous, and differential concepts as found in the various specializations within the field. We believe these concepts can be readily and acceptably taught in a single, basic methods course to all students beginning their graduate study in the field of social work.

THE SOCIAL WORK CURRICULUM STUDY AND ITS IMPLICATIONS FOR FAMILY CASEWORK[1]

Werner W. Boehm

THE RELATION of the Curriculum Study of the Council on Social Work Education to family casework is but one facet of a larger question: What is and what should be the relationship between social work education and social work practice? The Curriculum Study has been very much concerned with this question. Its statements both on the nature of social work and on the nature of social casework seek to reflect the evolving character of the social work profession and the changing nature of its practice as it "responds to changing needs in society."[2] In other words, the Curriculum Study and all of its projects were designed with one purpose in mind—to identify the curriculum content needed to enable graduates of schools of social work to become practitioners effectively equipped to help people in the mastery of emerging, as well as current, problems of living.

No attempt is made in this paper to do more than sketch some of the major considerations of the Curriculum Study. The full implications of the Study for family social work will be grasped only when the published reports have been carefully examined and studied.[3]

[1] Published in *Social Casework,* October 1959. Presented at the Biennial Meeting of the Family Service Association of America, Washington, D.C., April 2, 1959.

[2] Werner W. Boehm, "The Nature of Social Work," *Social Work,* Vol. III, No. 2 (1958), p. 18.

[3] Since this paper was given, *The Social Work Education Curriculum Study Projects* (13 volumes) has been published. See particularly Vols. I and X.

I should like, first, to state several basic premises that underlie all other considerations in this paper.

1. The Curriculum Study reaffirms the position now held in social work education that the social casework sequence is generic. In other words, this sequence contains the concepts, principles, and techniques characteristic of the casework method regardless of the setting in which casework is practiced. Hence, the Study does not focus on family casework per se, nor does it single out social casework as it is practiced in family agencies. The Study also affirms the position that the setting in which it is practiced affects the use to which the casework method is put and that there are variations in the application of this method from setting to setting.

2. There is much more to family social work than the practice of family casework. There is general agreement, I am sure, that family social work should include "participation in community planning, group education, contribution to professional education, and research." [4]

The discussion in this paper is limited to social casework as the primary method of service utilized in the family agency.[5]

3. The Curriculum Study takes the position that social casework ought to be family-centered regardless of whether it is practiced in family agencies or in other settings. "Family-centered casework might be defined as casework based on an understanding of the social, physical, and emotional needs of the family as a unit for the purpose of helping the family members attain the best personal and social satisfactions of which they are capable." [6]

The Relationship Between Social Work Education and Social Work Practice

It is axiomatic that the content of the social work curriculum ought to stand in some relationship to social work practice. Unless what the student learns in a school of social work is applicable to his later practice of social work, the school is not doing its job. These statements, however, do not indicate the complexities of the questions that must be answered. Should the schools prepare

[4] *Scope and Methods of the Family Service Agency*, Family Service Association of America, New York, 1953, p. 3.

[5] "The Content of Family Social Work," an FSAA report, *Social Casework*, Vol. XXXVII, No. 7 (1956), p. 320.

[6] Frances H. Scherz, "What Is Family-Centered Casework?" *Social Casework*, Vol. XXXIV, No. 8 (1953), p. 343.

students for practice as it now exists or should they prepare them for practice as it might be in the foreseeable future? Should the schools prepare each student for effective practice in a specific setting or should they furnish him with the basic equipment in terms of knowledge, attitudes, and skills which will enable him to practice in any setting on the assumption that he will obtain further training through agency-centered educational experiences? The answers to questions such as these determine the relationship between practice and education.

The frequently heard criticism that schools do not prepare students to be effective practitioners is serious enough that it should not be dismissed with rationalization or projection. On the contrary, the validity of such a charge should be examined carefully. Intelligent examination of the charge is virtually impossible, however, unless both practice and education are clear about what is expected of each. It is not enough to say that education and practice are partners; the terms of the partnership have to be spelled out and must be mutually agreeable. If the field of practice expects the schools to produce a finished product, certainly there will be major disappointment, for social work education at present expects the graduate to develop into a full-fledged professional person through practice. On the other hand, if the schools were content to gear curriculum precisely to practice as it exists today, the practicing agencies would have every right to be critical since the graduate would be ill-prepared to relate his professional equipment to the needs of practice tomorrow.

By the same token, the schools cannot afford to prepare social work students for a kind of practice that is so different from what is currently being done that any resemblance between what the student learns in school and what he can use on the job is purely coincidental. Hence, the principle that should govern the relationship between practice and education may be stated in this way: the realities of current practice must be heeded, but these realities must be seen as including not only what practice *is* but also what practice *may become* both in the light of present problems and in the light of problems that can be anticipated in the forseeable future. Only if this principle is followed can social work avoid the danger of stagnation on the one hand, and of utopianism on the other.

According to this view, which is the view adopted by the Curriculum Study, a good social work curriculum is one that provides for stability but also makes allowances for change. Fortunately, social conditions do not change so quickly, nor are they perceived so rapidly, that there is nothing but flux in social work education. A certain degree of cultural lag reinforces stability and continuity; but care should be taken lest the claims of stability and continuity be used to camouflage resistance to changes in curriculum content which should ensue from emerging social needs.

One of the several ways whereby the social work curriculum can meet the requirements of stability and continuity as well as of change is through establishment of educational policies that are broad and flexible and that incorporate an educational philosophy of social change. Another way is by the creation of a curriculum with a sufficiently broad conceptual framework to incorporate both prevailing and emerging social needs. Such a framework would remain relatively stable but would also leave room for more specific concepts that might be needed from time to time.

A third way is the adoption of an educational philosophy that clearly articulates the relationship between formal professional education and staff development. Such an educational philosophy would postulate that it is the task of professional education to provide the student with the basic body of knowledge, attitudes, and skill in appropriate areas of content, with a view toward helping him develop a generalized approach toward problem-solving; it is not its task to provide the student with all the facts and techniques required to deal effectively with the specific professional problems he is likely to encounter in the course of his career.

Thus, professional education can only be basic education. It can only lay the groundwork for the student's ongoing self-development, attained through his own efforts and through staff development. Staff development complements professional education by helping the professional social worker apply general knowledge and skill to a specific professional situation and deal with the specific body of problems that prevail in a given agency.

Impact of Societal Trends on Practice

Responsiveness to social needs is one of the indispensable characteristics of social work practice. What social workers are doing now and will be doing in the future, and what they ought to do better now and in the future, must be related to the changes that society is undergoing.

The Curriculum Study takes the view that individual needs are met through social institutions—the family, the school, the church, social welfare programs, income maintenance programs, and so on. The Study does not take the view that social welfare needs are residual in the sense that social welfare agencies attend primarily to emergency functions and will be eliminated or cease to exist once the regular social institutions, that is, the family and the economic system, are again working properly. The Study agrees with Wilensky and Lebeaux, who hold that social services are needed because of the inevitable complexity of modern life and are, therefore, not reserved for any one segment of the population, such as the poor or the sick, but potentially are required by any member of society and should be available to any member of society.[7]

If one takes for granted that urbanization and industrialization are the two major characteristics of American society today, certain changes in social relations can be identified which immediately or in the near future will have an impact on the functions of social work as a profession that seeks to be responsive to societal needs. Students of society have identified the following phenomena as effects of urbanization and industrialization: [8]

1. Social relations tend to become impersonal, utilitarian, superfical, and transitory. Relationships with relatives and friends and acquaintances become segmental, that is, they pertain to only some aspects of living, such as work or home, and no longer involve the total person.

2. Social tolerance, the blasé attitude, spreads. Given a heterogeneous population having mainly impersonal contacts, tolerance, or better, indifference, is inevitable.

3. The city dweller loses himself in an anonymous world. He is surrounded by strangers who are physically close but socially distant. But he also can rely heavily on his immediate family, friends, and acquaintances. This gives the individual a double refuge. He can free himself from the close moral control of the intimate primary group and escape into a sea of strangers.

[7] Harold L. Wilensky and Charles N. Lebeaux, *Industrial Society and Social Welfare,* Russell Sage Foundation, New York, 1958, pp. 117–119.

[8] Partially reproduced or paraphrased from material in Wilensky and Lebeaux, *ibid.,* pp. 117–119.

4. Social life becomes atomized; the individual stands apart, loses a sense of participation, becomes susceptible to manipulation. Social contacts may be numerous, but they are superficial.

One should not infer, however, that all these changes in society and social living will necessarily and automatically produce disruption and disorganization in human life. Some of these changes will be easily absorbed; others will not. All one can say at this point is that urbanization and industrialization have created a *potential* for social disorganization which must be recognized by a service profession such as social work. Furthermore, social work must recognize the tremendous potential for rendering preventive services.

I should like to cite only a few of the changes with which social work must reckon in the immediate future. New immigrants, such as Puerto Ricans, must be absorbed into our urban society. Large populations, shifted to other areas in the city as a result of slum clearance and housing developments, must be accommodated. Ways must be found to compensate for the impoverishment of social life attendant upon the depletion of rural areas. The new middle-class groups in the suburbs are searching for a new identity both as communities and as individuals. As a nation, we face the urgent and critical problem of integrating Negro pupils into the public school system. Profound changes in our way of living will probably be wrought by the new technology developed as a result of atomic energy. Finally, there is the impending shift in our world outlook which will include not only a picture of this globe but a widened concept of outer space and other planets as coming within our reach. Although these and many other changes cannot be clearly defined at this point, they will have to be anticipated and planned for.

The Nature of Social Work

In the process of the Curriculum Study, the identification of societal changes made it possible for the study group to arrive at a description of the nature of social work which reflected the thinking and trends in social work practice and was also attuned to emerging social needs.

In order to answer the question, "What is the nature of social work?" we first examined the ultimate goal of social work, its functions and its activities. The ultimate goal of social work may be defined as the enhancement of social functioning wherever the need for such enhancement is either socially or individually perceived. Social functioning encompasses those activities considered essential for performance of the several roles which each individual, by virtue of his membership in social groups, is called upon to carry out. All role performance requires reciprocal activity or social interaction between individual and individual, individual and group, and individual and community.

All helping professions subscribe to the view that man must be seen as a whole. However, both the complexity of man's functioning and the increase of scientific specialization have made it necessary for each profession to take one aspect of man's functioning as the primary focus of its activities. This does not imply that man can be divided into separate components or that there cannot be or ought not to be overlapping among the activities of the several professions.

The functions of social work fall into three categories: restoration of impaired capacity; provision of individual and social resources; and prevention of social dysfunctioning. Individuals, singly and in groups, on the one hand, and social environment on the other, are seen as components of an interactional field. Social work as a profession is viewed as having an obligation to intervene at any point in this interactional field, or in any aspect of the relationship between individuals and their social environment where, in the light of an assessment of the individual and social factors involved, professional activity will result in improved social functioning.

This professional obligation is discharged through the use of one or more of the professsional methods of social work—casework, group work, community organization, administration, and research. Each method consists of a variety of interrelated professional activities which can be grouped into four categories: assessment of the problem, planning for the solution of the problem, implementing the plan, and evaluating the outcome.

In sum, the Curriculum Study suggests that to understand social work as a profession we need to look at two things: its perspective and its focus of activity. The perspective of social work is a view of man and his environment as a field of interacting forces. Its focus of activity is professional intervention *only* in that aspect of man's functioning which lies in the realm of social relationships or of social role performance. Social work shares the perspective with most helping professions. The focus on social relationships, however, is suggested as the *distinguishing characteristic* of the social work profession.

The Nature of Social Casework

Clarification of the nature of social work made it possible for the study group then to clarify the nature of social casework. This step was undertaken by the persons assigned to the casework project of the Study, who made an analysis of the practice of social casework.[9] By relating this analysis to the formulations contained in the statement on the nature of social work, the casework project group arrived at the following description of the nature of social casework.

Social casework is a method of service which seeks to intervene in the psychosocial aspects of an individual's life for the purpose of helping him to improve, restore, preserve, or enhance his functioning in the performance of any social roles he has to fulfill. This intervention takes place in the context of a professional relationship between the worker and one or more individuals whose interaction has some bearing upon the social roles that are impaired. This intervention occurs at a point in time when individual or social resources and opportunities either are insufficient or their interaction is faulty to the extent of hampering or threatening to hamper effective or potential social functioning.

Hence, social casework does not deal with intrapsychic and somatic forces per se or with sociocultural forces per se. Neither does it disregard them. It is concerned with the ways in which intrapsychic, somatic, and sociocultural forces combine to find expression in social functioning. It assumes that social circumstances bear upon the internal forces of man, and vice versa, and that the social functioning of an individual is determined by the interaction between social circumstances and somatic and psychic factors.

In this view, diagnosis involves identification and assessment of those internal and social factors which have produced or may produce dysfunction in a one social role or a number. Treatment involves helping the client, who may be an individual or a family group, in the utilization of somatic, psychic, social, and cultural resources put at his disposal for the purpose of enabling him to

[9] Werner W. Boehm, *The Social Casework Method in Social Work Education: Vol. X of the Social Work Education Curriculum Study Projects,* Council on Social Work Education, New York, 1959.

eliminate or reduce dysfunction or to enhance his functioning in social roles. These resources may include service programs of social agencies, the professional relationship itself, other professional personnel, latent or unused capacities of the client and members of his family, or a combination of the various factors.

Curriculum Content Pertinent to Family Casework

A better understanding of the nature of modern society and the impact of urbanization and industrialization upon family living naturally influences the concepts of the role of social work and social casework in society. These concepts, in turn, make it possible to describe the nature of family casework and the curriculum content pertinent to it.

Three observations may be made:

1. The practice of family casework is directed toward the enhancement of social functioning. Social functioning reveals itself most readily in the intimate social group of the family, and family interactions largely determine the quality of a person's social functioning. Hence, focus on the family is essential for good casework practice.

2. To understand family interaction and to treat it, one must accept the fact that the interactions among family members are so numerous that not all of them can be understood, let alone treated. Thus, a way must be found to identify among a large number of interactions those that are crucial, positively and negatively, for effective social functioning.

3. Despite the advocacy in the literature and in gatherings of social workers of a shift in focus from the individual to the family, this shift has seldom been made in actual practice. Perhaps the reason for this failure is that our conceptual equipment is too inadequate to encompass all the phenomena that need to be considered in an attempt to achieve family diagnosis and family treatment. As Pollak suggests: "Persons with a psychological orientation traditionally have directed attention to the single individual. To understand pluralities in psychological terms demands a tremendous increase in observations and, in the analysis of these observations, an increase in integrative effort. In family agencies, the shift from a psychologically oriented concern with individuals to a similar con-

cern with groups, therefore, imposes a great burden on the caseworker and on the psychiatric consultant." [10]

It is clear that good family casework practice requires an understanding of those psychic, somatic, social, and cultural factors that affect individual members of a family and the family group as a whole. There seems to be a number of reasons why the attempts of caseworkers to ascertain which of these factors operate in the creation of stress and how they operate have not been so successful as one would like. One reason is the lack of a casework typology. There are no diagnostic categories into which types of family malfunctioning can be placed. One possible reason why such a typology has not been developed is that we lack a theoretical framework for somatic, psychic, and sociocultural factors, which would enable the worker to view family disturbances systematically. Another is that social casework knowledge in relation to the description of these factors is unevenly developed. We are much better able to understand psychic factors than social factors because we are much more conversant with psychoanalytic theory, in particular with the psychology of the ego and its structural and functional relationship to id and superego. Also, psychological theory is much more systematically developed than is social theory. Moreover, social caseworkers perhaps are less oriented to the use of sociocultural theory because they do not always perceive problems in these terms. Pollak points out that phenomena for which technological terminology is not available to the practitioner tend to remain unconsidered.[11] Perhaps the uneven development and the lesser availability of sociocultural theory account for the fact that schools of social work have only begun the process of extracting from sociology and cultural anthropology those concepts that seem pertinent to an understanding of the multiple causation of social functioning.

What do the findings of the Curriculum Study indicate should be done about this problem? The Study recommends that all social work students be given an understanding of individual behavior, group behavior, and social process. It also spells out some of the specific sociocultural concepts that are particularly pertinent to the goal and functions of social work. Undoubtedly, a broadening of the theoretical base of social work would help provide the worker

[10] Otto Pollak, commentary on "Family Diagnosis," *Social Casework,* Vol. XXXIX, Nos. 2–3 (1958), p. 83.

[11] Otto Pollak, *Integrating Sociological and Psychoanalytic Concepts,* Russell Sage Foundation, New York, 1956, p. 198.

with usable knowledge of psychic, somatic, social, and cultural factors. Even if it can be assumed that graduates of the future will possess more of this knowledge and will be better equipped to use it, it is doubtful whether this knowledge alone will result in better family diagnosis and family treatment. More than a wider array of theoretical concepts is needed, even though these concepts are also necessary. We shall be in a better position to know what is needed when we understand what is really involved in family diagnosis and family treatment.

Family interactions consist of an array of activities, a multitude of behaviors so large that it is impossible to assess them all or to treat them all. Hence, family diagnosis and family treatment are impossible unless a way can be found to isolate from the many interactions in the family those that are crucial for social functioning. What is needed is a theoretical construct that will fulfill two conditions: (1) It must provide a link between social and cultural factors on the one hand, and psychic and somatic ones on the other; and (2) it must enable the worker to single out from among a great number of interactions those that are particularly pertinent to social functioning. There is reason to believe that the social-role concept fulfills these conditions.

Concept of Social Role

The concept of social role provides a means for defining more precisely what is meant by social functioning. It permits analysis of social functioning through breaking it down into a number of task clusters which correspond to certain roles such as the roles of husband, wife, parent, and child. No role can be carried out in isolation, but requires reciprocity and relationship. For example, where there is a husband, there must be a wife. Thus, an accurate picture of family interaction requires an understanding not only of the ways in which the role of each member is actually performed but also of the expectations each has of his own role and the roles of the others.

Each social role is composed of a number of activities, a few of which seem to be so essential for the role that impaired performance or failure to perform them is an indication of social dysfunctioning. For example, a husband is expected to work for a living and to provide economic support—alone or together with a wife. He is expected to share in family decisions about leisure time, work problems, purchases, and so on; and he is expected to participate in giving love. The wife is expected to engage in reciprocal activities in the same areas. Thus, the role concept makes it possible to identify crucial tasks which, if not performed or inadequately performed, may make for family stress and lead to family problems or social dysfunctioning.

Once the tasks essential for the fulfillment of each role have been identified, it is still necessary to assess the impact of psychic, somatic, and sociocultural factors on how they are performed. This determination is made somewhat easier because the crucial tasks involve only a relatively small number of interactions rather than all possible interactions in the family. Let us assume, for instance, that one of the crucial tasks of the father in child rearing is to provide discipline. We know that there are marked differences in child rearing not only from culture to culture but also from class to class. We also know that somatic and psychic factors make a difference in the way a father participates in the disciplining process.

The caseworker's use of the concept of social role can never eliminate the need for him to consider also the psychic, somatic, social, and cultural factors in the genesis and present status of the client's problem. All the role concept can do is to specify what is meant by social functioning, to help the caseworker identify crucial roles in social functioning and the essential activities within these crucial roles. By narrowing the range of phenomena to be considered, the role concept facilitates an understanding of these phenomena in the light of the interaction of psychic, social, somatic, and cultural factors.

I should like to emphasize that the concept of social role is only one of a large array of concepts needed for effective family casework practice. The casework project of the Curriculum Study has developed three arrays of concepts: the agency, the worker, and the client. Here I have dealt only with the client and have covered that area only partially by discussing social role. With reference to the client, we also deal with the concepts of stress and problem—concepts that are differentiated on the assumption that not all stress leads to problems and that the stress-mastery pattern of the client in the past gives some indication of the way he will deal with the present stress situation. If he deals with it effectively, there is no problem.

The casework project has also attempted to describe the core problems encountered in the several fields of practice in which the casework method is used. In family social work, the core problem is inadequate performance of the interrelated roles of the members of the family in the family interaction. Inadequate performance may be the result of the stress arising from the addition of persons to the existing role network in the family or from the temporary or permanent elimination of members from the role network. Both these changes require a reshuffling and redistribution of the existing roles among the members of the family so that effective family interaction can continue. Stress may also come from the extrafamilial network of relationships and roles. Another source of stress may be changes in the quality of family interactions due to psychological, physical, or social factors. These stresses may produce changes in expectations and perception to which effective adaptation on the part of the several family members may not be forthcoming. Lastly, stress may result from differences in expectations of role performance, differences in definition of the same role on the part of the members of the family, as well as differences in perception of the role performance and of disagreement about the degree of freedom each member of the family has to perform his roles.

The casework method is used to provide resources and services in the form of role support given to members of the family. It may consist of redefining roles, reallocating role functions, eliminating stresses in the social, psychological, or physical realms, or increasing the stress tolerance of one or more members of the family group.

This description of the casework method has the advantage of bringing within one conceptual framework the problems recently identified as characteristic for family social work.[12] In addition it suggests a treatment method which, while making allowance for and being in harmony with the techniques of support and modification, does not maintain the sharp distinction usually made between these two sets of techniques, but seeks to pave the way for identifying a unitary method of casework with more specific social characteristics.

[12] Clark W. Blackburn, "Family Social Work," *Social Work Yearbook, 1957*, National Association of Social Workers, New York, 1957, p. 248.
"The Content of Family Social Work," *op. cit.*

Future Concerns

Two things now stand out sharply. First, the social caseworker must be more alert than ever before to changes in the quality, flavor, and content of family living, and their impact upon the tensile strength of the family. Consequently, he must be even more engaged in clinical and preventive activities. The family-centered caseworker of the future will have to have a better understanding of family interactions, family strengths, and family weaknesses, and their relationship to individual social functioning. Such concepts as social contagion and social infection may make possible social prevention through isolation or neutralization of contaminating factors in the family group. Thus, in time, through study and research, what now are but vistas and hopes—which do credit to our imagination—may yet become the tools that improve our skills in helping people.

Second, the caseworker must acquire more understanding of how people are affected by social and cultural factors. It would be a mistake, however, to assume that better understanding of the social and cultural dimensions of human behavior will free the worker from the necessity of achieving a greater depth of understanding of its psychological dimensions.

It is known from experience, confirmed by recent studies such as the one by Hollingshead and Redlich,[13] that vast groups of people in need of help go unaided. Social necessity as well as our professional ethics enjoin us to come to their assistance. We have learned something about the relationship between motivation and treatability, and we have begun to see that there may be a correlation between class position, motivation, and treatability. Perhaps social workers must develop their own knowledge about how to reach people who are now unreachable, rather than borrow it from other disciplines. What can we do about motivating members of lower socioeconomic groups? Do people in the lower-income groups react with conflict and guilt to stresses in the same way as people in the middle- and upper-income groups? Are there different types of stresses to which they are more vulnerable? Is the phenomenon of sociopathy, now so frequently encountered in daily life, an inevitable result of the changes in social living mentioned earlier? Is

[13] August B. Hollingshead, Ph.D., and Frederick C. Redlich, M.D., *Social Class and Mental Illness*, John Wiley & Sons, New York, 1958.

what we call "character disorder" but a middle-class designation of this phenomenon? Does the same phenomenon manifest itself otherwise in the lower-income groups? What about those families and individuals who are motivated to get help, but for whom available treatment personnel, be they psychiatrists, psychologists, or social workers, are woefully inadequate? Do we need to take a look, then, at whether diagnostic and treatment methods can be developed which are economical of time and yet are truly helpful? Do we need to do a better job of deploying personnel and find better ways of organizing our social services?

These questions and many others are a challenge both to education and to practice, for they suggest changes and improvements in curriculum content as well as in practice methods. Finding answers to these questions is a joint task for practice and education. We are helped in this task by our credo and our convictions. Our credo calls upon us to look for the strength in people and not for their weakness, and we are guided by our conviction that, even in a society as perplexing as ours, individuals can find a way of living their lives which, at one and the same time, is socially useful and individually creative.

TRAINING GOALS IN PUBLIC ASSISTANCE [1]

Corinne H. Wolfe

THE ESTABLISHMENT and development of the public assistance programs vividly illustrate Nathan E. Cohen's statement in regard to professional social work: "In the same way that our past and present have been intimately tied up with the economic, political,

[1] Published in *Social Casework,* February 1956.

and social climate which prevailed, so too our future will be markedly affected by the immense forces growing out of a dynamically changing world."[2] The objectives of the public assistance programs are (1) to relieve financial want, and (2) to help people to maintain or rebuild their personal strengths. For some persons, the goal of service will be to return them to self-support; for others, to increase their ability to plan constructively for the future. For all, the ultimate goals are the preservation of wholesome family life and the opportunity to participate in community life to the best of their ability. In all likelihood, the public assistance programs will continue to be a major force in the maintenance of the economic and social well-being of large numbers of people in our society.

If the full potentialities of the public assistance programs are to be realized, staff members who are able to provide extensive and skilled services are needed. The effectiveness of social and economic rehabilitation programs is dependent upon sound administration directed toward providing adequate services to their clientele and toward increasing the skill of their staffs both in working with clients and in working with the community for the purpose of developing resources to meet social and economic needs. When the administrative structure of the public assistance agency is good, the caseworkers are able to assist clients in a constructive and helpful way to achieve social and economic rehabilitation.

The training goal for public assistance staff is to ensure the availability of staff who have knowledge and skill to provide social services for each client which are appropriate to his needs and wishes, in the course of providing financial assistance. State public assistance agencies have demonstrated throughout the years, in a variety of ways, the importance of employing trained personnel. The constructive services provided by public assistance staff and the kind of knowledge and skill needed by staff to fulfill the social objectives of the program are coming to be more widely recognized. In order to attain the full potentiality of the public assistance program, the agency must provide in-service training so that the staff is enabled to render the agency's services in a constructive and helpful manner. Training must be undertaken on three fronts: more intensive training for currently employed staff, supplementary train-

[2] Nathan E. Cohen, "Professional Social Work Faces the Future," *Social Work Journal,* Vol. XXXVI, No. 3 (1955), p. 79.

ing for workers advancing into supervisory and administrative positions, and concentrated training for new employees.

Present Status of Staff Development Programs

The Social Security Act, as passed in 1935, provided that financial assistance be available to every person in the nation who met the eligibility requirements of the state programs. This made it obligatory for public assistance agencies to provide staff "coverage" so that persons in need could make application in the towns in which they were living. This meant, in 1935—and it is true to a large extent today—that staff members were employed who had had no basic training in social work although there was general agreement that the public assistance programs were to be administered in accordance with social work principles. The social work profession has not been able to provide a sufficient number of trained persons for employment in the public assistance programs during these twenty years. The fact remains, however, that social work knowledge and skill are needed by persons who administer public assistance programs and those who provide services to their clientele.

The real concern of state public assistance agencies for helping staff members to develop the skill necessary for helping families and individuals is indicated by their establishment of planned staff development programs as an integral part of agency administration. An analysis of state plans, made in June, 1953, revealed that 30 public assistance agencies had staff members assigned full-time to the planning and direction of their staff development programs; 26 agencies had staff assigned part-time to the planning and direction of such programs; 4 agencies did not have any staff members assigned for this purpose.[3]

The staff development programs of the public assistance agencies, for the most part, have included plans for in-service training for new staff members, supervision, institutes, conferences and meetings, and provision for educational or work-study leave. Recognizing that staff training in social work expedites proper and efficient administration, the Bureau of Public Assistance early developed a nation-

[3] "Selected Characteristics of State Staff Development Plans," monograph, Bureau of Public Assistance, Social Security Administration, U. S. Department of Health, Education, and Welfare, Washington, D.C., June 1953. (Mimeographed)

wide policy under which educational leave for employees of state and local welfare agencies is considered an administrative expense if the leave granted is for the purpose of developing more competent personnel. Federal participation in such expenditures has been on the same basis as holds true for other administrative expenses of the public assistance agency, that is, 50 per cent reimbursement. Some states have been able to take advantage of this policy; others have not. This method has not been successful in developing sufficient numbers of trained workers for the country as a whole. In a special study made by the Bureau of Public Assistance for the twelve-month period ending August 31, 1953, twenty-seven public assistance agencies reported that 131 individuals had returned to the agency after completing a period of full-time educational leave. Of this number, 110 received either stipends or pay.[4]

In some states, it has not been possible for the public agency to grant educational leave because of the state laws that prohibit "giving a gift" to an individual from state funds. Recently, a ruling has been obtained which places responsibility on government for the provision of competent individuals to deal, under the sponsorship of the government, with problems of other individuals. This is a significant precedent ruling inasmuch as it establishes a base for the training of personnel for public social services. The ruling, which was obtained by the Director of Public Assistance in West Virginia from the State Supreme Court, is concerned with the use of state funds for educational purposes. This ruling clearly identifies expenditures for training as a necessary cost of government, and says that the granting of funds to an individual is incidental to the purposes of the training. The following is an excerpt from the opinion:

> . . . Defendant contends that the payment of the sum for which the requisition was drawn would constitute a gift of public funds for a private purpose, and therefore would be in violation of provisions of Article X of the State Constitution. We think there is no merit in the contention. It is true, of course, that the employee will receive a special benefit from the expenditure. That, however, is not the test. We have no difficulty in finding that the funds are to be expended for a public purpose. Of special concern to the State, in fact, to any government, are the health and welfare of its

[4] "Educational Leave Programs of Public Assistance Agencies, September, 1952–August, 1953," Bureau of Public Assistance, Social Security Administration, U. S. Department of Health, Education, and Welfare, Washington, D.C. (Mimeographed)

youth. Obviously, the successful and efficient exercise of such a governmental function covering such a broad and specialized field requires the services of a great number of specialized leaders and workers. It also requires experimentation in new methods of assistance. Thus the necessity for the State to encourage and assist individuals in preparing and qualifying themselves for such services. The cost to the government is returned to the public in the better health and welfare of its people. It is no objection to such a program to say that a certain individual may fail to render services to the State after having agreed to do so on condition of receiving assistance. The program must be viewed as a whole, in the interest of better health and welfare, not measured by the mistake of some one of its administrators in selecting some individual for the schooling or training who may, after receiving assistance, dishonestly refuse to serve the State. . . .[5]

State agencies have been creative and imaginative in providing ways and means for their staff members to obtain the necessary knowledge and skill. The development of training centers for the orientation of new staff is an effective administrative device for providing the basic minimum of knowledge needed. In some state agencies, a centralized training center has been used. Other states have depended upon day-by-day supervision which, in the main, does not provide sufficient means for training new staff. For the most part, introduction to the job is provided by centralized training units under the direction of a trained and skilled social worker who, by individual and group supervision, can teach some of the basic material needed by the beginning caseworker.

In some states the development of supervisory training programs has proceeded in an imaginative way. In one state, a year's in-service training program is offered to the potential supervisor before he is actually promoted to a supervisory position. The content of the training program has been carefully developed. Considerable attention has been given in agency staff development plans to sound principles of teaching and learning. Some states have made constructive use of teaching resources, both within and outside the agency, by utilizing consultants in specialized areas. Some agencies have developed, in co-operation with schools of social work, summer courses directed toward filling the gaps in professional knowledge. Human growth and development, community resources, problems of disability, unmarried parenthood, economic and social development, and community planning are types of subject matter which have been covered in some training programs. The state agencies

[5] 81 S.E. (2d) 670

have demonstrated, through the actual work of their staff, that giving training through sound supervision has resulted in the development of workers who, though not professionally trained in social work, can provide sound services, particularly in the areas of environmental planning and the use of community resources. These demonstrations have also shown that it is wise for an agency to invest sufficient time and staff for teaching its personnel how to render the social services of the agency.

Agency training consultants are generally in agreement that public assistance caseworkers must have (1) knowledge of the society in which we live and of the basic forces that determine our cultural goals and aspirations; (2) understanding of the relationship of these goals to our political, social, and economic structure, and understanding of the changing forces that affect the individual, the community, and the society as a whole; (3) knowledge of normal human growth and personality development; (4) knowledge of behavior that is abnormal, and, to some degree, of how people may react in times of stress such as the loss of parents, loss of security, illness, or physical disability; (5) capacity to respond with empathy; (6) ability to evaluate controversial situations; (7) ability to obtain facts, to make an objective analysis of them, and to reach decisions.

Staff development programs are directed toward helping staff members acquire the requisite knowledge and skill through focusing on the agency's program, its objectives and services, its eligibility requirements, the use of community resources, and the skills needed in carrying out the services the agency provides. The individual staff member must learn how to use his knowledge of human behavior, how to use the social resources within the community best suited to the situation that the client faces, and, to a certain degree, he must understand the intricacies of human relationships as they affect his work with clients.

Agency staff development programs cannot cover all the educational needs of social work staff. The profession of social work had its origins in apprentice training. Theoretically, therefore, one might assume that full education could be accomplished through in-service training. However, agency staff development programs are job focused, and professional education must be focused on the student in relation to his growth and development. For this reason, staff development programs per se cannot be a substitute for professional education.

Despite the increase in the number and quality of agency staff development programs, the continued work of schools of social work, and the emphasis placed on preparation of personnel for public social services by the Council on Social Work Education, a serious shortage of personned in the public welfare field still exists. The number of social workers continues to be far short of the number of social work positions in the nation. Trained workers in public assistance agencies are in even shorter supply. Approximately 75,000 persons were employed in social work positions in 1950. Of this number, 30,000 were employed in public assistance programs. In 1950, only two out of ten of these 30,000 had had any professional training as contrasted with four out of ten in the over-all social work field.[6] A 1954 study conducted by the American Public Welfare Association indicated that 2,658 individuals in 13 states would be interested in and available for training in social work if funds were available.[7]

The cost of education for social work, like that for other professions, is high. The need in public assistance agencies for a different method of financing social work education has been apparent for some years. The Committee on Personnel and Training, advisory to the Bureau of Public Assistance and to the Children's Bureau, and the American Public Welfare Association, over a period of years, have made a strong recommendation to the Bureau of Public Assistance that the federal government pay the full cost of training selected persons for public assistance agencies. The need for such a method of financing social work training for work in public assistance programs is evident. The experience of psychiatric social work, medical social work, and child welfare has shown that persons are attracted into these programs by educational grants.

Long-Range Planning for Training

Recently state public assistance agencies have been undertaking evaluations of their program objectives and have given intensive consideration to the changing character of public assistance case loads in the light of the fact that old-age and survivors insurance

[6] *Social Workers in 1950*, monograph, American Association of Social Workers, New York, 1952.

[7] Unpublished study of the American Public Welfare Association Committee on Personnel and Training.

is taking an increasingly large part in meeting income maintenance needs. As part of the evaluation of their objectives, they are also defining the areas of knowledge required and the skills that staff members need in order to carry out these objectives. They are also beginning to develop training plans which, over a long period, will ensure an adequate number of qualified personnel to administer public assistance programs more effectively. Some states are administering, in addition to the public assistance programs, a program of social services for families and individuals who are not in financial need, in order to provide counseling and other services to all persons in the community who may desire them. The provision of social welfare services by public agencies, irrespective of the client's financial need, is coming to be an accepted responsibility of government. In the past several years, various statements of worker qualifications and services that should be available in public welfare agencies have been developed.[8] State public welfare agencies are now considered a permanent part of governmental structure and their services a continuing responsibility of government. Long-range plans must be made if the objectives of the current programs or of the projected programs of the future are to be realized. If a sufficient number of trained staff is to be secured, public agencies must develop long-range plans for the recruitment, selection, and training of staff. Such long-range planning involves the total administration of the agency, with respect both to its on-going programs and to its projected programs. There is agreement that staff are needed who can carry mature responsibility in providing services to those who need help.

The staff members of a public welfare agency must be as well qualified as those of any other social agency. In August, 1954, a group of public welfare program directors from both public assistance and child welfare programs met for a two-week workshop to learn about personality assessment as a part of the selection process and to determine some of the personal and professional qualifications that the public welfare job demands. It was agreed that the personal qualities needed by staff in the public welfare

[8] See American Public Welfare Association pamphlets on the public assistance worker, the child welfare worker, the medical social worker, and so on. See also "Draft Report on Services in the Aid to Dependent Children Program," Bureau of Public Assistance and Children's Bureau, Social Security Administration, U.S. Department of Health, Education, and Welfare, Washington, D.C., August, 1954. (Mimeographed)

agency are the same as those needed by persons who seek admission to a school of social work. There was also consensus that the person who is employed before enrolling in a school of social work doubtless needs to be more mature than the person who goes directly from college to a school of social work. The person who is to be employed by a public assistance agency not only should be educable, but should also have received a bachelor's degree and should possess the intelligence and personality characteristics that will justify the agency's making further financial investment in him, whether through training on the job or through educational leave and work-study plans. Emotional maturity and the capacity to use oneself in a professional helping relationship are essential.

Specifics of Planning for Attaining the Training Goal

In order to attain its goals in relation to training currently employed staff, preparing persons for promotion to responsible positions, and giving effective help to newly employed staff, a public assistance agency's administrative structure should include provision for the following:

1. A clear plan for gradually raising the standards in qualifications for all positions. For example, the agency could start with a plan for raising the qualifications for basic supervisory and administrative positions. If an agency does not at the moment require that all supervisors have social work training, it might set the goal of requiring that at the end of a specified period, perhaps five to ten years, anyone promoted to a supervisory position must have completed his social work training.

2. The development of recruitment and staff selection methods that will enable agencies to obtain those persons best suited for social work—both as to intelligence and as to personality. This objective might be achieved by use of the team approach—the merit system, the agency personnel director, the program director, and the staff development consultant all working together.

3. An adequate salary scale commensurate with the responsibility to be assumed in each position. The salary scale should also give recognition to educational achievement.

4. Educational leaves, work-study plans, and other devices to ensure that, within the time stipulated, staff would have the opportunity to meet the basic requirements set up by the administration.

Working out such plans on a sound basis requires that the agency make an analysis of the present staff members as to age, education, length of service, and requirements for service under the law. This analysis should be made in the light of the possibility that the current program will be expanded, and that therefore long-range planning will be needed in order to raise the qualifications for each position.

5. Selection of the most mature staff members for assignment to agencies in rural areas where frequently one person is called upon to act as caseworker, group worker, community organizer, and administrator. The salary should be commensurate with the scope of responsibilities the worker must assume.

6. A planned program of staff development under the direction of a staff member who gives full time to this assignment. This program should include staff orientation, continuing supervision, refresher courses, and so forth. Attention should be given to the staff members who, because of age or other factors, will not be enrolling in schools of social work, or obtaining professional education on a credit basis. One way in which this could be done is through making a state-wide training plan, or even a plan for several states, in which short courses are conducted by agency staff members or faculty of colleges or schools of social work. Also, consultants in special areas of practice can be brought into the training program.

7. The establishment of agency policies, rules, and regulations that will further the objectives of the program and the determination of the optimum size of work loads for both caseworkers and supervisors.

The following is an illustration of how one state agency initiated a long-range plan for improving staff and for determining training priorities. About five years ago, the staff members of this agency were not using all the available educational leave stipends. At the same time the agency was faced with the necessity of finding replacements for the considerable number of persons in case supervisor and county director positions who would shortly be retiring. Since replacements were difficult to secure, the agency decided to see if it could discover among its staff persons those who had the qualities needed for supervisory and administrative positions and who could be trained to step into the prospective vacancies. Out of the agency's review of employed staff came the beginning of an interesting long-range plan for increasing the numbers of qualified staff.

The agency first reviewed the educational background, length of service, and evaluations of all professional staff. A plan was then drawn up for obtaining a pool of supervisors.

A first step was the amendment of the official merit system qualifications for the supervisory position; this amendment provided that, after a specified period, a person would not be considered for promotion to the position unless he had had at least one year of social work training. The time selected for enforcing this qualification was a period during which a large number of staff members would be retiring and the agency would be able to send to schools of social work, either through educational leave or work-study plans, approximately 25 persons a year. In the year following the raising of the qualifications for the supervisory positions, 65 persons applied for the 25 stipends. Some of these applicants were already supervisors who, under the plan, could remain supervisors without further education, since the plan provided for blanketing-in the persons already in these positions. Others were persons who were interested in being considered for supervisory and administrative positions. By its administrative action the agency had expressed its conviction that these positions require social work training.

Since the adoption of the plan, the agency has moved steadily ahead in obtaining, training, and retaining qualified personnel for supervisory positions. The agency has also developed a comprehensive orientation and training program of one year's duration for prospective supervisors. It is now considering a similar plan for securing qualified county directors, by providing educational opportunities both on the job and in schools of social work.

In some states, trained social workers have been given a selected case load made up of the most difficult cases. Another state has established a system of specialized case loads in which the most difficult cases have been assigned to the best qualified staff members. In instances where these workers were untrained, they have been supervised by professionally trained persons. The use of differentiated case loads has of necessity been limited to large agencies where such assignments are possible. One state has long set the requirement of social work training for supervisory and administrative staff. At present 31 of the 35 state and local supervisors have had such training. In another state, the training plan established for obtaining staff and providing opportunity for further education has resulted in the state's having 51 casework supervisors who have at least one year of specialized training, of whom 15 have completed their professional training. One hundred and four of the caseworkers have had at least nine months of training. All of the superintendents of public welfare who have been appointed in recent years have had at least nine months of graduate training as well as appropriate experience.

These various experiences illustrate that by undertaking training plans now, we shall be able to make better use of present staff and to provide for their training on and off the job. They show also that public agencies are now selecting staff, both for employment and for promotion, on the basis of their current professional equipment or their potentialities for making use of professional training.

Summary

The urgency of securing trained personnel for public assistance agencies is clear, and ways of obtaining such training for currently employed staff, for staff being prepared for supervisory and administrative positions, and for new staff must be developed. The development of in-service and staff development programs has resulted, to a considerable extent, in providing the public agencies with staff equipped through knowledge and skill to administer the assistance programs. In order to realize the goals that have been set, there must be intensive work on the part of total administration in obtaining and maintaining competent staff. Administrative planning, including the determination of sound policies that make it possible to carry forward social work concepts, and the administrative establishment of case loads geared to the purpose of the agency and to the needs of the clientele, must be carefully developed. In order to attain the goals of public assistance, all agencies, both public and voluntary, as well as the social work profession, must discover ways and means of developing qualified staff for all public social services.

AN ATTEMPT TO CONSTRUCT A CONCEPTUAL FRAMEWORK FOR SUPERVISION[1]

Fred Berl

ALTHOUGH MUCH has been written about supervision in social work, the emphasis in such articles is usually on one or two aspects of the subject. Both the educational and the administrative elements have received considerable attention, with some writers viewing these functions as antithetical to each other and others believing that they can be harmoniously combined. Attention has also been given to methodological aspects, usually in the context of a particular setting or helping method.

In the seminar on which this article is based the members noted that little attempt has been made to analyze supervision as a generic social work operation or to construct a conceptual framework that would have application to all settings, regardless of the methods used. The need for such a framework was recognized and the group, therefore, assigned itself the task of constructing a model. The framework presented here should be regarded as the attempt of one group to relate the basic elements of supervision to each other. It is hoped that this attempt will underline the need for a conceptual framework and will stimulate further efforts to construct one.

In the seminar we first undertook to identify the components that are essential to an understanding of the operational practice

[1] Published in *Social Casework,* July 1960. Based on a doctoral seminar on supervision led by the author in the spring of 1958, at the National Catholic School of Social Service, Catholic University of America, Washington, D.C. There were eight members in the seminar, representing various fields and methods of social work practice. The members were Rev. John Bicsey, Mrs. Stephany Keyser, Marta Korwin, Robert Lanigan, Hortense Lilly, Mrs. Grace Llewellyn, Genevieve O'Leary, and Dr. Daniel Thursz.

called supervision. We identified four components: (1) the institutional, (2) the methodological, (3) the educational, and (4) the psychological. This paper will present a discussion of these components and of the interaction between them.

The Institutional Component

Social workers have a tendency to define supervision as a professional, rather than an institutional, operation. As a professional operation, supervision has certain defined norms and values, but these do not exist in vacuum; they are an intrinsic part of the norms and values of our society. It is true that a profession has an identity of its own, within the larger society, but it is not divorced from the larger entity. Supervision, therefore, should be viewed as an institutional, as well as a professional, operation. A social agency has responsibility to provide certain services to eligible clients in the interest of the welfare of the community as a whole. The staff members of an agency therefore have a special responsibility—one that goes beyond the responsibility of citizenship and community membership—to perform certain services and to develop methods appropriate to the purpose of the services.

An agency, in establishing methods of control, has two major purposes: the first is to make services available and the second to set standards for these services. The methods of control tend to become institutionalized in the structures and processes of the agency. Supervision plays a specific role in the institutional control of both the availability and the standards of service.

What is this role? Supervision itself is not a means of creating services or of determining standards. The services and standards of an agency are influenced by many other factors, such as professional methods and professional values (to which agency personnel contribute), social norms and values, and the social reality. The latter is subject to change as social needs and social attitudes change. The institutional component of supervision, therefore, encompasses those aspects that are concerned with the control of service and standards. Such "control" does not imply a mechanistic function but, rather, an integrative one. The control stems from the supervisor's understanding of the social forces and processes that have an influence on the agency's program.

In carrying responsibility for integrating and controlling the various institutional elements, the supervisor is subject to certain characteristic tensions. These tensions are related to (1) the supervisory function, (2) the supervisory role, and (3) the supervisory process.

1. *Tension related to the supervisory function:* Each agency and each community must attempt to establish an equation between traditional operations on the one hand and new values and goals on the other. An agency that is future-oriented may still have deep roots in the past, even though it is working toward change. It must utilize various processes of communication to establish a balance between the two forces. An agency cannot follow its vision of the future exclusively, but must also take present-day realities into account. The latter are related to hard facts of community need, budget limitations, availability of staff, and so forth. If an agency refuses to deal with certain realities on the ground that doing so would impede the attainment of new goals or the establishment of desired professional standards, it stands on a weak social base. Such refusals obviously are not likely to be helpful in attaining the new standards. If we understand the real meaning of a social institution, we shall also understand that tension is a necessary part of its very functioning. One might describe the tension as a conflict between the ideal and the reality.

2. *Tension related to the supervisory role:* The supervisory role, which prescribes both equality and inequality between professional colleagues, invites tension. The role of supervisor is one of equality in relation to such essentials as client service, community welfare, and the advancement of professional knowledge. The same role prescribes inequality in relation to job responsibilities, authority, and status. The supervisor, therefore, has the task of handling this dual requirement in a way that does not nullify either aspect. There is the danger that a supervisor may place so much emphasis on the authoritative elements that the equality of purpose will be lost; at the other extreme, he may minimize the authoritative elements to the extent of failing to discharge his essential institutional responsibilities.

Various psychological and sociological patterns for reducing the tension inherent in the dual task suggest themselves. One is the *primus inter pares* model, that is, the pattern in which a person is accepted by other members as the superior of his group. A supervisor may be in the fortunate position of being accepted as a leader, not only because of his status but because staff members have placed him psychologically in a superior position, recognizing his competence and professional helpfulness. Another model is that of *esprit de corps* which emphasizes the unity and common purpose of the group; the differentiations in status and authority are minimized, and the leadership often comes to be viewed as that of the group's own choosing. Still another model is the one of the "boss," with a division of labor; the emphasis here is on the value and importance of everyone's job in the total undertaking. In order to function as the "boss," the person must live up to certain rules and norms in relation to fairness, competence, and so forth. It would seem that these, as well as other models, may be used in social agencies in discharging supervisory requirements and achieving effective group functioning.

3. *Tension related to the supervisory process:* The supervisor's conception of supervision and his actual experience in the process are not always identical. There may be differences between his concept and that of his supervisee's in relation to expectation, responsibilities, purposes, and so forth. Also, the supervisor's role and responsibilities are defined by the norms and structure of the agency. The experience of the individual supervisor, however, does not always conform to these institutional expectations. It is a mistake to consider the institutional norms and ideals as characteristic of the individual experience. It is also a mistake to consider an individual experience as a basis for defining norms. In order to understand certain tensions that are involved in supervision, it is necessary to understand the degree of discrepancy that may exist between the institutional norms and the individual's own experience. A certain degree of tension is to be expected. Obviously, the way to reduce the tension growing out of such differences is by attempting to reduce the gap between the institutional demands and the individual's demands. Both the agency and the individual may need to make modifications in their concepts and requirements. Such modifications often result in the establishment of new norms for the agency and for the profession.

The above discussion of supervision as an institutional operation may suggest that the seminar group supported a relativistic philosophy. But this was not the case. Our reasoning was as follows: The chief aim of supervision is to help workers gain the capacity to perform adequately. It seemed to us that a clearer understanding by social workers of the institutional elements in supervision would help sharpen the understanding of the professional elements. There has been a tendency in social work to emphasize the professional elements and to neglect the institutional ones, with the implication that the latter are "unprofessional." It is true that certain relativistic standards are used in the practice of supervision, but these standards are not necessarily dominant. However, institutional elements, such as the functions of the agency, community needs, the agency's resources, and the training of the staff, enter into supervisory practice with its goal of helping workers to perform adequately. Institutional standards obviously must be related to professional standards. Although standards of "adequate performance" may vary considerably among agencies, professional standards, and the values forming them, have a high degree of homogeneity.

The Methodological Component

Method is essential to social work practice. It represents an attempt at conscious professional control of the multiple factors that enter into an agency's program. Traditionally, this control has been exercised through the interplay between board members, administrators, supervisors, and practitioners. Each of these segments of an agency may play a part in determining standards of supervision.

In most analyses of the responsibilities of the supervisor, two functions have been singled out—the administrative and the teaching. There has been disagreement about the respective weight that should be given to each, with some persons placing greater emphasis on the administrative aspects and others urging that supervisors be freed from the burden of carrying the administrative ballast.

Conceptually, both the administrative and the teaching responsibilities are essential elements of supervisory practice in a social agency. Since an agency is responsible for the results of its services, it must set up administrative controls to assure that standards of practice are maintained and it must devise methods for evaluating the service given. The very need of agencies to maintain standards of service is the major motive for developing educational programs —both within and outside the agency. The seminar group believed that, ideologically, the administrative and teaching functions of supervision are not divisible. This assumption seemed valid because of the common frame of reference for both these functions. Teaching, as well as administration, is a method for focusing, limiting, and enhancing service. The responsibility for determining, through administrative methods, the usefulness of a worker in a particular field—or in the total professional field—influences the nature and form of the teaching methods used. Vice versa, the availability of teaching opportunities, as well as the results achieved, influence administrative decisions about providing certain services.

Essentially, the administrative goal of an agency is to square the responsibility for meeting community needs with the availability of agency resources, which include staff able to maintain professional standards of service. In supervision, the administrative processes are formulated empirically. The variation in agency programs and in community conditions makes it necessary to rely on empirical methods. Such realities as client needs, community pressures, and limitations of resources are determining factors in establishing administrative processes and methods. In the endeavor to understand supervisory practice, it is necessary to be aware of this empirical element in administrative methods.

The teaching function of supervision, on the other hand, is more clearly conceptualized by the profession and has a firmer scientific underpinning. Because developmental goals for staff members are defined, teaching tends to be systematic; it can subordinate irrelevant variables. A systematic teaching approach in supervision can bring cohesion to elements in practice that are unstable, such as variations in agency policy, changes in programs, and so forth. The major enemy, so to speak, of systematic teaching is the frequent change in community conditions and administrative policy. This unpredictable element of change, with which the board and the administrator are constantly struggling, creates an obstacle for the supervisor. Teaching requires a certain degree of stability.

It seemed to the seminar group, in view of the points discussed above, that supervisory practice should combine administrative and teaching functions. Three supervisory stages might be used to facilitate the worker's development. The first would aim at individualization of the worker's unique potentials, with the aim of helping him carry responsibility for service. The second aim, through the medium of teaching, would enable the worker to move toward independent functioning. In the third stage, the aim would be to clarify learning goals for the worker and to motivate his self-advancement.

At its best, the supervisory method can provide necessary agency controls and at the same time further sound professional development of staff members. When the supervisor has conflict between the two roles, the integration of the administrative and teaching functions is not achieved. The supervisor may then resort to efforts to control and manipulate staff members and to rationalize about deficiencies in the agency.

Much has been said in recent years about the undesirable features in supervisory practice. It seems likely that a clearer understanding of its diverse elements may help to improve methods and reduce dissatisfactions. One test of the adequacy of a supervisory method might be the extent to which it achieves the goal of individualizing the worker and of enabling him to function on a higher level. This goal transcends the purely professional goal, since it encompasses basic values of our society. Another test of a supervisory method might be the effectiveness of the work of staff members. Greater objectification is needed in all parts of social work practice, including supervision. Such testing, however, should take place under optimal conditions because of the many variables in supervision and the high degree of subjectivity about it.

The Educational Component

Some learning is implicit in the performance of any professional service. In a social agency, the learning becomes particularized because of the standards set for the performance of various services. Although supervisory operations have an essential place in fostering the learning of staff members, these operations are only a part of the total educational framework. Staff members draw on many other sources, both within and without the agency, for knowledge and enhancement of skill. In any consideration of staff development, one must be aware of the total framework of educational resources and processes.

In analyzing the supervisory operations, we agreed upon an approach that seems central to the learning needs of staff. This approach consists of a constant and a number of variables. The constant may be defined as the process by which staff members are helped to move from less to greater adequacy in knowledge and skill. Such progression is the common aim of all educational endeavors. Also, in the educational process there are recognized stages of moving from less to more adequate performance.

Within this constant, we identified certain differential characteristics in social work learning. The major differential is in the subject matter itself. The complex content and the requirements of the helping process place unusually heavy demands on the learner. Mastery of content is closely allied to mastery of skills. It is difficult to determine whether this close relationship is necessitated by the character of social work learning or whether it stems from tradition.

Another differential in this process is that it involves the learner in a "living experience." It is true that all learning demands some personal involvement, but the involvement in social work learning is particularly intense. It requires a correlation of intellectual grasp and emotional development.

In social work one needs to learn in order to perform and to perform in order to learn. In the beginning stage, the learner has feelings of inadequacy and a need to rely on someone with superior knowledge; he also gains security from the stability of an organizational structure and its processes. He then moves into the stage of mastering the subject matter and of establishing a pattern of functioning. In this stage he must make many shifts and readjustments in his patterns of thinking and acting. As a result, he tends to be critical of external power, whether it is represented by the supervisor or someone else. Later, he has less need for dependence and develops greater ability to function as part of an established structure and to meet the demands of the job.

In addition to the constant and its differential characteristics, a number of variables in social work learning were identified by the seminar group. One variable is the *situational* element, that is, the functions, services, policies, philosophy, and morale of a particular agency. Another variable is the *technical* nature of the assignments given and the responsibilities expected from the learner. A third variable is the nature of the *relationship* between the learner and the supervisor, that is, the elements in their interaction that foster or impede learning.

It is as important to be aware of the variables in the learning process as of the constant. These variables may create problems in teaching but they are the very stuff with which the supervisor must deal in furthering the learner's development. The type of assignment and the level of skill required help to particularize learning. The specifics are the means of feeding into the learning process the elements that are needed at various points in the worker's development. Supervisors have developed much technical know-how about utilizing agency structure, policies, services, and so forth to advance the competence of staff members.

In utilizing these variables for generic learning, the supervisor should be aware of two major requirements. One is that he adapt the demands of the assignment to the stage of the worker's learning. The other is that he be aware of the interplay between the relationship elements and the total learning process of the worker. The relationship can be a catalyst for speeding up, or slowing down, the learning process. The relationship is the base for learning, since it helps the learner assimilate and integrate all other aspects.

The Psychological Component

The application of psychological principles is essential in the provision of services for which the social agency exists. The supervisor, therefore, needs to have a sound grasp of psychological theory, not only to assure that adequate services are given, but also to handle the supervisor-worker relationship. An important aspect of learning in social work is the opportunity provided in the supervisory relationship for the worker to experience psychological processes similar to those required of him in giving adequate service to clients.

One psychological factor in supervision is the degree of harmony between the supervisor's personality and the role he must assume. By definition, this role carries a strong element of authority. The authority delegated to him may initially provide a sufficient base for him to perform effectively for a time. His effectiveness will not continue, however, unless he earns the right to the authority by demonstrating his competence in relation to various aspects of his job. Persons who have difficulty in carrying an authoritative role are likely to have difficulty in meeting the role expectations of the supervisory position. Able and competent persons sometimes have conflict about carrying this role, and their uneasiness is reflected in negative reactions on the part of the persons they supervise.

Ability to carry a particular social role requires a certain degree of maturational development. If we apply this principle to the supervisory role in the social agency, the question of maturational standards arises. Considerable study will be necessary to determine what psychological qualifications are needed by persons who are expected to meet the role requirements of the position.

Another psychological factor in the supervisory relationship is the complementarity of roles. Complementarity is implicit in the very nature of the social agency and its organizational structure. The supervisor and the worker are necessarily dependent on each other in order for each to discharge his functions. The worker's dependence on the supervisor is generally recognized as well as the risks involved in the dependence. To a large degree, such dependence is institutionalized and cannot be changed by decision on the part of either the worker or the supervisor. The institutional nature of the supervisory relationship places some limitations on the worker's independence and, in reverse, some responsibility on the supervisor to handle the dependence. A point that is often overlooked, however, is that there is also a mutuality of dependence; that is, the supervisor also depends on the worker. In order to make his own job a reality and in order to function effectively, the supervisor must rely on the participation of the worker.

In the teaching process, too, there is complementarity. The content of the worker's learning is largely the social data he has gathered and the problems with which he is attempting to deal. The supervisor, in attempting to understand the data, learns from the worker in much the same way as the worker learns from the client. Each must be able "to listen" in order to be of help. The participation of supervisor and worker is based on a mutuality of interests and an acceptance of their complementary roles. Such mutuality and complementarity do not conflict with their specific roles or with the definitions of their respective responsibilities. Helping, learning, and teaching are linked together in one interacting psychological process.

Transference and countertransference phenomena can be expected to occur in the supervisory relationship, as they do in other relationships. In the supervisory situation, however, the reactions are heightened by such factors as the power and control of the supervisor, the dependence and insecurity of the learner, and the closeness of the relationship. These factors may tend to stimulate anxiety and hostility on the part of both participants. Special note should be made of the authoritative element. The worker may react to the supervisor's authority with fear, and defeat his own learning by becoming overly independent or rebellious. The supervisor, in reaction, may then assert undue authority, thereby setting up a vicious circle.

In the course of gaining greater independence, the learner will experience certain transference phenomena that are similar to those characteristic of the maturational process. The process of separation and of establishing independence will be accompanied by anxiety and projection. The supervisor, as well as the learner, is involved in the process and will have subjective reactions.

Interaction

It is evident in the foregoing discussion that the components that enter into supervisory practice form an interlocking process. No one of the four—the institutional, the methodological, the educational, and the psychological—is paramount.

The social agency itself is a complex structure, often made up of many organizational units and staffed by persons discharging various functions. The clients, too, must be considered part of the total configuration, since the agency exists for the purpose of extending help to them in meeting social problems. The concept we wish to suggest here is that the field of transaction in an agency includes both the social problem to be dealt with and the helping methods.

Any problem experienced by the client group is the result of a chain of interrelated forces and events—psychological, interpersonal, and social. Social work is moving away from the former tendency to view the "problem" in terms of the individual client, with emphasis on his psychological difficulties. The trend is toward broadening the theoretical base and toward developing new technical methods for working within the broader framework. The current literature reflects this trend.[2] A similar trend toward enlarging the theoretical

[2] As illustrations, see:

Nathan W. Ackerman, M.D., *Psychodynamics of Family Life,* Basic Books, New York, 1958.

John P. Spiegel, M.D., "The Resolution of Role Conflict within the Family," *Psychiatry,* Vol. XX, No. 1 (1957), pp. 1–16.

Seymour Fisher, Ph.D., and David Mendell, M.D., "The Communication of Neurotic Patterns over Two and Three Generations," *Psychiatry,* Vol. XIX, No. 1 (1956), pp. 41–46; "The Spread of Psychotherapeutic Effects from the Patient to His Family Group," *Psychiatry,* Vol. XXI, No. 2 (1958), pp. 133–140; "Approach to Neurotic Behavior in Terms of a Three-Generation Model," *Journal of Nervous and Mental Diseases,* Vol. CXXIII, No. 2 (1956), pp. 171–180; "A Multi-Generation Approach to the Treatment of Psychopathology," *Journal of Nervous and Mental Diseases,* Vol. CXXVI, No. 6 (1958), pp. 523–529.

Viola W. Weiss and Russell R. Monroe, M.D., "A Framework for Understanding Family Dynamics," pp. 175–198 of this volume. Reprinted from *Social Casework,* January and February 1959.

Gardner Murphy, Ph.D., "New Knowledge about Family Dynamics," pp. 93–105 of this volume. Reprinted from *Social Casework,* July 1959.

Frances H. Scherz, "What Is Family-Centered Casework?" *Social Casework,* Vol. XXXIV, No. 8 (1953), pp. 343–349.

M. Robert Gomberg, "Family-Oriented Treatment of Marital Problems," pp. 198–212 of this volume. Reprinted from *Social Casework,* July 1956.

and operational base has been taking place in the psychiatric field.[3]

The wider field of transaction in social work suggests the need for a re-evaluation of supervisory practice. Supervision in many instances is still geared to the methods developed at an earlier period when the focus of the helping services was more limited. Supervision, in a sense, has been isolated from the main stream of technical developments. Much of the current criticism of supervision may stem from the fact that the emphasis in supervision is still on helping the worker acquire skill in a single operation, with little effort to have him participate in other processes and in the wider responsibilities of the agency. Supervisory practice should be related to the agency's total operation and to forces and events that shape its program and the helping methods.

This broader concept of supervision does not imply that standards of performance should be lowered. The agency's expectation of types of performance must still be made specific. However, greater individualization of responsibilities for particular workers may be indicated as an agency program becomes more diverse and relies less on a single helping method.

In our seminar discussions of the components of supervision, we made reference to a number of areas of tension. We agreed that tension is inherent in the supervisory task, which involves the integration of many, and sometimes conflicting, elements. As mentioned earlier, the supervisor must function in roles that prescribe both equality and inequality. He must deal with both future-oriented values and reality limitations of the present. He must weigh his own individual experience in teaching against the agency's patterns and methods. In addition, he must develop a pattern for bringing these interacting elements into some sort of harmony so that the services of the agency are effectively rendered. Such interactional transactions always create tension, but the degree depends on the supervisor's ability to integrate the various components.

[3] Alfred H. Stanton and Morris S. Schwartz, *The Mental Hospital,* Basic Books, New York, 1954.

August B. Hollingshead and Frederick C. Redlich, *Social Class and Mental Illness: A Community Study,* John Wiley & Sons, New York, 1958.

Otto Pollak, *Integrating Sociological and Psychoanalytic Concepts: An Exploration in Child Psychotherapy,* Russell Sage Foundation, New York, 1956; "Relationships between Social Science and Child Guidance Practice," *American Sociological Review,* Vol. XVI, No. 1 (1951), p. 63.

Maxwell S. Jones and others, *The Therapeutic Community: A New Treatment Method in Psychiatry,* Basic Books, New York, 1953.

Tension should reduce with successful experience. In relation to workers, supervision also has certain tension-producing elements, such as the anxiety involved in learning and in working under authority. However, it also has some tension-reducing elements. Tension tends to diminish as the worker gains mastery of the subject matter and as he finds a balance between the interacting forces that affect his performance.

Despite the fact that tension for both supervisor and worker is a reducible factor, it should be recognized that a certain degree of tension is inevitable. Overemphasis on the tension, with attempts to short-cut or eliminate the supervisory process, would tend to undermine client service, staff learning, and the advancement of professional knowledge. Denial of the tension, however, might lead to the same undesirable ends, since such denial would result in ritualistic enactment of roles on the part of both supervisor and worker.

The major problem in supervisory practice is the need for the participants to find and maintain a balance between the tension-provoking elements inherent in the process. This problem, in a sense, is the problem faced by all individuals in the process of daily living. It comes into sharper focus in a professional operation because of the specific demands made on both supervisor and worker to render a community service, to maintain and advance standards of service, and to observe professional ethics.

Supervision has been blamed for the existence of many problems, including the creation of disabling anxiety in the practitioner group. Supervision has also been lauded as a valuable educational device, one that provides the practitioner with needed emotional support while he is mastering content and skills. Our seminar group recognized that objective standards for evaluating the shortcomings and values of the process would be difficult to establish. Our appraisal was that the values outweigh the shortcomings. The important values lie in the maintenance of client service, in the improvement of performance on the part of the practitioner, and in the provision of a framework through which he can find a balance between the interacting processes that are part of professional performance in a social agency setting.

AN EVALUATION OF SUPERVISION[1]

Lucille N. Austin

THE PRESENT ORGANIZATIONAL structure of social agencies lodges responsibility for certain administrative and staff development functions in the supervisor. This delegation of administrative responsibility has an understandable rationale. The supervisor, as a member of the administrative personnel and as the person who has a close working relationship with the practitioners, has seemed to be in a strategic position to develop a sound interrelationship between agency services and staff development. From time to time the question has been raised as to whether the supervisor carries too heavy and too complicated an assignment. In general, the hope has persisted that he could perform both the administrative and teaching functions and keep his respective roles from interfering with each other. Currently, however, it seems that the supervisor's assignment needs to be re-evaluated, both because of its inherent complexity and because of new professional developments.

During the past twenty-five years the persons entering the field have been, to an increasing degree, graduates of schools of social work. This trend has resulted in higher standards of professional performance on the part of graduates in all social work functions—in practice, in administration, and in social work teaching. A more adequate conceptualization of relevant knowledge and a clearer formulation of methods in these various functions have resulted in more rapid professionalization of social work students. These technical advances have provided a sound basis of learning for the student and have enabled him to assimilate knowledge and

[1] Published in *Social Casework,* October 1956. Presented at the National Conference of Social Work, St. Louis, Missouri, on May 21, 1956.

to internalize standards of performance. As a result, the school graduate today is in a position to assume considerable responsibility for his own work. Although this professionalization has made some things easier for the graduate, it also has imposed new responsibilities; to refine one's skill in any of these specializations requires an absorbing interest and particular aptitudes on the part of the person performing the function.

As more school graduates have entered the field, criticism of present ways of working has increased. Supervision has taken the brunt of this criticism. Practitioners believe that they are not permitted to be sufficiently responsible for their own work and that as long as they are described as "supervisees," they are not accorded professional status. Supervisors, administrators, and social work educators also have had a growing concern about the relatively small number of leadership people which this work situation is producing.

If the present agency organizational structure is not providing the conditions for creative work and for accompanying satisfactions for practitioners and if it is not facilitating the discharge of the administrative and teaching functions adequately, some changes seem to be in order.

Status of the School Graduate

The new school graduate who takes a position in an agency is accepted as an accredited social worker—but with many reservations. Emphasis is placed on his youth, on his inexperience, and on the many things he has yet to learn.

No one will deny, least of all the new worker, that he has much to learn and that experience will improve his skill. Today's graduate, however, is entering the field with a considerable degree of professional knowledge and skill. He has had training in delineating the basic casework processes of study, diagnosis, and treatment. He has had field experience in which he has utilized a variety of treatment methods and techniques under skilled direction. He has learned and used important content from psychiatry and the social sciences. He has gained ability to think logically and scientifically, has learned how to use the professional literature, and has been introduced to research methods. He is familiar with the history and the philosophy of the profession. Education in the master's program, in both class and field instruction, has notably improved in recent years, and the student is reaping the benefits. The employing agency can expect him to be competent in basic casework treatment, and to know when to consult and to ask for direction. On this basis, the graduate has a right to expect to be welcomed as a professional colleague and not to be treated as an advanced student.

The "internship" concept, which implies that the new worker must have a period of continued learning in an agency, has never been implemented by a systematic educational program. The concept, however, affects the status of the worker during his first two or three years of employment. Unless the internship is formalized and becomes a part of a degree program, there would seem to be question about retaining it. If certain agencies that provide a specialized service find it advisable to construct a further educational program, they should be clear about its specifics—the length of the training, the content, and the standards for completion. This might be defined as a "residency" program. The present undefined status of agency training results in vague commitments, on the part of both agency and worker, and is therefore unsatisfactory to both.

Whether the school graduate entering practice will advance in skill and professional expertness is determined by the strength of his own motivation, by the available sources of learning, and by his own ethic of accountability, as well as by the agency's way of holding him accountable for his work. Self-direction must be the main driving force. One characteristic of a profession is that the individual members accept, by virtue of their personal and professional ethics, the responsibility for maintaining and improving their services. Today, much is known about experiences that strengthen ego development and aid in the internalization of standards. Not the least of these experiences is that of being given responsibility commensurate with one's ability, and being aware of the expectation that the obligations will be fulfilled.

The objectives of the new worker—and the profession's objectives for him—are to increase his competence, to be given status, and to reinforce his own ethic of responsibility. In what ways are present agency structures failing to accomplish these objectives? Can the objectives be implemented in other ways?

Problems in the Present Supervisory System

The problems in the present system seem to go beyond the issue of good supervision versus poor supervision. It seems that certain complicating factors are inherent in the agency structure that assigns to the supervisor the two major functions of administration and teaching. This system, which was undoubtedly useful in the early days of the profession, seems less appropriate now when a higher degree of professionalization has been achieved. At the risk of overlooking positives, I shall present some of the negative factors in the present system. Among them are these: (1) the assimilation of knowledge and the internalization of standards by the worker are weakened by an overemphasis on external controls; (2) the caseworker's professional contacts are too limited; (3) the assignment of two major functions to the supervisor leads to a concentration of power in one person; and (4) the dual function results in an overcomplex assignment for the supervisor.

1. *Assimilating knowledge and internalizing standards.* The present system, which places responsibility on the supervisor for setting standards of work and for following up on the worker's performance, has tended to reduce the worker's own responsibility, although it was designed to do the opposite. Unintentionally, social agencies seem to have shifted from an emphasis on faith in and support of the worker's capacity to internalize standards to an emphasis on external means of control. Stress tends to be placed on the supervisor's responsibility, rather than on the worker's own responsibility for his work. The supervisor's responsibility for the evaluation of workers, which is part of his administrative function, further emphasizes his standard-setting role. The psychological danger is that he may become an externalized superego, and thereby invite from the worker the responses of fear, dependency, hostility, or conformity. Evidence of these reactions is clearly presented in Dr. Babcock's historic paper.[2] Today's graduates are asking for more responsibility and for more confidence in their competence.

2. *The limitation of professional contacts for the worker.* A further result of the supervisor's discharging two functions is the limitation of professional contacts for the caseworker—a limitation of his professional object world. Too many kinds of problems are discussed with one person, and the caseworker's contacts with other members of the administrative staff tend to be too superficial or on a too informal level. In reality, several spokesmen are needed to interpret and develop ideas related to the many aspects of an agency

[2] Charlotte G. Babcock, M.D., "Social Work as Work," *Social Casework*, Vol. XXXIV, No. 10 (1953), pp. 415–422.

program. Healthy young people welcome and can use more than one working relationship. They need to be known by more than one person in order to advance their careers. Hence an overshadowing relationship to a supervisor can be a constricting professional experience.

3. *The concentration of power in the supervisor.* The concentration of power in the hands of the supervisor, by virtue of his two functions, places him *in reality* in too much control over the worker's fate. It is true that the supervisor can make it either hard or easy for a worker to progress. The lodging of so much responsibility in the supervisor contributes to the previously mentioned negative reactions of workers, since it tends to re-create the parental situation. The supervisor is presumed to know more than the practitioner; he is presumed to "know best." In his evaluative role he has the power to give rewards and punishments. Such concentration of power encourages infantile fantasies and arouses fear in the young person that he can never attain the superior status of his parent.

This power structure also has a negative effect on the supervisor. In his wish to do his work well and to satisfy agency expectations, he may easily fall into the role of the overcontrolling and overprotective parent. As a teacher he may tend to hold the reins too tightly, losing sight of his enabling role; he may drive the worker as hard as he drives himself. If he is insecure about his teaching ability, he may shift to the role of critic or overemphasize his administrative authority. He cannot easily move into practice in order to refresh his knowledge and thus improve his teaching, since such a step is viewed as a demotion in the hierarchy.

The realistic limitations of the supervisor's knowledge, as well as the subjective factors that color the worker's attitudes, point to the need for an open, rather than a closed, network of contacts for the caseworker.

4. *The supervisor's dual function.* The dual function assigned to the supervisor, each assignment demanding special skill, makes it next to impossible for him to give each one its proper attention even if he has the skill and aptitude for both. As a result the caseworker may not be as well oriented to his job as is desirable. There is no question that the functions of administration and teaching are interrelated and must be integrated. The question is whether they can best be integrated by assigning them to one person—the super-

visor. It may not be possible to separate these functions, or it may not be wise. This question has been raised before but, to date, the answer has been against separation. There is reason to look again at the possibility and the wisdom of such a course. Let us examine each of the functions with the idea of considering the possibility of separating them and of establishing new alignments of responsibilities for the administrative personnel of an agency.

The Teaching Function

Supervisors have made an outstanding contribution to the development of teaching methods in social work, as well as in other professions. This tribute may sound like a contradiction of the foregoing analysis of problem aspects of their job but in actuality it is not. The teaching function is the one that supervisors have liked better and to which they have given greater attention. It is a demanding task, since it carries responsibility for generalizing and conceptualizing within the framework of particular case situations. A special skill is needed to carry this responsibility, since the ideas discussed are for use and have an effect on the welfare of human beings. The case discussion method, in the individual conference, provides the practitioner with the opportunity to explore ideas that will influence his handling of a case. There is no substitute for it in the social work learning situation. The teaching personnel of an agency, therefore, should be carefully selected for skill in discharging this function. Not everyone can teach. This assignment is sometimes carried by persons who do not have special aptitude for teaching or who have not had sufficient help in developing their teaching skills. The present burden—and opportunity—for social work teachers to help the practitioner think in conceptual terms demands of the supervisor greater ability and leadership than were necessary in the past.

The way might be cleared for an improvement in the teaching function if agencies recognized the many complications, for both the supervisor and the caseworker, that exist in the present situation in which the caseworker is *required* to learn from the supervisor. This authoritative element is entangled with the authoritative element inherent in the supervisor's administrative responsibility for staff evaluation. The kind of authority appropriate for discharging an administrative function may not be appropriate in a teaching situation. The administrative authority may becloud the educational relationship, in which the learner utilizes the "authority" of experts in acquiring knowledge. Any teacher can offer the learner his knowledge for consideration, but he cannot ensure its use. The responsibility for using the educational resources must rest with the caseworker. Archibald MacLeish states: "There is no record whatever of the teaching of creativity. The creativity of others will release one's own creativity if they are the right 'others,' and if he himself is right to receive them at the moment he comes to them." [3] It is well to remind ourselves that casework is an art. It is also a profession, not a trade.

The Administrative Function

If we look at the supervisor's performance in his administrative role, another picture emerges. In a review of articles published in THE FAMILY (later SOCIAL CASEWORK) from 1935 to 1955, Ellen Walsh noted that seventy-seven articles were devoted to supervision.[4] Of this group, forty-eight discussed some phase of the teaching aspect of supervision. There were six articles on the administrative aspects of supervision; of these, only two were written in the last ten years [1946–1956].

The lack of attention to administrative aspects of supervision is pointed up by Bertram Black. He says: "Too few supervisors know how to make use of these valuable [administrative] measures as tools in controlling case loads of workers, in estimating quantitative performance, and in gaining clues to changing quality of casework." [5] Sidney Berkowitz notes that administrative responsibility has long been recognized as part of the supervisor's job but that it has not been adequately defined or sufficiently integrated into the supervisory process. He says: "If we are not willing to unite the administrative and teaching functions in casework supervision, we should have the courage to separate them clearly and decisively." [6] Supervisors frequently indicate that they do not like the adminis-

[3] Archibald MacLeish, *Art Education and the Creative Process,* published for the Committee on Art Education by the Museum of Modern Art, New York, 1954, p. 5.

[4] A paper on current problems in supervision prepared by Ellen Walsh as an assignment in the doctoral program of the New York School of Social Work of Columbia University.

[5] Bertram J. Black, "Tools and Techniques of Administration," *Social Casework,* Vol. XXXI, No. 6 (1950), p. 229.

[6] Sidney J. Berkowitz, "The Administrative Process in Casework Supervision," *Social Casework,* Vol. XXXIII, No. 10 (1952), p. 423.

trative responsibility. There is reason to believe, therefore, that although they are designated as administrators with line authority, they have never functioned comfortably in the administrative role. The administrative responsibility, when combined with the teaching responsibility, seems to take second place.

Many supervisors tend not to hold firmly to agency rules and regulations. They see the worker's problems and are inclined to make exceptions and compromise with requirements—in a sense, they become corruptible. In doing so, they make it as difficult for the worker to internalize work requirements as do the supervisors who are too strict.

It is probable that the lack of interest in administrative processes, on the part of many social workers, can be partially attributed to the present form of agency organization. Many caseworkers have a limited concept of the administrative function. They view it as a management operation, and consider administrative responsibilities an interference with their casework practice. They have little or no contact with administrative personnel other than the supervisor and little or no knowledge of the vision and skill required of the administrative group in developing a total program and in maintaining quality of agency service.

In the present organizational structure, the supervisor is usually the key representative of the operating unit in administrative deliberations. This system tends to limit communication between workers and members of the administrative staff other than the supervisor. Such representation on policy matters affecting program is questionable, since supervisors for the most part are not in direct contact with clients. It circumvents real participation by the practitioner group in that it prevents the administrator from securing the direct reactions of the practitioners—both their contributions and their criticisms. As a result, the administrator operates in a peculiar kind of vacuum in many social agencies and therefore often fails to give true leadership. The small agency has a distinct advantage over the large one, since the total staff has closer relationships with the board and community and the practitioner group usually has more frequent contacts with the executive and the board.

Suggestions for Realignments of Functions

If we consider the possibility of separating the teaching and administrative functions now carried by the supervisor, several basic questions must first be resolved. To date there has been little study of the issues and little experimentation with new organizational forms. The issues involved would present a suitable subject for research in agencies. Such studies should endeavor to find ways (1) of diluting the power position of the supervisor and of giving him greater freedom in exercising his educational function, and (2) of placing more responsibility on the administrator for management of the casework program and for the evaluation of the caseworker.

I shall try, in a purely theoretical way, to project some of the possible means by which the supervisor might be freed to carry out his basic responsibility for staff development and for enabling the workers to perform as adult, responsible persons.

It might be well, in this theoretical discussion, to avoid the use of the term supervisor. Instead, we might think of a new kind of position, held by persons who would be responsible for staff development. Such persons would be members of the agency's administrative staff but would not hold line authority. They would work in a service unit and would be responsible to the administrator of the unit. They would offer responsible casework leadership to the practitioners, using appropriate educational methods—didactic as well as discussion methods. They would have responsibility to follow through with the caseworkers, not in an authoritative administrative role, but in an educational role, testing the validity of ideas for use in the context of the case and of the client response. They would have responsibility for helping the caseworker with countertransference problems when they were present and for helping the caseworker in his over-all professional development. They would share responsibility with the caseworker for conceptualizing method and for formulating generalizations deriving from a particular case or group of cases.

They would also share responsibility with the practitioner for major casework decisions, especially for those decisions involving critical issues in the lives of clients. They would be responsible for communicating formally any opinions they might hold about the worker's competence, both to the worker and to the administrator of the unit, but they would not carry major responsibility for staff evaluations and for recommendations about staff reassignment or continued employment.

Obviously, both case discussion and case management must always be bounded by the policies of the agency. Separating the teaching function from the adminstrative function does not imply that policies could be ignored by the staff members responsible for teaching.

The new graduates, as well as experienced caseworkers, would use these persons for help in case study and in other professional learning experiences. These experiences might be supplemented by casework and psychiatric seminars, staff workshops, and psychiatric or other specialized consultation. Group methods of learning might be used more extensively, although I do not believe that the aims of professional training in social work can be achieved solely through the use of group methods—through so-called group supervision.

Under this projected plan, it can be assumed that a new staff member would want and need a greater number of conferences during his first two years than in subsequent ones; for some time to come, however, such case discussion will continue to be important for workers at all levels of experience in the interest of developing method. It might be possible, under certain circumstances, for a worker to seek educational help from staff development personnel other than the one he works with regularly, especially if the others have developed expertness in particular kinds of cases.

In order to use this type of staff development profitably, the new graduate should be adequately prepared for his professional responsibilities. He should come from the ablest group of college students and be given the best form of master's education that the profession can offer. The agency, therefore, should assign its best teaching personnel to work with students in their field placement. It is unrealistic to expect inexperienced field instructors to give leadership in social work teaching and to pass judgment on the suitability of students for future membership in the profession.

If the staff members who traditionally have been responsible for supervision were relieved of their administrative assignment, not only would they be able to give fuller attention to the education of the practitioner group but they might conceivably have some time available for casework practice. There would be advantages in this arrangement, since competence in teaching casework is always enhanced by direct practice.

Let us now look at possible restructuring of the administrator's position. The administrator in charge of a unit presumably is equipped to give casework leadership and to implement the casework program. In our proposed plan, he would assume the administrative responsibility for the program or, in a large unit, he might delegate administrative responsibility to administrative assistants. Each member of the casework staff would be assigned to work with the administrator or one of his assistants.

The administrator—or his assistants—would work directly with the casework staff and with students, both through group meetings and through individual conferences, for the purpose of developing and interpreting program, of formulating policy, and of setting work requirements. He would hold the caseworkers responsible for work production and for their professional casework performance. He would have an ongoing relationship with each caseworker and with the educational staff members, so that he would know about the casework performance of the worker. He therefore would be in a position to help the worker utilize the agency's educational resources appropriately.

One of the major administrative problems in social work centers around the evaluation of staff. The fundamental purpose of evaluation is to determine whether the worker meets the standards and requirements of the agency. Evaluation has also been used as an educational tool, that is, as a means of defining areas for the worker's improvement. This educational use should not be confused with its administrative purpose. Evaluation involves a joint concern, on the part of both the worker and the agency, about professional performance. The worker's own ethic of holding himself accountable for his work must be linked with the agency's accountability for its stewardship. The accountability of a profession working under the auspices of social agencies is different from that of a profession composed of private practioners. In social work, the ethic of accountability holds within it the concept of answerability, that is, the expectation that any staff member may be called upon to explain his actions to clients, to various persons affiliated with the agency, and to the public at large.

In spite of this recognized agency responsibility, it seems that the evaluative process in social work has been used to overcontrol the caseworker. Because the worker feels he is expected to meet rigid criteria, evaluations have placed a particularly heavy burden on him. Standards of service can have meaning to the worker only if the ethic of professional performance is internalized and if it is supported by a professional climate. How, then, can the agency's responsibility for evaluation best be implemented?

In the projected realignment of functions, I would place on the administrator the responsibility for assembling the data, for making the appraisal, and for holding the evaluation discussion with the caseworker. The appraisal, however, would not be based only on his own opinion. The data would include the administrator's own evaluation of the caseworker's performance, reports from the educational or other administrative staff, and the caseworker's self-evaluation. The caseworker's own appraisal, written or presented verbally, would be the point of departure for the administrator. The caseworker would not only be allowed, but would be expected, to speak for himself. In order to promote a fair and objective evaluation, the caseworker would be asked to submit samples of case records. A random sampling for futher study might be selected by the administrator. These sets of records might be evaluated by members of the educational staff, perhaps by one person who had worked with the caseworker and at least one who had not. Such focused reading of the caseworker's records at the time of the formal evaluation would be one way of securing an objective rating. Case reading, of course, would be an ongoing responsibility of the educational staff members for the purpose of developing standards of practice and identifying casework problems for staff attention.

In a large agency, the evaluation report of the unit administrator would be submitted to the central administrative personnel and, as routine procedure, would be discussed with the caseworker by appropriate persons.

Experimentation with ways of using a review group for evaluation may be indicated, especially at the point where major advancements for the caseworker are being considered. The review group would be advisory to the administration. It might not only appraise case records and other evidence but also conduct an evaluative interview with the worker. The advantage of such a plan would be an increase in objectivity. The use of oral and written examinations for promotion, such as those used in the public services, is another method worthy of consideration. Various patterns of evaluation undoubtedly would evolve if attention were directed to finding methods consonant with professional objectives.

Being evaluated should be a formal experience but not a formidable one. At first glance, the suggested changes may seem to carry more frightening elements for the caseworker than "taking his chances" with a supervisor. The suggested plan, however, may offer him greater security because of its broader base and its objectivity. Criteria for evaluating casework performance as well as clear statements about agency standards would need to be further developed. Evaluations, of course, would include items that are concerned with professional behavior, observance of administrative requirements, and the worker's contribution to the agency and the community. Professional writing and other professional activities might well be added. Other aspects of the evaluation process would also need to be reviewed: How often should an evaluation take place? How should it be related to salaries? What is a useful number of classifications for the practitioner positions?

Even under the present organizational structure, it seems to me that evaluations should be made only at certain pivotal points in the caseworker's professional development and at certain reasonable intervals to assure him of his progress. The principle of automatic salary increments should operate within the minimum and maximum salary range for a job classification. It is probable that there are too many classifications for the practitioner positions and that too much emphasis is placed on moving from one classification to a higher one. Progression from one to the next should be assumed, except in unusual circumstances.

Reasonable average standards of performance, rather than exceptional standards, should characterize agency norms. Professional recognition, and eligibility for the higher brackets in the agency's salary range, should not be closed to the majority of adequate practitioners; they carry the bulk of professional service to clients.

Summary

The graduate caseworker today must be given, and must be expected to take, responsibility for his own work. He must be accorded the status of an accredited professional worker. The present organizational structure of agencies tends to confuse the work situation for both the caseworker and the supervisor. It seems to me that a new alignment of the functions of the teaching personnel and the administrative personnel would help clarify the worker's responsibilities and also give recognition to the special skills and obligations involved in each of these functions.

The exact division of responsibilities between the educational personnel and the administrative personnel cannot be determined without further study. It may differ somewhat according to the size of the agency and the setting. If a new alignment does take place, the two major functional positions may well need new titles. If the title of supervisor is retained, it appears to be more appropriate for the position of administrator, although another title might be preferable. For the educational personnel position, the title of consultant would not be accurate, since a consultant's function is different from the functions I have outlined for the educational person.

I have presented many controversial points with conviction that there is need for analysis of the problems inherent in present practices and an urgent need for change.

A CONCEPT OF SUPERVISION BASED ON DEFINITIONS OF JOB RESPONSIBILITY [1]

Frances H. Scherz

THE POINT OF VIEW expressed in this paper is that the job of casework supervisor is, in essence, an administrative job. Both of the major components of casework supervision—teaching and management—are administrative functions. I should like to discuss in some detail the job responsibilities of a supervisor and a caseworker, the specific performance requirements of each of these jobs, and the effects of the differences between the job responsibilities of these two positions on the content of supervision and on the supervisor-caseworker relationship.

[1] Published in *Social Casework,* October 1958. Presented at the National Conference on Social Welfare, Chicago, Illinois, May 16, 1958.

The following suggested definitions of job responsibility are based on two specific premises. First, the caseworker, whose job assignment is the giving of direct service to clients, must assume the primary responsibility for his own work and for his own continued professional development. Second, the supervisor, by nature of his job assignment, has the primary responsibility for facilitating the work of the casework staff. Both the caseworker and the supervisor are responsible for implementing the purpose and function of the agency, although their job assignments are different. The point at which these two jobs meet is in the mutual concern for giving effective service.

The executive staff of the Jewish Family and Community Service of Chicago presented to the supervisory staff the following propositions: (1) that the core of the supervisor's job is administrative leadership; (2) that the caseworker bears the major responsibility for his own work. Meeting together as a group, the executive and supervisory staffs were asked to examine job content and supervisory practice in the light of these propositions. The willingness of the staff members to be freely critical of the agency's established practices and procedures created an atmosphere in which everyone could react to and consider and work together on the propositions. The group is continuing to examine the formulations presented in this paper, their applicability to supervisory practice, and the traditional professional attitudes that further or impede their implementation.

Although the point of view that supervision is inherently an administrative function is a departure from the usual concept that supervision has two distinct components, teaching and administration, the two specific premises are neither new nor startling. The literature is replete with discussion of the roles of the supervisor in teaching and management. The long history of attempts to interpret and implement these roles is one of trial and error. A great deal of both positive and negative emotion has been associated with these efforts.

Basic Assumptions

Basic to the considerations presented in this paper is the assumption that every professionally trained staff member has some measure of competence. By this is meant that, upon completion of training in a school of social work, a caseworker is presumed to be able to meet the requirements for the position of Caseworker I, as described in many agency classification plans and in such statements as *A Guide to Classification of Professional Positions and Evaluation Outlines in a Family Agency*.[2] Moreover, a caseworker who has had work experience is hired on the basis of his presumed ability to meet designated job classification requirements. The agency is responsible for delineating in relation to the worker's level of experience the job assignment in regard to such specific matters as the nature of the case load, qualitative and quantitative standards of practice, explicit recording requirements, routines, evaluation procedures, and the agency resources available for help in carrying out the job. Supervision is one of these resources. Within this framework, the agency assumes that the caseworker will use his knowledge and capacity to the best of his ability and that he will use all of the available professional resources in the interest of continuing to increase his capacity for giving effective service.

These assumptions about competence and self-responsibility have been neither clearly understood nor wholeheartedly accepted. For example, although schools of social work state that the new graduate has some ability to perform in a job, they, as well as agencies, have stressed the need for the recent graduate to have "very close supervision" for the first several years of practice. Relatively little emphasis has been placed on the beginning caseworker's ability to perform and to take responsibility for further developing his capacities. Rather, emphasis has been placed on the quality and quantity of supervision, as if the caseworker's development proceeds in direct ratio to the kind and extent of supervision. This concept is highly questionable. We know that the most effective learning is learning that is self-motivated. It is stimulated by normal impulses toward growth and reaches its highest level when associated with self-responsibility for achievement. Even in the instance of an externship, it is unsound to have the achievement of the educational goals largely dependent on supervision as the main medium for learning.

The new graduate does not entirely accept the fact that he has the ability to perform on a job. His doubts are revealed in his anxiety to be given "good supervision." Nor is this anxiety confined to the worker who is seeking his first casework job. Much of it stems

[2] Family Service Association of America, New York, 1957.

from the wish to be helpful to people, but some of it is related to the inordinate value falsely placed on supervision as a means of learning and of assuring good service.

Responsibilities of the Supervisor

Essentially, supervision is a job of administrative leadership. The agency is responsible for designating the job responsibilities and requirements for supervisors at various levels of experience. Since schools of social work cannot provide specific training in supervision within the master's curriculum, the agency has to establish an in-service training program for the beginning supervisor. In hiring a supervisor with experience, the agency assumes that (1) he has the degree of competence in casework practice that is required to facilitate the work of casework staff; (2) he is able to transmit knowledge effectively; (3) he is capable of assessing the performance and the professional developmental needs of casework staff; (4) he has a body of knowledge about differential supervisory methods which he can apply discriminatingly; and (5) he understands authority and uses it appropriately.

The agency expects the supervisor to continue to develop his skills in casework and supervisory practice. He is not necessarily expected to be the most skilled practitioner in the agency. He is expected, however, to re-examine casework concepts, to acquire new knowledge about human behavior as it emerges, and to encourage the casework staff to examine and experiment with new concepts and techniques. He is expected to use the resources both within and outside the agency to enhance his casework knowledge and supervisory practice.

The supervisor is not expected to have achieved mastery in all the areas of casework knowledge. His lack of knowledge in certain areas may make him unable to be of assistance to casework staff in dealing with some cases. Both the supervisor and the administrative personnel to whom he is accountable should accept the fact that he has both strengths and limitations and that he may have "blind spots" in respect to certain cases and in his supervisory methodology. Such acceptance should make it possible for the supervisor to handle these variations in his knowledge comfortably, and should free him and the staff to use other helpful resources appropriately. The supervisor is not expected to work with all members of the casework staff with equal ability or ease, but he is responsible for using his reactions to different staff members and their ways of working in a disciplined fashion.

Certain responsibilities that by tradition have been attached to the supervisor's job no longer seem valid. The supervisor has been held accountable for the specific service given in a case, for knowing the total case load, and for promoting the competence of casework staff. In the wish to provide good service, agencies have fostered the idea that the supervisor is responsible for the service given in a case by calling him, not the caseworker, to account when the community complains. Not only has this concept increased the worker's unwholesome dependence on the supervisor and the supervisor's overcontrol of the worker, but it also has served to place the supervisor in the untenable position of a buffer or protector between caseworkers and other administrative personnel. At times it is necessary for the supervisor to be specific and direct about what must be done in a particular case in order to avoid serious consequences. This is clearly an appropriate use of supervisory authority, but it should not be thought of as sharing with the caseworker the responsibility for the case. The supervisor is not responsible for, and cannot share responsibility with, the caseworker for either the kind or the quality of service given in a case.

The supervisor cannot know the total caseload to the extent that he can control the quality of service or prevent errors, nor should he attempt to do so, since the management of cases is the caseworker's responsibility. Similarly, the supervisor cannot make caseworkers competent by injecting knowledge into them. The quality of casework service in an agency depends upon the quality of casework staff. The latter, in turn, is highly influenced by the caseworker's motivations for giving the best service of which he is capable. The supervisor can and should serve as a vital resource in the caseworker's own achievement efforts. Indeed, the supervisor is responsible for providing leadership in this area.

Another traditional concept of the supervisor's role that requires re-examination is that the supervisor's primary job responsibility is teaching. A nod is given to the so-called administrative aspects of supervision, which are considered less important and somewhat distasteful. As a teacher, the supervisor has been in conflict about discharging various administrative duties, including evaluation of workers, since these seem to intrude like a foreign body into the benign teacher-learner relationship.

The teaching component in the supervisor's job has been stressed because he has been held responsible for the casework service given and for the level of competence of the casework staff. The evaluation of his own supervisory competence has often been related to the success or failure of his supervisees. If, as has been stated here, the caseworker is responsible for his own work and is largely responsible for his own continuing development, and if the supervisor's job is one of administrative facilitation, it becomes manifestly impossible to separate the teaching and management components of supervision. They are fused together and form an integrated unit.

Specific Job Responsibilities

Within the framework described above, the specific job responsibilities of the supervisor may be described as follows:

1. The supervisor is responsible for (a) knowing how effective the caseworker's service is, (b) assisting the caseworker to give service according to the standards of the agency, and (c) assisting the caseworker to develop further skill in giving effective service. Beyond this, he is responsible for developing ideas and content which will influence the standards of casework practice in the agency.

The supervisor learns how effective the caseworker's service is and how he may assist the worker in implementing and enhancing the service by evaluating the worker's request for supervision. In preparing for a discussion with the worker, the supervisor needs to assess the purpose and validity of the request in terms of its appropriateness to the case and to the worker's level of skill and experience. Although it is not possible, in this paper, to describe the specific supervisory methodology to be used in a variety of situations, one important principle can be noted: the supervisor should teach the concepts relevant to the handling of a case rather than the specifics of what the worker should do. The basis for conceptual teaching is the educational principle that a person can learn to apply his knowledge to a variety of situations more rapidly, more effectively, and more creatively when his learning is based on general theories and ideas than when it is based on specific knowledge gained in one case which he attempts to apply to another. In following this principle, the supervisor does not teach the specifics of practice in a given case but teaches, instead the various possibilities, both theoretical and practical, that might affect the nature of service. Although these possibilities can be thought through in the supervisory conference, the caseworker is left with the responsibility of deciding what particular concepts or techniques are best suited to the management of the case and how and when they are to be applied. This is not to say that there may not be an occasion when a caseworker requests and uses supervision that is specific, but such an occasion should be considered special and unusual.

Basing his judgment on the caseworker's level of experience and skill, the supervisor has to decide when to offer assistance, when to leave the problem with the caseworker, and when to suggest the use of other agency resources in the interests of the case. Conceptual teaching requires of the supervisor a greater degree of casework knowledge and more self-discipline than the teaching of specifics case by case. For example, the supervisor should consider with the caseworker the problems that are impeding service rather than teach all the dynamics in the case or how the case is to be handled. Should a further supervisory conference seem advisable, it is the supervisor's responsibility to set the purpose and time for it. When action in a case is imperative, however, the supervisor must use his authority to see that it is carried out.

The supervisor can also estimate how effectively service is being given by frequently reading a sample of the caseloads of his supervisees for the purpose of observing trends in quality of service, the workers' areas of competence, and problem areas that require supervisory consideration. Reading for the purpose of observing trends should enable the supervisor to assess areas of competence and limitations. The worker should be told of both kinds of observation. I should like to stress the value of letting the caseworker know about his successes since so frequently the supervisor is inclined to stress the failures. When problems are noted, the supervisor should assess whether they are due to the worker's lack of sufficient data, to his lack of understanding of psychological concepts or techniques, to his difficulties in understanding or responding to manifest or concealed meanings in the material, to his lack of awareness of his reactions to people, or to his inability to tolerate or manage the variety of emotions expressed. Are his problems related to working with the different phases of a case—intake, social study, evaluation, and treatment—as well as to his differing abilities in dealing with various problems and personalities? Trends in the quantity of his production are equally important to note.

It is obvious that the supervisor's reading to discover trends cannot be effective unless the agency sets recording requirements that are clear, specific, and feasible. The casework staff needs to understand the purpose that recording serves in relation to the supervisor's responsibility for facilitating service. The supervisor is responsible for orienting the caseworker to the agency's recording requirements and for dealing actively with the worker if there are problems in meeting recording requirements.

Knowledge derived from a continuous examination of trends through case reading, as well as from requests for supervision by the caseworker, enables the supervisor to understand the caseworker's characteristic ways of working and learning and his level of ability to give service. It enables the supervisor to formulate differential supervisory plans related both to service needs and to the caseworker's ability to meet these needs according to the job expectations for his position classification.

In thinking through a possible supervisory plan or in making a decision that no supervisory intervention is required, certain questions must be answered by the supervisor. Do the trends in performance appear to be within normal expectations for the caseworker's level of experience, and, if so, are certain problem areas best left untouched while the caseworker accumulates knowledge and experience or can development be facilitated by supervision? Are there special areas of difficulty in groups of cases that can be singled out for consideration with the caseworker? How serious are particular difficulties as they affect service in a single case or a group of cases?

The supervisor is responsible for taking action when the need for such is indicated by general trends or by the developments in a specific case. Such action requires self-discipline on the part of the supervisor. He must judge how important the problem areas are in relation to service to the client and also to the worker's job requirements. He must permit the worker some freedom in making errors and should contain his concern until he knows their consequences in terms of service. A supervisory plan should be specific and should be discussed with the caseworker, so that there is mutual understanding about the specific areas to be worked on and the time to be devoted to this purpose.

The supervisor should plan, in relation to each of his supervisees, the particular supervisory methodology and the learning resources to be used. How does the caseworker learn best? What are the indications for limiting his teaching to a circumscribed area or for extending it beyond what the caseworker recognizes or asks for? What should be handled by didactic teaching? Which learning blocks does the caseworker need to become aware of; which are best left untouched? What other resources in the agency does the supervisor need to call upon in working with the caseworker?

A third way in which the supervisor can facilitate or enhance service is by using the knowledge gained from an examination of trends to determine when individual supervision is most useful and when a group process is preferable. Although it is not possible within the limitations of this paper to describe in detail the various uses of groups, I should like to emphasize the supervisor's responsibility for leadership in assessing the need for a particular type of group and for bringing this need to the attention of the appropriate administrative personnel.

2. The supervisor is also responsible for facilitating the work of the casework staff through using agency procedures and routines in such a way that a smooth flow of service is assured. He orients the casework staff to the management aspects of the job. He takes leadership in initiating staff discussion of management operations and in implementing agency policies. He conveys to the executive staff his observations in regard to the casework program, the quality of practice, the developmental needs of staff, and so forth. He encourages casework staff to bring questions and ideas concerning program, practice, and operations to appropriate personnel in the agency.

3. The supervisor is responsible for evaluating the casework staff in accordance with agency classification requirements and for making appropriate recommendations in relation to salary changes, promotions, separations, and so on. In many agencies, evaluations are expected to serve two main purposes: (a) the assessment of performance as a basis for salary changes, and (b) the assessment of the worker's progress and his future developmental needs. When used in this way, the periodic evaluation serves an educational as well as a practical purpose. The caseworker often shares in the evaluation process, and the written document shows the results of joint consideration between caseworker and supervisor. Material about the caseworker-supervisor relationship is frequently included. Using the evaluation process as an educational device is highly questionable.

The written periodic evaluation is an *administrative* document to be prepared only for the purpose of making judgments about changes in salary or job assignment and about reclassification or separation from the agency. Hence, the written evaluation is a statement concerned specifically with the performance of the caseworker in accordance with the requirements of the job. It is not concerned with describing the difficulties the worker has overcome or the areas that he will be expected to work on in the future. It is not concerned with how the caseworker learns or the nature of the supervisor-caseworker relationship. If the supervisor and worker have engaged in continuing evaluation for any length of time, the written document should contain no surprises for the caseworker. It may vary in length from a very brief statement indicating that the caseworker has met agency requirements to a full assessment at a point of reclassification or marked change in performance.

The evaluation that represents an administrative judgment is written by the supervisor without prior discussion with the caseworker. It is objective insofar as it is based on accepted criteria for performance; it is subjective insofar as it represents a judgment. Whenever possible, the judgments of the supervisor and of appropriate administrative personnel should be pooled to ensure objectivity, but the supervisor has primary responsibility for collecting the data and making the assessment. The significant data on which an assessment is based are the trends in performance judged in relation to the designated requirements of the job. The written evaluation may well be used as the basis for discussion between caseworker and supervisor of the worker's present performance and his developmental needs. The caseworker should discuss with appropriate personnel his questions about or disagreements with the written evaluation.

In summary, since supervision is essentially an administrative job, the functions of teaching, management, and evaluation cannot be separated from each other nor can they be assigned to different persons within the agency. Individual supervision should remain as one part of an agency's staff development program. Groups may serve certain training purposes or may be used to implement certain aspects of the agency's work. The core of the supervisor's job is giving administrative leadership to the casework program.

The Caseworker

The caseworker has the primary responsibility for giving direct service to clients to the best of his ability and within the job requirements for his level of experience. He must assume the major responsibility for his own performance and for continuing to acquire knowledge and skill. The new or beginning staff member should be given orientation to the agency, to the specifics of its program, policies, and resources. But he also needs to be granted freedom to take responsibility for his own work—freedom to use his capacities and to discern and work on those areas in which he needs to develop further.

1. The caseworker is responsible for identifying his areas of competence, of partial ability, or of limitation. This includes identifying gaps in his theoretical knowledge or in the application of theory to practice, his special skills or problems in psychosocial evaluation and treatment, his special abilities or limitations in dealing with various problems or personalities, and his acknowledgment of personal reactions that enhance or interfere with his service. Making these identifications takes time; it can be accomplished only through his continuous experience in integrating theory and practice. The caseworker should use the supervisor as an aid in this process, but the latter cannot share responsibility with him for the quality of his casework or for the service he gives. Freedom to perform means taking responsibility for success, for failure, and for errors, seeking assistance in the interests of effective service, and deciding both the specific help he needs and which of the available resources he will use. He may choose to use the supervisor or other personnel the agency provides.

The caseworker has not been clear about his responsibility for his casework practice. As indicated previously, he has been confused because he has thought of case management as a responsibility shared with the supervisor. He has become resentful because he has felt that the supervisor was really directing his cases. Moreover, he has felt guilty over withholding from the supervisor difficult or "pet" cases. He has not felt the need to think through as clearly as possible the specific aspects of a case that are puzzling him and that may require supervisory consideration. He has tended to ask for help in general terms, with the result that the sheer mass of supervisory teaching has made him feel dependent and out of control in the management of the case.

The caseworker learns to recognize his skills and his gaps in knowledge not only by day-to-day work on cases, but by formulating concepts derived from an examination of groups of his cases. Such examination is the base for increasing his knowledge of his areas of mastery and the areas for continuing professional development.

As the caseworker gains experience in noting and assessing the trends in his work, he should be able to work skillfully and securely in the areas of his competence and to accept his limitations without loss of self-esteem. When the caseworker and supervisor work together appropriately, the caseworker is free to use supervision at any level of experience without the burden of dependence, hostility, or guilt. He is thus comfortable about seeking assistance in cases in which his limitations might seriously interfere with giving service. He can also use the supervisor's help in considering parts of a case, or a group of cases, for the purpose of conceptualizing his techniques, re-evaluating certain casework concepts, or experimenting with new or different concepts or techniques.

From the outset of his employment in the agency, the caseworker, whether beginning or experienced, should know that he will be held accountable for his work—for formulating his own thinking about a case prior to seeking supervisory assistance, for deciding what specific areas in which cases require supervisory consideration, and for examining the trends in his work. His purposeful use of supervision is more important than the frequency with which he seeks it.

2. The caseworker is responsible for his own continuing professional development. In a work situation, learning is not a specific goal in itself, but is related to the goal of increasing one's ability to provide effective service. Personal growth cannot be set as a job requirement, nor is it an appropriate area for supervision. As the caseworker identifies his own developmental needs, he should decide where and how these are to be met—how much reading he needs to do, what institutes or classes he might attend, and when to use supervisory help or other resources in the agency. Initially, the supervisor may encourage the caseworker to use a variety of resources; with experience, he should gain assurance and skill in choosing appropriate resources without necessarily channeling his requests through his immediate supervisor.

Accepting this concept will mean making changes in supervisory methodology. Making an assessment of the worker's educational needs has long been considered an important part of the supervisor's job. Supervising the new or beginning worker closely has been justified on the basis of helping him to develop his capacities. Thus, emphasis has been placed on the caseworker as "learner" rather than as "doer," and the worker has viewed himself as a learner for an unspecified number of years. Once it is clear that the caseworker has complete responsibility for doing his job and for developing his own skills, the supervisor should observe how the worker performs and learns before making a specific plan for supervising him.

This confusion about the caseworker as learner, or worker, has resulted in considering the more experienced worker an "independent worker" who may ask for "consultation" rather than for supervision or who may use the supervisor for guidance in certain questions of agency policy. When the caseworker is held responsible for his own work, there should be no question of dependence or independence, supervision or consultation at any level of experience. Rather, there should be a differential use of resources based on the complexities of the case material and on the caseworker's demonstrated abilities in relation to job expectations.

Viewing the supervisor as the major, and in some instances the sole, medium of continuing professional development has hampered the worker's achievement of professional maturity. His feelings of dependency and hostility have been stimulated, and he has reacted by "flight or fight." The supervisor has tended to become overcontrolling and protective. Under the plan suggested here, there is no reason to fear organizational confusion or the undermining of what has been in the past a rigid and hierarchical agency structure. The caseworker should be able to judge when the supervisor's knowledge will be useful to him and when consultation with other personnel will be appropriate. Being able to use the agency resources freely should enhance his ability to render good service.

3. The caseworker is responsible for managing his job assignment—handling his case load in such a way as to serve as many people as possible, organizing his time so that he can meet production standards, assembling statistics, and so on. Case recording is an integral part of giving direct casework service. The case record is a working tool designed for the caseworker's use, a means by which he pulls together his data and thoughts about a case in order to formulate plans, check or recheck his assessment, evaluate the effectiveness of his service, and plan for the future of the case. From his case records the worker should, with supervisory assistance, be able to identify the trends in his practice and the areas in which he needs to develop greater skill.

In summary, the caseworker's job requires that he be responsible for the quality of his casework service to clients, for the maximum development of his capacities, for the management of his job in the interests of giving as much service as possible, and for using the resources the agency provides to implement and enhance his service.

The Supervisor-Caseworker Relationship

The supervisor-caseworker relationship should be a positive one, based on knowledge and respect for each other's competence and job responsibilities. Clarity about these responsibilities should do much to minimize such problems as dependence, hostility, independence, and so forth. Dependence is not in and of itself evil, but the unwholesome, childish dependence which is stimulated when job responsibilities are ill-defined and ill-used has created problems in both casework and supervisory practice. Mature interdependence, which results from the appropriate use of the strengths of others without loss of self-identity, is highly desirable in the complicated process of serving people through casework. Control by the supervisor when confused with authority also creates problems. Administrative leadership requires the use of one kind of authority; casework practice requires another.

Much has been written and said about the anxiety created in the supervisor-caseworker relationship. Certainly, when the supervisor controls or protects the worker and removes the responsibility that belongs to him, the latter responds with conflicted emotions that are often expressed as anxiety, feelings of pressure, resentment, and the like. Normal anxiety is desirable in a work situation. The wish to succeed, the concern about meeting job requirements, the desire to give good service, concern about a new setting or agency, the feeling that a case is not going well—all are useful anxieties in stimulating self-motivation for meeting responsibilities. Normal resistance to change, which is always present in learning and doing, and periods of regression under particular stress or under the impact of trying to integrate new material, are familiar behavioral manifestations in both caseworkers and supervisors and need not cause concern. The intensity and persistence of these phenomena offer clues to the need for intervention and assistance. Some dependence, frustration, and displacement of feelings will always exist in working relationships but are of concern only when they become predominant or persistent.

Problems in these areas are exacerbated when the caseworker's performance or characteristic ways of behaving are assessed in personal or clinical terms rather than in relation to his job responsibility and the agency's requirements. Again it must be emphasized that it is the supervisor's responsibility to use supervision in the interests of facilitating service and to assess the individual only in relation to his work.

If the concepts outlined in this paper are to be implemented, the executive staff of an agency must take leadership in defining job responsibilities and requirements. It must also facilitate a different type of supervisory practice.

The staff of the Jewish Family and Community Service of Chicago has begun to test these formulations in practice. Thus far, the caseworkers have expressed satisfaction with the clearer definitions of job responsibility and a feeling of relief that evaluations are used solely for administrative implementation of salary scales. The supervisors have said that they know more about a caseworker's abilities in a shorter time than previously and, therefore, are better equipped to plan for differential supervision. They are keeping track of the various uses of supervisory time made by casework staff in the hope that this information will clarify the areas in which supervision can be useful and also the appropriate nature and size of a supervisory load.

The process of learning new ways, unlearning old ways, and combining what was useful in the past with what is done in the present is painful but exciting. Specific applications of these formulations must be tested, and new applications must be developed. It is to be hoped that the continued development and testing of new concepts will add to the growing body of knowledge of the practice of supervision. It is a practice that utilizes special methods and processes and that requires specific abilities and training.

Index